LEAN SPD

Creating and Sustaining Lean Sterile Processing Departments

John Kimsey

Contributing Editor
Dan Johnson

Published by John Kimsey
2022

Lean SPD is authored by and self-published by John Kimsey.

Many thanks to Dan Johnson for his contributions and editorial assistance as a friend and colleague. Additional thanks to Amanda Marcrum for her proof reading and editorial assistance.

Front cover photo courtesy of Carl Sharp and STERIS Corporation. Back cover photo courtesy of Charles Williams. Cover design by Leah Dodd.

To all the Sterile Processing Professionals worldwide.

May this book help you advance your professional career.
You are truly unsung heroes of healthcare.

Contents

Introduction

First, we would like to say thank you for taking the time to read our book. Sterile Processing books are not exactly thrilling New York Times best sellers, so we assume you are an industry professional looking to improve your knowledge and expertise. Excellent! The time and effort we have put into writing Lean SPD is a labor of love and our attempt to share our knowledge and expertise with you. Whether you are a sterile processing technician, supervisor, manager, director or anyone else interested in improving their departmental performance, we hope this book provides useful insight and guidance. For clarification, we will use both SPD (sterile processing department) and CS (Central Sterile) to mean the same thing. Canadians use MDRD for Medical Device Reprocessing Department while other countries utilize CSSD for Central Sterile Services Department. We have chosen SPD since it is a common theme amongst most hospitals and widely utilized and understood. We will also use the Operating Room abbreviation OR throughout the book.

For us, our interaction with sterile processing departments usually starts with a phone call and a hospital perioperative executive asking us how we can help them address issues with their sterile processing department. The story is usually the same: citations from The Joint Commission, instruments backlogged in the department or quality issues that result in daily firefighting to keep OR procedures on-time. The hospital sterile processing department is unable to meet their Customer's expectations and the hospital is looking for help to fix it.

Conversely, we are occasionally invited to tour sterile processing departments that never call us, are meeting their Customer expectations on a consistent basis and for the most part have reliable, consistent and predictable operational performance. Why the difference?

While the answers vary from leadership to resources to dysfunctional hospital environments, the call to action seems to be the same. Sterile processing departments traditionally focus on ensuring clinical compliance and adherence to AAMI standards, certification of their technicians and working day in and day out to meet the daily needs of their Customers. "Make sure the OR has what they need today" is a common mantra. What is missing though is a structured approach to planning, executing, managing and continuously improving the department.

We have met numerous SPD managers, toured hundreds of sterile processing departments, helped hundreds more and find a common thread lacking throughout the industry – leadership development. Often, the SPD manager and supervisors are promoted technicians who performed well as technicians and were given the chance to advance their career. While training and education may have been common for the technicians, once they were promoted to a leadership position, they were expected to figure things out on their own. There was never a structured leadership program to guide them through how to manage an SPD, how to manage people or how to manage a process that is becoming more and more complex and critical to patient safety and care.

Occasionally, the hospital recruits the help of their internal "process improvement", "operational excellence" or "lean team" to help the department. Sometimes they hire an outside healthcare consulting firm, perioperative consulting firm or lean expert to help them. Other times they call a sterile processing expert or company specializing in sterile processing. What seems to be needed is a combination of all the above. Sterile processing departments need to leverage the expertise of non-healthcare operational experts, lean methodologies, healthcare requirements, industry regulatory guidelines and leadership development experts to help them create leaders who are qualified and capable of successfully managing the department and meeting their Customer's needs.

In this environment, we have strived to provide a sterile processing focused guidebook that combines the best of lean methodologies and sterile processing requirements into an easy-to-read approach to managing an SPD. The book is not meant to be an all-encompassing guide to everything an SPD leader needs to be successful, but rather a focused text on utilizing lean principles to create a successful operational structure.

We have also made sure adequate attention has been given to lean management practices in addition to more traditional lean production methodologies. Lean management is perhaps the core value the book focuses on as we believe it is the underlying foundation of any successful department and as previously stated a lacking element in many sterile processing departments.

Knowing that there are numerous “lean” books on the market, Lean SPD is not a traditional lean book full of Toyota Production System stories and Japanese terms, although we do share a few. Instead, we have taken the approach of presenting lean concepts and best management practices in a simple to understand manner focused specifically on the sterile processing environment.

To make things fun, we have included a novel style story of a local sterile processing manager, Rob, attempting to improve his department using lean concepts. Rob represents a typical sterile processing manager faced with a department that works hard day in and day out to make sure the OR has what they need but continuously faces challenges and never-ending complaints from their Customer. Rob’s journey is not intended to imply all sterile processing managers have these problems but rather provides an entertaining “example” of how the methodologies being presented can be utilized in real life.

We have also included case studies from actual sterile processing departments that highlight real life utilization or non-utilization of lean methods. These case studies are all based on real examples and experiences from our time working with hospitals. Just as a picture may tell a thousand words, a case study can invoke a thousand thoughts in a more efficient manner than trying to explain a concept through literary means. An entire book could be written with nothing but case studies!

Occasionally you will run across a Japanese lean term. Don’t worry. We try to explain them as we go and if needed, we have provided a chapter with Lean Terms and Definitions you can refer to.

In summary, this book is our attempt to share our experience and knowledge with the thousands of sterile processing leadership and staff who are interested in improving their departments and expanding their knowledge and understanding of lean. We hope that the information is useful and presented in a manner that is easily understood and applicable to sterile processing departments. In fact, as we review the book ourselves, we have wondered if the material is too "easy" and critiqued as basically common sense versus a more technical dive into lean principles. To this end, we believe that lean in and of itself should be viewed as common sense approaches to continuously improving daily operations and solving problems. Lean does not have to be complicated and neither does managing a sterile processing department.

One important note to add is that even simple common-sense applications are sometimes hard to implement and follow. Self-discipline and continuous motivation to hold oneself and a department accountable to doing the common-sense simple things is often harder than it seems. Managing people is an art and a full-time job itself, let alone ensuring they are actively participating in and building a lean culture. In fact, we could have written a full book on managing people and effective leadership and we strongly recommend that all leaders make efforts to improve in their leadership skills. While leadership is a major theme in Lean SPD, it is limited to the lean attributes of leadership. Leadership skills such as motivating staff, positive feedback, mentoring and coaching, accountability, discipline and many other leadership skills have been left to other books, courses and HR professionals more qualified than us.

We would also like to acknowledge that Lean SPD is not a clinically focused book addressing adherence to AAMI guidelines and regulatory audits. While clinical requirements and regulatory compliance is mandatory for every sterile processing department, we have found that a Lean SPD department that is structured properly will be better suited to successfully meet their clinical requirements. In fact, this is an important concept to remember as you read through the book. For a sterile processing department to be operationally, clinically and financially successful, it must have a structured operational and management system that plans, controls and improves daily performance. This is the "common sense" lean approach we are sharing.

Lastly, as we review and make final edits to Lean SPD, we realize that we could spend the next five years continuously improving our book but need to make the decision to release it in hopes that those who read it today can start their lean journey sooner rather than later. Perhaps we will find ourselves releasing version two with updated case studies, new and improved material and further details on how to successfully implement lean based on feedback from people such as yourself. We also found that we had utilized the word "ensure" over 120 times. We've since substituted some of those instances for words like confirm or guarantee but the point hit home that lean is about the word ensure. Lean ensures work is completed as expected, ensures people do what they should be doing and ensures work activities are standardized. Lean ensures that processes and people work together to continuously improve. Lean is all about ensuring everyone knows what to do, when to do it, how to do it, and variances are identified and addressed. Ensure, guarantee, confirm are all great words to start using in our vocabulary when talking about our sterile processing department performance.

We hope you enjoy the material, find multiple actionable items that improve your department and utilize the book to improve your professional knowledge and expertise.

Sincerely,
John Kimsey and Dan Johnson

Introduction

Chapter One: Introduction to Lean

Our Job is NOT to reprocess surgical instrumentation.

Our Job is to CONTINUOUSLY IMPROVE how we reprocess surgical instrumentation.

City Hospital: The Problem

Scene: Karen, the OR Director, has called Rob, the SPD Manager, to her office to discuss the department's performance. Unknown to Rob, two OR Service Coordinators are also waiting for him in Karen's office.

"Come on in Rob," Karen remarks from her desk without getting up.

Rob enters and immediately senses that this is not going to be a good meeting. Deana and Beth are sitting cross armed at the small round table in the corner.

"Hi Deana, Beth," Rob politely offers. No response.

"I've asked Deana and Beth to join us today to discuss what we can do to address the issues we're having with the sterile processing department," Karen turns from her computer screen and faces the table where Rob has sat down next to Beth.

"While there's many things you do that I appreciate and I know your staff works hard, we have to find an answer to the issues we keep having day after day. I've asked Deana to share what the Ortho team is feeling. I have also asked her to quantify things and not just make it an emotional plea."

Rob sinks into the chair, knowing what is coming.

"We can't keep working this way," Deana begins as she lets loose for the next 90 seconds. "Three cases today didn't have the instruments we needed and when we called SPD all they could tell is that they'd look for them. After ten minutes, I went down there and was shocked at how many trays were sitting in the department; no wonder people can't find anything. It took me and your staff another ten minutes of looking before we found one sterile tray in the core but not put back on the shelf yet and another tray in the sterilizer."

"That tray wasn't on the case cart preference list," Rob interjected before being cut off.

"That doesn't matter. We needed it," Deana shouted back visibly upset having to listen to Rob defend why the trays were not done.

"Deana, let me take over," Karen suggests. "Rob, we understand that you're under pressure and have staff issues and such, but we have to find a solution. The surgeons aren't happy. Here's what I would like for us to agree to. First, you must reduce the backlogs in your department. Find a solution and let me know what you need to make it work. As you know, the solution can't be hiring more people. None of us can hire more people. Second, we have issues with quality that need to be addressed."

"We had another dirty instrument today," Beth adds.

"Ok, I get it," Rob concedes.

"Rob, this is serious. Can you excuse us ladies?" Karen asks Deana and Beth.

Alone in the room, Karen looks at Rob for a moment of silence that pierces his heart. Rob wonders if he is about to be fired.

"90 days Rob. Do what you can in 90 days, and we'll meet again. I need you to give me data, numbers, something to show that the department is getting better. Something to show that there's a light at the end of the tunnel. The surgeons are talking to my V.P. and it's not going to be pretty if we don't do something." Karen appears equally stressed.

"Ok, I'll work on it." Rob speaks as if he has just received his final warning.

"I'm here for you Rob, but I need to know what your plan is. Let's meet every week if you want, but I'm serious about the data. We need something concrete to show that we're making changes and improving."

Rob realizes that his department is barely getting by everyday but isn't quite sure what to do. Maybe a good night's sleep will reveal a solution he thinks to himself.

~~~~~~
~~~~~~

Lean in Healthcare

Since the early 2000's the view that lean manufacturing concepts, such as the Toyota Production System, could work in healthcare settings and specifically major hospitals has not only proved to be true, but in some cases, very successful. Unfortunately, the number of successful implementations and sustained improvements in healthcare from lean methodologies seems to have been outnumbered by numerous attempts, failures and un-sustained improvements. This experience is not unique to healthcare. Many of the same challenges have been faced during Lean implementations in all industries allowing us to learn from the struggles of others. In this context, Lean SPD explains not only the lean tools and methods so frequently quoted, talked about, implemented, and sometimes dismissed, but enlarges the conversation to include a sustainable and all-encompassing lean system that greatly increases the success rate for implementing lean. Perhaps most importantly, substantial time is spent on defining lean management principles that build the lean foundation to sustain operational improvements that the lean tools strive to implement.

Let us first start with a high-level overview of lean principles and their application to the sterile processing department. We will differentiate two basic categories of lean: Lean Production and Lean Management Systems.

Lean Production

Plenty of definitions of lean or lean production exist online with elimination of waste as the predominant theme. For a typical SPD, simply stating they must eliminate waste to be lean does not generate excitement or explain what they need to do. A simple definition that has proved useful as well as applicable for explaining lean production to SPD leadership and staff is as follows:

"Lean Production is a method of work that improves quality and efficiency while meeting Customer requirements."

It is encouraging that there are SPDs and leadership teams that have successfully implemented lean methodologies that led to improved quality and improved efficiencies simultaneously. Unfortunately, many sterile processing departments face daily backlogs of instruments, Customer complaints and frantic telephone calls, variance in work practices between staff, errors and rework and constant fire fighting to get through the day while the OR struggles to understand why their instruments are not ready when needed. Lean Production aims at creating a predictable work environment in which variance in product and service quality as well as cost is minimal, and the Customer requirements are consistently met.

To help understand Lean Production in the sterile processing environment let us breakdown the issues stated in the previous paragraph and learn how lean production has successfully been utilized to improve performance.

Issue: Backlogs of Instruments

A key attribute of Lean Production is Continuous Flow or the ability of a process to maintain flow without any product sitting, waiting, or unnecessary backlogging. To address backlogs, lean production identifies when the work is to be completed and aligns resources to maintain a continuous flow or as close to continuous flow as possible. For sterile processing departments, this means aligning resources such as staff and equipment to be available when the dirty instruments begin showing up in decontamination and maintaining the flow of those instruments through the department without undue waiting.

Issue: Customer Complaints and Frantic Telephone Calls

At the heart of lean is the Customer Requirement and any process or operation that is experiencing any type of Customer complaint should pay attention to the Customer requirements and how well their process can meet those requirements. Lean Production identifies Customer requirements, measures those requirements and focuses on creating processes and operations that support achieving those requirements. Failures such as Customer complaints are tracked, prioritized, analyzed for root cause and eliminated. Implemented changes become the new Standard Work and SPD Leadership actively follow-up on staff and process performance to ensure they are sustained.

Issue: Variance in Work Practices Between Staff

An SPD technician from a large, unionized, Level 1 Trauma hospital once commented that their process should not be based on "the way I do it" but rather on "the way we do it." What a perfect saying to support Lean Production's focus on Standard Work. Sterile processing work is becoming more technical, more complicated and more regulated every day. The need for standardization is an absolute must and key to ensuring quality and predictable outcomes. Saying you have Policies and Procedures is easy to do but instituting Standard Work Instructions is difficult. Lean Production develops Standard Work Instructions that detail the "how to" steps of performing specific activities such as cleaning lumen instruments or creating sterilization loads and then ensures the staff are trained, knowledgeable of and follow the Standard Work. No staff member should have to decide how to perform his or her job.

Issue: Errors and Rework

Errors and rework are classic waste in Lean Production. While perfection may not be achievable, the patient having surgery is expecting it. Not only do errors and rework represent quality issues and potential adverse patient outcomes, they increase the department's resource needs, lower productivity and increase the cost of healthcare. Lean Production drives out waste such as errors and rework through Standard Work, real time performance measurements, active root cause analysis, implementation of process improvements, sustainable leadership follow-up and continuous improvement.

Issue: Constant Fire Fighting

For many people in healthcare, not just SPDs, the objective seems to be the outcome: a healthy patient, a successful knee replacement, a tumor removed, a life saved. While the outcome is important and the efforts of millions of healthcare workers to produce positive outcomes can be applauded, Lean Production is more concerned with how you get to the outcome. In fact, how you get there will have a direct impact on the outcome itself most of the time! In our years of working with hospitals around the world, we have found that sterile processing departments that take care of their processes to eliminate waste and meet Customer requirements through Lean Production and Lean Management Systems (i.e. focus on the processes required to achieve the outcome) have far better outcomes than those departments who only focus on the daily outcome. Additionally, Lean departments not only have better outcomes, but they also accomplish it using less resources at a lower cost per unit. Unfortunately, many SPDs struggle each day to meet the OR's requirements and resign themselves to fighting the same fire over and over every day with the only consolation that in the end, surgeries were completed, and they were able go home knowing the outcome was achieved. Lean Production focuses on creating predictable and efficient processes that meet the Customer's requirements.

The following case study is a simple example of a Lean Production concept implemented that meets the Customer requirements while removing waste through efficient utilization of SPD staff.

~~~~~~

Case Study – Lean Production with OR Supply Carts

A typical SPD was tasked with serving a 24 OR Customer as well as multiple hospital floors and clinics while simultaneously finding ways to reduce operational expense. While the department implemented many changes in their on-going effort to achieve their objectives, one simple process improvement provides a perfect example of Lean Production concepts.

Twice a day the department sent a staff member to the OR to inventory three separate OR supply carts located in three different OR cores. The staff member would walk to the OR, visually record items needing replenishment, walk back to SPD to pull the needed supplies and then return to the OR to restock the supply cart. If you are already knowledgeable on Lean, you are probably thinking this is going to be Kanban case study but it is not. We will talk about that later. Instead, this is a case study on Customer Requirements and finding ways to reduce waste.
~~~~~~

Charged with finding ways to get the work done within their budget, the department started to question every activity they did and how it related to their Customer's requirements. When they reviewed the OR supply cart activity, they asked the most important question first: What does our Customer expect and require from us? Their answer was simple but enlightening. The Customer always wanted the supplies on the OR supply cart for when they needed them. The Customer did not care how the task was fulfilled. Encouraged to put aside any preconceived ideas and design a lean process to meet the Customer's requirement but utilizing the least possible resources, the team quickly realized three opportunities existed. First, the staff walked to the OR twice, once to count what was needed and once to refill the cart. According to lean, walking or movement is a waste when it is not actively adding value. Thus, walking to the OR twice is waste. Secondly, after reviewing what items and in what quantities they were restocking, the department realized that they typically restocked less than 20% of the items on the cart each time and often those items only needed a few individual pieces to meet the par level. Lastly, they realized that no one required them to stock twice a day.

Within an hour the team had decided to implement immediate changes without engaging a full Kaizen team or spending more time analyzing the situation. They felt this qualified as a quick fix but, as with any implementation, would need measurement to prove success. Their solution was to only restock the OR supply carts once a day instead of twice, push an SPD resupply cart to the OR and restock the OR carts from the SPD cart, thus eliminating one round trip walking and adjust par levels to ensure that the OR always has what they want.

The team's implementation worked perfectly, and the OR never knew anything had changed. Importantly for the staff, they felt satisfied that they could successfully take the Customer's requirements and translate those into a lean process that minimized waste while creating a predictable and sustainable process that produced positive outcomes. Quick wins like these, help build confidence and team engagement in further implementing Lean Production.

~~~~~~

Lean Management Systems
Implementing Lean Production concepts, reducing backlogs, eliminating waste and finding ways to improve operations is great if the progress is sustainable. This is where Lean Management Systems come into play.

"Lean Management Systems provide tools to sustain lean production, expose waste and operational issues, and create continuous improvement."

Lean Management Systems provide the structure in which Lean Production can be implemented and sustained. All too often, organizations rush to implement lean tools to gain operational improvements only to find their improvements vanish over time as the department returns to pre-lean performance. This lack of sustainability and/or inability to effectively implement lean methods is usually a sure sign that the Lean Management Systems needed to maintain the changes were not implemented at the same time. Without these systems, any operational changes made are at high risk of backsliding. Lean Management Systems are thus focused on sustaining lean production improvements through controlled and monitored operations while identifying and addressing continuous improvement opportunities. Essential to the Lean Management System is the concept of Daily Management defined as routine, fact-based, goal oriented and active leadership to manage operational performance.

Daily Management includes:

- Process management that directs team members through Standard Work, Production Boards to visually display actual to planned work accomplished, identification of problems encountered at the place of work and Key Performance Indicators or Measurements (KPI's) to monitor and display overall performance against plan
- Occurs at the Genba (Genba defined as the place of work or the actual SPD work area. See lean definitions) by walking the floor and observing the details of the process as they happen
~~~~~~

- Ensures all processes and results are reviewed several times per day and variances or problems are noted
- Ensures adherence to Standard Work
- Ensures decisions and changes are made through fact gathering and analysis
- Clearly and visually communicates operational status to real time targets resulting in greater attainment and satisfaction
- Uses the Kaizen and PDCA methodologies to solve problems
- Aligns teams and their leaders

Characteristics of Lean Management Systems are best described by David Mann in his 2015 book *Creating a Lean Culture – Tools to Sustain Lean Conversions Third Edition*. David discusses four primary elements to an effective Lean Management System. While David's book is not specific to healthcare, the principles are very applicable to sterile processing departments.

- Visual Controls – Part of the implementation of lean is to install a system to help flow and measure the work performed. This is accomplished using visual controls such as:
    - Kanban signals instead of par level counts or supply rounding schedules
    - Steady work pacing signals and production boards or "gas pumps" instead of daily quotas that show the actual work accomplished versus the plan
    - Quality charts that immediately identify when work does not meet the Customer's expectations

  There is no set format for visual controls but rather unlimited options that are usually designed to meet the specific operational need. While the content matters, it is just as important that the format is developed by the individuals using it so that it indicates what is most important to the team and is easy to use. Whether tracking planned versus actual production, material refill rates or staff scheduling "heijunka" boards, the controls should indicate results against the expectation and capture any reasons for variances. Visual controls should be updated by the staff member performing the work when possible and should be at short intervals (several times per shift as an example). The results of the controls should help identify and drive corrective action.

- Standard Work for Leaders – The discipline in fulfilling and following standard work by the leadership team is the most critical element to maintaining lean changes. Leader Standard Work puts the leaders in position to drive performance, sustainability and improvement. In simple terms, Leader Standard Work defines the key activities the leader is to do throughout the day to ensure the department is performing to plan and, if not, why? Properly set up, the leader can see all that is happening from a few feet away and take corrective actions to address incorrect processes, interrupted work and defect occurrences in real time. Leader Standard Work will need to be created and modified as the lean transformation progresses because, early on, the leader may still have to conduct tasks to support the more conventional management model. As the lean environment stabilizes, the new roles begin to become clearer and make more sense.

- Daily Accountability Process – Part of the leader's standard work, the Daily Accountability Process provides the structure to take the data gathered and turn it into actionable steps to further improve the process. It begins with the routine review of each work element on a short-interval schedule and the recognition of problems. Immediate action items are implemented to keep the workflow on schedule followed by discussions with the team at the daily huddles. The final accountability step is the assignment of tasks to further investigate and correct the causes of the problem.

- Discipline – the best tools and processes available will not mean a thing unless YOU have the discipline to follow through with correct practices. In doing so, you set the example for others, no matter if you are a shift lead, supervisor, or SPD Manager.

Lean Management Systems reach beyond the traditional department manager as well by incorporating structured routines for on-the-floor team members all the way up to executive levels. The Roles of Leadership in a Lean Transformation are shown below as relative percentages. While the percentages are approximate, they do provide a baseline to measure current time allocation against identification of improvement opportunities.

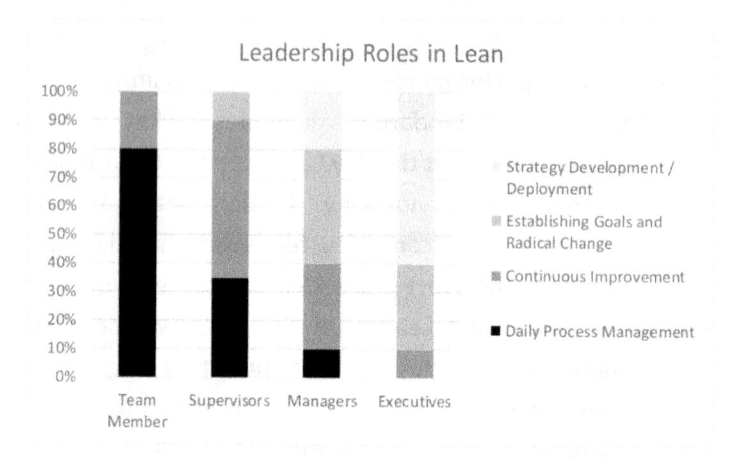

- Team members – Daily Process management (80%) and Operational Kaizen or Incremental Continuous Improvement (20%). Teams and employees are responsible for following the Standard Work, recording actual progress to plan throughout the day and recording problems as they occur and help solve problems.

- Team Leaders / Supervisors – Operational Kaizen or Incremental Continuous Improvement (55%), Daily Process Management (35%), and establishing Goals and Radical System / Operational Change (10%). Team Leaders manage the status of and align resources as needed to accomplish the work required, review the data collected on their routine rounds, prepare and conduct daily huddles, train team members in new roles, lead Kaizen problem solving and audit the workplace and processes at the Genba.

- Management – Establishing Goals, Radical System / Operational Change and System Wide Kaizen or Continuous Improvement (40%),

Operational Kaizen or Incremental Continuous Improvement (30%), Strategy Development and Deployment (20%), and Daily Management (10%)

- Executive – Strategy Development and Deployment (60%), Establishing Goals and Radical System / Operational Change (30%) and System Wide Kaizen or Continuous Improvement (10%)

We dive deeper into the details of Lean Management Systems for sterile processing a bit later but offer the following case studies to help stimulate the thought process.

~~~~~~

<u>Case Study – Decontamination Flow Improvement Sustained</u>

A large teaching hospital with over 30 ORs and a decontamination area equipped with seven instrument washers and three cart washers was experiencing severe backlogs in decontamination. The room would routinely fill with dirty case carts to the point that one staff member spent most of their time moving the carts in a conga line through the area to make room for the next one coming off the dirty elevator. Occasionally, the supervisor would realize the backlogs were beyond acceptable and move more staff to decontamination but was often content with the backlog remaining until the evening hours when surgeries were completed, and the flow of dirty case carts ceased. Due to continued OR complaints about the service and turnaround times provided by the sterile processing department, a sterile processing lean consultant was asked to help implement change to improve flow and service levels.

After an initial review, the team identified several issues causing the backlogs and their ability to maintain a continuous flow through the area. Staffing levels were aligned with the incoming flow of work which required additional staff in decontamination between 10AM and 5PM. A "do what you want" mentality to the room workflow was replaced with specific work assignments. A "Navigator" assignment was created with responsibility for maintaining flow
~~~~~~

while the rest of the staff were assigned to specific prep sinks with the sole responsibility of cleaning instruments staged at their station. Expectations for work performance including quality and productivity were developed in Standard Work and reviewed with the staff. A staff member volunteered to be the first Navigator and the system was implemented. Within two weeks the backlogs had virtually vanished and the staff member previously responsible for moving the carts through the conga line was assigned to a more productive task.

More importantly, Visual Controls and Management Systems were implemented and followed up on. The navigator recorded incoming dirty case carts by the hour as well as backlogs on visual wall charts and the supervisors were tasked with monitoring the department flow every hour with specific staffing standards based on the number of dirty case carts to be processed. Eventually, two changes occurred that highlighted the effectiveness of the Lean Management System and Leadership Standard Work. First, backlogs began to develop again in decontamination. This time though, the visual documentation was reviewed on a weekly basis by the SPD Manager who then questioned the Supervisor who admitted they had not followed their Standard Work and had not staffed the room adequately. The supervisor was held accountable and learned their lesson because the process had a built-in accountability check at the SPD Manager's level. The second event occurred when backlogs vanished completely between 10AM and 3PM but suddenly showed up late in the afternoon in numbers unforeseen. The SPD leadership team was able to trace the change in flow to delayed case cart delivery from the OR by comparing case end times to their recorded arrival pattern of dirty case carts. With data in hand, the SPD Manager presented their findings to the OR leadership team and a solution was found and implemented to ensure timely delivery of dirty case carts. Again, the Lean Management System actively monitored and identified opportunities for improvement and sustained the improvements implemented.

~~~~~~
~~~~~~

<u>Case Study – Decontamination Flow Lost</u>

A major city hospital was experiencing similar backlogs throughout the sterile processing area and, after continual complaints from the OR, hired a sterile processing lean consultant to help. Backlogs in assembly grew throughout the week reaching over 300 instrument trays at 7AM by Thursday morning. Due to the continual backlogs in assembly, no one ever paid any attention to decontamination until the lean team began to review the workflow from start to finish. Beginning in decontamination the consultant and team members found that backlogs also occurred frequently in decontamination. There was no standard process or workflow in the area as staff worked differently depending on who was assigned. What the leadership team thought was happening in the area was not happening at all.

Like the previous case study, the team identified several issues causing the backlogs and their ability to maintain a continuous flow through the area. Supervisors agreed to increase staffing levels to align with the incoming flow of work by sending more staff to decontamination when case carts begin to backlog. The "do what you want" mentality to the room workflow was replaced with specific work assignments including a navigator with the responsibility of maintaining flow while the rest of the staff were assigned to specific prep sinks with the sole responsibility of cleaning instruments staged at their station. Expectations for work performance including quality and productivity were developed in Standard Work and reviewed with the staff. A daily room set-up checklist was created to ensure daily cleaning, washer testing and workstation stocking was completed. An experienced staff member was assigned to be the first navigator and the system was implemented. After a successful first week that saw reduced backlogs and completion of daily tasks, the supervisor was tasked with follow-up as part of their Leader Standard Work and the consultant moved on to the next area of opportunity.

Very different from the first case study was the lack of a Lean Management System, Visual Controls and actual leadership follow-up and accountability. There was no recording of incoming workloads or backlogs, the supervisors did not follow their Standard Work and even worse the SPD Manager never felt compelled to follow-up on the supervisors' performances. Two weeks later the consultant did an audit of the implemented changes and found that the daily room set-up checklist had not been completed in over a week and no one had ever followed-up with the staff on its duties to complete it. Backlogs were again building in decontamination, and when questioned, the supervisor stated they needed the staff in assembly. This response was in light of the fact that the entire leadership team had agreed to create and sustain a continuous flow in decontamination first and then work on assembly. Due to the lack of a Lean Management System and no accountability at any level, staff and the supervisors returned to their old way of doing things and completely disregarded the improvements implemented. Who was to fault? Everyone was unfortunately. All levels of leadership failed to hold themselves and their direct reports accountable and, without active follow-up, the staff reverted to the path of least resistance and the routines they were comfortable with.

~~~~~~

Lean is Good Business, Not Another Program

You have heard the talk before in break rooms across the nation that the latest management improvement program is just another program, project or initiative that will change, fade away or become obsolete soon enough so why bother or get excited. Lean has also fallen victim to this thinking, though not without good cause. Many lean transformations, lean projects and lean Kaizen events have been just a temporary leadership pet project only to fade away when immediate results are obtained or sustained. This does not have to be the case though. Lean should not be viewed as a program, project or initiative. All things have end dates. Lean should simply become the way business is performed, the way people work and the way the business continuously improves in meeting the ever-changing Customer requirements while efficiently utilizing their resources.

A great story from Toyota that helps stimulate thinking that lean is not a one-time event comes from Shigeo Shingo. Mr. Shingo led many of Toyota's
~~~~~~

initiatives to improve performance that eventually led to the Toyota Production System.

Mr. Shingo shared the following. "In 1969 I visited the body shop at Toyota Motor Company's main plant. Mr. Sugiura, the divisional manager, told me they had a 1,000-ton press that required four hours for each set-up change. Management had given Mr. Sugiura clear instructions to better that time. Together with the foreman and plant manager I set out about seeing what could be done. We took special pains to distinguish between internal and external set-up time. After six months we succeeded in cutting set up time to 90 minutes. When I revisited the shop later, Mr. Sugiura had some rather startling news for me. Management had given him orders to further reduce set up time to less than three minutes! For an instant I was dumbfounded at this request. But then an inspiration struck, why not convert internal set-up time to external set up time? A number of thoughts followed in rapid succession. On a conference room board, I listed eight techniques for shortening set-up times. Using this new concept, we were able to achieve the three-minute goal after three months of diligent effort. I named this concept SMED (Single Minute Exchange of Die). SMED was later adopted by all Toyota plants and continued to evolve as one of the principle elements of the Toyota Production System. Its use has spread to companies throughout Japan and all around the world." Shigeo Shingo 1983, Page 24-25 Fundamentals of SMED.

The point to reinforce is that no matter how good you think you are today, tomorrow will reveal new challenges that will require a non-stop continuous focus on improving operational performance. I am positive that the Japanese workers in Mr. Shingo's story all worked long hours to reduce their set-up times from four hours to 90 minutes and felt very proud of their efforts. They worked tirelessly, thought outside the box so to speak and changed the mindset of what a die exchange should be like. To then have someone come and tell them to improve even more must have been a bit disheartening, but that is the reality of the world we live in. If you are not continuously improving, then someone else will and take market share away from you. Toyota never viewed their production system as a program or one-time management initiative. They viewed it simply as how they ran their business. It made sense to them to do it no other way than to continuously improve.

Fast forward to American healthcare and we find that lean is still considered a program, a process improvement Kaizen event, something management implements to cut costs, etc. It should not be. We hope that through this book you will find that lean is a systematic way of doing business that may have a beginning but should never have an end. Lean is more than a set of tools. Lean is a way of thinking and a way of living and working. The tools should be secondary to a deep passion for continuously striving to meet and exceed Customer requirements, eliminating waste or unnecessary costs, improving staff satisfaction and continuously improving processes.

Once you understand the power of lean, you will soon realize that lean can become a major culture change for your organization or department that requires much more time and effort than simply assigning a team to a process improvement project. Yes, it can be work but the rewards and benefits can be great for those who succeed. Multiple hospitals have already begun the lean journey working hard to transform from a traditional healthcare provider that was physician and outcome focused to a Customer centered philosophy focused on process. Their experiences have shown that the journey is indeed a major culture shift that has taken years to implement and sustain. While lean does not guarantee financial success, perfect operations or 100% happy Customers, it does position your department or organization to become a leader in quality, efficiency and other metrics that support positive results.

The LeapFrog Group collects data points from numerous hospitals on quality, efficiency and other data points and provides baseline and comparison points for hospitals to judge how well they are performing. The combination of quality and resource use into one matrix is a perfect representation of lean principles in meeting Customer requirements of quality while eliminating waste through effective resource use. The lean journey's focus is to be the hospital depicted by the large dot in the upper right-hand corner of the graph below; a leader in both quality and resource use!

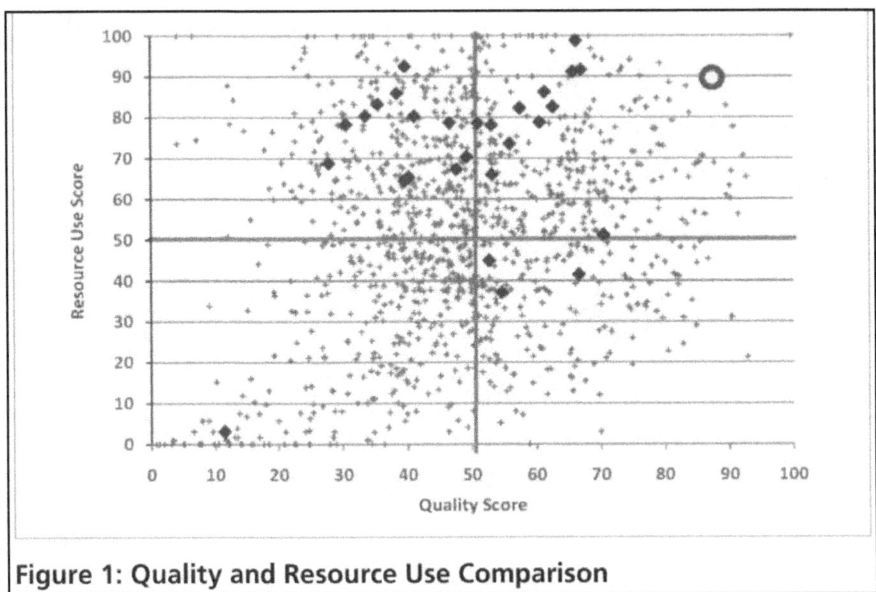

Figure 1: Quality and Resource Use Comparison

In summary, Lean is good business and, best of all, lean evolves. You may find new ways to do business that improve performance, reduce cost, improve staff and Customer satisfaction and make your sterile processing department a better place to work. In doing so, you are creating a lean department and may just have a new lean tool named after you!

Lean – The Buzz Words

Lean is flush with buzz words, Japanese vocabulary and glossaries of terms which we also have in the back of this book! As you encounter a lean term or word in this book, feel free to jump to the Lean Terms and Definitions to find the definition and description of the key concepts. While utilization of some technical lean terms or Japanese terms is used, this book tries to present lean concepts in easy-to-understand terminology that makes sense to SPD leadership and staff.

Chapter Two: Introduction to Lean SPD

HOW DO YOU KNOW YOU'VE BECOME A TRUE LEADER?

1. YOU DON'T TRY TO BE RIGHT; YOU TRY TO BE CLEAR.

2. YOU TRY NOT TO HAVE THE LAST WORD.

3. YOU NO LONGER TRY TO SHOW THAT IT WAS YOUR IDEA. YOU EMPOWER OTHER PEOPLE TO OWN THE IDEA.

What exactly would a Lean SPD look like? A fun method to jump start the creative juices and get everyone thinking how their department could be lean is to visualize the perfect SPD. In this exercise, it is best to have a scribe taking notes while the rest of the staff share their dream of the perfect department. Of course, some guidance is beneficial so that participants provide valuable input that helps drive improvement versus random conversations or non-productive negative comments. Let us look at a fictional department sharing their vision of the perfect sterile processing department.

~~~~~~

City Hospital: The Perfect SPD Conversation

Scene: Rob, SPD Manager, has gathered the first and second shift technicians and supervisors into the assembly area of the SPD in City Hospital. After last week's meeting with Karen, Rob is under pressure to find ways to improve his department and is attempting to jump start the conversation with his staff.
~~~~~~

"Welcome everyone. Today I'd like to start a journey that really has no end," Rob opens the conversation. "I say no end because I truly believe that operating an SPD department is a continuously changing challenge where we have and always will have opportunities for improvement. Like any journey, whether it's a family vacation, a weekend hike or a business venture, it's always best to know your destination and what you're shooting for. So, for fun, I'd like to propose that our journey is to become the perfect SPD!"

The staff shuffle their feet while mostly staying quiet, except for the few normally vocal ones. "No one can be perfect," Rachel shares openly with a pessimistic tone in her voice.

"Let's talk about the OR. They're far from perfect! How can we be perfect when we have to work with them?" Richard claims.

"Ok, I hear you guys but this isn't about the OR and this isn't about the absolute idea of perfection," Rob replies. This is about a journey to become the best we can. Yes, the OR is not perfect but let's first look in the mirror and fix our issues before we start trying to fix other peoples' issues. No one is going to listen to us complain about the OR's performance when we can't show that we're capable of managing our own performance. So, have some fun with the exercise and try defining what the perfect SPD would look like, operate like, and we can throw in what a perfect OR, perfect Customer, perfect hospital might look like as well."

Rob knows that there are certain staff members whom he can count on to give professional and valuable input if they feel encouraged and not overrun by other more vocal, and usually, more negative staff. So, he starts the discussion himself and then calls on staff as needed to make sure everyone is involved and engaged.

"How about we start with this?" Rob begins. "Every morning in the perfect SPD the OR staff comes down to our department and asks what they can do to help us." Everyone laughs. "Write it down on the paper," Rob asks of the staff assigned to take notes. "Let's have some fun with this! Richard, what's something else that a perfect SPD would have?"

"Well, not only would the OR want to help us but they'd return all the instruments in the correct trays after each surgery so we wouldn't have to go looking for them." Richard shares as he starts to engage in the conversation.

Melissa adds, "They'd also clean and spray the instruments like they're supposed to and get the case carts to us as soon as possible. It's so frustrating when I have to try and clean dried, caked on blood that's been sitting for hours."

"Excellent! Let's keep sharing but remember to focus on the perfect SPD." Rob feels the team is starting to open up and continues to lead the conversation. "How about the perfect SPD having enough staff to keep up in decontamination so we never have more than two case carts backed up?"

"I think the perfect SPD would have enough staff in decontamination to start cleaning the case carts immediately when they arrive. Why have a backlog at all?" Latisha speaks up.

"Ok, excellent Latisha. Let's write down that the perfect SPD has enough staff to keep up with the incoming work. Vlad, what do you think the perfect decontamination would look like?" Rob deliberately asks his often quiet but influential second shift technician who frequently requests to work in decontamination.

"Well, I think it would be very clean, have everything we need to do our job, washers that never break down, temperature that's cool so we don't sweat to death and OR staff that ask us politely to quick turn instruments they need right away." Vlad, short for Vladimir, looks at his second shift teammates and adds, "What do you guys think?"

"I don't know about decontamination but I get so frustrated sometimes not being able to complete a single task without being interrupted by someone needing something, the phone ringing or someone at the window to pick-up a tray," Jackie shares while looking a bit frustrated.

"That's an excellent point Jackie," Rob continued. "Let's write that down. The perfect SPD would allow us to work uninterrupted in a clean environment with equipment and supplies readily available and working."

Rudy, a young second shift technician new to the department suddenly speaks up. "I think the perfect SPD would be able to pick case carts without the OR cancelling them or sending so many unused supplies back to us. It's such a waste of time to pick so many items, take them to the OR, have them bring them back and then we put them back on the shelf." Everyone who has ever picked case carts voices agreement and soon the conversation is fully underway.

Rob notices that not everyone is speaking up but the momentum is gaining and he is happy that the staff is not only voicing their frustrations but are beginning to state their ideas as a future positive state versus focusing on the current negative state. "What about how we actually do our work?" Rob questions the group. "Would the perfect SPD have staff doing things in the same standardized way?"

The group readily agrees that things should be standardized but that is not how it is today. "I think everyone works roughly the same way, but we all have our own preferences," Rachel shares.

Melissa almost cuts Rachel off. "There's no way we're doing things the same. Just watch each other. I totally agree that we should have a standard way to do things and everyone gets trained to do it that way."

"When do we have time for training?" Richard sarcastically adds. "We have to work our butts off just to keep up."

"Time out guys. This is supposed to be a fun, vision building session to describe the perfect SPD, not complain about things that aren't working. Let's take what we just said and turn it around for the positive." Rob realizes he is running out of time and wants to end on a positive note. "So, the perfect SPD would have time for training. Let's add that to our list. Plus, the perfect SPD would have standard work instructions that everyone follows. Along with that, I'd like to add that the perfect SPD would have supervisors who have the time to follow-up with their staff and help make sure staff members can do their job the right way, which will make us more successful."

"I'd like to know what successful means!" Roberta adds. "All I hear is how poorly we're doing or what mistakes I've made."

"That's on me," Rob quickly responds. "I'll take responsibility for that. Let's add that a perfect SPD provides feedback on performance both for the department and for individuals, sets clear expectations for all and provides a structure for leadership and staff to work together to address issues and improve."

The scribe looks at Rob and remarks, "Hmmm can you repeat that?" Everyone laughs.

The meeting continues with staff suggesting valid and some not so valid perfect SPD ideas. Afterwards, Rob takes the scribes notes and returns to his office and begins to summarize what the perfect SPD looks like from his staff's initial feedback and comes up with the following bullet points. He has chosen not to include every suggestion to keep the conversation professional and focused so "more pay", "more time off", "free lunch" and "windows looking outside" were left off the final list.

The Perfect SPD

- Sets clear expectations for all
- Provides feedback on departmental and individual performance
- Provides a structure for leadership and staff to work together to address issues and improve
- Supervisors follow-up with their staff and help ensure they can do their job properly

- Has enough staff to keep up with the workload
- Provides adequate time for training
- Follows standard work instructions
- Only pick case carts and supplies that are used
- Staff can work uninterrupted
- Environment that is clean and orderly with proper environmental controls
- Has the needed supplies readily available and in working condition?
- Equipment that is maintained and working
- The OR asks how they can help SPD
- The OR would return all the instruments to the correct trays
- The OR would spray the instruments within enzymatic soaking solution after surgery

~~~~~~

While this is a fictional story, the process Rob went through with his staff is a valid means to start a lean journey without even using the term lean! Using the definitions from Chapter One, it's easy to draw parallels between Rob's list and Lean Production and Lean Management Systems.

"Lean Production is a method of work that improves quality and efficiency while meeting Customer requirements."

"Lean Management Systems provide tools to sustain lean production, expose waste and operational issues, and create continuous improvement."

Every bullet point from Rob's list supports improving quality and efficiency, meeting Customer requirements, exposing waste, sustaining lean production and creating continuous improvement. To meet Customer requirements, the department must first understand what the Customer's expectations are and then translate those into clear expectations for staff performance. To confirm the department can meet those expectations, adequate resources, equipment and staff must be available and capable of performing the tasks required. To train staff and ensure consistency, standard work instructions should be
~~~~~~

developed and implemented. Improving quality and efficiency will require supervisors to follow-up with staff to ensure they are following standard work and have the necessary tools to perform their tasks. Quality and efficiency is measured and improved as feedback is provided and the leadership team and staff work together to address issues and challenges that arise. As issues are addressed and improvements implemented, staff can focus on value added work without interruptions, equipment is maintained in working condition and the department is cleaned and kept in an orderly fashion. As the department continues to improve and can quantify their performance to their Customers such as the OR, the Customer relationship improves. Lastly, the OR begins to understand their impact on the overall process and having experienced improved service levels begin to work with the SPD department in a positive manner.

Unfortunately, the journey from holding a staff meeting to fantasize about the Perfect SPD to changing the department's culture and operational performance is often a confusing and difficult path to follow. While it may be easy to identify the perfect department and what you as the leader or staff member wants, understanding how to go from point A to point B is tough. Even for those who understand lean concepts, implementing lean in the sterile processing environment to move from today's performance to tomorrow's perfect SPD requires a structured approach that is sustainable.

Having successfully and unsuccessfully applied lean methodologies to numerous SPD departments, the following eight steps have emerged as a template to creating a perfect or Lean SPD.

The Eight Steps to Creating a Lean SPD

1. **Customer Requirements (Lean Management System)**

   A perfect or Lean SPD identifies their Customer's expectations, how well they are meeting them and exactly what, where, who and why they are not meeting them.

2. **Measurements (Lean Management System)**

A perfect or Lean SPD measures their performance in real time and historically can identify an off-schedule or off-plan situation immediately and take action to correct.

3. **Developing a Lean Operational Plan (Lean Management System)**
A perfect or Lean SPD develops a detailed operational plan and ensures everyone knows what should be happening, when it should happen, how long it should take and what the results should be.

4. **Developing Leadership Routines (Lean Management System)**
A perfect or Lean SPD clearly identifies what leadership routines or activities should be performed on a regular basis to ensure operations are performing to plan and variances to expectations are identified.

5. **Problem Solving (Lean Management System)**
A perfect or Lean SPD utilizes a systematic approach to solving operational problems.

6. **Employee Engagement (Lean Production)**
A perfect or Lean SPD has 100% employee engagement in actively finding ways to continuously improve Customer satisfaction and operational performance.

7. **Eliminating Waste (Lean Production)**
A perfect or Lean SPD understands operational waste, exposes it and finds ways to eliminate waste from their processes to improve operational performance.

8. **Continuous Improvement (Lean Production)**
A perfect or Lean SPD never stops improving, never stops striving to raise the bar of performance and never stops finding ways to improve Customer satisfaction, employee engagement and operational performance.

These eight steps become the basis for our Lean SPD as depicted below.

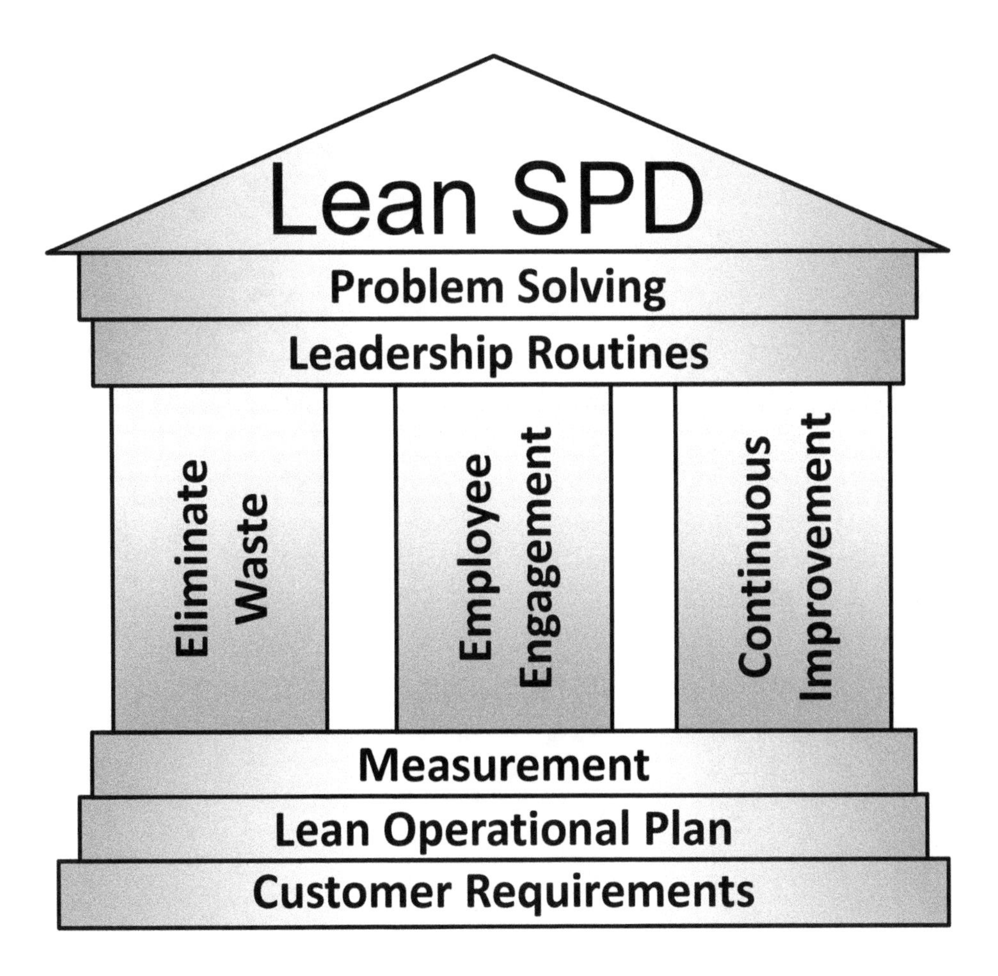

Chapter Three: Customer Requirements

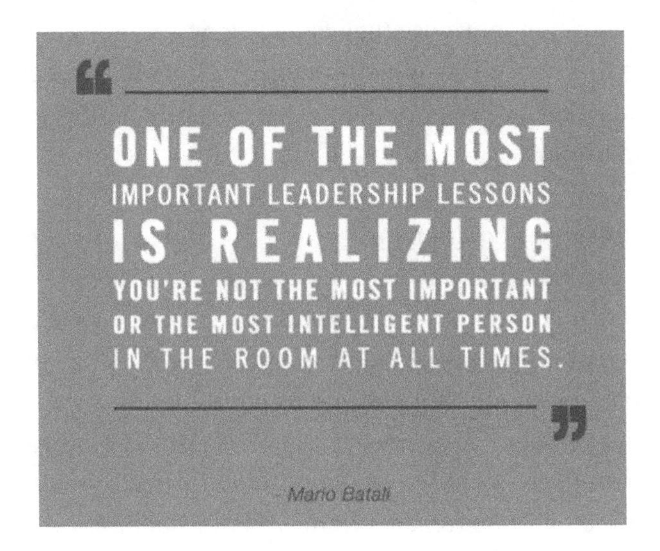

A typical sterile processing department may have several Customers for which they provide a variety of services. Knowing and understanding the requirements of your Customers is imperative to achieving a successful Customer / supplier relationship.

Most often the primary Customer of a SPD is the Operating Room or OR. Establishing a relationship with the OR based on mutual respect and mutual trust will result in mutual benefit. Communication is the key to establishing this relationship. Requirements must be clearly and succinctly expressed by the Customer, the OR for example, and capabilities clearly communicated by the supplier, the SPD. When doing so, avoid vague or general terms and focus on brief and concise expectations.

Over time Customer requirements can and will change, new requirements added, and supplier capabilities improved or compromised. Frequent ongoing communication should be scheduled. It is important to keep everyone involved in these changes and the effect such changes may have on quality and delivery.

In the case of the OR staff, expectations are often expressed in terms of convenience or completeness. Some typical requirements expressed by the OR staff include "on time", "complete" and "sterile". As a supplier, the sterile processing department must use their knowledge to determine and communicate the most efficient methods by which those requirements can be met. Understanding Customer requirements is a prerequisite to meeting the Customer expectations.

Identifying Customer Requirements

It is truly amazing how many SPDs have never taken the time to meet with their Customers to identify what their requirements are. While the requirements for the OR may be intuitively stated by the SPD staff as "complete and sterile trays" for example, you may be surprised by the OR's perception of what their requirements are. While working with a hospital to improve their sterile processing workflow, a surgical doctor remarked to the SPD Manager that his requirements were "I want what I want when I want it!" With unclear and unrealistic requirements like this, it becomes easy to see why SPDs struggle with improving their Customer satisfaction scores.

Similarly, OR perceptions of how long it should take the SPD to reprocess an instrument tray can vary from one hour to eight hours depending on the situation and person you are talking to. With perceptions and / or expectations not clearly identified and agreed upon, SPDs will be shooting in the dark so to speak in their quest to create a satisfied Customer.

There are three steps to identifying your Customer's expectations.

1. Identify your Customers
2. Define your Customer's expectations
3. Mutually agree on achievable and sustainable expectations

Identify Your Customers

To effectively identify all SPD Customers, the department must understand the difference between external Customers and internal Customers. External Customers are those Customers whom you provide completed services and products to. Examples for an SPD would include the OR, Emergency Room, Labor and Delivery, Clinics, Nursing Floors, Endoscopy, Cysto and any others who receive a service or product produced by SPD. Internal Customers are defined as any person or process that receives or is part of the steps required to complete the final service or product. Examples of internal Customers include the assembly area being a Customer of the decontamination area by stating their expectations on how instruments should be clean and decontaminated prior to being given to assembly. Department management and hospital management are internal Customers as well as the SPD staff themselves.

Define Your Customer's Expectations

Defining your Customer's expectations will require a face-to-face meeting between the SPD Leadership and the Customer. While the SPD Leadership may be certain they understand and know their Customer's expectations because they live with them every day, they should not underestimate the power of a face-to-face meeting to clarify those expectations. The face to face meeting will accomplish more than just defining service and product expectations. It will begin the on-going dialog between Customer and supplier that is vital to a positive long-term relationship. In fact, there is only one thing more powerful than a supplier asking the Customer what their expectations are and that is to deliver on those expectations!

When meeting with a Customer, there are a few best practices to take into consideration:

- Keep the conversation focused on the Customer.
- Openly state the purpose for asking the questions.
- Do more listening than talking.
- Ask what is most important to the Customer and what specifically they value.
- Ask open ended questions.
- Do not be defensive. Take criticism graciously.
- Ensure understanding of why the Customer has their requirements.
- Do not be afraid to ask clarifying questions and/or lead the Customer when they are unsure.

Remember, this is not a sales meeting to prove how great SPD is but rather an opportunity to gather information on the Customer requirements. Be prepared to assist the Customer as well. Many times, the Customer has never tried to articulate their requirements and may be unable to clearly state them in a manner that assists in defining the expectation. For example, the OR can state that their expectation is for instrument trays to be 100% complete all the time. This is an acceptable expectation but one that should have added clarification. 100% complete instrument trays under what circumstance and what expense? Ask the clarifying question of whether the SPD will be allowed to purchase back-up instrumentation to keep on hand should the OR return trays missing instruments or with broken instruments? Will the SPD be able to hold instrument sets while they wait for the missing instrument to be found? Will the SPD be able to substitute instruments? Will the OR allow non-critical instruments to be left missing? Will the OR assist in defining what is critical and what is not a critical instrument? As you see, one simple expectation opens the door for healthy dialog on the actual processes involved in meeting the Customer requirements and often leads to a mutual understanding of what is required to meet that expectation.

<u>Mutually Agree on Achievable and Sustainable Expectations</u>

Having met face to face with their Customers and clarified expectations, the sterile processing department must determine their department's ability to fulfill the Customer's expectations. A certain level of trust and mutual understanding must be established between the SPD and their Customers at this point to ensure both parties understand potential roadblocks to success. While the lean principles explained in the following chapters will assist in providing a roadmap to meeting Customer requirements, the following three key factors can be considered before agreeing to achievable and sustainable expectations.

1. Capability of the SPD Department
    - Adequate technical proficiency
    - Adequate workforce skills
    - Sufficient processing capacity
    - Demonstrated ability

2. Commitment of SPD Department and Customers
    - Concern for each other's success
    - Common / mutual goals
    - Honesty and integrity
    - Courtesy and respect
    - Cooperative and flexible
    - Explain actions which impact the other
    - Effort to become familiar with the others' processes
    - Promote open, two-way communication

3. Consistency in Performance
    - Honor commitments
    - Deliver expected performance
    - Follow through on what is said
    - Timely response
    - Open exchange
    - Effort to understand as well as be understood

Having developed mutually agreed upon Customer expectations, the next step is to communicate these expectations to the SPD staff and ingrain them in the operational culture and belief system. Better yet, have the staff involved in the expectation meetings so they are part of the experience and the solution. This is the first step in developing a Lean SPD and drives to the heart of every successful lean implementation: cultural acceptance and change. Without a culture of engagement, acceptance of the lean principles and a driving force of meeting Customer requirements while minimizing waste, the lean implementation will fail. SPDs must demonstrate a commitment to improvement efforts and meeting their Customer's expectations. In fact, their Customers are amongst the most demanding and work in life and death situations. To be successful, the SPD's staff must be aware of their Customer expectations, understand how their daily activities impact the expectations and participate in the continuous improvement efforts aimed at meeting those expectations. Staff contribution and engagement is critical to the department's success.

Developing the SPD Charter

A simple and effective manner to communicate external Customer and internal Customer expectations as well as start the cultural change process is to develop an SPD Charter. The SPD Charter is a brief document no longer than one page. It clarifies the SPD's purpose and function and acts like a job description for the entire team. The Charter often describes the responsibility of the team to the rest of the organization. It provides structure on how the team operates and helps focus on meeting Customer expectations.

Using a Charter provides direction and helps guide the team toward their defined goals. In addition, the Charter helps others within the hospital understand the SPD's purpose and operational focus. The increased awareness of the SPD team's purpose can be utilized to encourage support from other teams within the hospital. A clearly defined and communicated Charter provides a foundation for the team's success.

The following page shows an SPD Charter utilized in a large hospital SPD department. Some charters focus only on External and Internal Customer requirements while others incorporate hospital mission and vision statements. Perhaps the most important aspect of any SPD Charter is in its ability to motivate both leadership and staff to continuously strive towards perfection. An effective Charter becomes part of the organization's DNA driving all operational performance measurements and team member's actions. Weekly departmental meetings and operational performance reviews should incorporate the Charter in their common language and updates. Staff should be able to recite the Charter and understand their impact on the department's ability to meet the Charter's objectives. An effective Charter sets the stage for creating the perfect or Lean SPD.

Example SPD Charter

Patient Expectations

- Complete, sterile and working supplies, equipment and instrumentation ready for surgery when required

Customer Satisfaction

- Average Customer satisfaction survey score of greater than 4.0 out of 5.0

Operating Room Expectations

- 100% instrument trays complete
- 100% instrument trays clean and sterile
- 100% instrument trays on-time
- 100% case carts complete
- 8-hour turn around for normal processing
- 4-hour turn around for terminal sterilization quick turns

Hospital Floors and Clinics, Plaza Clinics and Outside Clinics

- 100% complete, clean, sterile instrumentation
- Orders fulfilled within 2 hours of receipt
- Daily pick-up of dirty instruments / items

SPD Operational Expectations

- Zero workplace injuries or health and safety issues
- < 10 trays on the shelf waiting to be assembled at 7am
- < 30 trays on the shelf waiting to be assembled at 3pm
- < 10 trays on the shelf waiting to be assembled at 11pm
- 100% compliance to work instructions and SPD policies
- > 90% productivity
- Average Staff Satisfaction survey score of greater than 4.0 out of 5.0

SPD as the Customer

Just as the sterile processing department should identify their Customers, define mutually agreeable expectations, and create their departmental Charter, they should also realize that they are a Customer as well. The SPD is easily identified as the Customer in traditional vendor relationships such as purchasing equipment, maintenance and repair, reprocessing supplies or temporary staffing solutions. Additionally, the SPD is an internal Customer within the hospital to departments such as Human Resources, IT, Biomedical, Facilities and Environmental Services. Each of these departments should meet with the SPD to understand the SPD expectations and define mutually agreeable expectations. This process will be easier if the participating departments are familiar with lean or implementing their own lean methodologies.

Examples of internal SPD Customer expectations that have proved helpful in facilities include the following:

- Human Resources: Time-based expectations to process a staff requisition, post opening, recruit applicants and provide candidates for selection. Too often, SPDs struggle through staff shortages while Human Resource departments take months to fill open positions. Conversely, SPDs have been known to be their own worst enemy in not submitting timely and complete paperwork with the needed justification to ensure adequate staffing is available.
- Biomedical: Time and quality-based expectations for equipment preventive maintenance and break down repair.
- Facilities: Time and quality-based expectations for facility maintenance and environmental controls such as airflow, humidity and temperature controls.
- Environmental Services: Time and quality-based expectations for departmental cleaning based on industry regulations and standards.

We have seen too many SPDs that struggle with receiving the internal Customer support they require to successfully manage their operations. Simple requests for adequate and scheduled cleaning of the department often falls on deaf ears with environmental services stretched too thin. If one truly believes the SPD should be as clean as the Operating Room (which we and others around the world believe to be true), then cleaning becomes a critical aspect of infection control.

If you find yourself struggling to receive the attention required as an internal Customer, try creating your own performance measurements and measure your internal Supplies performance. This may provide you with the evidence and metrics needed to instill a sense of urgency and change.
Having determined both external and internal Customer requirements, we now move to the next chapter and discuss measurements.

Chapter Four: Measurements

> **"In God we trust, all others bring Data."**
>
> **Deming**

Step two in our Eight Steps to a Lean SPD addresses measurement of performance. Most sterile processing departments measure something. It may not be the right thing to measure but they measure something. At a bare minimum, there is the finance report which measures how much money was spent versus budget. Beyond that, the list of potential SPD measurements is quite long with some measurements being very valuable while others offering zero value.

At this point in the process of becoming a Lean SPD, our fictional SPD has listed the attributes of a perfect SPD and we identified our Customer requirements in the last chapter. The question then becomes; how can the department know if they are meeting their Customer requirements and making progress towards the perfect SPD?

In reviewing the attributes of the Perfect SPD that our fictional department came up with, you will notice that most of them are process related.

The Perfect SPD

- Sets clear expectations for all
- Provides feedback on departmental and individual performance

- Provides a structure for leadership and staff to work together to address issues and improve
- Supervisors have time to follow-up with their staff and help ensure they can do their job the proper way
- Has enough staff to keep up with the workload
- Provides adequate time for training
- Follows standard work instructions
- Only pick case carts and supplies that are used
- Staff can work uninterrupted
- Environment that is clean and orderly with proper environmental controls
- Has the needed supplies readily available and in working condition?
- Equipment that is maintained and working
- The OR asks how they can help SPD
- The OR would return all the instruments to the correct trays
- The OR would spray the instruments within enzymatic soaking solution after surgery

After reviewing the Perfect SPD list above, you will probably realize that most if not all SPDs do not measure these types of processes and whether they are moving towards or away from the Perfect SPD. For example, are you measuring how well your staff follows standard work instructions? Do you measure how effective your leadership is in giving feedback on departmental and individual performance? Do you measure interruptions?

Most SPDs measure outcomes such as number of errors, productivity, trays processed and budget. While measuring outcomes is important and assists in identifying progress and opportunities to improve, the lack of process measurements results in performance variance that results in less than desired outcomes. Here is an important point to understand.

- Measuring and managing process improves outcomes while measuring outcomes simply provides insight into whether your processes are working.

It makes sense to measure processes as well as outcomes. Ignoring process measurement is the equivalent of ignoring the root cause and focusing instead on symptoms. A Lean SPD should thus be focused on measuring and managing their processes to improve their outcomes.

Another important point in Lean is the understanding that lean systems expose waste. Measurements can be a useful tool in understanding how much waste is currently in the department and how well waste is being eliminated or accumulated. Later, we will explain the eight wastes of lean in more detail but for now think about how well you are using measurements to expose waste in your processes. Are you identifying how long instruments sit waiting? Defects and time spent on rework? Excess motion of staff? Excess transportation of instruments? Underutilized staff knowledge and ability?

In summary, operational measurements can be grouped into three categories:

- Outcome measurements
- Process measurements
- Waste measurements.

Measurements in General

The concept of managing operational processes through measurements has been around as long as modern manufacturing and comes from many sources. In the early days of the development of the Toyota Production System, it was learned that real time communication of results and progress with employees helped to engage and motivate them. Toyota began measuring operational performance and posting charts throughout their manufacturing plants not with the intent of driving more production but sharing information. Toyota found the results to be outstanding.

Measuring operational performance and sharing the information with employees can be a powerful cultural change agent. Given the right leadership and environment, measurements can motivate staff and leadership to continuously improve, ensure Customer satisfaction and improve operational efficiencies. Unfortunately, we have seen many organizations post their performance measurements only to find that the graphs and results become "wallpaper" that no one pays attention to. This should not be the case. While Leadership roles will be discussed in more detail later, it is sufficient to say that the staff's attention to posted measurements is a direct correlation to the leadership team's emphasis and importance they place on those measurements. If the leadership team does not pay attention to them, then the staff will not either.

If you are going to measure performance, then make sure that you place a value on meeting your objectives and institute consequences for poor performance. As individuals and organizations, we have a natural tendency to be motivated and perform according to how we are measured. Thus, it is important to institute the right measurements or else you may get staff performing a bit different than you expected. Examples of measurements missing the mark include:

- If efficiency is the primary measure, then staff will naturally strive to be efficient at the tasks they perform but may not follow standard work or complete the tasks that are a departmental priority.
- If the number of instrument trays completed is the primary measure, staff may select the easiest and quickest trays to work on without regard for priority or actual need.
- If the number of equipment cycles is the key measure, then focus will be on running more equipment cycles with less than full loads and without regard to actual operational needs.

The correct measures accurately capture department and individual performance as well as directly linked to the process and outcomes desired. These linked performance factors should be tracked, posted and discussed and corrective action should be taken to adjust less-than-desirable trends and result in appropriate and timely recognition and reward.

Timely reviews of the measurements are equally important. Too often, managers look at performance indicators too infrequently such as once a month. By then, the data is "old news" and they are focused on the current issue of the day. A manager or employee who is aware of poor performance early can make appropriate corrections and impact results quickly. Timely, consistent review of performance measurements is necessary for success. As a rule of thumb, performance measurements should be reviewed more frequently at the staff and department level and less frequently at the executive levels.

Ultimately our goals should be to provide our Customers with the best quality product, at the volume required, at the proper time and at the proper cost. Effective performance measurement for SPD processes help to establish the difference between perception and reality. They provide data, historical and real-time, and can be used to predict future outcomes. The use of consistent metrics can help measure the impact of improvement. They provide a baseline against which to measure performance and track whether improvements are temporary or sustained. They weave accountability into the initiative and provide a tangible picture of the organization's efforts.

Measurements must present data in such a way that drives us to act. They should identify what needs to be done, who needs to do it and how well the objectives and goals are being met. They should further the understanding of the processes and motivate the team or individual to action and improvement. Only then are performance measurements meaningful to you and your Customer.

There is a rule of process improvement that states, "We can't change what we don't measure," and its corollary, "Don't measure what you won't change." It is important that measurements be properly focused on elements of the operation that reflect what you value and want to improve. For example, if Customer satisfaction is valued by your SPD, then there must be a way to continually measure that value. First, identify what steps in your processes are critical to Customer satisfaction. Next, correlate your processes to the elements that are critical to improving Customer satisfaction. This will help focus staff attention and improvement efforts on areas that actual improve Customer satisfaction.

Outcome Measurements

Outcome Measurements are by far the most common and perhaps easiest to collect and report. They represent the final product or service, the Customer experience and the culmination of everyone's efforts. They are often the ultimate measurement to be held accountable for. Outcome measurements are frequently used to determine bonuses, rewards, individual and departmental recognition. They are utilized to compare departments and institutions to benchmarks or each other. They are the final grade, the visible reflection of your work and the standard by which success or failure is determined. In short, outcome measurements are extremely important to us for obvious reasons.

They are not the best measurements to compare a process to. As stated earlier, outcome measurements are simply a reflection of the underlying process, the symptom of an effective or dysfunctional operation, and an indication of our core ability to perform. Lean operations do not rely on outcome measurements but rather utilize them as an indication of how well their process measurements are successfully managing their operations.

An outcome measurement that has recently been highly visible is the number of automobile recalls due to defective parts. The outcome measurement is the defective car. Announcing that 200,000 automobiles will be recalled (outcome measurement of quality) simply says that a process earlier on broke down. Quality was not managed; decisions were not managed, and the process was not able to effectively correct the defect early enough to avoid the mass recall. Similarly, in the SPD, tracking the number of defects the OR experiences is a valuable measurement but is simply a measurement of a process breakdown days or weeks earlier.

Outcome measurements do support the general measurement goals of driving organizations to take action and motivate individuals to find ways to improve. They are also a valid indicator of overall process effectiveness and whether improvement initiatives are working, and improvements sustained. Outcome measurements provide a valid "voice of the Customer" measurement. In short, Outcome measurements are valuable but should be combined with process and waste measurements to create a balanced measurement scorecard.

So, what are the most beneficial outcome measurements for a SPD? While every SPD may be slightly different, serve different Customers and have different circumstances, the following outcome measurements are commonly shared amongst most sterile processing departments:

- Instrument set quality (defects)
- Complete instrument sets
- Complete case carts
- On-time delivery
- Customer experience
- Customer satisfaction
- Staff satisfaction

Instrument Set Quality (Defects) – Instrument set quality measures how your product (instrument sets) met the Customer requirements and performed according to specification. To effectively measure instrument set quality as an outcome measurement, three questions need to be answered:

- What constitutes a defect?
- How will the defects be identified and reported?
- How will the defects be measured?

<u>What Constitutes a Defect?</u>
In the simplest form, a defect is anything that does not meet the Customer requirements. For instrument sets, this can include missing instruments, dirty instruments, broken instruments, wrong instruments, incorrectly labeled instruments, non-operable instruments and non-sterile instruments. Defects highlight a process breakdown in the actual reprocessing of the instruments. Decontamination, prep and pack (assembly), or sterilization did not perform their task correctly and thus produced a bad product. To determine what constitutes a defect, most SPDs can create lists quickly and accurately on their own. Though it is recommended to take the time to sit down with your

Customer and have them agree to the defect list as well. It will only help to strengthen the bond between SPD and their Customers and may highlight issues that were not thought about before.

How Will the Defects Be Identified and Reported?

Here is where the process tends to break down. In numerous SPDs we have worked in, it is commonplace to hear the statement "The OR doesn't report all the issues so we track what we can." How you identify and record defects is critical to the success and believability of the measurement. If you are only receiving what the Customer is willing to tell you, then you only have half the story. Too often when the OR is asked why they do not bother reporting all the issues they have one of two responses: 1. "We're too busy to worry about the issues that aren't critical" or 2. "SPD doesn't do anything to fix the problems so why should we take the time to report them."

Here is where the rubber hits the road. First, the SPD department must take the defect data and make sustainable changes to improve performance and then report this improvement to their Customer. If the SPD is not going to make the effort to improve then how can the OR be blamed for not reporting issues. Remember the sayings, "We can't change what we don't measure" and "Don't measure what you won't change?" SPDs need to look at themselves in the mirror and honestly answer these two questions. I doubt any department would say they do not want to improve performance and reduce defects, but the truth is many SPDs are having the same defect issues today as they did yesterday, last week, last month and last year. The perception of the OR is that they are not doing anything about it. Here is where perception is greater than reality. If you are continuously improving but still having quality issues, then your Customer may not believe you are doing anything to improve unless you tell them. Perception can only be changed through communication, and communication takes effort. So what to do?

First, set up communication channels between the SPD and its Customers, especially the OR. Second, communicate your measurements on a regular basis with your Customers along with the action plans that you have implemented based on their feedback. Third, gain their trust. Any time the OR invests in reporting issues, big or small, their effort should be seen as valuable and acted upon. Fourth, make improvements that change the underlying processes and employee behaviors that will change the outcomes. Do not simply tell your staff a mistake was made and that they need to be more careful next time. Dig into the root causes and find a better way to do the job that reduces quality issues. We will address Problem Solving skills later in the book, but for now the point is to gain your Customer's trust. Let the OR know that it is worth their time to report any quality issues they uncover.

Reality may be different though, and your Customer may not agree to take the time and report all the quality issues and simply look to you to figure it out. What to do now? In this situation, SPDs have taken it upon themselves to go and collect the data themselves by rounding in the OR. While this may increase the labor required by the SPD, it does show the Customer that the department is serious about identifying and reporting all quality issues by taking the time and coming to their Customer. Take time to round all first cases and record everything you learn. Then throughout the day return to your Customers and follow-up on the products and services you are providing to identify both the good and the bad. Record everything you can about the issues and use the data to investigate root causes.

One example that seemed to work well for one hospital was the case cart quality sheet placed on every single case cart. If any issue was found with the instruments, supplies or case cart in general, the OR could record the issue on the case cart quality sheet that was taped to the top of the case cart. Since every case cart was given a sheet and every case cart returned to the SPD, a reliable method of receiving the feedback good, bad and indifferent was already in place. The SPD needed to convince the OR it was worthy of the time necessary to record the issues on the provided sheet. Once recorded, the SPD would take action and report back on implemented improvements.

How Will Defects Be Measured?

Measuring defects can be accomplished a few different ways with the most common decision being what to use as the denominator in the calculation. The three most common forms of instrument set quality measurements are:

# of Defects Reported Today

$$\frac{\text{\# of Defects Reported Today}}{\text{\# of Sets Processed Today}}$$

$$\frac{\text{\# of Defects Reported Today}}{\text{\# of Instruments Processed Today}}$$

- # of Defects Reported Today: This measurement is purely a defect count. It is easy to understand and highlights the fact that zero is the objective while giving no indication as to the scope of the issue in comparison to the volume of work. Three defects in one day may be a poor day for a small SPD processing only 80 instrument sets but an acceptable day for a SPD processing 600 instrument sets.
- # of Defects Reported Today / # of Sets Processed Today: This measurement is the most common of the percentage measurements. It can be stated as a defect rate (1.5% defects for example) or the inverse as a quality rate (98.5% quality for example). While the defects reported today have no operational correlation to the sets processed today (they would have been processed on a prior day) it is still a valid indicator of quality trends and performance. Using the # of Sets as the denominator also aligns more with the Customer experience since they typically evaluate the situation by how many of their sets had issues.
- # of Defects Reported Today / # of Instruments Processed Today: This measurement favors the SPD department by creating a very large denominator of individual instruments processed and thus dramatically increased the quality percentage as compared to using #

> of Sets instead. While the SPD department may conclude that # of Instruments is a valid measurement since each instrument represents an opportunity for a defect, the resulting percentage becomes so small that staff is often led into complacency.

To show how each of the three different measurement methods can visually present the same data in a very different view, we have graphed the following data for each. The data represents a large SPD department processing 400 trays a day with an average of 3 defects per day. Each graph seems to tell a different story, but the numbers are the same. The # of Defects graph is the easiest for Customers to understand and gets right to the point. On Day 5 we had six errors. The second graph, Defects per Set, is harder for the Customer to translate into their experience as Customers can not relate to a 99.5% quality experience. They just know they have experienced problems. The third graph, Defects per Instruments, needs to have the Y-axis scale changed to see the fluctuations in daily results as the Customer could never understand how their actual experience relates to such a good graph where quality is 99.9%.

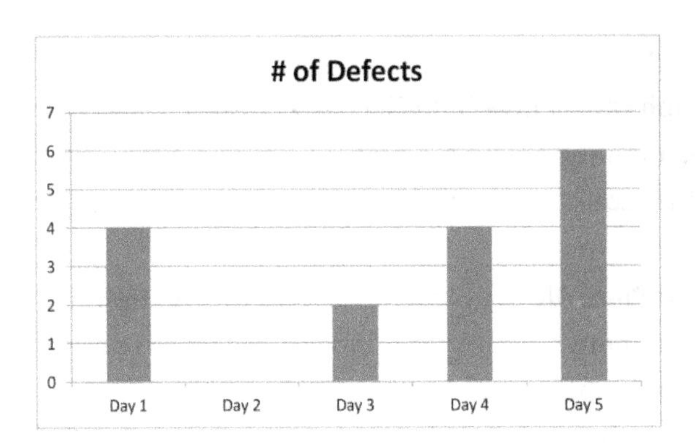

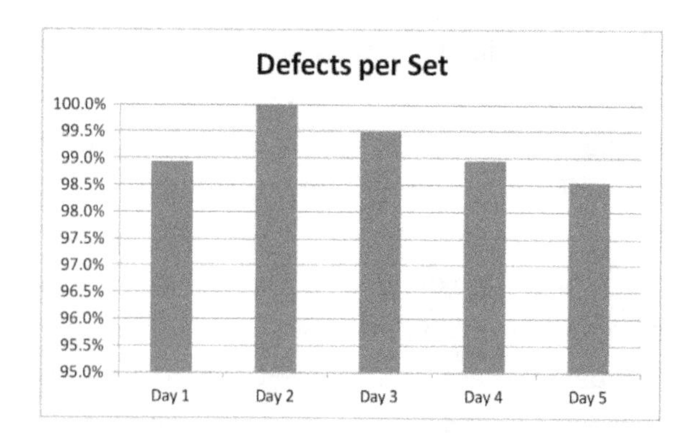

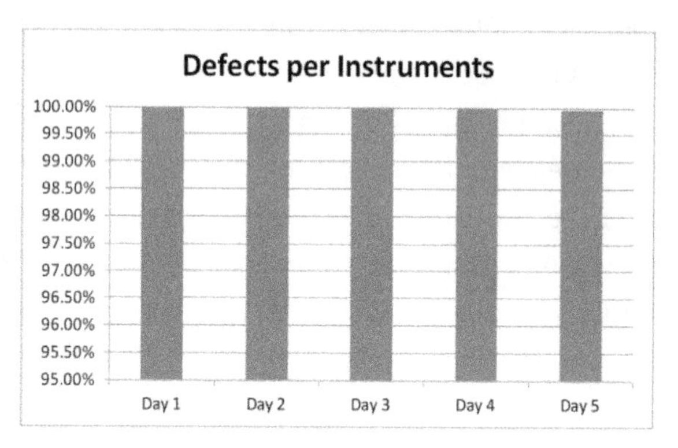

The above graphs are simple but effective graphs to show trends and actual performance. In the spirit of Six Sigma, we'll share a few notes on additional information that could be useful when presenting data graphically.

- **Goal or Plan**: Always present the goal or plan for the performance measurement. In the graphs above, the goal is not shown but rather assumed to be zero defects or 100% quality. In other measurements, the goal may not be obvious and thus needs to be depicted either graphically or written into the title area.
- **Baseline**: It is sometimes beneficial to state the baseline against which current performance should be measured. This would provide a reference point for the viewer to understand if current performance has improved or deteriorated against the starting point. The easiest method to state a baseline is to build it into the graph.

- **Upper and Lower Limits**: For some measurements, there may be an acceptable or planned variance in performance. To indicate how far the performance is allowed or expected to vary, the upper and lower limits should be graphically shown. If performance exceeds either of these limits, the process has either increased in variability (which is bad) or performance in general has improved or deteriorated from the original starting point. Upper and lower limits should be adjusted as performance changes over time.

The graphs below show a goal, baseline and upper and lower limits graph for a backlog measurement. In the graph on the left, actual performance shows a high variability with values above and below the limits. High variability performance is a symptom of a non-stable process. Stable processes, as shown in the graph on the right, remain within their upper and lower limits and provide a predictable environment.

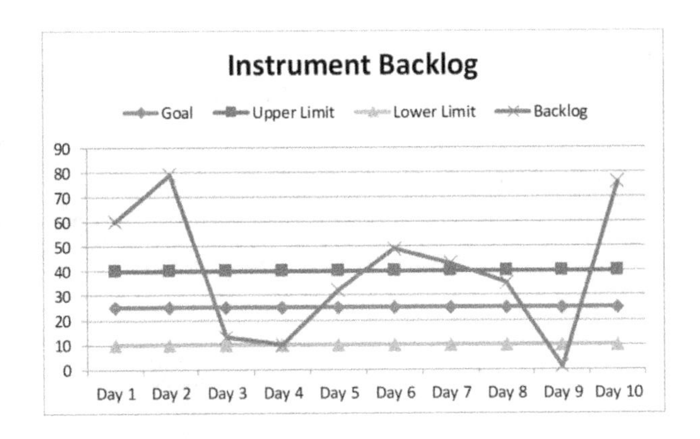

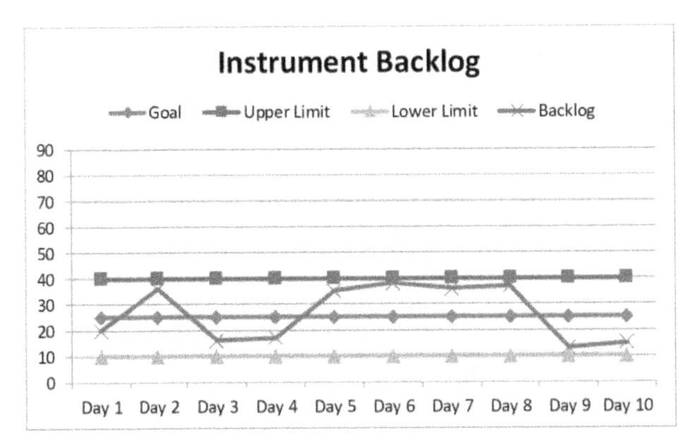

When implementing lean or any process improvement, it is important to build predictability into the process as well. Improved performance that varies widely from one day to the next is just as annoying and problematic as poor performance in general. Lean, as well as Six Sigma and other methodologies, strives to eliminate process variance and create controlled environments. It has been proven to work, even in sterile processing departments! Below are actual before and after results from a six-month lean process improvement project at a mid-sized SPD serving 20 operating rooms, two hospital towers, multiple clinics, OR support functions and hospital durable medical equipment. Notice that the implementation of lean methodologies helped improve overall performance while simultaneously reducing the variance between minimum and maximum fluctuations. As described earlier, the baseline performance for Quality was unknown because the OR was not reporting issues and the SPD was not actively following up and tracking them down.

Performance Measurements	Before Lean Min-Avg-Max	After Lean Min-Avg-Max
Instrument Set Backlog at 7AM	0 - 63 - 146	2 - 12 - 31
% Complete Instrument Trays	90% - 96% - 99%	93% - 97% - 99%
% Complete Case Carts	42% - 76% - 96%	89% - 97% - 100%
Productivity = Hours Per Tray	0.93 - 1.37 - 2.16	0.80 - 1.00 - 1.20
# of Quality Errors per Day	Insufficient Data	1 - 5 - 8

Complete Instrument Sets –Complete instrument sets measure the number of instrument sets assembled complete versus the total number of sets assembled daily. This measurement is one that the SPD can track internally without input from the Customer. For departments using electronic instrument set assembly via software, the data is most likely already available and easily accessed. The one weakness of this metric is the accuracy of the person assembling the instrument set. If he or she incorrectly assembles the set missing an item but indicates in the system that it is complete, you will have incorrect data. Experience though has shown that the number of staff errors of this nature are very small compared to the number of sets assembled and should not deter the measurement being utilized. Thus, the actual definition is better defined as the number of instrument sets recorded as complete versus the total number of sets assembled daily. When an instrument set is found to be incomplete but marked as complete in the system, it can be categorized as a defect.

An additional attribute to this measurement would be the number of instrument sets received from the OR complete versus the number of instrument sets completed by SPD. An example would be 70% of instrument sets are received from the OR complete while 90% are completed by SPD. This represents an improvement of 20 percentage points by the SPD department. Additionally, it highlights the OR's ability to return the proper instruments to the proper sets after use to improve the workflow and remove waste from the processes within the SPD in trying to find the missing instruments.

This measurement is typically shown as a percentage of complete sets with the ultimate goal being 100% complete. Another option is to report the actual number of Instrument Sets not completed with the goal being zero. Various process management decisions can also play into this measurement such as whether implants should be counted as a missing instrument when they are not stocked for replenishment but ordered after use. Additionally, decisions could be made by the SPD leadership team to hold instrument sets in their department for a period of time to locate missing instruments before finishing the assembly process.

The graphs below show both the % Complete Instrument Set option as well as actual # Incomplete Instrument Sets with Goal and Lower/Upper Limit lines to show current performance ranges. In both cases, the Goal represents the appropriate Lower or Upper Limit. Leadership should have process improvement initiatives in place to eventually raise or lower the Goal and Limit towards the ultimate goal of perfection. Additionally, when any measurement is outside the red limit line, leadership should require a detailed review and root cause analysis to further understand operational issues. Both graphs represent the exact same data set as well.

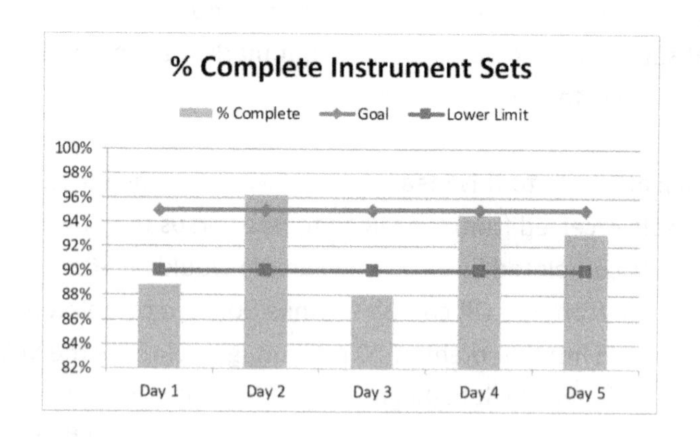

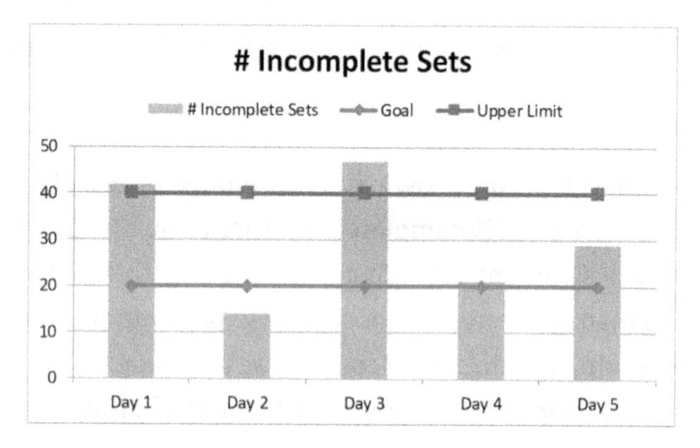

Complete Case Carts – Complete case carts can be measured various ways. Three options are shown below. The first two graphs focus attention on the case carts and whether the cart is complete or not. The third graph focuses attention on the number of items missing from the case carts. Percentage graphs are great at stating the measurement in terms of overall performance while raw data graphs such as # Incomplete are great at highlighting the actual extent of the issue being addressed. No matter which graph, or combination of graphs, is utilized the action steps required to improve performance towards the goal and eventual perfection would be the same. Leadership should understand the reasons why actual performance is below or above goal and how it can be improved. For complete case carts, this usually requires an understanding of what specific items are missing, the reason they are missing, and what action can be taken. From the graphs below, it would seemingly make sense to focus attention first on supply issues due to the high number of supplies missing.

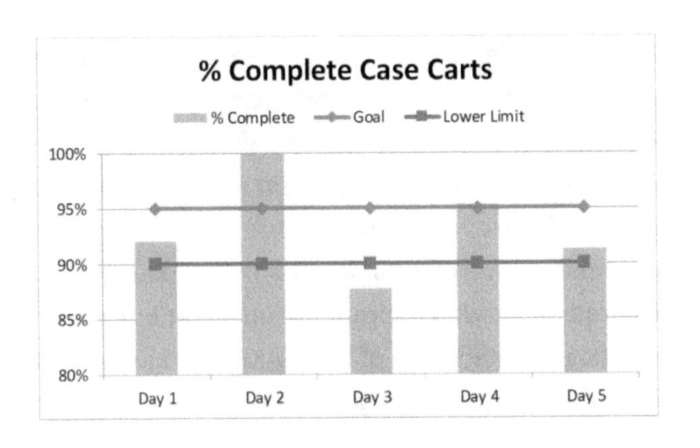

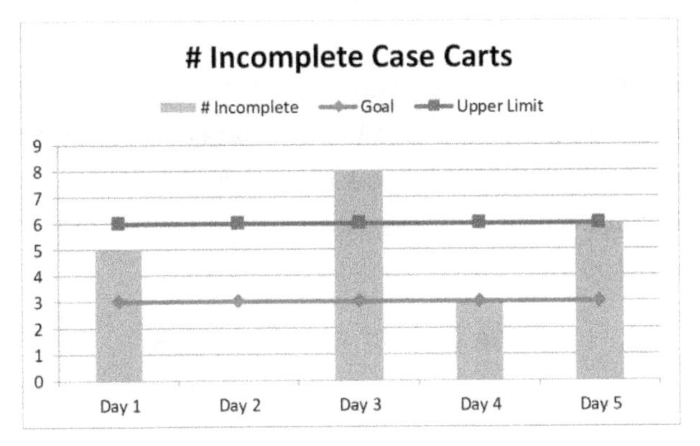

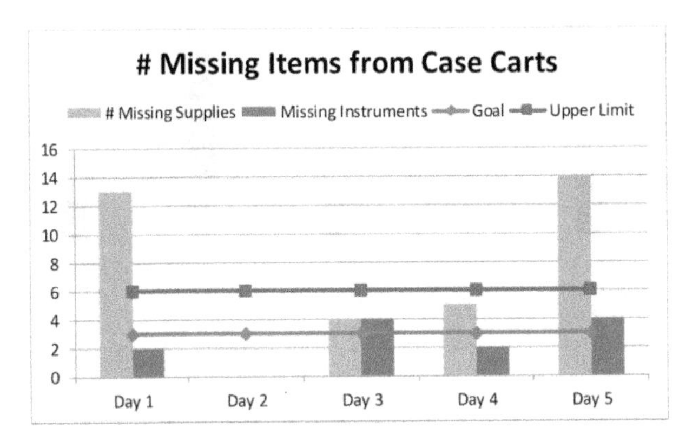

On-Time Delivery – On-time delivery measures how well the SPD is meeting the Customer requirements for delivery of items. Whether this is for case carts, quick turn instrument trays or floor items, the department's delivery performance should be measured. How this data is captured and recorded is dependent on the department's processes. Instrument tracking systems could be utilized to provide time stamps for reference. Document tags, see Lean Definitions, could be utilized to record plan and actual delivery or pick-up times to determine whether requirements were met. An example would be a quick turn requirement for an instrument set needed for a surgical case later in the day. The OR uses the instrument set, hands off the set to SPD at 10:45AM with a needed time of 1:30PM for an afternoon case. The document tag (piece of colored paper with appropriate information) would be completed indicating the start time of 10:45AM, instrument set name, need time of 1:30pm and destination such as OR #5. There would be a time stamp at each step of the way for decontamination, assembly, sterilization and delivery to the OR. The document tag would be returned and entered into the measurement database for tracking. The follow graph is an example of a late delivery / pick-up graph showing the raw data of late performance. Notice that even though Day 2 showed 100% complete case carts in the previous graph, they delivered three case carts late in this graph.

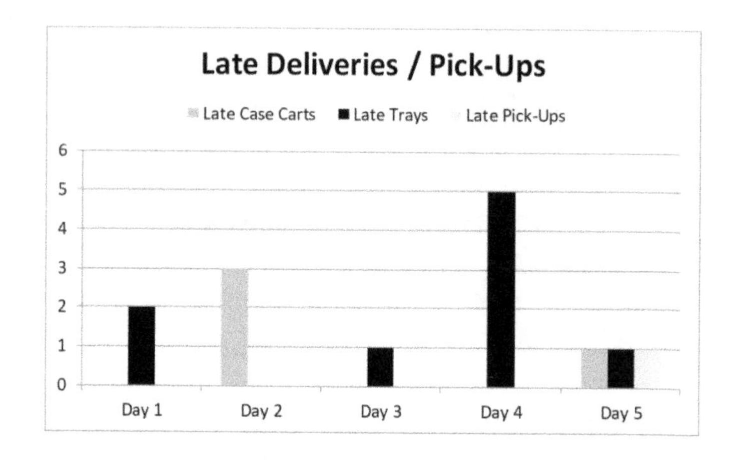

Customer Experience – Customer experience measures how well the SPD department fulfills the Customer's requirements on a per event basis. This measurement is an excellent one to share with your Customers for the simple reason it speaks to their experience. An example is the OR experience where the measurement is number of surgery cases with no issues versus total number of surgery cases. Whether the issue is a late delivery, an incomplete instrument set or incomplete case cart they all are accounted for in the Customer experience. This measurement is more difficult to score well on as the denominator in the percentage calculation is the number of OR surgeries. Like other measurements, Customer experience can be stated as a percentage or a raw score as shown below. In both circumstances, the Customer has set the current goal of no more than three negative experiences or surgical cases with an issue each day which represents approximately 5% of the cases. Based on these graphs, this SPD has some work to do.

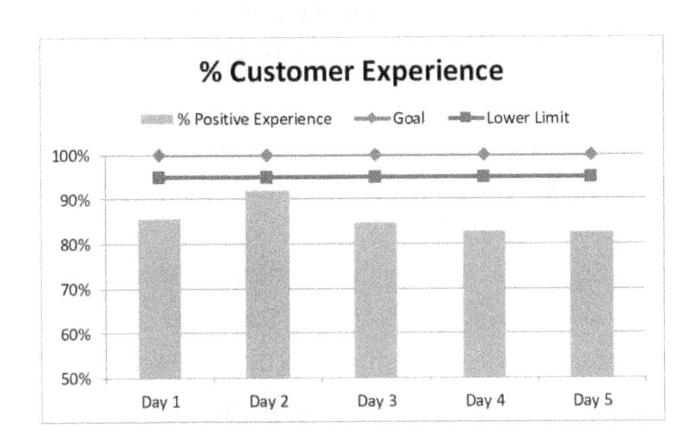

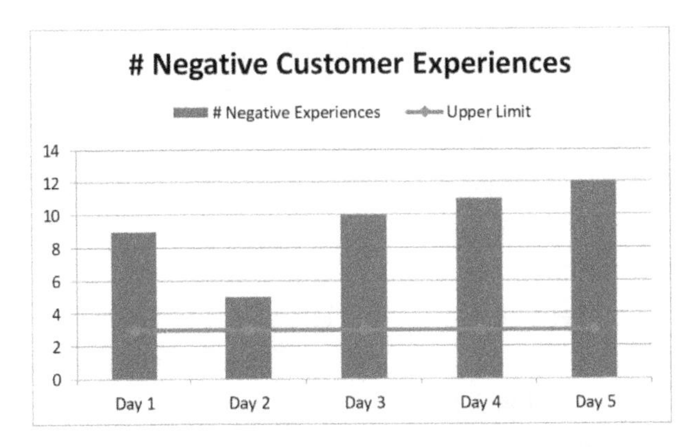

Customer Satisfaction – Customer satisfaction is usually tied to surveys or direct Customer feedback. The frequency of the feedback can be set by the hospital or SPD department. Frequent feedback allows for early identification of trends and movement either positive or negative in Customer satisfaction. Early identification enables the SPD leadership team to address issues before they affect a larger population as well as reinforce positive operational performance that is improving satisfaction. At a minimum, it is recommended that Customer satisfaction be surveyed at least twice a year for the entire population of Customers. On a more frequent basis, random samples of Customers can be surveyed.

Customer surveys help you identify Customers who are unhappy with the service or product being supplied and more importantly the reasons for their dissatisfaction. Conversely, surveys help identify advocates who are happy with your service and can help improve relationships with other Customers. A Customer survey enables you to identify trends and help you make better decisions to improve the overall Customer experience. They help identify Customer likes, dislikes, and the specific areas of improvement that exist.

For example, what does the average Customer think about your delivery and turn times? How well is your staff providing Customer service? Surveys let you hold employees accountable to the level of service they are delivering and empowers your staff to meet objectives based on Customer needs.

Once you have decided to survey your Customers, you will first have to decide who to survey as well as what questions to ask them. For a typical SPD department, their OR is their largest and most important Customer, so it is recommended to start there. Within the OR, there are surgeons, OR leadership and OR staff with each group having slightly different perspectives of the SPD's performance. Historically, surgeons have had a very low response rate to surveys and simply tell leadership to fix the problem if they perceive one to exist. OR leadership and staff have typically provided more than enough survey feedback to create a valid and actionable to do list for most SPDs. It is suggested to utilize the weekly morning in-service time on late start day to survey the OR staff and leadership when they are all together. In this setting, simply have them fill out the survey immediately, give them 5 minutes, and then do not let them leave until they have completed it.

For Customers other than the OR, take the time and talk to them about the possibility of surveying them throughout the year and come to an agreement on frequency, whom to survey, and what type of questions to ask. For the OR, we have included a sample OR Customer survey below showing the horizontal and color-coded graphical display results. This survey is broken into four sections: Instrument and Trays, Case Carts, SPD Service, and Service Scores.

A few tips on developing surveys includes creating a scoring scale using odd numbers such as the five options shown below. A common and effective five category scoring method is Excellent, Good, Average, Fair and Poor. The last survey example below utilizes a scale of 1 to 10. All surveys should also provide the opportunity for your Customers to write personal comments to help explain why they are scoring the way they did.

Sample OR Survey Results

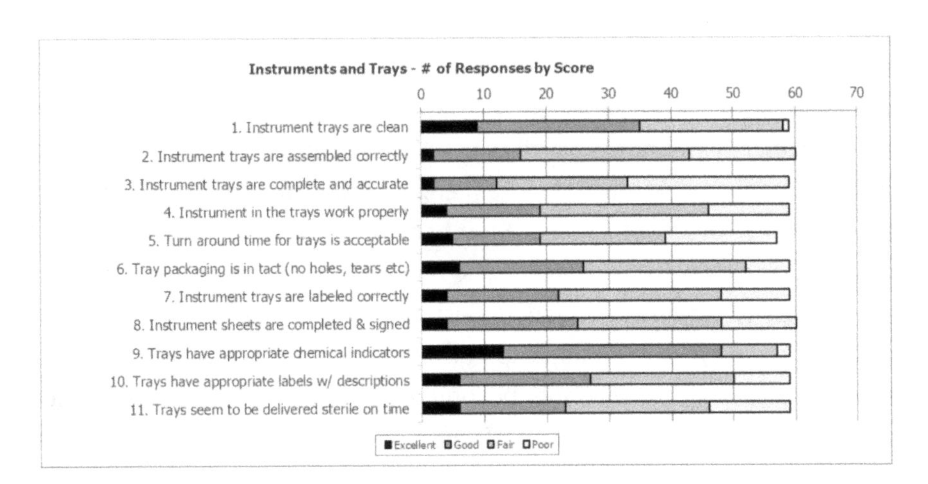

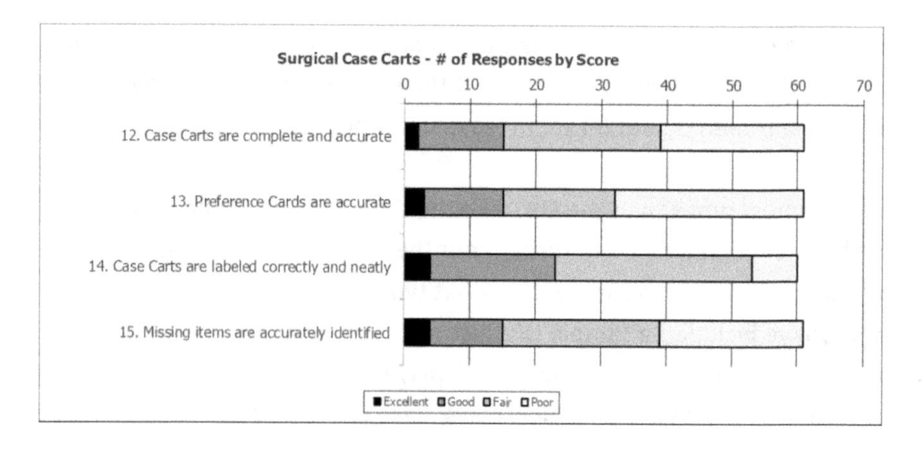

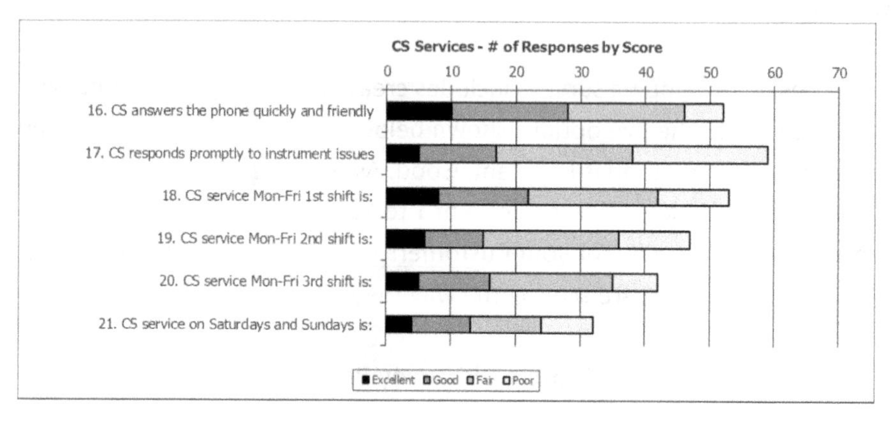

Staff Satisfaction – Staff satisfaction measures employee satisfaction with their working environment as well as their level of engagement. Successful lean organizations develop and sustain engaged staff participation in a continuous improvement culture. Staff become engaged when they are happy with their work environment and feel valued. Happy and engaged staff is more likely to provide outstanding Customer service and produce quality work. Thus, the cyclical relationship between staff satisfaction and Customer satisfaction and quality can either become a positive reinforcing experience or deteriorate into a negative culture. Thus, staff satisfaction is just as important to measure and manage.

The questions you ask your staff are important to determine beforehand. You may even include them in developing the survey and work this into the perfect SPD conversation early on. The sample survey results shown below include five categories of Education, Environment, Leadership, OR, and Service. Similar to the Customer satisfaction survey, the survey should be administered twice a year covering the total population with random sample size surveys throughout the year as desired.

Sample SPD Staff Survey Results

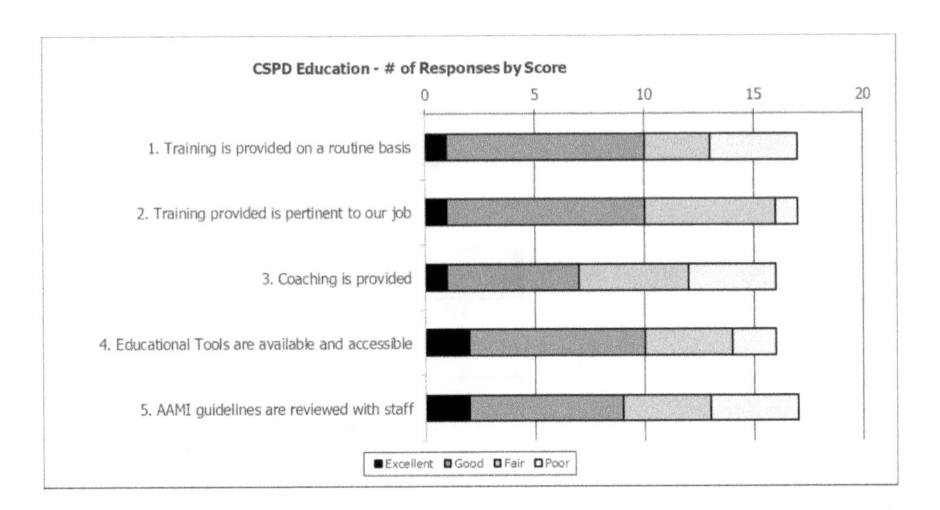

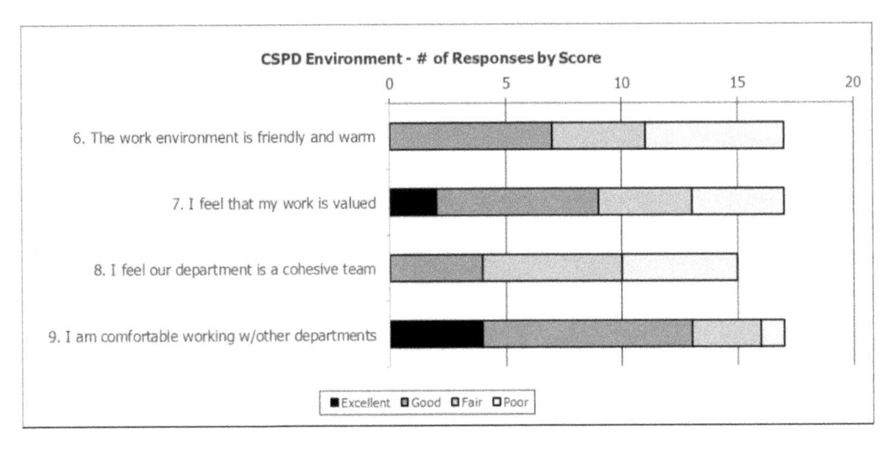

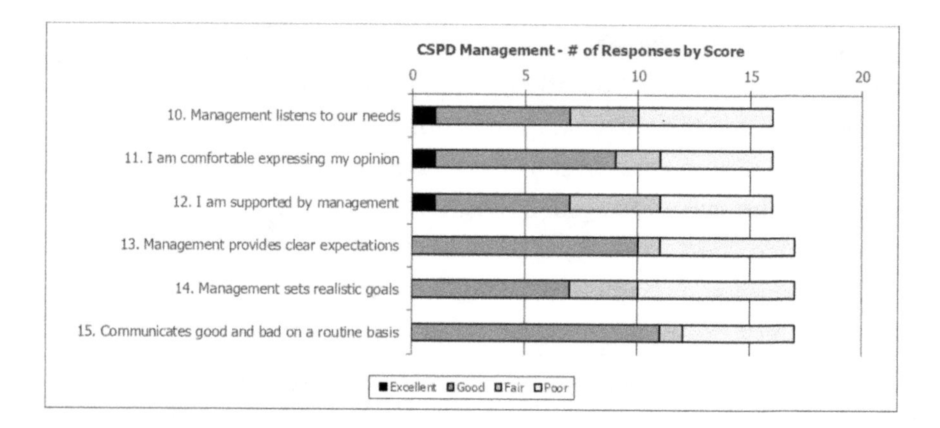
CSPD Management - # of Responses by Score
0
5
10
15
20
10. Management listens to our needs
11. I am comfortable expressing my opinion
12. I am supported by management
13. Management provides clear expectations
14. Management sets realistic goals
15. Communicates good and bad on a routine basis
Excellent
Good
Fair
Poor

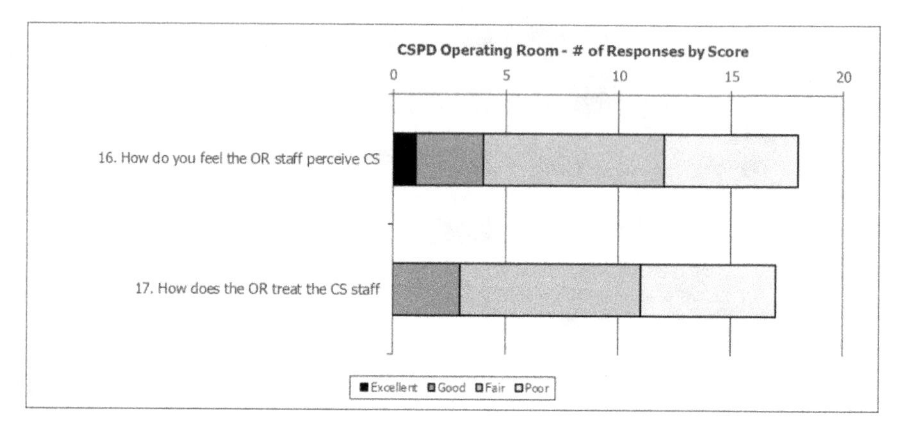
CSPD Operating Room - # of Responses by Score
0
5
10
15
20
16. How do you feel the OR staff perceive CS
17. How does the OR treat the CS staff
Excellent
Good
Fair
Poor

Process Measurements

Process measurements represent the heart of lean. They may not be easy to measure or track and may require additional daily leadership and staff effort. They may be difficult to improve, but they provide the best opportunity and information to improving operational performance. Occasionally, process measurements are duplicates of outcome measurements as well. To better understand process measurements, it is beneficial to understand the concept of process handoffs and task management.

The following graphic displays a generic process of four steps with three internal handoffs. Each blue section represents an activity that should be completed according to standard work. The red sections represent a transfer of the product from one task and one work area to the next task and work area. While each blue section traditionally has or should have standard work instructions clarifying how the work should be completed according to quality, quantity and timeliness guidelines to meet Customer expectations, each red section should also have handoff expectations. Stated another way, each blue section is the internal Customer of the previous blue section. Thus, Step 2 is the Customer of Step 1, Step 3 is the Customer of Step 2 and Step 4 is the Customer of Step 3. Utilizing Lean principles, each process should perform in a manner to meet the Customer expectations. While the entire process is working towards the ultimate Customer requirements, process measurements are focused on ensuring each step of the process also not only meets the ultimate Customer requirements but also the internal Customer requirements.

Example of Four Step Process with Three Internal Handoffs

Using this principle, let us take a look at the typical workflow to reprocess surgical instrumentation to identify the work activities and handoffs. Then we can determine what Process Measurements can and should be tracked.

Example of Seven Step Process with Six Internal Handoffs

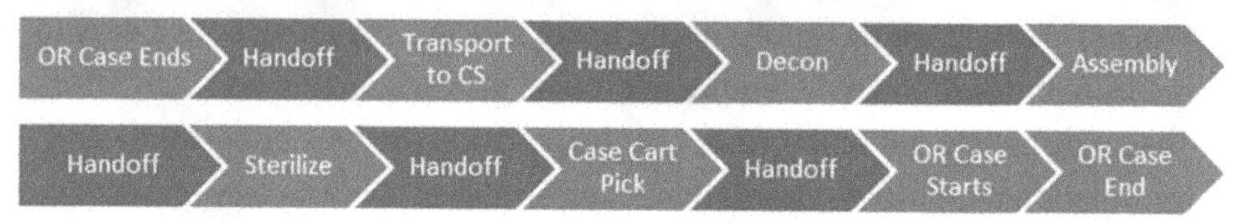

Based on this simple process map, the potential Process Measurements for reprocessing surgical instrumentation include the following.

Potential SPD Process Measurements for Surgical Instrument Reprocessing

- OR handoff compliance
- Transport adherence to standard work and delivery of instruments
- Transport handoff compliance
- Instrument set backlog in decontamination
- Decontamination adherence to standard work
- Decontamination handoff compliance
- Dirty instruments caught in assembly
- Instrument set backlog in assembly
- Complete sets received from OR
- Complete instrument sets
- Assembly handoff compliance
- Sterilization compliance
- Sterilization handoff to case cart pick
- Case cart pick compliance to standard work
- Case cart pick handoff to OR
- Productivity
- Task completion

In reality, not all of these potential measurements will be measured, but we want you to understand the concept of process measurement and then apply it where it is needed the most.

In looking at this list, it is a bit overwhelming to think that this is a simple listing of the multiple processes that are happening in a typical SPD. Two main concepts stand out though: 1. The need to implement and measure compliance to standard work instructions and 2. Set, manage and measure handoff expectations. These two concepts form the guiding principle behind process measurements. Let us take a few of these and provide some real-life examples.

OR Handoff Compliance – Keeping to the process mentality, the first step in any process is the receipt of raw materials from a supplier or previous process. SPDs are in a unique position where their raw materials, such as dirty and used instrument sets, are received from their Customer. Using lean methods though, the receipt of dirty and used instruments from the OR for example should follow and adhere to agreed-upon expectations. This concept applies to every handoff within any process. The previous step in the process understands the requirements of the next step in the process and makes sure they meet those expectations. For a traditional manufacturing or assembly line process this could encompass timing of delivery of materials, quantity of materials, quality or state of materials such as correct size, functionality and presentation. Within the sterile processing environment this starts with the OR handing off dirty instruments to the SPD.

Handoff requirements from the OR to SPD are based on AORN recommended guidelines for instrumentation handling and end of case handling. Best practices call for the OR to remove gross bioburden at point of use and dispose sharps appropriately. At the end of the case they then return instrumentation in a safe method to the proper instrument tray taking care to not damage anything and apply a soaking solution to maintain moisture levels and inhibit bioburden from drying. Whether this is performed by the scrub technician, circulator or surgical services support staff is at the hospital's discretion. Whether it is done should not be a discretionary decision but rather standard work for instrumentation handling.

The process measurement is how well the OR is complying with the standard procedure. Typically, decontamination receives the OR's used instrumentation and is where compliance is measured. Since it is a dirty environment, the measurement should be as easy as possible and focus on the non-compliance or non-conforming instruments sets. The following two graphs give an example of how this measurement can be visually displayed.

Note: Remember the measurement saying, "Don't measure what you won't change." This saying applies greatly to the OR Handoff Compliance Measurement. If you find yourself in a situation where the OR is not willing to participate and take ownership of their handoff for end of case instrument handling, then this measurement becomes a futile exercise. Do not let a situation like this stop you from utilizing measurements in general. Typically, ORs who are not willing to participate in improving the instrumentation process usually state two reasons: 1. SPD needs to fix their issues first, or 2. We are too busy turning over our rooms, and that is the higher priority. Reason #1 is a good one. SPDs need to worry first about their internal processes before asking their Customer to change theirs. Remember the perfect SPD exercise and the staff's immediate desire to point the finger at the OR? Well, you can only do that after you have fixed your own house. For reason #2, there could be numerous reasons ranging from valid to invalid. Unfortunately, there is no easy answer except to focus on improving the SPD processes as best as you can and utilize clinical and operational measurements to prove your case and how it adds value to the organization.

Example of OR Handoff Compliance Measurement

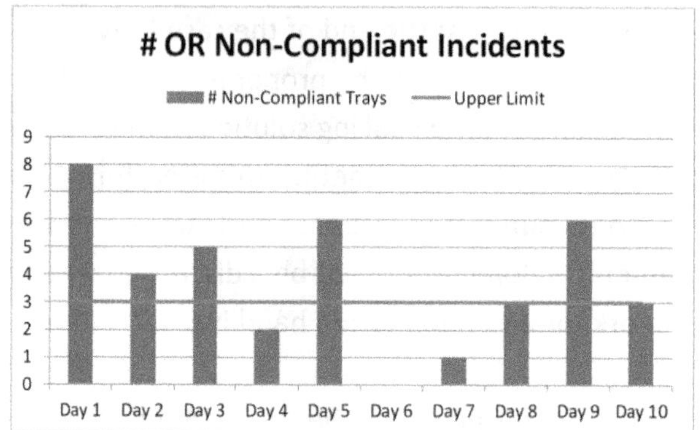

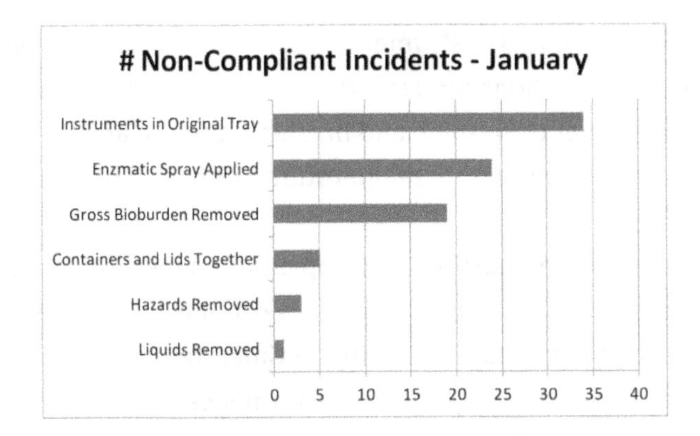

Decontamination Adherence to Standard Work – Adherence to standard work is critical throughout any process and can be improved and managed using employee engagement, supervisory routines, and measurements. Employee engagement refers to a work culture where employees care about how they perform their tasks and they self-monitor themselves to the standard work. Supervisory routines, explained in-depth later in this book, refers to active on-the-floor follow-up with specific attention paid to ensuring staff are following standard work. Measurements are utilized to capture staff's adherence to standard work either manually or electronically. This is where technology can greatly assist both the staff member attempting to perform the standard work as well as the leadership team attempting to monitor and measure adherence to standard work.

In decontamination for example, a typical standard work requirement would require the staff to scan incoming case carts and instrument trays, break down case carts and containers, remove filters, properly wash case carts and containers in the cart washer, stage instruments at the appropriate sinks for either hand washing or manual prep for automated washing, follow manufacturer's instructions for use in pre-cleaning instruments, utilize correct washer cycles and wear the appropriate personal protective equipment. Each decontamination is different, but this example provides a baseline to discuss the difficulties in measuring how well staff are adhering to the standard work for the area.

How can we be sure that all instruments are scanned? How can we confirm staff is following instructions for use? How can we ensure staff is effectively pre-cleaning instruments, flushing and brushing lumens, and using the correct amount of enzymatic in properly temperature-controlled water?

Before we answer these questions and implement a method to measure compliance, it is best to first understand how often the measurement should be completed. Options include 100% of the time, routine samples such as every 10th item, or as needed based on performance. How often you measure compliance depends on the level of quality or precision required, the criticality of task, or current issues being faced.

If the process or task being performed requires the staff to execute at a very high level of precision or it will negatively impact a patient's life, then 100% compliance measurement is recommended, and standard work must be followed. If the task being performed is important to quality but is not experiencing any current issues, then routine audits may fulfill the need to measure. As needed, measurements are usually utilized for processes that typically operate within quality parameters and can accept small levels of variance in performance; however, measurements occasionally need additional attention due to new staff, new techniques or occasional process drift. Frequencies should only be utilized for processes that are by design error proof, are very difficult to vary from the standard work and/or have very little impact on Customer requirements should the standard work be deviated from.

For decontamination, most SPDs rely on staff to self-monitor themselves with an annual competency check as a refresher. For those who prefer to move beyond self-monitoring and utilize lean concepts to truly understand actual compliance and thus actively manage it, we have a few suggestions.

Leadership Audits for Compliance Measurements

We will talk more on leadership routines in a later chapter but need to introduce the audit concept at this point to complete the measurement discussion. In almost every lean implementation project, most of the time is spent with the supervisory team responsible for on-the-floor management. Their presence on the floor overseeing people and process becomes a pivotal success point to every Lean SPD transformation. Considerable time is spent teaching them how to "see" the work being performed through the lens of lean. This includes seeing waste, seeing opportunities for improvement, questioning why things are the way they are and, in this case, seeing compliance to standard work. Having a supervisor spend 5 to 10 minutes observing the work in decontamination throughout the day with various staff often leads to surprising findings for leadership teams not accustomed to it. Frequent quotes such as "They're not supposed to do it that way," or "That's not how I told them to do it!" are often heard. Comments such as these inevitably led to discussions on why processes and people drift from standard work and what the supervisor's role is in ensuring compliance.

Leadership audits for decontamination compliance to standard work provide valuable information and can easily be converted into a Process Measurement. A simple method is to have your supervisors visit decontamination throughout their shift and spend 5 to 10 minutes observing the work being performed. If staff is following standard work, then they score the observation as compliant. If variance is observed, they score the observation as non-compliant. This provides an opportunity to provide real time coaching. For this work, supervisors must know and understand the standard work themselves and spend enough time observing to determine compliance!

Leadership audits do not provide 100% compliance or else the supervisor would spend their entire day watching staff in decontamination: however, they are effective as routine samples or as needed compliance checks. Using the Toyota concept of the Kamishibai board, audit cards can be scheduled throughout the month to provide a valid sample size compliance check for decontamination compliance to standard work. Since decontamination can have multiple standard work instructions, the audit cards can be specialized to focus in on specific activities such as scanning, instrument pre-cleaning, or manual washing compliance. The card itself has bullet points from the standard work to ensure the observer checks the appropriate compliance. It is also color-coded red on one side for non-compliance and green on the other for compliance. The cards should be randomly drawn on a weekly basis with every week having an agreed upon number of compliance audits. After completing the audit, the card is placed in the visual audit board for the day of the month with either green or red facing outward so that all staff can see if they passed the daily audit. Decontamination would have its own audit board.

Process audits add value by ensuring leadership is spending time observing work practices, ensuring standard work is reviewed, creating a culture of compliance, helping sustain process improvements and providing a visual compliance scorecard. A sample of a decontamination audit card is shown below along with the sample process measurements.

Example of Standard Work Compliance Audit Card – one side green one side red

Decontamination Pre-Cleaning Audit

1. Is enzymatic soak water clean, properly diluted, and water temperature within range?
2. Are instruments soaking for 5 minutes and is the timer consistently utilized?
3. Are lumens first flushed with water prior to using brush?
4. Are hinged instruments properly opened and positioned in tray?
5. Are all instruments visually inspected and gross bioburden removed?

Decontamination Pre-Cleaning Audit

1. Is enzymatic soak water clean, properly diluted, and water temperature within range?
2. Are instruments soaking for 5 minutes and is the timer consistently utilized?
3. Are lumens first flushed with water prior to using brush?
4. Are hinged instruments properly opened and positioned in tray?
5. Are all instruments visually inspected and gross bioburden removed?

Example of Standard Work Compliance Audit Measurement

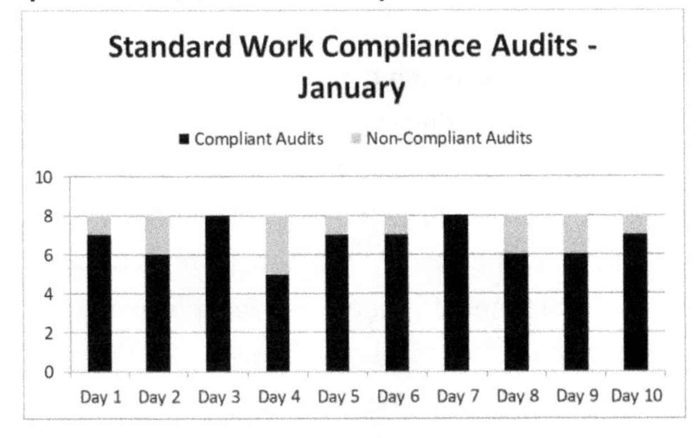

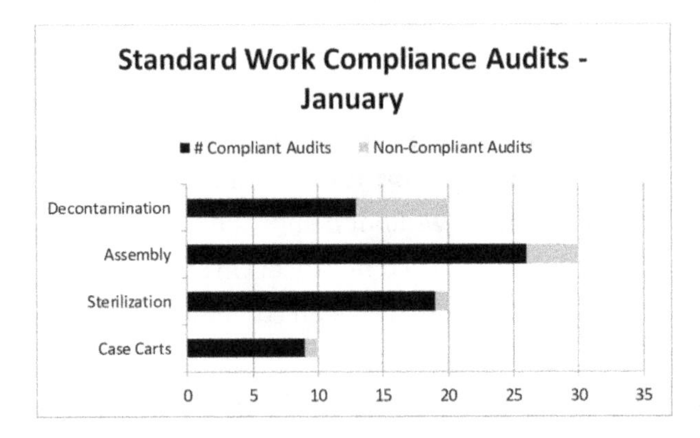

<u>Technology Solutions for Compliance Measurements</u>

While every SPD can and should implement leadership audits, to further ensure compliance to standard work often requires an investment in technology solutions such as instrument tracking. Instrument tracking systems have evolved significantly over the years and offer much more functionality than simply tracking location of instruments. In fact, using the terminology instrument tracking is no longer representative of the power these systems now offer. Current software solutions on the market incorporate aspects of workflow, staff, inventory and equipment management. They provide point of use information access, help prioritize work, manage the completion of daily tasks and assist in managing compliance. With the right database structure, they can also provide unlimited reporting and query functionality.

To improve decontamination compliance to standard work, technology can provide the actual standard work instructions at the workstation where the staff are working based on scanning the instrument set. Process steps can be converted into questions requiring staff interaction or confirmation that the step has been completed. Compliance to scanning and Standard Work can then be tracked electronically. As with every technology solution, collecting the data is of no use if no one uses it. The best systems provide visual displays and controls so that real time information is available and usable to drive real time action. Alerts, text messages, audio alarms or flashing displays bring immediate attention to tasks out of compliance.

Examples of technology improving decontamination compliance include the following:

- Decontamination scanning: Reporting showing process scans being skipped. For example, an instrument set scanned to the OR and then scanned into assembly without being scanned in decontamination.
- Decontamination process compliance: On screen requirement to acknowledge specific step has been completed such as "Ronguers individually inspected for bioburden."
- Decontamination task compliance: On screen reminders of task requirement, on screen confirmation that task is completed and on-screen notification when task is not completed. This works well for daily cleaning tasks or washer testing for example.

Visual presentation of the data from technology solutions will vary depending on the software being used, but it should follow the same logic as previous measurements with percentage and/or raw data graphs including goal and limits as applicable.

Dirty Instruments Caught in Assembly – This measurement is an internal departmental measurement on how well decontamination performed their task of cleaning and disinfecting instruments. Any "dirty" instrument found during the assembly process should be recorded and tracked to determine root cause and drive potential process improvements. Frequently, staff may be hesitant to report such an incident officially as it may come across as "tattle telling" on their staff members working in decontamination. If this is the case, then further work on creating a culture of continuous improvement and meeting Customer requirements will be required to overcome the staff's fear of reprisals. Instead staff should view the incident as a "good catch" that prevented a possible negative patient outcome.

The actual measurement and data collection is straight forward with the usual information collected being date, instrument set name, instrument set unique identifier if using a tracking system, individual instrument name and the person identifying the dirty instrument. Leadership may then trace the instrument back to a specific individual or group of individuals that processed the instrument in decontamination for further follow-up as needed. The measurement should then lead to a root cause analysis and process improvement initiatives to address potential process breakdowns. Pareto analysis may prove useful to identify trends with specific instrument sets, specific instruments, specific days or specific staff.

Example of Dirty Instruments Caught in Assembly

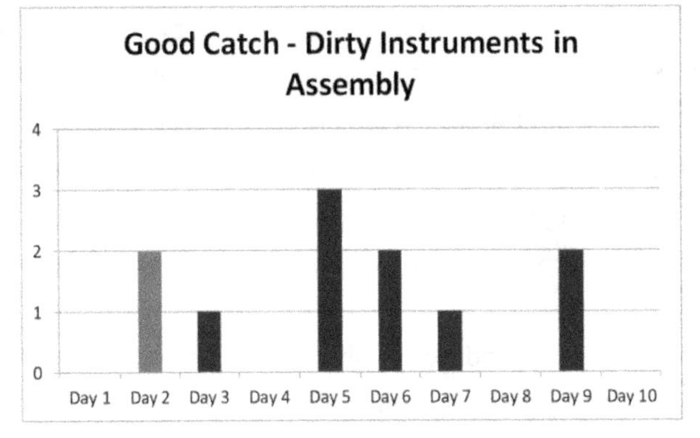

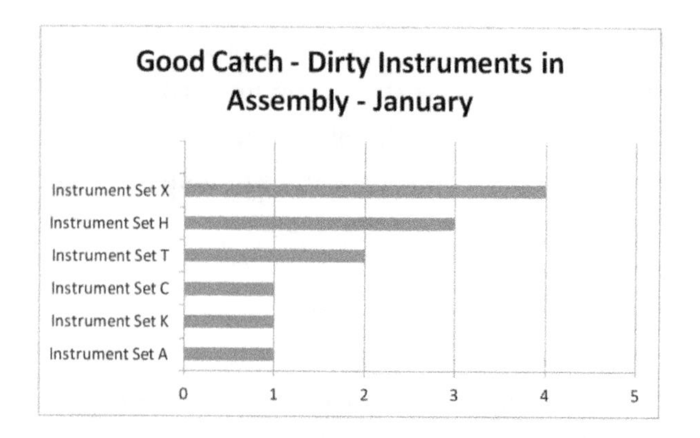

Instrument Set Backlog in Assembly – Assembly and decontamination backlog provides valuable insight into how well the department can maintain continuous flow through the department and keep up with the incoming workloads. Excessive backlogs result in longer total cycle times (time required to process an instrument set from decontamination back to sterile storage) and unhappy Customers as their instruments sit unsterile and thus unusable in the sterile processing department. As a process measurement, excessive backlogs potentially represent workloads greater than expected, insufficient staff or resources, lower than planned productivity or poor process management. Conversely, lack of backlogs does not necessarily mean everything is going perfect as workloads may be less than planned, excessive staff or resources are being utilized or work arrivals have changed, and a tidal wave of work is looming in the near future! Assembly backlog is also a waste measurement in that it is measuring one of the eight wastes of lean – Waiting.

Assembly backlog is measured by simply counting or scanning all the instruments sets waiting to be assembled. Measurements should be compared to targets established for various points of the day such as shift change. Shift change targets are useful if they align with supervisory shift changes as well. This provides the supervisor a measurable indicator to manage their shift as if they were running a "small business" focused on maintaining manageable backlogs to meet their Customer requirements. Typical SPDs with shift changes at 7AM, 3PM, and 11PM should normally see minimal backlogs at 7AM, peak backlogs at 3PM and manageable backlogs at 11PM.

The following graphs give an example of basic backlog graphs. This example shows an SPD that is not able to keep up with the workload during the week, Day 1 – 5, and utilizes the weekend to catch up. Their goal should be to manage their backlog daily to meet their goal of only 25 instrument sets in backlog every morning at 7AM. More information on managing continuous workflow to achieve the desired backlog goals is shared later in the book.

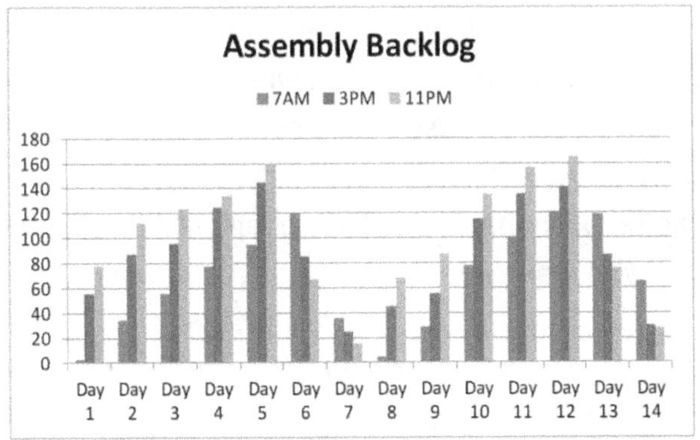

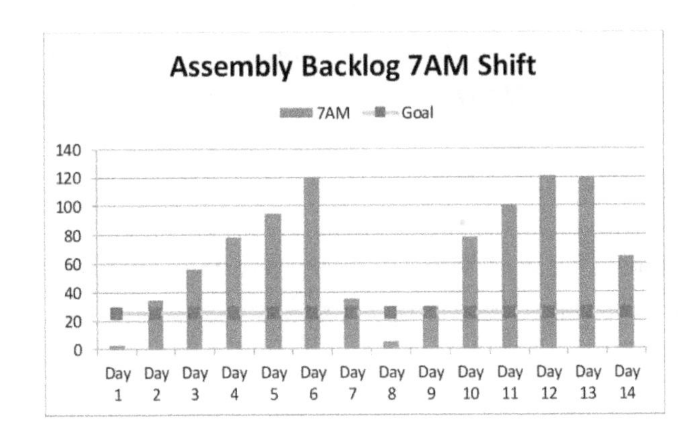

Complete Sets Received from OR – This measurement is a process handoff measurement of how well the OR returns the correct instruments to the correct instrument tray. When combined with the measurement of complete instrument sets, the SPD can measure how well they take non-conforming instrument sets and turn them into conforming quality ones. Typically, handoff measurements are best measured at the time of the handoff for immediate feedback; but in the case of dirty instruments returning to the SPD in the correct tray or not, this measurement will normally not be identified until the assembly process. If RFID tags were to be attached or imbedded into individual instruments, the actual measurement could happen in the OR at the end of the case or in decontamination without anyone counting the instruments. Simply place the instrument set over a RFID reader and with the correct software you would know immediately what is in the set, what is missing from the set and what extras have been placed in the set. For now, we will be happy with manual or instrument tracking measurements.

This measurement is one that may not be able to drive action to change processes or practices depending on the involvement of the OR. With room turnover being a priority in every OR, taking the time to ensure every instrument is returned to the correct instrument tray is not high on the OR's radar of standard work. Many OR staff do a great job of returning most the instruments to the correct set but may stop at that. Thus, if you measure it but find that no one is going to take action to improve it, you should focus your attention elsewhere. If it does become a valid measurement, then here are two examples of how it can be visually presented as well as how to show SPD value add in completing incomplete sets.

Example of Complete Sets Received from OR

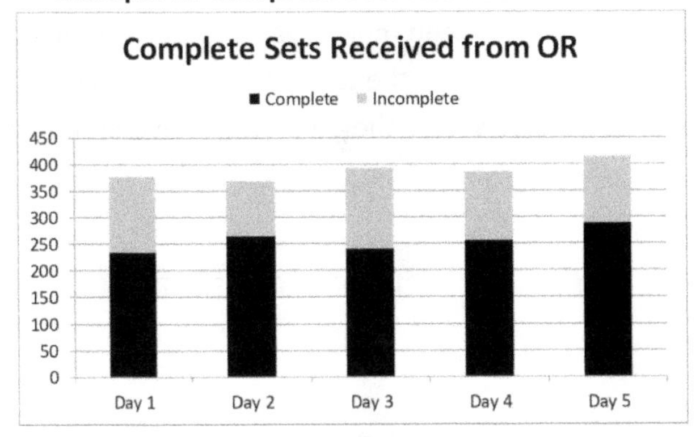

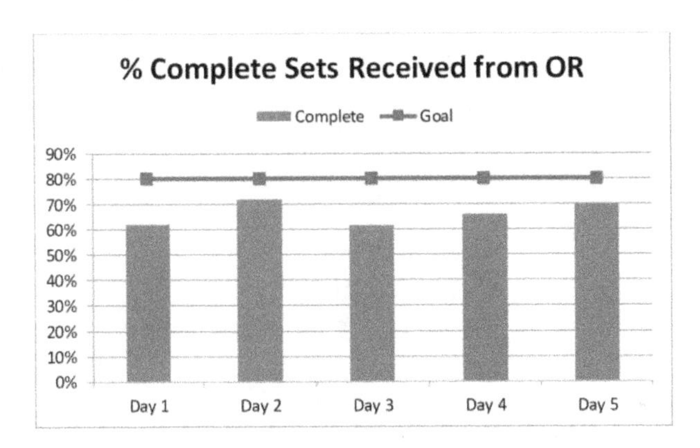

Example of SPD Ability to Complete Sets Received from OR Incomplete

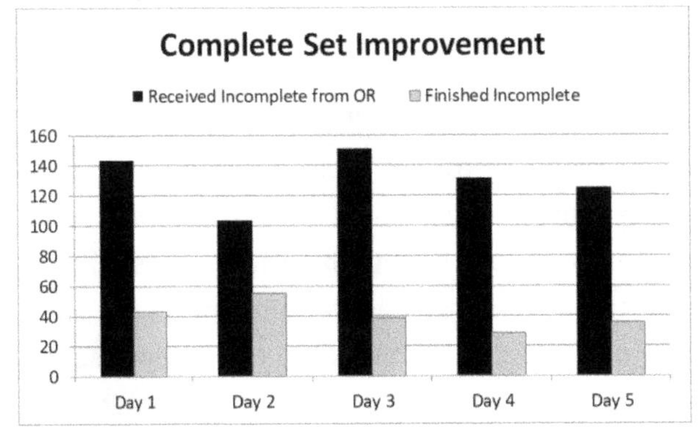

Complete Instrument Sets – This process measurement is normally identical to the outcome measurement and measures the number of instrument sets assembled 100% complete versus the total number of instrument sets assembled. The same graphs from the outcome measurement are shown below.

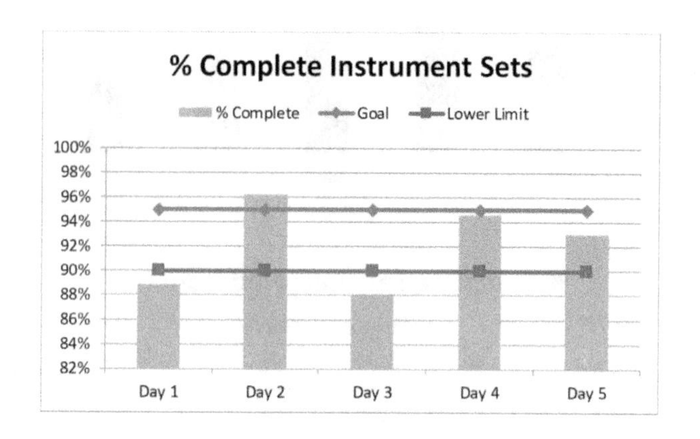

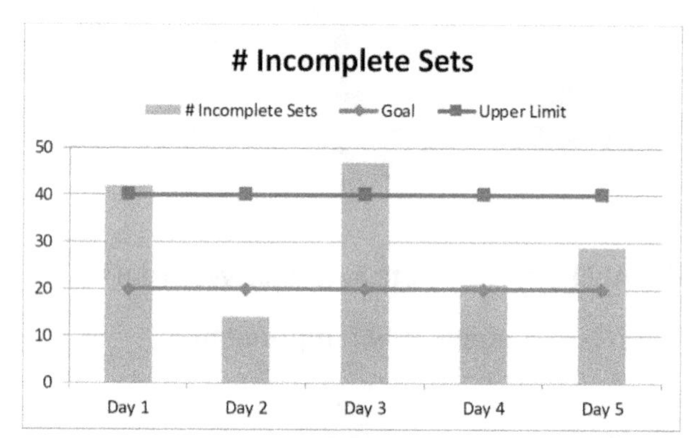

One variation of complete instrument sets that is focused more on process than final outcome is first pass complete instrument sets. First pass is defined as the staff's first attempt to complete the instrument set before either handing off the incomplete set to sterilization or placing in a non-conforming status for further processing. This measurement is dependent on the internal processes the SPD is currently following. Process variations include the following:

- All instrument sets can be sent to sterilization no matter their status.
- Only complete instrument sets or those only missing non-critical instrument can be sent to sterilization.
- All instrument sets unable to be completed after first pass are placed in a non-conforming status for further follow-up
- All incomplete / non-conforming instrument sets are sterilized but then held in SPD for completion unless requested for use by the Customer.

Once the SPD decides on their internal process, then a process measurement can be utilized to determine how well the process is performing and be complied with. In traditional manufacturing operations, non-conforming product is taken offline for either rework, root cause analysis, recycled or scraped. For an SPD, the only available options are to send the non-conforming product to the Customer or hold it for future completion when the necessary parts are available. Thus, the first pass complete instrument set process measurement allows the department to understand how well they are resourced and equipped to complete instrument trays by the initial staff member attempting the work. Factors that affect their ability to complete the set include availability of extra back-up instruments, ability to sort through other used instrument sets that may contain the missing instrument and ability to quickly reorder and receive the missing instrument.

One hospital was facing this exact process improvement challenge when their instrument set inventory consistently had over 100 instrument sets incomplete. With the help of their instrument tracking system they could quickly measure incomplete instrument sets. They were able to find a solution to completing sets on the first pass through the department. They wanted to not only improve their outcome and Customer facing measurement but also their internal process measurement. The following process measurement graph shows both first pass and final Customer facing measurements. Both measurements could be graphed separately or jointly.

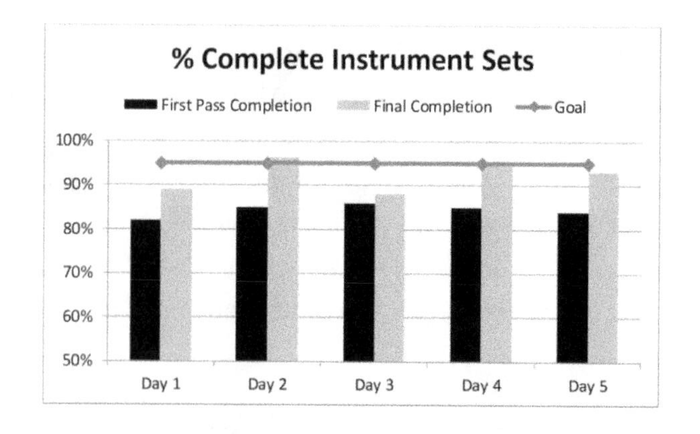

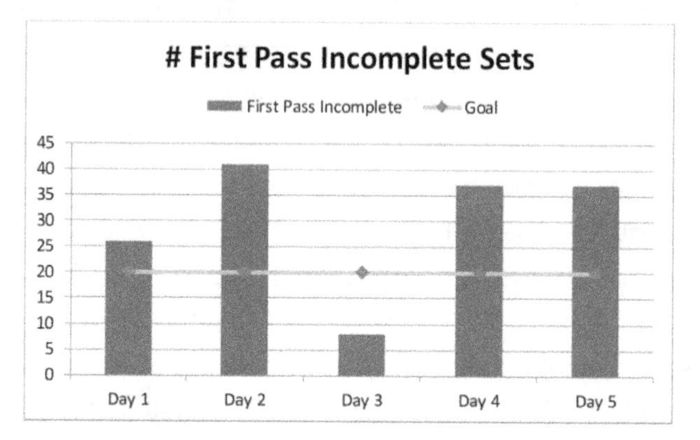

Sterilization Compliance – Sterilization compliance calculates either the number of errors in adhering to standard work or the percentage of opportunities successfully completed correctly. Typical sterilization standard work includes selecting the correct cycle to meet instrument instructions for use and the correct documentation, checking parameters of the cycle by possibly signing the cycle tape, documenting and correctly handling load results and biological indicators. Compliance can be tracked for both accurate completion of the task as well as timely completion of the task. For hospitals with instrument tracking systems, most of these tasks are now captured electronically while other hospitals maintain paper records and documentation. Instrument tracking systems that have evolved into workflow management systems are also able to accurately track timely completion of tasks such as one hour and three-hour biological reads with the system providing warnings when the tasks are due or past due. Measurement graphs are shown below. Due to the critical nature of sterilization, the goal is 100%.

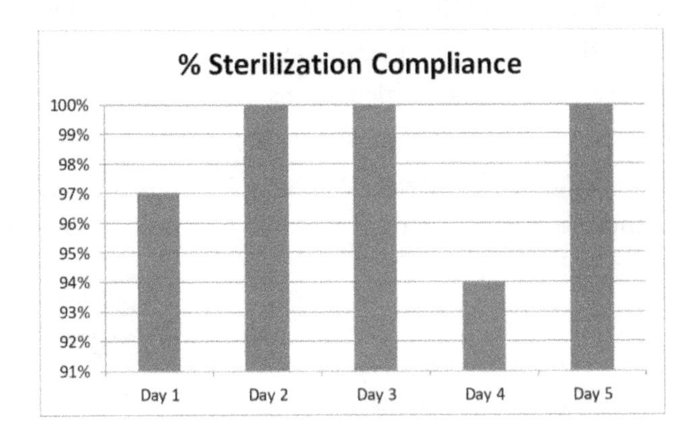

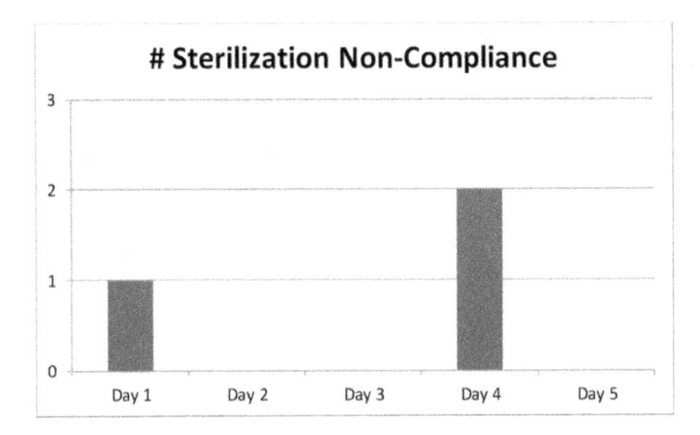

Productivity – Productivity is often a confusing measurement with multiple definitions and measurements found throughout the industry. In simple terms, productivity measures the rate of output versus unit of input. People often state productivity in terms of assembling four trays per hour or picking five case carts per hour but these calculations are statements of throughput or how much output is being accomplished in a given time. Productivity compares actual throughput to the expected or standard throughput. To better understand the full picture of productivity, let us first look at a fictional SPD employee's activity.

Activity	Assemble Major Basic Tray	Talk to Friend	Assemble Power Drill	Personal Break	Assemble Delivery Set
Actual Time	20 Minutes	2 Minutes	15 Minutes	2 Minutes	6 Minutes
Standard Time	15 Minutes	None	10 Minutes	None	10 Minutes
Category	Work	Lost Time	Work	Lost Time	Work
Efficiency	15/20 = 75%	n/a	10/15 = 67%	n/a	10/6 = 167%
Utilization	41 Minutes Worked / 45 Minutes Paid = 91%				
Productivity	35 Standard Minutes Earned / 45 Minutes Paid = 78%				

The above graph helps explain the difference between efficiency, utilization and productivity. Efficiency is a calculation of how efficient one is when performing a task. In the example above the staff member was not efficient assembling the major basic tray and power drill achieving scores of 75% and 67% but was very efficient when assembling the delivery set at 167%. We are assuming that quality was maintained in all activities. Efficiency only looks at the specific time spent on a specific activity and ignores any lost time or other time that the staff spent. To calculate efficiency, divide the standard time for the activity by the actual time spent on the activity.

Utilization calculates the amount of time during the day or given time period that a staff member is working. Utilization does not care if the staff is efficient but only looks at whether he or she is working. Often in SPDs that are facing backlogs of work, opportunities exist in improving utilization first before addressing efficiency opportunities.

Productivity is a combination of both efficiency and utilization. Productivity divides the standard time earned or completed during the time period by the total time at work including lost time. To be productive you must actively be working and produce work within the standard time for each activity.

For SPDs, productivity can be measured at both individual and departmental level. The example above depicts an individual measurement. Tracking individual productivity can be a cumbersome task though. Instrument tracking systems that have evolved into Workflow Management systems provide electronic means of tracking individual tasks completed and can automatically compare the task to the standard time for efficiency calculations. Frequently though, not all tasks are scanned and thus the data is incomplete.

To overcome this measurement dilemma, remember the 80-20 rule and do not attempt to measure every task or activity. Measure those tasks that account for 80% of the department's workload such as decontamination, assembly, sterilization and case carts. Manage the remaining 20% through on-the-floor follow-up. One method to assist in managing all non-measurable or hard to measure activities is to group them together into one work assignment. Activities such as answering the phone, answering the door, running items to the OR, unloading washers, fulfilling floor orders and others can be assigned to one person working in a utility position. The remaining measurable and major activities are then assigned to individuals and productivity tracked. Whether you capture the data electronically or manually, everyone's daily productivity could resemble the following:

Example of Daily Productivity for Individual Staff

Activity	Standard	# Units Completed	Standard Minutes Earned
Decontaminate Tray	5	12	60
Assemble Tray	15	12	180
Case Cart Assembly	12	6	72
Floor Runs	30	1	30
		Total Minutes Earned	342
		Total Minutes Worked	450
		% Productivity	76%

Example of Daily Productivity for Individual Staff

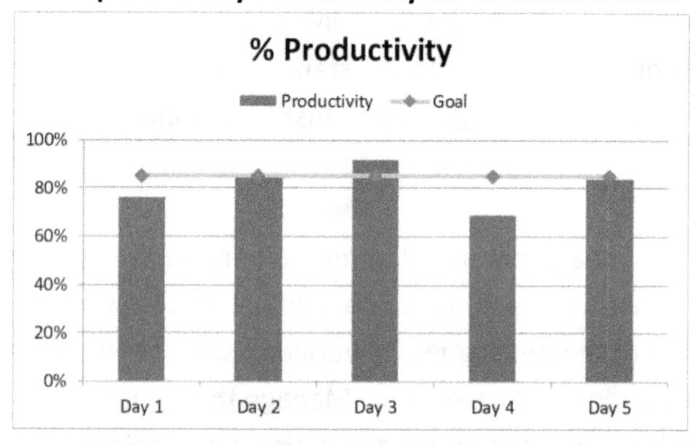

For sterile processing departmental productivity measurements, one of the most consistent and comparable departmental measures is SPD hours worked per instrument set completed. Various departmental productivity measurements abound including SPD hours worked versus OR minutes, SPD hours worked versus patient days and SPD hours worked versus budgeted hours. While some may focus more on a financial benchmark or revenue generating patient benchmark, the one that makes the most sense is hours worked versus instrument sets completed.

The determination of the denominator, instrument sets completed, is utilized as it represents the largest volume indicator in the department and thus is the key volume indicator. Key volume indicators are utilized as baseline volume measurements when capturing all the volume becomes too tedious and non-value adding. If the goal or target is set utilizing the same denominator, then the measurement is justifiable. To calculate the goal, determine the total amount of labor required to complete all the tasks in the department and then divide that by the number of instrument sets that will be completed in the time period. The following graphs depict a typical SPD Hours per Instrument Set measurement as well as the corresponding % productivity measurement.

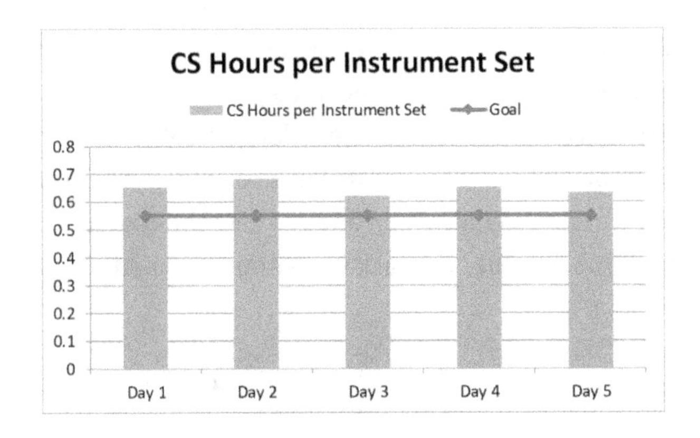

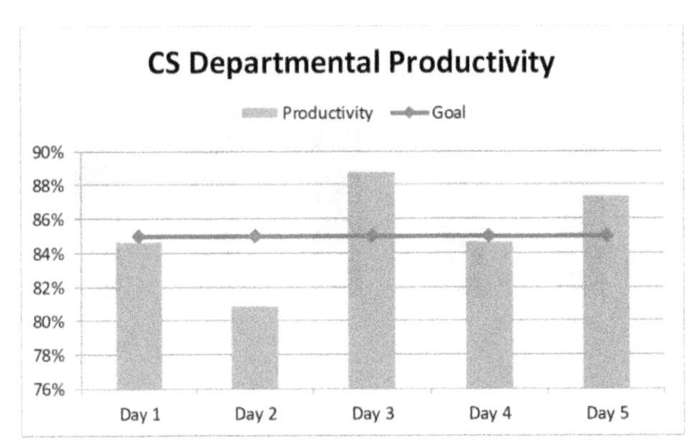

Task Completion – Task completion measures how well the required tasks or activities have been completed and or completed on-time. There is nothing magic about this measurement except that it is an indication of how well the department embraces a culture of adherence and doing what they need to do when they need to do it. Tasks could include daily cleaning of decontamination, recording environmental readings such as humidity and temperature, daily washer testing, daily sterilizer testing and so on. Ensuring these tasks are completed should not solely rely on human memory and discipline but also incorporate a systematic process control to measure compliance and identify opportunities for improvement. Remember the bathroom cleaning checklists you see in public bathrooms? Those are a form of a task completion tool that can be measured. Historically, task management has been a pen and paper documenting exercise, but with the recent scanning technology and workflow management systems coming to market, this process can now be managed electronically. Systems can schedule tasks to be completed, provide visual or other indicators when a task is due and send warning signals when a task is not completed. The actual measurement shows whether the task was completed and whether it was completed on-time.

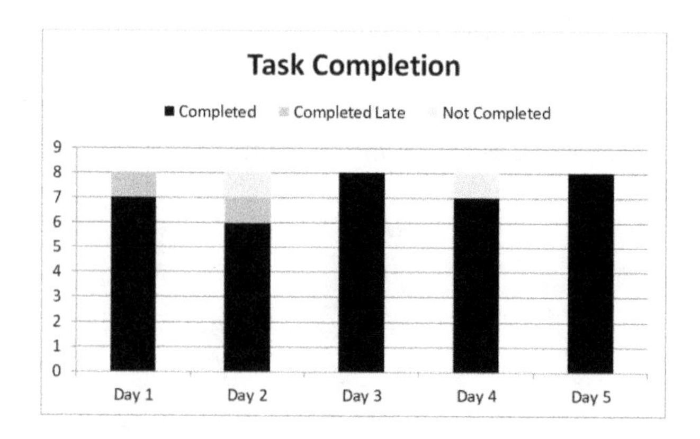

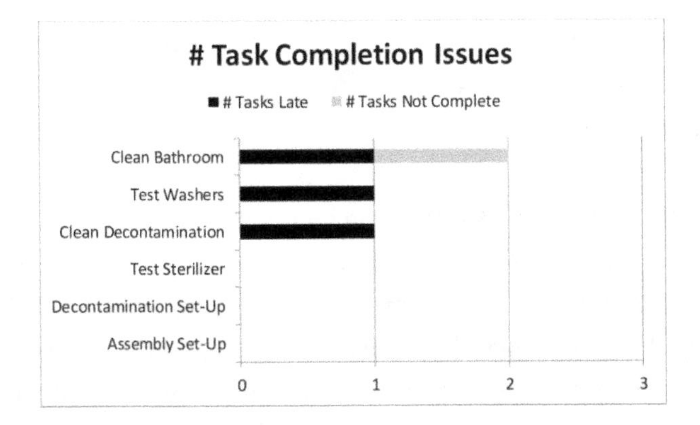

Waste Measurements

Generally speaking, waste measurements are the most difficult and least utilized form of measurement. The exception to this is the utilization of budgetary measurements to determine if associated costs are greater than planned and thus an easy indicator of waste in the process. This is a poor plan! Like outcome measurements, budgetary measurements are usually an indicator of a symptom and rarely give a clear picture of the underlying root cause issue. True waste measurements help pinpoint opportunities to eliminate waste by clearly measuring a specific waste. The problem usually lies in the department or individual's ability to capture the data.

Waste measurements can also be closely related to or identical to outcome and process measurements. An instrument set that was found to be defective by the OR would trigger an outcome measurement of the defect but could also result in reprocessing the instrument tray, using a second instrument tray, delaying the surgical procedure, phone calls from the OR and a special delivery of the required item. All these activities are considered waste and, if measured, could become a waste measurement. An example would be tracking and measuring the number of special deliveries to the OR that could have been avoided if the proper requirements were clearly identified in advance and supplied as needed on-time. Reducing the number of special deliveries through process improvement eliminates waste in the process. The process measurement of dirty instruments caught in assembly is also a waste measurement because the dirty instrument must be returned to decontamination and cleaned a second time. All error type of process measures usually leads to a waste measurement as someone or something is affected by the error.

There are many types of waste that can be identified but are not readily tracked. While implementing lean in SPDs, it is typical to identify excess walking or movement, backlogs, rework, poor design causing people to spend more time looking for things all of which are waste. In these cases, process improvement initiatives are implemented to eliminate the waste and sustain the improvements going forward. Is it necessary to measure the waste first? No. If you can identify it, then go ahead and eliminate it. For some forms of waste there may not be an obvious solution and measuring it will help determine if efforts to reduce it are working or not. Remember the perfect SPD discussion earlier? Try using that discussion to identify work, processes, tasks and headaches the staff would like to eliminate and then measure how well the department eliminates it. It may surprise you how similar staff headaches and complaints are to root cause wastes. Make their work life easier and you will probably have eliminated process waste at the same time.

Waste measurements can also be departmental and thus provide a global measurement of waste in the department. Going back to our perfect SPD discussion, what if you could identify the labor required to do the work if everything was perfect and there was zero waste in the process? You actually can. Take pen and paper or open a spreadsheet and list all the activities the department performs, how often they are performed and how long it should take to do the work. There is one important rule. Only count the activities that add value to the work. For a sterile processing department, typical value-adding activities are cleaning, assembling, packaging, sterilizing and delivering the item to sterile storage. Any additional activities beyond these could be considered waste in the eyes of your Customer. While this example is over simplified, the point is to identify the value-adding labor time it takes to meet the Customer requirements and compare that to the amount of labor you are using. Following are some examples of Waste Measurements, but you are encouraged to determine your own.

Potential Waste Measurements for an SPD include.

- % Value-adding labor
- Rework
- Returned unused items
- Phone calls
- Special deliveries

% Value-Adding Labor – As explained above, this measurement compares actual labor utilized versus value-add labor required. This measurement can be for a specific product, process or the entire department. At the departmental level, determine your value-adding labor requirements for all activities and then pick one key volume indicator, usually instrument sets, as the denominator. Then measure your total actual labor utilized versus actual instrument sets processed and compare. There should be opportunity for improvement as a perfectly Lean SPD may not exist. Once found, you can start your lean journey to reduce the gap.

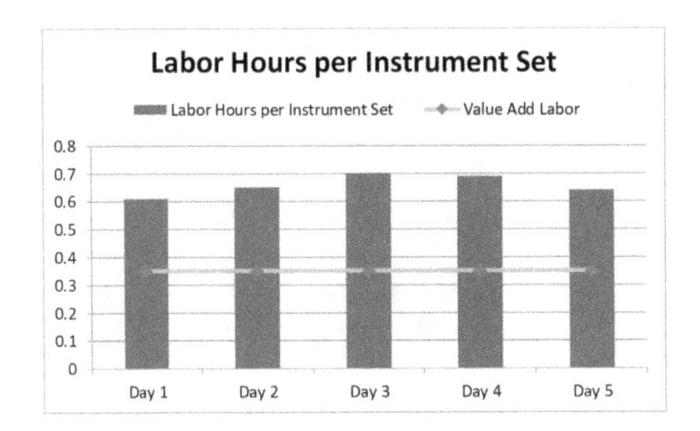

Rework – Rework waste may be identical to the process measurement of defects assuming a defect drives rework or at least duplication of work. Rework can also be internal such as dirty instruments caught by assembly and returned to decontamination for rework. Whether you measure these items as process or waste measurements is not critical as long as you are measuring them.

Returned Unused Items – Every SPD that is responsible for picking case carts has the task of putting away any unused items returned by the OR. This is partly due to patient safety concerns where the doctor calls for additional items just in case, they need them but is also due to inaccurate case cart picking lists or doctor preference cards. It is common for hospitals to allow preference cards to become outdated and inaccurate due to lack of available staffing and/or poor process management. The result is 20% to 30% items picked for a case to be returned unused requiring labor to restock the items. Two measurements are useful here. First, track the total numbers or percentage of items returned and then provide a Pareto analysis for the highest returned items. In the actual example below, the hospital immediately addressed the issue of OR gowns being returned and reduced their returned items by 400 a week. They then addressed which items they were pulling for case carts that were also stocked in the OR rooms causing the nurses to return the case cart items since they were using the item from the room stock.

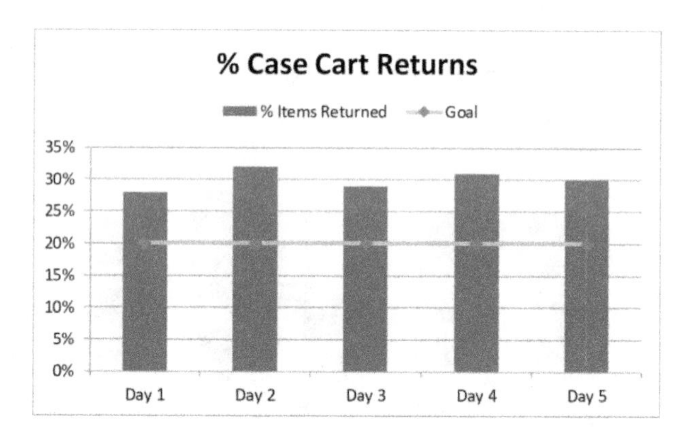

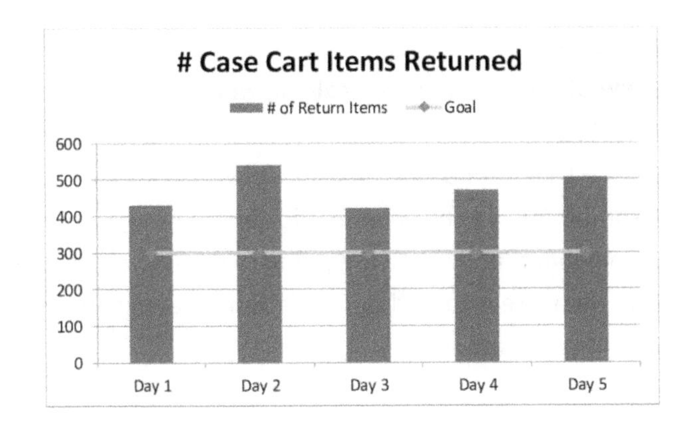

TOP 20 ITEMS BY VOLUME	RETURN	PICKED	% RETURN
90010000701 GOWN SURGICAL DISP BARRIER XLG	-239	822	-29.08%
90010002949 GOWN IMPERVIOUS SURGICAL XXLG	-165	247	-66.80%
90010000726 SPECIMEN CUP	-112	197	-56.85%
90010000328 DRAPE SHEET 3/4	-107	250	-42.80%
54226800 GLOVE TRIFLEX REG 8	-106	510	-20.78%
90010002178 SUCTION LINER 3000ML DISP	-67	410	-16.34%
541060001 SPONGE LAP X-RAY 8X18 ST CA/40	-57	229	-24.89%
54383150 BLADE SURGICAL #15	-54	128	-42.19%
54887010 STOCKING COMPRESS MED PR	-54	159	-33.96%
90010004140 LIGHT HANDLES	-53	127	-41.73%
113002100 SYRINGE 10 CC LUER LOK TIP	-51	182	-28.02%
90010000079 CAUTERY PAD REM ADULT	-50	216	-23.15%
545180001 CULTURE AEROBIC TRANSETTE 3-R	-49	76	-64.47%
540740401 SPONGE GAUZE 4X4 ST BX/50	-46	106	-43.40%
54165160 FOLEY CATH 16F 5CC	-46	103	-44.66%
90010000089 SUCTION EVACUATOR	-46	51	-90.20%
90010004333 STAPLER SKIN APPOSE ULS 35 WID	-46	135	-34.07%
54189000 CATH TRAY	-42	91	-46.15%
54102000 SPONGE X-RAY 4X4 STER 1350/CA	-41	93	-44.09%
90010000758 CULTURE ANAEROBIC BBL/BD	-40	63	-63.49%

Phone Calls – Phone calls are usually a sign that something did not go according to plan. The OR needs something they cannot find or do not have. SPD is late in delivering something. Information was not shared in the proper manner resulting in a phone call. Some phone calls may be part of the agreed upon process but in general you may find most phone calls are either a symptom of waste or simply waste themselves. Even if the phone call is considered to add value, can the information and communication be automatically generated, sent earlier, standardized, electronically distributed or some other way to improve and/or eliminate the need for a person to initiate the call? Measurements can either be simple checkmarks by the phone or a review of the actual phone call log weekly.

Special Deliveries – Like phone calls, special deliveries are usually a sign and symptom that something was not planned for or did not go according to plan. This is waste somewhere, and if you are going to eliminate it then you will probably need to measure it to find out what is happening, where it is happening and why it is happening.

Where to Start

While there is no shortage of measurement options for SPDs, it can be overwhelming to initially start. Here is where your measurements can be grouped into two categories: Key Performance Indicators (KPI's) and Mini-Metrics.

Key Performance Indicators (KPI's)

KPI's are a widely overused term in business today. Too often they are taken to represent any performance measurement. In fact, KPI's are the core metrics that your business uses as the most important guideposts to keep you on track, enabling you to manage, control, take action and achieve results. Most SPD KPI's are common to all SPDs since the core functions of sterile processing are the same. They track the day-to-day operational measures and give near real-time feedback on critical-to-success performance factors of quality, schedule and cost. KPI's are generally charted in the positive, such as % complete versus the negative % incomplete to support a positive culture. They should also provide a balanced view of the department's performance and be regularly communicated and reviewed. Lastly, every staff member should have a thorough understanding of every KPI measurement and how his or her personal performance impacts each KPI.

Recommended KPI's for sterile processing departments include the following.

- Backlogs
- Instrument set quality
- Complete instrument sets
- Complete case carts
- Productivity

Mini-Metrics

Mini-metrics represent performance measurements focused on change management or defect elimination and are used only when needed. They represent the current process improvement focus, recently implemented process change or current Customer priority. Use them when you need them and then move on to another measurement. Mini-metrics help to focus efforts on identified process improvement opportunities and are typically used for a short time before being updated as new opportunities come into focus.

Mini-Metric Examples

- Overtime – Used to bring overtime usage and its associated costs in alignment with goals
- Items returned unused – Used to address specific issues with returned items
- Instrument sets missing instruments on recurring basis – Focused on specific services or sets
- Employee turnover – Used as an indicator of staff dissatisfaction and retention efforts
- Loaner set deliveries – Used to track vendor adherence to loaner tray delivery guidelines
- Others – There may be endless opportunities. When a problem is discovered or suspected, establishing a short-term mini-metric can help you focus and resolve the issue.

~~~~~~

Case Study – Vendor Mini-Metric

Unreliable instrument vendors can cause significant problems for an SPD and its ability to properly serve their Customers. Late deliveries of loaner sets often result in a disruption of workflow as staff scramble to reprioritize the workload in an effort to get the loaners prepared for an upcoming case. Inadequate documentation of required processes can also result in the improper processing of vendor sets. For departments experiencing these issues, it is advisable to create a vendor mini-metric. Keep in mind the earlier statement, "Don't measure what you won't change" and truthfully consider if you have the political backing to affect an operational change. To implement a vendor mini-metric focus on vendor, delivery lead time, documentation and surgeon. Track each vendor's delivery time versus scheduled case time to determine adherence to agreed-upon lead times and determine vendors out of compliance. Documentation adherence includes instructions for use for cleaning and sterilization. Surgeon tracking will help determine if late deliveries are vendor driven or doctor driven. If all late deliveries come from the same doctor, then there is a good chance the doctor's office is ordering the vendor trays late.

~~~~~~

Case Study – Overtime

A large university teaching hospital with over 30 ORs and a unionized SPD staff found themselves implementing process improvements to reduce backlogs. Serving both an adult and children's OR suites, operating 24/7 and traditionally scrambling every morning to provide the required instrument sets to the correct OR, the SPD leadership team initiated a series of process improvements to improve throughput and reduce the daily 7AM backlogs and morning rush to find instruments the OR needed.

In doing so, they created operational plans for throughput for each shift based on standard work times and staffing levels and as backlogs rose above acceptable levels overtime was mandated. While mandating overtime is never a fun thing to do, it was deemed necessary given the current circumstances.

Immediately, the staff started to pay attention to the backlog levels and posted goals for acceptable levels for each shift to avoid mandated overtime. During the initial implementation period, staff filed a formal complaint to the union that overtime was excessive, and the mandating was unwarranted and inappropriate. Their complaint was not supported by measurable data or facts but rather staff feedback and feelings.

Leadership responded by utilizing a mini-metric to measure overtime and the impact of their decision to mandate overtime if backlogs were above acceptable limits. With data in hand they presented their findings to the staff directly in a transparent manner to foster team building. Surprisingly to many staff, total overtime had decreased since mandating overtime was instituted. The difference was that all staff were now working overtime instead of only those who chose to work overtime. The mini-metric was continued and tracked for a period of time until mandating was no longer required and the backlogs had been managed to acceptable levels.

~~~~~~

Case Study – Missing Instruments

An SPD was asked to find a way to improve their complete instrument sets measurement and turned to a mini-metric to help. The complete instrument sets measurement had been tracked for years with results bouncing between 85% and 90%. They had been given the challenge to increase the percentage to 95%. Diving into the data required them to start to track complete instruments sets in various mini-metric measurements looking for trends. What they found surprised them. One of their most productive assembly staff members was the worst at completing instrument sets. Apparently, their measurement of individual productivity was the driving force behind her performance to the point of not spending any time at all attempting to complete the sets missing instruments. As soon as they created a balanced measurement of quantity and quality, this employee's complete instrument set percentage improved helping the entire department's performance improve.

~~~~~~

Chapter Five: Lean Operational Plan – Resource Requirements

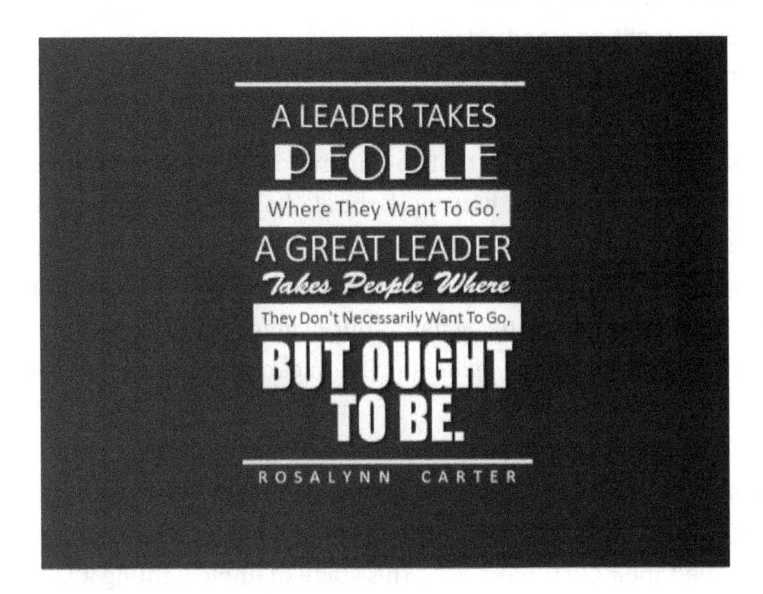

Step three in our eight steps to creating a Lean SPD focuses on developing a Lean operational plan. A perfect or Lean SPD develops a detailed operational plan and ensures everyone knows what should be happening, when it should happen, how long it should take and what the results should be.

The importance of developing a plan prior to performing any work is crucial to successfully implementing and sustaining a lean environment. Remember that a lean system is one in which opportunities for improvement or waste is exposed. The system must be able to expose the waste for action to be taken to eliminate it. To expose waste, actual performance must be compared to expected or "waste free" performance. Thus, the importance in developing a lean operational plan is in developing a waste free plan or at least a plan to which actual performance can be measured against.

The basic elements of creating a lean operational plan are covered in the following chapters and include:

- Determining resource requirements
- Building a value stream
- Implementing standard work
- Drive for continuous flow

Each of these elements helps create an operational blueprint for how the department should operate, how work should flow, and what must happen for success to be obtained. All too frequently, we have been consulted to assist a struggling SPD only to find they have no plan for how to be successful. Asking the simple question of "What's your plan for today" is most enlightening to how well the leadership team can predict and plan for success.

Departments better able to predict their workloads and daily operational requirements are also better able to plan to handle those workloads. The better they plan, the better their outcomes. The better their outcomes, the more satisfied their Customers are. This stage of implementing a Lean SPD is all about being proactive and not reactive, understanding the environment, preparing in advance and being in control of the work versus being controlled by the work.

This concept of creating and working a plan is no different in healthcare than in any other business or industry. In fact, all successful businesses have some sort of operating structure by which they plan and control their activities to create a desired outcome. These operating structures vary in size and complexity but typically have the following elements:

- Forecasting – Projecting business into the future. How many items, instrument sets, case carts or other items did we receive and process last year and what is our forecast for the future? What seasonality do we need to consider? What procedural volume changes are expected which might impact the future items to be processed?

- Planning – Determining what is needed to handle the work. How much work needs to be completed? In what time frame? What are the required steps or activities required to complete the work? How long should each activity take? How much equipment is needed? What are the space requirements? How many people will be needed? What training is required? What regulatory and compliance standards impact the plan? What are the required quality standards?

- Executing – Implementing the plan. Who is going to perform the work? When is the work expected to be done? What are the priorities for the work? How should changes in the schedule be communicated? How will staff members know what standards of performance they are expected to meet?

- Follow Up – Active monitoring of the work. Is the work on schedule or off schedule? Are there any problems? What additional resources are required? What adjustments to activities need to be made to stay within the plan? What opportunities for improvement have been identified?

- Reporting – Comparing actual results to planned results. How well were resources used? How much of the plan was completed? What equipment and materials were used? What problems occurred during the process? What were the variances to plan, quality issues and other opportunities for improvement?

- Evaluating – Determining action items to improve performance. Should the work be done differently? Is training required? What waste can be removed from the process? Do people need to be moved to different areas at different times of the day? What equipment changes need to be made? What additional materials are needed? How well is the equipment performing?

The eight steps of a Lean SPD incorporate these elements with the first two steps of identifying Customer Requirements and Developing Operational

Measurements setting the stage for developing a Lean operational plan. At this point, it is time to dive into forecasting our Customer workloads and determining our resource requirements.

Forecasting Workloads

Before we can determine our resource requirements, we need to forecast the work to be completed. Every SPD must be able to forecast the amount of work they are required to complete for a given time period. For most, this starts with understanding the OR case volumes and then relating that volume to surgical trays, peel packs and other items they must process. Added to this volume are the additional tasks the department performs and can include activities such as building case carts, processing medical equipment and picking up and delivering items to customers. Once the department understands the volume of work they must accomplish, they then move to the next step of determining resource requirements.

It is surprising though how many SPDs do not or are not able to forecast their workload. Technology certainly helps here, and instrument tracking systems are invaluable in collecting raw volume data that can be useful in forecasting workloads. Even without technology though, departments can and should forecast their workloads as accurately as possible to improve their ability to effectively plan how to handle the work.

Where to start can be a daunting task so let us break it down into common SPD categories of work that are easier to handle. While the following information is not inclusive of all possible work a SPD may perform, it does provide examples of the process to follow in forecasting workloads.

It is worth making a valuable comment before moving on. When forecasting workload, first determine how the forecast will be utilized to confirm you are capturing the data in a format that is usable. The easiest example of this is in forecasting surgical instrument tray volumes. If the forecast is to be utilized for staffing requirements, then the complexity and number of instruments in the tray may be the most accurate forecasting attribute to determine staffing requirements. The more instruments in the tray and the more complex the tray is then the longer it will take a staff member to reprocess. Simple trays with few instruments will take less time. If the forecast is to be utilized for equipment requirements, such as instrument washers or sterilizers, then the physical size of the tray may be more important. Larger trays take up more space in the equipment chambers and thus drive more capacity requirements without regard to how many instruments are in the tray. In either scenario, an average may be utilized as well. The point is to think through how you are going to use the data to confirm you are collecting the right data for starters. This is referred to as "starting with the end in mind."

Differences like those described above will affect the final resource requirements but also are dependent on how detailed or exact the final resource requirement is expected to be. Sometimes a "back of a napkin" exercise can produce a result just as valid as a two-week detailed study. Other times a detailed analysis is required to avoid inaccurate forecasts and/or provide enough justification for a CFO to approve the resources required while feeling confident that the decision is accurate.

It is also valuable in reiterating the need to justify resource requirements through verified data collection. The statement "We can't keep up and need more people!" has echoed through many administration hallways only to be ignored until data is provided to back-up the claim. Hospitals are no different than any other business in that they must balance their resource spending against incoming revenues all the while prioritizing requests from multiple departments for increased budgets. Prioritizing who receives the limited resources and how much they receive should not be a decision based on feelings but rather data. Successful SPDs are those that utilize data to demonstrate their needs based on actual workloads, accurate forecasts and reasonable standards that are managed. SPD managers unable to present data in this manner often find themselves frustrated at the lack of resources they are given. Managers must understand that until they can measure their performance and prove their ability to effectively oversee the resources they already have, they will not be able to gain the confidence of the executive suite.

OR Surgical Instruments

By far the largest single workload driver of every SPD is the OR surgical instrument volumes. Forecasting this volume may seem simple and straightforward but entails a few twists and turns that can dramatically affect the outcome. Starting with the end in mind, let us first look at how we will use this data:

- Staffing requirements for decontamination, assembly, sterilization and transportation
- Equipment requirements for sinks, sonic washers, instrument washers, cart washers, assembly tables, steam sterilizers and low temperature sterilizers
- Space requirements for all the above plus staging areas and storage areas

Let us look at the easiest and most efficient method to collect and forecast OR surgical instrument volumes. First, the workload is usually split into two categories: trays and peel packs or small items. The definition of these categories is where the fun starts and will play a crucial role in setting up an instrument tracking system. Since trays and peel packs often have very different labor, equipment and space requirements, it is best to clearly determine the differentiation between the two categories. Small, wrapped items or large peel packs with multiple items start to blur the line between the two, but each hospital will need to clearly draw the line at some point. For those using an instrument tracking system, a typical differentiating factor is used. Any item that is individually and uniquely tracked through the system and counted as inventory is defined as a tray, and everything else is a peel pack.

Know that our end result is to be able to effectively predict our future workload and then plan to handle that workload. Here is a typical breakdown of OR surgical instrument volumes that will provide valuable data:

- # of trays processed for a period of time
    - # of trays requiring normal processing
    - # of trays requiring expedited processing
    - # of trays that are vendor or loaner trays
- # of peel packs processed for a period of time

Most SPDs can come up with this data. For those diving a bit deeper into their workloads, the following breakdown can provide further value:

- # of trays or sterilization loads for steam sterilization
- # of trays or sterilization loads for low temperature sterilization
- # or percentage of trays that are containerized versus wrapped
- # or percentage of trays by size (extra small, small, medium, and large)

These data points will provide the basis for determining resource requirements in the next section.

An interesting and sometimes valuable data point to calculate is the number of instrument trays processed per surgical case. Whether the number is 4, 5, 6 or 9 trays per case, it can provide a baseline to compare future operational changes as well as start discussion on tray optimization. Reducing trays per case from 6 to 5 for an average hospital performing 50 surgical cases per day immediately results in a reduction of workload through the entire system of 50 trays per day. This reduction results in reduced labor, equipment and space requirements as well as potentially alleviating immediate use sterilization due to insufficient instrumentation inventory. Instrumentation optimization is worthy of an entire chapter or even a book to itself, but we will simply use it as an example of a lean initiative.

Clinics and Hospital Floor Instruments

Clinics and hospital floor instruments are often managed and processed somewhat separately from the OR surgical instruments. The separation is often a combination of the SPD managing their processes and workloads efficiently as well as ensuring the instruments are returned to the correct owner at the end of the day. Often, averages can be utilized in determining labor, equipment and space requirements for this category and thus the data collection is usually a simple count of trays and singles or peel packs.

- # of clinic / floor trays
- # of clinic / floor single or peel pack items

Case Carts

Tracking and forecasting case cart volumes is utilized in determining labor, equipment and space requirements for cart washers, picking case carts and staging space. Traditionally a simple count of case carts provides the data required for determining resource requirements. Variations may exist if multiple sizes of case carts exist and/or if multiple case carts are utilized for single cases or single case carts are utilized for multiple cases.

- # of case carts processed
- Average number of case carts processed in cart washer
- Average number of case carts processed per OR surgical case

Medical Equipment

For an SPD, medical equipment usually refers to IV pumps, feeding pumps, SCA's and other durable medical equipment that requires cleaning. Some SPDs handle this workload while others do not. For those that do, a simple item count and/or item count by category is sufficient for determining resource requirements.

- # of equipment processed
- # of equipment by category if the categories vary in labor, equipment or space requirements

Supplies

Additionally, some SPDs handle supply restocking or other supply activities. Activities like these may lend themselves to per item counts or per occurrence counts. An example would be the restocking of case cart supplies daily taking 60 minutes while averaging 360 items to put away. The workload forecast can be either 360 items per day or 1 occurrence per day. When determining resource requirements such as labor, this will translate into 360 items per day at 10 seconds per item or 1 occurrence per day at 60 minutes per occurrence.

- # of items stocked
- # of occurrences

General SPD Activities

Forecasting workloads does not stop at instruments and the core functions of the SPD. Every activity the department performs should have a forecast of workload so that a total departmental plan can be developed, and resource requirements calculated. Examples of general SPD activities that will require some type of forecast include departmental cleaning, staff training, meetings, equipment testing, customer service activities and perhaps other activities. For each activity, determine if the forecast will be a per item count or a per occurrence count. A few examples are listed below:

- # staff huddles – per occurrence
- # staff competency training sessions – per occurrence
- # of sterilizer testing – usually per occurrence but could be per sterilizer
- # of washer testing – usually per occurrence but could be per washer
- # crash cart restocking – per cart
- # of floor deliveries – per delivery
- # of floor pick-ups – per occurrence if done all at once or per delivery if done individually

Forecasting Workload Summary

Forecasting workloads is the start of developing a lean operational plan and determining resource requirements and thus is the first place mistakes can happen. Incorrect data at this stage will carry through the entire operational plan and execution with potentially detrimental impacts on patients or departmental performance. Workloads forecasted too high will result in overstaffing, too much equipment and space and a non-lean environment.

Forecasts too low will result in backlogs, inability of the department to complete the work required, staff forced to take short cuts or activities not being completed. Initially, many managers view the data collection as a one-time event and grudgingly comply and then happily forget about it once they are done. Unfortunately, this should not be the case. Data collection is best when it is continuous, automated as much as possible and provides data as needed to determine resource requirements while also utilizing track trends in changing conditions.

The graph below provides an example of the type of data and format that could be utilized at this stage in collecting. This format will carry over nicely to the next step of determining resource requirements.

Forecasting Workload Example

Activity	Unit	Frequency	Volume
OR Trays	Tray	Weekly	1300
OR Quick Turn Trays	Tray	Weekly	22
OR Loaner Trays	Tray	Weekly	78
OR Peel Packs	Peel Packs	Weekly	500
Clinic Trays	Tray	Weekly	70
Case Carts	Carts	Weekly	250
Steam Sterilizer Loads	Load	Weekly	96
Low Temp Sterile Loads	Load	Weekly	65
Medical Equipment	Items	Daily	10
OR Supply Restocking	Occurrence	Daily	1
Crash Cart Restocking	Cart	Monthly	5
Sterilizer Testing	Occurrence	Daily	1
Washer Testing	Occurrence	Daily	1
Daily Staff Huddle	Huddle	Daily	1

The use of weekly versus daily will be determined by whether you consider daily to equal five days per week or seven days per week. If you are processing 250 trays per day Monday through Friday and only 25 trays per day Saturday and Sunday then you can either average the total over seven days for 185 trays per day or average the total over five days for 260 trays per day.

We've found that leaving the frequency at Weekly and list the total tray count as 1300 is the simplest method and takes out the confusion of whether Daily is five or seven days a week.

Determining Resource Requirements

Determining resource requirements for most SPDs focuses on four items: labor, equipment, supplies and space. The forecasted workloads identified in the previous step drive the requirements for labor, equipment and supplies and these together determine the space requirements. Note: For our discussion, surgical instrument inventory will be considered an OR equipment resource requirement and not an SPD requirement.

Determining resource requirements is more than just determining what you need to run the department. Remember the cry for help, "We can't keep up! We need more people!"? Now is the time to truly identify what you need to keep up. Even more importantly though for a Lean SPD is to determine how lean the department could be. Remember that lean is all about exposing waste and identifying opportunities for improvement. Simply asking for more people because you cannot keep up has not identified waste or opportunities. Rather it is a simple statement that says you cannot keep up if you continue to do things the same way you are currently doing them. There is a saying from the executive offices that goes like this: "We don't need managers who report the news; We need managers who change the news." In other words, an effective manager can assess the situation and act to change the outcome rather than simply reporting how the day went. This changes the cry for help to, "We can't keep up, but I'll find out why and let you know what we can do to change the situation."

For a Lean SPD, this process starts in the planning phase and determining resource requirements in a way that sets the lean baseline against which to measure actual performance. Lean departments will continuously improve and thus continuously update their plan, but we must start somewhere. For each section below, the objective is to determine resource requirements for a lean or perfect SPD as well as current operational capabilities. In other words, what resources would we need if we were the leanest SPD around and what resources do we need today based on our current performance. The gap between these two represents the waste or opportunity to improve in the current process without any further lean improvements.

Labor Requirements

For labor, a simple Excel based staffing model can be utilized to determine staff requirements. The spreadsheet should list every activity the department performs, the frequency it is performed (daily, weekly or monthly), the volume or number of times it is performed, and the time standard required to perform the activity. This is very similar to the volume forecasting example just reviewed and it should be! Just add an additional column and you will have the example below.

Labor Requirements

Activity	Unit	Frequency	Volume	Time Mins
OR Trays Decontamination	Tray	Weekly	1300	6
OR Trays Assembly	Tray	Weekly	1300	15
OR Quick Turn Trays	Tray	Weekly	22	20
OR Loaner Trays Decontamination	Tray	Weekly	78	6
OR Loaner Trays Assembly	Tray	Weekly	78	10
OR Peel Packs Decontamination	Peel Packs	Weekly	500	-
OR Peel Packs Assembly	Peel Packs	Weekly	500	2
Clinic Trays Decontamination	Occurrence	Weekly	5	30
Clinic Trays Assembly	Tray	Weekly	70	6
Case Carts Picking	Carts	Weekly	250	15
Steam Sterilizer Loads	Load	Weekly	96	15
Low Temp Sterilizer Loads	Load	Weekly	65	8
Medical Equipment	Items	Daily	10	3
OR Supply Restocking	Occurrence	Daily	1	60
Crash Cart Restocking	Cart	Monthly	5	25
Sterilizer Testing	Occurrence	Daily	1	35
Washer Testing	Occurrence	Daily	1	10
Daily Staff Huddle (20 people)	Huddle	Daily	1	200

You will notice that some of our activities have been duplicated to account for various process steps. OR trays are now shown as OR trays decontamination and OR trays assembly to better reflect the different activities being performed, different time standards, different standard work instructions and physically different locations. Clinic trays have also been split into clinic trays decontamination and clinic trays assembly with the additional change in the unit of measurement. Clinic trays decontamination shows occurrence while clinic trays assembly shows Tray. While there is no set rule to determine the unit of measurement, how the activity is performed will often lead you to determine which unit of measurement makes the most sense. In this example, all clinic trays show up at the same time due to the pick-up schedules and one staff member goes to decontamination and processes the trays. Based on data collected from daily observations, the workload is approximately the same every day and requires 30 minutes to process all of the trays. Instead of breaking down the time into a per tray amount of approximately 30 seconds per tray the decision was made to treat the activity as one occurrence and plan for 30 minutes.

Once all activities have been listed in a manner that makes sense for determining resource requirements, the next step is to determine the time standard. Here is where a few definitions can help.

- Fastest Time: The fastest time observed to perform the activity by an experienced and trained staff member following standard work

- Standard Time or Reasonable Expectation: The time required to perform the activity by an experienced and trained staff member following standard work, working at a normal pace and including allowances for personal needs, fatigue and unavoidable delays.

- Average Time: The average of all observations or actual staff performance including all variances, interruptions, personal fatigue and any other delays.

Which definition you choose to favor will depend on what outcome you are trying to accomplish. For a Lean SPD, you will want to use all three! The fastest time can be used as a baseline to judge current performance to determine the potential opportunity that exists. Standard time can be used for actual staffing requirements and staff expectations. Average time is used to calculate current performance and lead discussions on opportunities for improvement and resource requirements based on reality.

In the spirit of lean, the objective is not to make people work faster, sweat more and go home absolutely fatigued. The objective is to find ways to work smarter, remove waste from the process and produce an environment that staff can work in comfortably. Keeping in mind that lean systems should expose waste and that lean is a journey and not a destination, SPD leaders will want to take time to appropriately explain why time standards are useful and needed to help forecast, plan, and manage the department. Remember, the reason we are setting time standards is to accurately plan our resource requirements to handle the forecasted workload and meet our Customer requirements. No hidden agendas. Let us return to our fictional SPD and play out this scenario.

~~~~~~

City Hospital: Time Standards Conversation

Scene: SPD Manager Rob has begun his Lean SPD journey and is about to introduce time standards to the staff as part of their performance measurements.

"Good morning everyone. Today's topic will be time standards. I realize that just saying time standards evokes different images for each of us, so I'd like to start with a few definitions. First, I'd like to hear from a few of you what you think time standards means."

"It means how long it should take to do a job and, if we don't do it, we're in trouble," Rachel speaks first. Rob realizes that Rachel is always quick to answer but usually a bit pessimistic in her responses.

"You are correct Rachel in that time standards represent how long it should take to do a job, but their objective is not to get you into trouble. Let me restate the question a bit. How do you think time standards can actually help us?"
~~~~~~

Latisha raises her hand and adds, "I hope they can help justify why we need more staff, so we're not always backlogged every day."

"It could help us plan better if we knew how long everything took, and then we could tell the OR exactly how long it would take to turn a tray so they're not always asking us if the tray is ready," Melissa states.

"Excellent Latisha and Melissa," Rob responds. "I agree with you totally. In fact, time standards will not only allow us to plan better but they will help us determine how we should be doing things. Remember your comment Melissa about everyone doing things differently? Well, to set time standards, we'll have to come up with the correct way to do our work first and then we can set a time standard. We'll include all quality steps, no rushing and no short cut taking, because quality is our first concern. Let me share a few different approaches that I've recently learned about."

"I'd like to look at identifying three different time standards," Rob continues. First, for some activities we'll determine the fastest time. This time will represent the best of the best, doing the job with no problems, no interruptions and representing the perfect SPD so to say. We won't expect you to work to the fastest time, but we'll use this to judge how lean we are, what our opportunity for improvement is and why we're X number of minutes slower than the fastest time. Vlad, you might be a good candidate to lead our decontamination standard setting as the fastest time in decontamination. Also, remember that the fastest time today may not be the fastest time tomorrow. Things will change. Processes may change and require us to take more or less time than before. We'll find ways to be better and remove waste."

"The second time standard is the one that you'll all be most interested in and that's what we'll call the standard time. This is slower than the fastest time because it is based on working at a normal pace and includes allowances for personal needs, fatigue and unavoidable delays. For example, let's say our fastest time for case cart picking is 8 minutes per cart set by Rudy who has been doing nothing but picking case carts for the past 3 months and knows it like the back of his hand. But the 8 minutes doesn't allow Rudy to catch his breath, go to the bathroom or slow down a bit after his 40th case cart. In short, the 8 minutes is the all-star time and we'll assume it's for an average size case with an average number of items to pick. We'll probably still use Rudy as our standard setter, but we'll look at his performance over the entire shift and realize that things happen that take him away from being the fastest. So, the Standard Time will be a standard that anyone who is picking case carts should shoot for while knowing that it is doable over the course of their shift. In other words, it's reasonable for someone who is experienced in performing the task and performs it on a regular basis to become proficient. So, for now if the fastest time is 8 minutes per case cart, then the standard time may be 10 minutes per case cart."

"The last time standard is our average time. We may not be able to come up with an average time for all our activities, but we'll probably focus on a few key areas such as tray assembly as well as our departmental performance overall. Since we can pull tray assembly data from our instrument tracking system and staff assigned to tray assembly are usually there for their entire shift, we can easily come up with an average time per tray. I pulled some reports from yesterday and we assembled 162 trays with a total of 7 people working 54 hours in assembly. That gave us an average of 20.25 minutes per tray. We'll use this number to determine what the gap is between our current average performance and the standard time as well as the fastest time. I'll make up the following numbers as an example, but I've talked with other SPD departments and have found that 4 trays per hour is a reasonable expectation for tray assembly. This assumes a variety of large, small, hard and easy trays and equates to 15 minutes per tray. If our average is 20.25 minutes and we determine the standard time to be 15 minutes, then we can say our gap is 5.25 minutes or 26% variance. I don't know what we'll find for the fastest time for assembly, but we do know that some of you have averaged 12 minutes per tray for an entire shift. I don't know if 12 minutes is valid because we haven't really implemented standard work, but if it was then we'd have a fastest time of 12 minutes."

"I can only go so fast without making errors and it sounds like you want quantity over quality. This just sounds like the hospital wants us to work faster," Jackie states in her typical frustrated manner.

"I have to share with you Jackie that I am not here to simply make you or ask you to work faster. You'll have to trust me on that. I am here to say that we need to prove to ourselves, our hospital and our patients that we are managing our work, ensuring quality and not wasting resources in the process. That includes making sure we work to a reasonable standard that we all participate in determining and then measure how well we're doing within those parameters. Remember, our lean journey is about eliminating waste, not about running around faster than we already do. Lean departments find that once they start to remove waste and find ways to work smarter that the work becomes easier. I'm here to ask for your open participation, to be curious and to join the journey and be a part of the solution."

Rob realizes the time has quickly gone and the staff need to return to work and ends with the following statement. "OK, our time is up but I wanted to end with this thought. Our lean journey is about meeting our Customer requirements and our first step is to develop a plan that helps us do that. I'd like to leave you with our first lean objective that we'll be working on over the next couple of weeks. Melissa, you've expressed concern about our backlogs and so have our Customers. So, reducing backlogs is our first priority. To do this, I'll be asking all of you to help me develop a plan to do just that. We'll need to forecast our work volumes, look at each step in the process, determine the time standard and then figure out how we can allocate the necessary resources to eliminate our backlogs and keep up with work. I would love to never have the OR call again at 7AM asking where an instrument tray is only to find it still sitting in our department. Sound good?"

No one answers but shrugs their heads in agreement. Meeting adjourned.

~~~~~~
~~~~~~

These types of conversations are never a one and done deal. They are frequent and constant during the initial lean implementation while culture shifts from traditional processing to lean processing. To finalize our labor requirements, the following final steps need to be addressed.

As a rule of thumb, a 15% variance between fastest time and standard time is an acceptable gap to plan for, but each department should evaluate their own circumstance. As for the difference between average time and standard time or fastest time, those gaps are always specific to the department. We have calculated SPD staffing requirements based on standard times and found departments operating as low as 65% to standard and as high as 95%. Occasionally, we find a department operating at over 100% to standard. When this happens, it raises the question of whether the standard is appropriate or correct and whether the staff is completing all tasks planned for and/or following standard work for the activities they are completing.

When implementing Lean in the SPD, the first step is to determine where you are compared to a plan. Whether you are going for the fastest time, standard time or average time plan, the important part is that you are measuring actual performance to the plan, identifying variances and taking action to reduce or eliminate the variance. At this point you will move into the lean principles of identifying additional waste, implementing a culture of Kaizen improvements and continuously improving the department's performance.

Having listed all activities, developed frequency and volumes and then added in time standards, the last step is to add in non-productive time such as vacation and absenteeism as well as productivity factor as needed. The productivity factor can be thought of as adjusting the time standard (either fastest or standard Time) to represent current performance or planned performance. This is assuming the department is not currently working to the planned time standards. If they are working to the planned time standards, then the productivity factor would be zero.

Equipment Requirements

The second resource requirement is equipment. Determining equipment requirements is a bit easier than determining staffing requirements. To begin, SPD leadership must determine the amount of work flowing through the department and the capacity of each piece of equipment within the process. It is worth noting the difference between capacity and throughput. Capacity refers to the potential amount of work a process or piece of equipment can produce. Throughput refers to the actual amount of work that is being produced. Typically, sterile processing departments find that their equipment or process capacity is greater than their actual throughput. This is usually due to lack of staffing, incorrect staff scheduling or lack of management of staff and processes. An example would be a single instrument washer in decontamination that has a capacity of washing 6 trays every 30 minutes or 12 trays per hour. But the actual throughput may be only 6 trays per hour if the decontamination staff is only able to prep and load 6 trays per hour. For our discussion, we will focus on determining capacity requirements, assuming the department will manage the process to ensure the equipment is utilized.

The first step is to determine the amount of work that is required to be completed for each category of equipment during a typical busy hour of the day. The basic categories of equipment include cart washers, instrument prep sinks, instrument washers, sonic washers, assembly tables, steam sterilizers and low temp sterilizers. Determining a typical busy hour of the day may require some thought or data collection but should not take too much time or effort. In fact, this is where the "back of the napkin" calculations can be accurate enough.

The first step is to determine the volume to plan for and whether you should use an average day, busy day, peak day or some other day. For equipment planning we have found that a busy day, not the peak day, is the best compromise for ensuring adequate capacity for most the working days while not overspending on equipment. The definition of a busy day is up for debate, but we have found that taking a day that represents the 80th to 90th percentile of all days is usually sufficient. The following Histogram gives a graphical example of choosing a busy day based on the 90th percentile of all days experienced. The graph depicts the number of OR cases per day as the key volume indicator for the SPD and the main driver for determining equipment requirements. If the department were to choose the average day, they would purchase and install equipment capable of handling workloads based on 26 surgical cases per day. Any day with more than 26 cases would theoretically create backlogs in the department. Since backlogs are generally not acceptable or desired, especially when bioburden is drying on the instruments and or the OR may require the instruments to be reprocessed quickly for a future case, SPDs should plan capacity to handle their busier days. In this example, the graph shows that the 90th percentile of all days falls at 33 surgical cases. Planning capacity for this volume ensures the department's equipment can keep up with the workflow for 90% of their days. The remaining 10% of extremely busy days will be managed by exception.

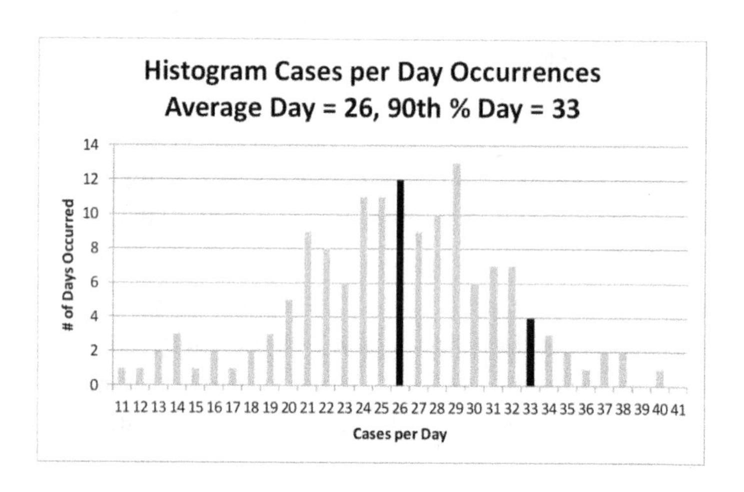

Now that we know we want to plan for a 33 surgical case day, let us break that down to actual equipment requirements. Here is where we get out our napkin and do a quick calculation. Rather than bore you with verbiage trying to explain this, here is a look at the napkin calculations.

- 33 Surgical Cases at 6 trays per case = 198 trays a day.
- The OR usually works from 7AM to 5PM or 10 hours so 198 trays divided by 10 hours = 20 trays an hour on average.

- An instrument washer can handle 6 trays in 30 minutes or 12 trays an hour thus we need 2 washers with a capacity of 24 trays an hour. A 3rd washer may be desired for redundancy in case one goes down for repair.
- Occasionally we receive five case carts at once representing 30 trays. 30 trays would require 3 washers with a capacity of 36 trays an hour.
- Decision = three washers capable of handling peak hours and providing redundancy on average days for maintenance and repair.

While the "back of the napkin" logic does require some insider knowledge of number of surgical cases, number of trays per case, capacity and cycle times of the equipment, the calculations are straight forward. You can then take this concept and apply it to every category of equipment.

Create a Balanced Process

The result of determining your equipment requirements should be a Balanced Process. The intent is to create a balanced flow of work through the department where no one area represents a significant capacity constraint or overabundance of capacity. Known as line balancing, the process ensures even distribution of work across all available resources, equipment and staff to meet the Customer demand and prevents the underutilization of some staff while overwhelming others at the bottlenecks. Line balancing prevents the delay of work completion and improves overall utilization of equipment and labor resources.

The graphs below depict a typical SPD that is not in balance and one that is in balance. The first two dark bars represent the average and peak number of incoming items into the department such as dirty instruments received in decontamination. The following lighter bars represent the capacity of each process step in the department. Shorter bars mean the process is under capacity and represents a bottleneck or capacity restraint. Taller bars represent over capacity and should be viewed as acceptable only if is not too over capacity or as a redundancy should the equipment go down for repair. While we have specifically addressed equipment in this section, line balancing obviously applies to the labor aspects of the process as well.

These graphs represent a common problem seen in many non-balanced SPDs. The major pieces of equipment have the capacity to keep up with the workflow but are constrained by the labor resources within the process and thus sit waiting for work.

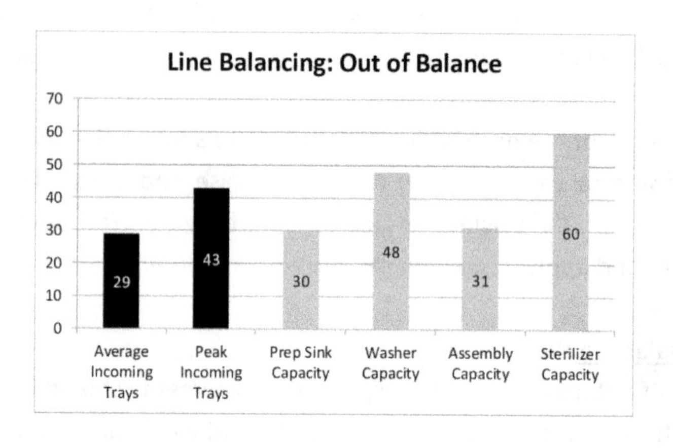

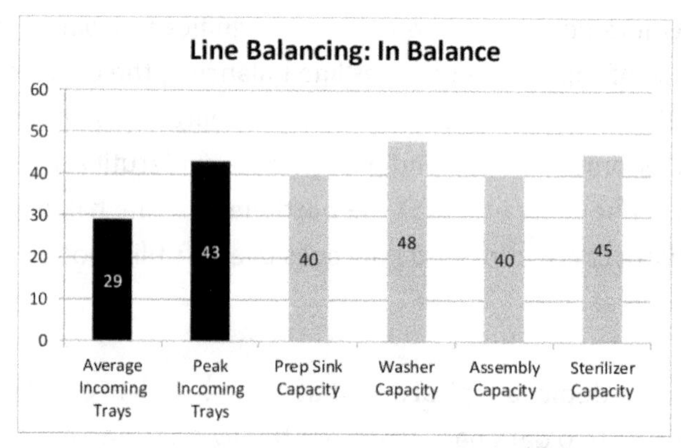

Inherent to any balanced process is the assumption that all resources, mechanical or human, are working as planned to a standard of performance. For equipment, this means that the actual demonstrated capacity is equal to its rated capacity. In other words, the equipment is performing as sold. For labor resources, this means that staff is performing similar functions utilizing the same practices within an acceptable range of productivity and quality. Lastly, a balanced line on paper does not guarantee that it will be a balanced line. Interruptions, repairs, staff shortages and poor process management all play a part in creating non-planned bottlenecks and out of balance processes. This is where active process and workflow management become critical to ensuring processes operate as planned or as close as possible.

Supply Requirements

The third resource requirement is supplies. For this, the easiest method to determine resource requirements is to understand usage rates for your supplies and then set up automatic reorder points to guarantee that the supplies needed are available. For a Lean SPD, there are three areas of focus to ensure your supply management is following basic lean principles and minimizing resource use while striving for Customer satisfaction. For our discussions, supplies will refer to only those specific to SPD operations and will exclude OR case cart supplies:

- Supply quality
- Carrying cost
- Ordering and stocking costs

Supply Quality is determined by required clinical requirements and/or regulations as well as Customer identified requirements for use. AAMI (Association for the Advancement of Medical Instrumentation) and other standards and regulatory bodies provide plenty of information and guidance on the clinical requirements for supplies. Once you have identified the supplies which are required you can review the manufacturer's instructions for use (IFU's) for proper clinical use. While supply chain management may push for the lowest cost solution, be careful to ensure that the product purchased is in fact clinically relevant and able to effectively meet the requirements of the application and use. Examples of improper decisions based on cost alone can be found in almost every hospital.

In one SPD, the lowest cost instrument cleaning chemistries were purchased for use in their automated instrument washing equipment. The manufacturer of the equipment had not validated the use of the cleaning chemistries so there were no FDA approved claims that the equipment and cleaning chemistries would effectively work together to achieve the level of cleaning and disinfection desired and required. Further process breakdown occurred when the department failed to implement regular equipment efficacy testing on the instrument washers and thus had no recorded data on whether the washers were in fact meeting the required levels of cleaning. After a consultation with the Customer, washer tests were implemented, and the results were less than desirable showing the equipment and chemistry combination was in fact not able to remove the basic levels of bioburden. Manufacturer approved and tested chemistries were introduced as a trial and the test results were immediately positive with a 90%+ pass rate. After further refinement of the actual cycle parameters on the machines, again not managed or controlled, the equipment proved to effectively clean and disinfect 100% of the time. While the new chemistries did in fact increase the cost per cycle, the clinical requirement justified the investment. The lesson learned was that lean does not always mean the least expensive option, especially when the least expensive option does not meet quality and Customer requirements.

Typical SPD Supply Categories

- Environmental decontamination: chemistries, towels, mops
- Instrument cleaning: automated and manual chemistries
- Cleaning and sterility assurance: washer tests, air removal tests, biologicals, integrators, indicators, indicator tape
- Low temperature sterilization sterilant
- Sterilization packaging: peel pouches, wrap, plastic covers, corner protectors, tray liners
- Personal protection equipment (PPE): decontamination PPE, scrubs, shoe and hair covers
- Miscellaneous: paper, pens, printer cartridges, labels, blue towels

For each of the categories above and specific supplies utilized, spending time to determine the clinical and Customer requirements for each is a valuable exercise to perform. Once the requirements are clearly identified, each product should then be tested or reviewed to determine its ability to meet the stated requirements on a consistent basis and how their performance can or should be tested.

Carrying Cost is a financial term indicating how much money is currently tied up in the inventory on the shelf. A company able to reduce its on-hand inventory cost from $2 million to $1.5 million would have made a lean improvement by utilizing fewer financial resources to meet their Customer requirements assuming everything else stayed the same. For an SPD, the carrying cost of their inventory may not be a very large financial number but in the spirit of lean, everything should be actively managed to eliminate waste. So, the question becomes how many supplies in inventory is the right amount of supplies? Is one day's worth of blue wrap or PPE best, or is one week's worth better? Obviously, one day's worth of anything is going to cost less and tie up fewer financial resources and thus have a lower carrying cost. The tradeoff though is in the costs associated with daily ordering, receiving, stocking and cost per unit. If keeping one day's worth of product on the shelf increases the per unit price while simultaneously increasing labor requirements due to daily ordering and receiving, then a decision must be made as to which option is less expensive overall. This is where a balanced scorecard concept or an overall team approach is effective in determining what's lean for the hospital versus what's lean for one department. The table below shows the daily carrying cost difference between ordering daily and ordering weekly. In the daily order option, the department places a $1,200 order every day and consumes the ordered supplies every day. The weekly order option shows the $6,000 order at the start of the week with the inventory being depleted throughout the week. The daily order averages $1,200 in carrying costs or inventory on the shelf value while the weekly order option averages $3,600 in carrying costs. Strictly speaking, one would assume daily ordering is the leaner method since it ties up less capital.

SPD Inventory Carry Cost Example

Option	Mon	Tue	Wed	Thu	Fri	Avg
Daily Order	$1,200	$1,200	$1,200	$1,200	$1,200	$1,200
Weekly Order	$6,000	$4,800	$3,600	$2,400	$1,200	$3,600

The example above assumes the same cost per unit with both ordering options. This assumption is often all the SPD Manager can do as they may not know the ordering costs associated with different quantities or unit of measures associated with product ordering or shipping. To further complicate the matter, many hospitals operate based on a central warehouse that may manage the ordering and inventory while releasing daily or weekly quantities from their bulk storage to individual SPDs within the system. Our intent here is not to write an entire chapter on supply management but rather give a foundation for an SPD Manager to speak intelligently and make educated decisions concerning lean supply management.

Moving to a balanced scorecard, the SPD Manager's decision to order daily or weekly may change as carrying costs may not be the most significant factor. Look at an expanded view of the same example with ordering, receiving, stocking and cost per unit added in. In this example an average of 421 items are ordered every day or week. While the balanced scorecard still shows a higher carrying cost for weekly orders, the cost per unit is less due to bulk purchases and less labor utilized in the overall process of ordering, receiving and stocking. Factoring the labor into the total average cost per unit with labor, the weekly order option starts to look more attractive.

SPD Inventory Balanced Scorecard Example

Option	Avg. Carrying Cost	Avg. Purchase Cost Per Unit	Weekly Ordering Labor	Weekly Receiving & Stocking Labor	Total Avg. Cost Per Unit with Labor	Total Annual Cash Flow Savings
Daily Order	$1,200	$2.85	$50	$200	$3.44	$0
Weekly Order	$3,347*	$2.65	$40	$160	$3.13	$34,892

*The weekly order average carrying cost is less when considering the average purchase cost per unit difference which was not known in the first example.

The question then becomes, is it more important to reduce inventory levels and carrying costs to $1,200 and free up the difference between $3,347 and $1,200 for use in other areas, or save $34,892 in annual supply spend? In this example, I am sure most CFOs would happily increase inventory carrying costs to improve their financial margins by $34,892! While this might be a simple example, the intent is for SPD managers to be more financially aware of the impact on supplies to the hospital both in carrying costs, cost per unit and associated labor requirements.

Ordering and Stocking Costs, as seen from the above example, refers to the inherent labor and process spending associated with ordering, receiving and stocking of supplies. Additionally, there may be holding costs and transportation costs depending on the hospital's processes. As the above example also shows, the costs of labor in the supply process may outweigh other supply metrics, such as carrying costs, especially when dealing with low cost items. For our lean discussion, we will focus on how you can create a lean supply ordering and stocking system utilizing the lean concept of Kanban as well as some good common sense.

Traditional, SPD supply ordering processes go as follows: Staff member walks the aisles of supply storage and visually looks at the supplies on hand and determines if more should be ordered. Technically speaking, there is usually a par level which triggers a reorder and the staff member is to count the number of items in inventory and compare to the par level. It is rare a staff member will count anything but rather eyeball the amount on hand and determine if he or she should order or not. Eyeballing is a form of lean in that the staff member has determined that counting does not create a more accurate result than eyeballing does, so why spend the time? While this may be one staff member's thought, it does highlight a basic point that staff will naturally drift towards finding the easiest way of doing something. Perhaps this is because as humans we all tend to give in to our tendency to be a bit lazy, but when harnessed properly it can lead to lean breakthroughs. Unfortunately, it can also lead to staff skipping process steps and short cutting quality which is not lean.

After visually determining what needs to be ordered and handwriting this information on a preprinted reorder sheet, the staff member logs into some type of order system and orders an amount that hopefully was predetermined. This system is heavily dependent on the staff member to determine what needs to be ordered and then to correctly order the item in the correct quantity. Mistakes may lead to out of stock situations, too much stock or the wrong stock. The supplies arrive and a staff member breaks out the product from shipping boxes and then places the items into inventory with or without regard for any type of first-in first-out system.

While this system has worked for years, it is a very outdated system in the general business world, and lean methodologies such as Kanban have devised methods to reduce the waste in the process. In the example just shared, waste is found in multiple areas. First, having a staff member walk the aisles counting or eyeballing supplies is waste. Having a staff member un-box items and place them into the same bin with other older items creates waste and the possibility of supplies expiring before they are used.

In our efforts to reduce waste and labor or eliminate them all together, let us first set some expectations that would guide our process improvements.

- Expectation #1: Supplies needing to be ordered would be automatically known and not require any counting.
- Expectation #2: Supplies would be ordered in a quantity that would maximize potential quantity discounts while also reducing any labor needed to breakdown larger boxes into smaller batches.
- Expectation #3: Supplies would be used on a first-in first-out basis to avoid supplies expiring while making it easy for the user to know which supply to pick.

Before redesigning our supply ordering and stocking process, let us review what Kanban is. Kanban is a signal to do something and is most utilized to signal that an inventory item needs to be replenished. While the actual signal can be anything, the most common form of Kanban utilized to manage supply inventories is a two-bin Kanban. Supplies are stocked in two bins with users pulling supplies from the first bin. Each bin is filled with a predetermined amount of supplies based on reorder amount, time to replenish and the cost analysis we reviewed previously. An example may be chemical indicators used inside of instrument trays that are packaged by the box and thus one bin would be one box of indicators. Once the first bin is emptied the staff places the bin on top of the supply cart or nearby specified location and begin pulling supplies from the second bin. Staff conducts regular walks to collect the empty bins and refill them. The bin itself is the Kanban signal. Visual counts are eliminated, reorder quantities are set, first-in first-out supply management is automatically implemented, labor time spent on counting and replenishing supplies is reduced, supplies are maintained at the predetermined levels and stock is usually always available.

Reducing labor even farther, automatic Kanban systems have been implemented where the signal is an electronic signal from a magnet placed on a board, an automatic weight signal from the bin or scanning systems that counts the items automatically and sends the signal to reorder when the quantity used reaches a threshold. These systems eliminate the need for staff to physically walk and pick up the signals. Grocery stores have perfected this system using electronic scans at the cash register automatically decrementing the inventory levels and automatically generating restocking orders for clerks to replenish the shelves as well as purchase orders to buy more items from the vendor.

In summary, the goal is to reduce the amount of labor spent in counting, ordering, moving and stocking supplies while ensuring the right quantity is ordered, supplies are never out due to human error, carrying costs and inventory levels are set and per unit prices are maximized.

Space Requirements

The fourth and last resource requirement is space. Space requirements are a culmination of the previous three requirements – labor, equipment and supplies – plus additional categories such as storage, offices, utilities and other items. Space is also about design and process flow. We have seen many SPDs, especially older ones, that are unfortunately too small to effectively handle their daily workloads. While this is usually due to years of surgical procedure growth and increase in instrument tray volumes beyond what the original SPD was designed to handle, too frequently the inefficient and inadequate design was simply due to lack of consideration for the actual work being performed. Other reasons such as financial limitations on space, space reductions due to other revenue producing departments needing space and other trade-offs often leaving SPDs cramped for space. In determining what space is needed for an SPD, the department's actual processes and workflows should be simulated and forecasted into the future.

Simulating SPD workflows first starts with a floor plan and activity listing of everything the department needs to do. Remember our activity listing described earlier? Here is another use for it! If you are starting with a blank slate and/or a new building project and now limitations have been set, then start with a rough idea of dirty and clean sides. Usually, a current floor plan or an architect's initial walled area is available as a starting point. Later in this book we will dive into the specifics of designing a Lean SPD so at this point we will hit the highlights only of the process you should go through.

We have found that the easiest way to determine space requirements through simulation is by starting in the OR with a dirty case cart exiting the room and traveling to decontamination. From there we follow the process through the entire department to determine requirements for equipment, supplies, people, processing areas, staging areas and anything else needed to efficiently process the instruments. The equipment simulations should have accounted for busy day volumes in determining the number of equipment so at this point you can focus on the small items like number of case carts in decontamination at once, where will the PPE be stored, how will hand wash items flow through the room and other process questions. Remember to go through your activity listing to ensure that every activity is simulated through your floor plan to determine space requirements.

Once you have gone through your activity listing, then stop and review your floor plan, utilize "spaghetti diagrams" to visually see the movement of people and product through the department and then, most importantly, ask yourself the question "why". Ask it over and over until you are sure that every item in the floor plan, every storage rack, every movement, everything and every space you have said you need you really do need. Here is an example:

An SPD Manager was designing his new SPD and planned space for multiple storage racks outside the washers on the clean side where assembly is performed. His current process allowed instrument trays to backlog in assembly to the point of needing multiple storage racks for placing the trays while they waited for a staff member to assemble them. He had planned five racks, each capable of holding up to 50 instrument trays each. He had just planned a space to backlog up to 250 instrument trays. Hopefully by now you realize that he was planning on having waste in his department! Waste of product waiting, waste of storage racks, waste of space, waste of clutter, and waste of multiple handling of trays was all part of his plan. To him, this was the reality he faced every day and thought nothing of it. If his department continued to do things the way they always had, then the space and racks would be required waste. If they decided to eliminate backlogs through line balancing and proper staffing by time of day, then the racks and space could be eliminated. A pair of outside eyes and knowledge of how lean could transform an SPD department was needed to help this SPD manager and department to see waste and how it was affecting their design decisions.

Chapter Six: Lean Operational Plan – Create A Value Stream

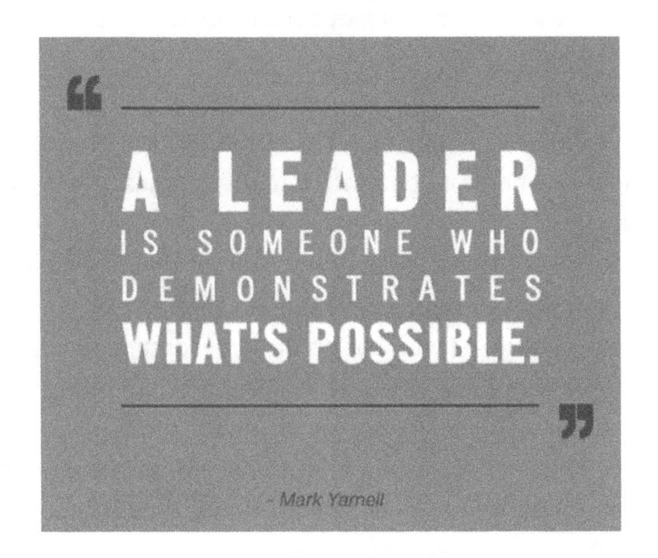

Our journey to a Lean SPD started by defining Customer requirements and creating a Lean SPD charter. Measurements were defined to help understand how well we are performing to expectations and resource requirements were calculated to understand what we need and the gap between what is needed and what is being used. Now it is time to dive into the processes and workflows that will turn the operational plan into reality. Whether you are designing a new process from scratch or trying to improve a current process, determining what, when, where and how activities are to be done is not only critical but mandatory if you are going to proactively manage the workflow.

Lean is often spoken about it terms of eliminating waste, engaging people and transitioning from a push process to a pull or flow process. At its root, Lean is first and foremost about seeing and exposing waste and then improving processes. Measuring performance is one method of exposing waste but it may not help pinpoint the exact process, activity or location that the waste is occurring. While every SPD desire to provide their Customers with the best quality products, on time and at a reasonable cost, the question becomes how do they systematically expose waste in a way that allows the department to make specific process improvements?

In this chapter, we will explore two lean tools that clarify the details of a process, exposing waste, identifying opportunities to improve while engaging staff in the process.

The first tool, Value Stream Map, depicts the overall process and is designed to identify and group process steps into three categories: Adding Value, Non-Value but Required Waste and Non-Value Waste. A Value Stream Map (VSM) views the workflow at the process step level rather than the individual activity or task level. For example, decontamination might be a single box on the VSM versus detailing out each activity that occurs in decontamination. The second tool, Process Flow Diagram, is designed to dive deep into the specific activities and tasks that occur within each process to understand the details and complexities of the workflow at its lowest level. Process Flow Diagrams (PFD) may cover one process area such as decontamination or attempt to cover the entire process through the SPD department.

A simple visual depiction of the differences between a Value Stream Map – Process Steps and a Process Flow Diagram – Detailed Tasks is shown below. A point of reference is that the Value Stream Map may identify waste within the overall process as well as within a specific process step but does not necessarily pinpoint the waste within tasks. In the example below, the process step assembly is depicted as adding value in the VSM but when it is detailed out in a PFD it becomes evident that there is waste within the value-added activity that can be removed.

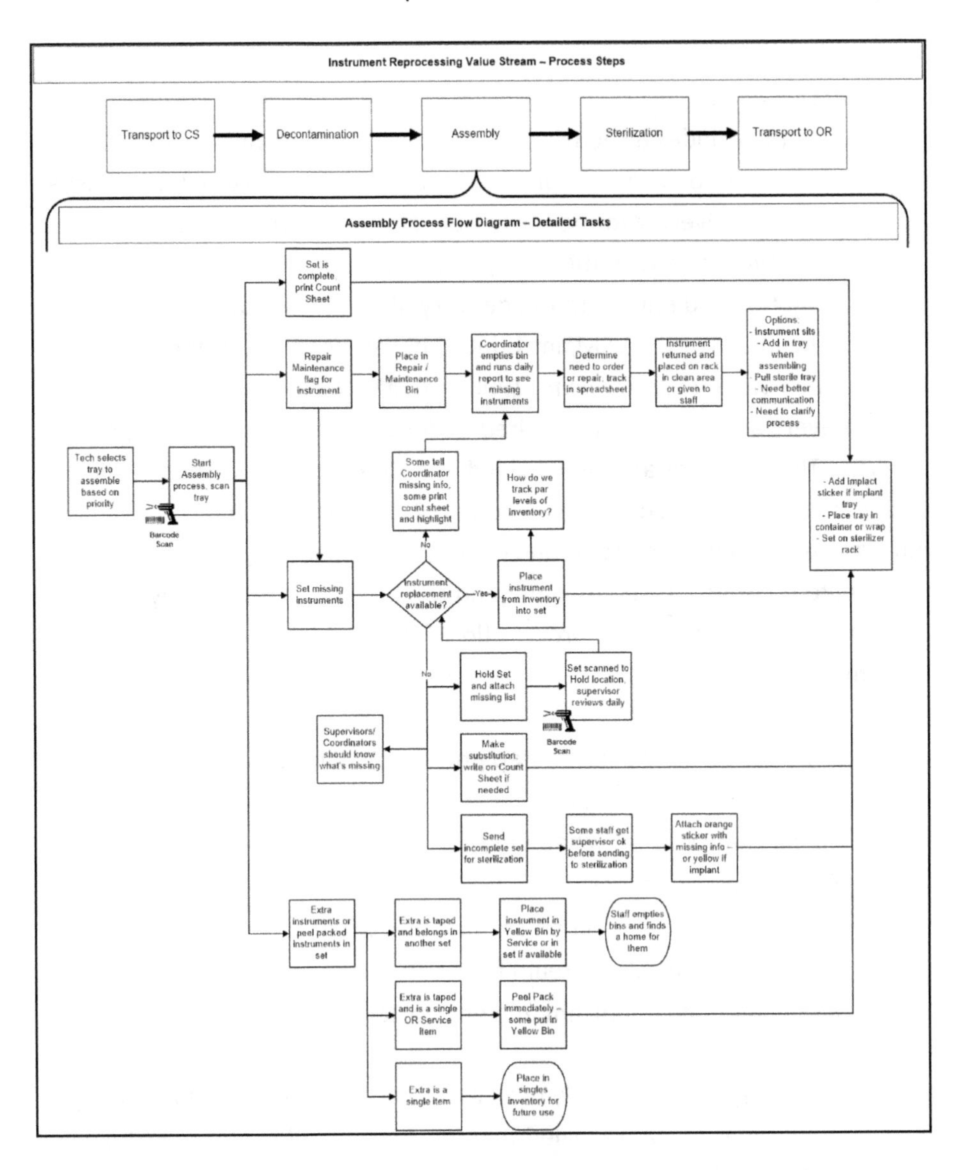
Instrument Reprocessing Value Stream – Process Steps
Transport to CS
Decontamination
Assembly
Sterilization
Transport to OR
Assembly Process Flow Diagram – Detailed Tasks
Tech selects tray to assemble based on priority
Start Assembly process, scan tray
Barcode Scan
Set is complete, print Count Sheet
Repair Maintenance flag for instrument
Place in Repair / Maintenance Bin
Coordinator empties bin and runs daily report to see missing instruments
Determine need to order or repair, track in spreadsheet
Instrument returned and placed on rack in clean area or given to staff
Options: - Instrument sits - Add in tray when assembling - Pull sterile tray - Need better communication - Need to clarify process
Some tell Coordinator missing info, some print count sheet and highlight
How do we track par levels of inventory?
No
Set missing instruments
Instrument replacement available?
Yes
Place instrument from inventory into set
- Add implact sticker if implant tray - Place tray in container or wrap - Set on sterilizer rack
No
Hold Set and attach missing list
Set scanned to Hold location, supervisor reviews daily
Barcode Scan
Supervisors/ Coordinators should know what's missing
Make substitution, write on Count Sheet if needed
Send incomplete set for sterilization
Some staff get supervisor ok before sending to sterilization
Attach orange sticker with missing info – or yellow if implant
Extra instruments or peel packed instruments in set
Extra is taped and belongs in another set
Place instrument in Yellow Bin by Service or in set if available
Staff empties bins and finds a home for them
Extra is taped and is a single OR Service item
Peel Pack immediately – some put in Yellow Bin
Extra is a single item
Place in singles inventory for future use

Value Stream Map

A value stream includes all activity, value added and non-value added, currently required to produce a product from initial raw material to a finished good as well as delivering to the Customer. For an SPD reprocessing surgical instruments, this starts with the transportation of used instruments to decontamination and ends with the delivery of sterile instruments to the OR for use. The intent of the VSM, introduced by James Womack and Daniel Jones in their work, *Lean Thinking*, 1996, is to illustrate using simple graphics or icons every action and step required to design, order and make a specific product. Those actions are then divided into three groups: 1. Those which create value as perceived by the Customer, 2. Those which create no value but are required by the systems and cannot be eliminated yet, and 3. Those that create no value to the Customer and can be eliminated. Its key purpose is to analyze and improve the process flow from the perspective of the Customer.

Womack and Jones described a 5-step process of lean transformation including:

- Find a change agent (champion)
- Find a sensei (teacher)
- Seize on (or create) a crisis to motivate action
- Map the entire value stream for all products
- Pick something important and get started

This roadmap began to be widely used and after follow-up investigation by Womack and Jones, it was revealed that most Lean implementations followed through with only four of the five steps. For various reasons, many lean initiatives disregarded the VSM step and instead dove right into waste elimination and Kaizen events. The results were often islands of excellence with little or no real improvement created for the Customer. Improvements failed to change the outcome, final quality or final value as perceived by the Customer. While islands of excellence in a sea of chaos may provide some benefits, taking the time to create a VSM is a recommended starting point on your journey to a Lean SPD.

Benefits of Value Stream Map:

- It helps you visualize the entire flow, not just a single process or what happens in your department.
- It helps you see waste and its sources.
- It helps develop a common language so that decisions can be made as a team.
- It shows the linkage between information and material flow including waste in the information systems used.
- It forms the basis of an improvement plan and becomes a roadmap for implementation.

One point that differentiates a VSM from other process mapping exercises is the inclusion of the information flows into the map. This includes how and when the Customer orders product, how that information is translated into resource requirements and how requirements are communicated to the staff to ensure the process produces what the Customer wants. Value streams are also specific to the product being mapped. For the typical SPD, a catalogue of VSMs might include surgical instrument reprocessing, case cart picking, crash cart fulfillment and delivery of instruments to Labor & Delivery or IV pumps to the Emergency Room.

Value Stream Mapping should be a team effort as well. Include all the stakeholders involved to be sure you are not creating "your view" of the process and thus miss important information, processes and perceptions. The VSM will help managers and team members see the process steps between different departments or teams, identify value and non-value adding activities, and take advantage of the opportunities to eliminate waste within the process. The result is a demonstration of the process steps including materials, information and key data.

The mapping is completed in two phases. The first phase maps the current state of the processes precisely as they occur today. Analysis is done to identify the value-added and nonvalue-added steps in the current state to identify improvement opportunities. The second phase creates a Future State

Value Stream map that defines business essential value adding activity, maintains the highest degree of flow and minimizing or eliminating non-value adding activities. It is important to note that there may be activities classified as "non-value adding" to the final product that should not be eliminated. Activities such as in-service training, safety meetings and inspections may be essential to the operation of your department even though they may not provide a direct value add to the production process. Your goal is to identify and eliminate unnecessary non-value-adding activity.

Creating the Value Stream Map

The first step in creating a VSM is to clearly define a specific scenario for a Customer. Womack and Jones noted in *Lean Thinking*, "The crucial place to begin any improvement effort is clear specification of the value of a product as perceived by the end Customer. Thus, mapping begins with the Customer requirements." For SPD this may be delivery of complete and sterile instruments sets to the OR.

Begin mapping your current process by walking the "Genba," the actual area where the work is occurring. Draw the process as you see it, not as you think or heard it should be. Pretend that you are the instrument set and follow its route through the department. Walk the floor following the process and observe, interview and listen. Begin with a quick walk to get oriented to the sequence of the process and the sense of the flow. After the quick walk, go back through and capture the detail of each step and the information associated with it.

Many Lean facilitators create their map beginning at the end where the product is delivered to the Customer and then work upstream. This way they see the processes that most directly link to the Customer and should set the pace for the work to be done.

Map the entire flow, door to door, not just your department. Handwrite your notes including what is done, by whom, what sequence and issues that prevent flow. Ask probing questions to truly understand the process as it currently exists. A list of possible questions to ask based on the lean A3 Problem Solving methodology is shown below. A3 Problem Solving is defined in more detail in a later chapter.

- What is the problem? What are the symptoms? What's the impact?
- Who owns the problem?
- What is the background? What are you talking about and why?
- What are the current conditions?
- What is the root cause of the problem?
- What is the specific improvement in performance you need to close the gap?
- What are possible countermeasures for the problem?
- How will you choose which countermeasure or fix to propose?
- What is the cost and benefit of the selected countermeasure?
- What is the implementation plan and schedule?
- How will you know if your plan is working?
- What problems are likely to occur during implementation?
- How will you ensure follow up and continuous improvement?

While these questions may go beyond the requirements to create a Value Stream Map, they do provide excellent insight into the process and issues that should be addressed when defining the Future State Value Stream Map.

Where possible, capture real process times using a stopwatch or clock to accurately depict the real process and not what you or others think it should be. Do not rely on estimates or file data as these generally prove to be wrong.

Value Stream Mapping usually crosses organizational boundaries and you will find that you are developing a view of the process that no one else in the organization has. This view helps prevent making isolated improvements at the risk of disrupting processes up or down stream. Magnified or more specific maps can be created later when focusing a kaizen activity.

Drawing the Value Stream Map

Begin with a Data Box which contains the basic requirements of the Customer. In our example, the OR is requiring SPD to reprocess 250 instrument sets per day over the course of 16 hours. Note that this Customer is requesting that there be no backlog of instruments left over at the end of the day!

CS Daily Demand	
# of Trays	250
CS Operating Hours	16
Items per Hour	15.6
TAKT (production rate minutes)	3.8

Add process boxes to indicate the flow of material. Remember the VSM is meant to highlight process steps not the individual tasks that will be captured in the process flow diagram. Use one process box for each area and think in terms of continuous flow. Where there is a break in flow include a new box. For example, in our assembly process box we include the detailed steps of obtaining the set, inspecting the instruments for cleanliness, testing functionality, adding chemical indicators and filters and containerizing or wrapping all in one process step. There is generally a stop in the flow before assembly where sets are staged following decontamination and another stop following assembly as items are staged for sterilization.

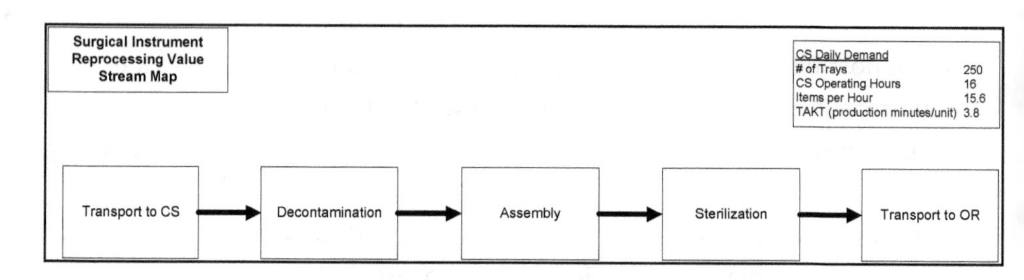

Next obtain the metrics and details of each process step. In our example, we show cycle time, number of trays per cycle, available minutes in the day, machine uptime experience and number of machines or people needed to maintain flow evenly throughout the day and on peak hours. Your process box may also include such data as scrap or quality rate, set instrument quantity, wait time, number of machine operators or any other data that may be relevant.

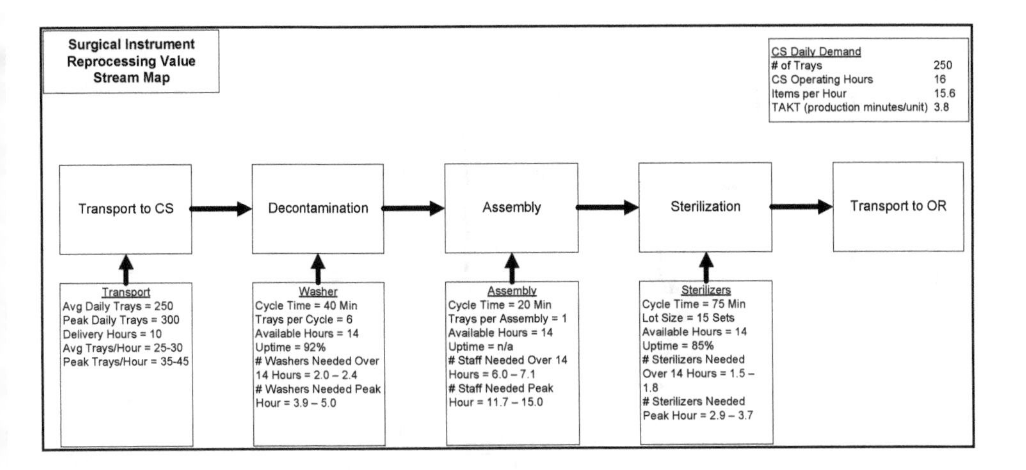

The next step focuses on the space in between the process steps. Here, identify what triggers the work to move from one process to the next and how the product is handed off. Also, include what signals the process to finish working as well as how they prioritize what they should be working on next. The space between processes is also where inventory or backlog accumulates. This may be where the OR holds soiled case carts, staging in decontamination or assembly or sets waiting to cool down before distribution back to the OR. Since backlogs typically represent waste we will use "warning triangles" to show the number of trays accumulated. At the bottom of the VSM draw a timeline depicting the typical process time the trays spent in each process and inventory backlog. This timeline will help you see the waste in the process, especially the time trays spent sitting in backlogs waiting. Compare the sums of the value-added process time and nonvalue-added wait or backlog times. You might be surprised. The shorter the timeline the faster your instrument trays are available for your Customer.

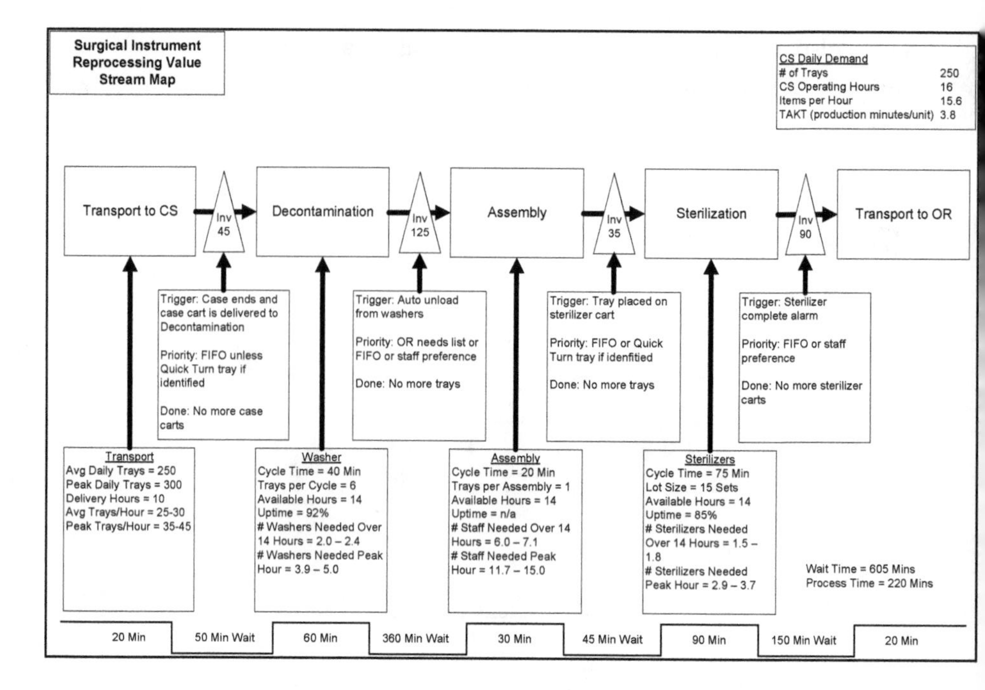

To finish the VSM, add the Customer and internal information / communication flows and call out any waste, errors and other opportunities for improvements in Kaizen flash bursts. You can always include additional information such as scheduling methods, inventory tracking, truck transportation, vendor sets or any other process that impacts the production of the value for the Customer.

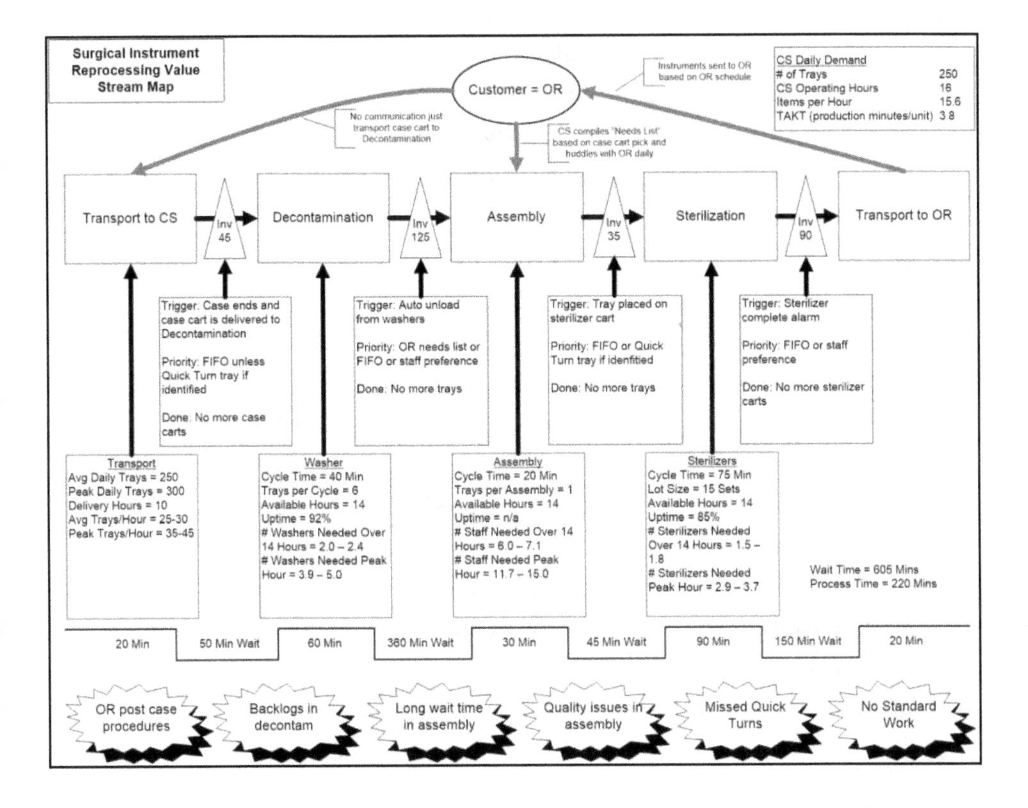

Once you have completed VSM walk the process again. Follow your first map closely to see any variances in the processes. Fill in the blanks. Add new insights you have based on your observations and any new metrics you have discovered or determined applicable. Put the finishing touches to your current state Value Stream Map.

Creating the Future State Value Stream Map

Creating the current state map is only the start of the journey. Value Stream mapping is a process improvement exercise and planning tool that identifies and eliminates waste. It allows you to envision and design a lean transformation for your processes and improve operational performance. The fun, or should we say work, begins when you create a future state value stream map and begin to change operational habits, culture and workflows. This is the point where you must engage your staff in the process if you have not already. Receiving their input and involvement is critical to gaining their buy-in to the future process changes that directly affect them. Value Stream conversations naturally focus on improvement opportunities and the difference between adding value and adding waste within the process. These discussions naturally lead to the development of a detailed process flow diagram as staff dive into the details of the issues they face every day and the waste within the process.

It is worth mentioning that many Value Stream Mapping exercises quickly become a full-blown process flow diagram session with every process step and task being documented. Be careful to keep your VSM at a higher level on your first attempt. There is plenty to do at 30,000 feet before diving down into the weeds. Use the VSM exercise as the prioritization step in determining where you should dive into the details and gain the most value from operational improvements. If this is the first time you have looked at your processes, you will probably find there is a lot to accomplish that cannot be completed all at once! Take good notes of the opportunities, prioritize and organize them and follow a structured implementation plan.

Typical improvements identified in the initial future state value stream mapping include shortening turnaround times and reducing backlogs by creating continuous flow, reducing defects, reducing motion and standardizing work. Future state mapping will also be done many times as you Lean your processes and get closer to a state of continuous flow and zero defects. Remember that lean is a continuous improvement journey that never ends!

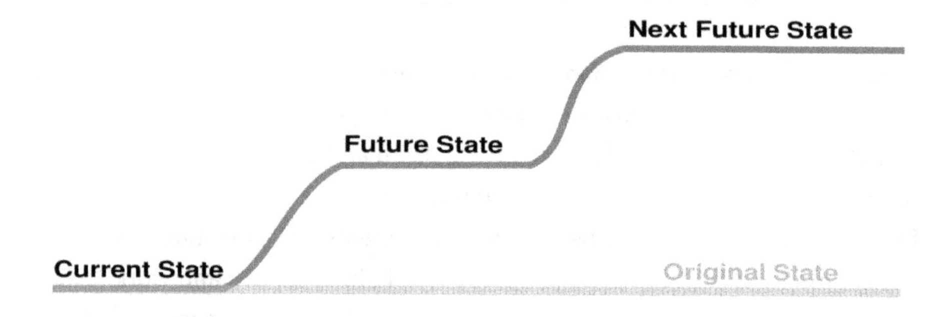

The following bullet points will help start the future value stream mapping exercise by providing some structure and guidance in focusing on the bigger picture first and then diving into the details with process flow diagrams:

- Is the production line balanced?
- Do we have enough resources?
- How can continuous flow or reduction in backlogs be achieved?
- If continuous flow is not possible, how do we create a "pull" system based on Customer demand?
- Should any process step be a "push" instead of a "pull"?
- Is the communication from the Customer sufficient for prioritizing workflow?
- Is the communication between processes sufficient for effective workflow?
- Are instruments and products handed off from process step to process step in a standardized and agreed upon manner?
- Are instruments processed to meet a specific Customer demand or processed to return to sterile storage to have readily available? Which method does the Customer prefer?
- What is the impact of inconsistent workload? Can it be managed? Are current processes capable of handling workload spikes?
- How is process performance measured? How do we know if we had a good day? What is the definition of a good day?

Notice that this level of questioning is macro and not micro. It is asking questions about the process performance, communication, hand offs and how to improve the big picture. It is seeing imbalances and disconnects between the process steps. It is evaluating what happens between the process steps and why backlogs exist and how long instruments are sitting and not moving within the department.

As the team begins to answer the macro questions and determines what is possible, they create the future state value stream map. Process improvements are depicted through reduced backlogs, improvements in equipment performance, reduced processing times, and other high level operational changes. These are then presented in the same graphical format. These improvements may be estimated opportunities or actual proven opportunities. Either way they represent work to be done, operational and potential cultural change, possible financial investment and benefit justification.

Future Value Stream Map with Changes / Future Improvements Outlined in Heavy Boarder

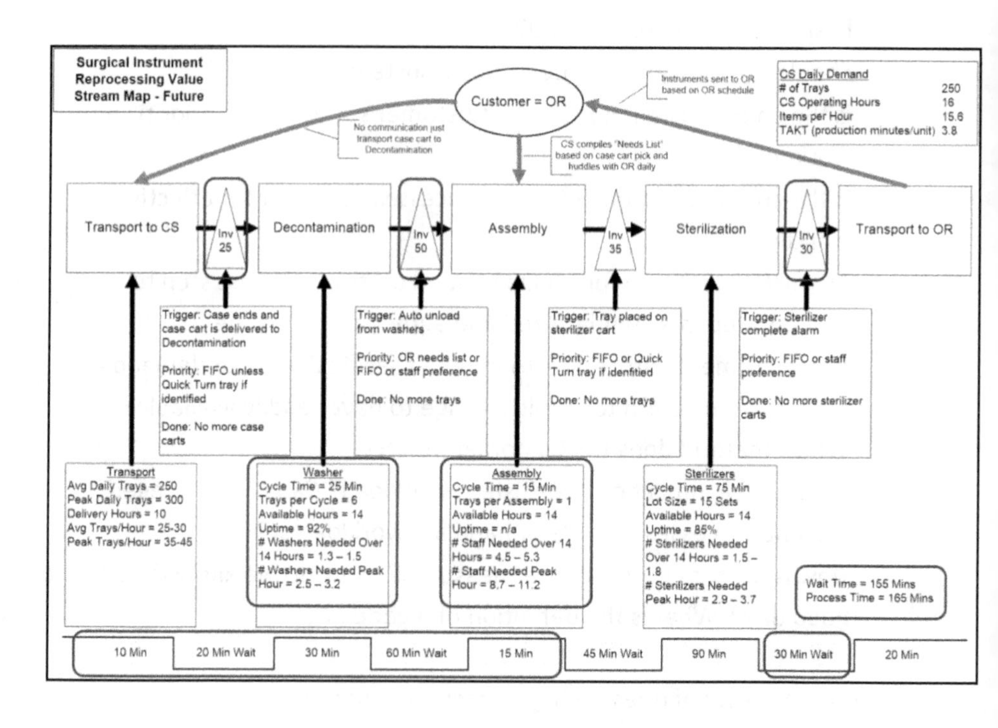

Process Flow Diagram

The second and most used process diagram is the process flow diagram (PFD), which graphically and linearly depicts the entire process or specific portions of it as the improvement effort dictates. In our process improvement work, both in sterile processing departments and non-healthcare companies, we have utilized PFDs the most and find them to be an invaluable tool in getting to the root of process issues while simultaneously engaging the staff.

There are many similarities between the PFD and the VSM as both provide a visual representation of the process and each activity on the process flow diagram is defined as value-added or nonvalue-added activity. Additional details are frequently documented on the diagram such as activity time, bottlenecks and constraints, quality issues, variance in process, staffing issues and any other wasteful activity and opportunity for improvement.

The primary difference is in the level of detail and graphical layout. VSMs are generally a single page depicting the process. PFDs provide detail on every activity or task within the process and thus expose the true complexity of the workflow staff experience. Completing a PFD helps identify all the actions required to process an instrument set through the entire reprocessing cycle while highlighting every opportunity to improve.

Process flow diagrams are best used when you want to accomplish the following:

- Engage your staff in identifying improvement opportunities in specific activities.
- Understand the detail of how a process works, variances in practice and lack of standardization.
- Uncover workarounds or hidden processes staff created to get the work done.
- Understand what happens versus what is supposed to happen.
- Identify specific improvement opportunities.

In short, if you want to know what is going on and create a comprehensive list of improvement opportunities, then take the time to document your processes with a process flow diagram. Fortunately, completing a PFD is a rather simple process. All you need is a large blank wall, a roll of paper 3' or 4' wide by 10' long, sticky notes and a black and red marker. If you do not have a long roll of paper, then tape together multiple flip chart papers.

To start, determine the boundaries of your process. Where will you start and where will you end. If you are attempting to diagram out the entire instrument reprocessing flow, then be prepared to have a very long process flow. Then determine the level of detail to be included. Some people prefer starting at a little higher level and then diving into the details later. I prefer to jump right into the details from the beginning. It is also recommended to engage the staff from the beginning and let them provide the details of what happens. Creating a PFD from how the manager believes the process works is usually very different from creating a PFD from the staff's view of how the process really works. For best results, bring in staff two or three at a time and let them explain how the process works. Ask them questions to ensure you are uncovering every possible action taken and encourage them to be honest in their feedback.

Each step or activity is written on a sticky note and placed in sequence. Arrows are drawn to connect the steps and represent the flow. You may also write directly on the paper but as the staff continues to remember and share, you may find it easier to rearrange and move sticky notes. Be sure to ask for variations in process and how each person performs the task. Usually you will find that each person may have a slightly different approach to how they accomplish a task. Document these variances. Discuss every point of waste and breakdown all the issues the staff face in accomplishing their tasks.

The black and red markers can be utilized to show the process in black and issues in red. Issues may include lack of standardization, variance in process, quality issues, backlogs, communication issues, equipment issues or any other waste the staff shares. Like the VSM, add timelines and how long activities take to understand opportunities.

The result is usually a very detailed diagram with a lot of red. Most people, especially executives in hospitals, never realize the complexity and steps required to process an instrument tray and ensure the correct instruments are supplied on-time to the OR. The following example of a PFD is too small to read but you will understand the level of complexity involved in following an instrument tray through the entire process. Notice the amount of stop signs and small "clip boards" at the bottom highlighting issues and opportunities. An example of one section detail was provided earlier in this chapter that is easier to read.

Process Flow Diagram of Instrument Reprocessing

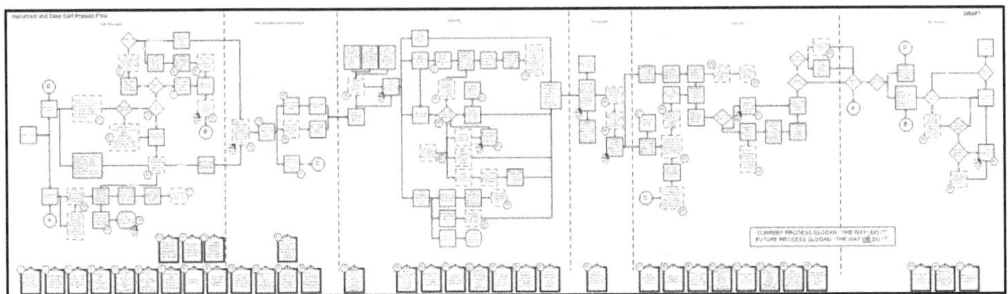

Once you have completed the PFD, you will want to digest the information and determine where and how to best start addressing all the issues uncovered. A helpful hint would be to start simple and small. Ensure that you can successfully implement an improvement opportunity and sustain those improvements. There are plenty of stories about well-intended process improvement projects that fizzled out after the identification phase due to lack of effective implementation.

One recommendation and proven approach is to start in decontamination and work your way through the process. Below is an example strategy that we have used successfully in the past. Lean methodologies are underlined to give you an idea of how easy it is to incorporate lean into the SPD environment and process improvement initiatives.

- Begin in decontamination with a daily room set-up checklist. The checklist outlines the daily cleaning and stocking of the room to guarantee the staff has everything needed for the day as well as organizes the area by cleaning out the supply locations. Create an actual checklist to be completed each day, either on paper or a weekly dry erase board, and document standard work instructions explaining how to perform the daily tasks and complete the checklist. Ensure staff is involved in developing the checklist and then train everyone who will work in decontamination and must complete the checklist. Lastly, create a daily supervisor follow-up routine to confirm sustainability of the checklist, identify further improvements and create accountability with both staff and supervisors while performing their tasks. If you are familiar with lean, you have probably just realized that the above plan utilizes multiple lean methodologies and we did not even use "lean" terminology! Setting up a decontamination daily checklist allows you to incorporate lean 5S methodologies in cleaning and organizing the area, creating standard work instructions, engaging staff in the process and creating supervisor routines to ensure follow-up and sustainability. While this sounds so simple, you will be surprised how many departments lose traction and have trouble sustaining a decontamination checklist.

- Having successfully mastered the checklist, next move to improving the workflow through decontamination by asking the staff what needs to happen to eliminate backlogs and make sure the work is being performed how it should be performed. This will lead to balancing labor to incoming workloads and creating some type of trigger to move staff in and out of decontamination as needed. By using standard work for activities within decontamination, you may possibly determine that a "navigator" position is needed to keep the flow moving while other staff remains at their workstations. Lastly, implement supervisor routines requiring them to physically go into decontamination to observe the work, identify improvement opportunities and sustain improvement and adherence to standard work.

- As the workflow improves in decontamination, move to assembly and follow a similar path of process improvement. Balance labor to workloads, create standard work for assembly tasks, set and measure performance standards such as trays assembled per hour per staff, minimize backlogs by creating continuous flow, reduce interruptions and allow assembly staff to remain at their stations. A "navigator" position may again be used to keep the work flowing and handle other activities. As always, create supervisor routines to identify opportunities to improve and manage the flow.

As you work through the department you may find that previously experienced backlogs slowly move from decontamination to assembly to sterilization and then eventually out of the department completely! While the process steps described above are simplistic in nature, they are never that simple to implement. Managing a positive culture and staff during transitions of change is never easy. If you have never held staff accountable to performance standards or standard work, you also face a learning curve to follow and possible push back to the change.

In the end, a PFD opens the door for these conversations with your staff and begin the journey from simply processing instrument trays to improving how you process instrument trays.

~~~~~~

City Hospital: Creating a Process Flow Diagram

Scene: Rob has started the department's lean journey but has so far been the only one who seems excited about it. According to what he has read and what seems to make the most sense at this point, he decides to create a high level VSM. With the help of two more senior staff who seem to understand process, they create a VSM from case cart pick through reprocessing and back to sterile storage. While the VSM provided a valuable starting point and
~~~~~~

identified a lot of product wait time, it gave the team a starting point for a deep dive that focused on their main Customer, the OR.

"Good afternoon everybody. First off, I'd like to thank those who worked overtime this weekend to cover for calls-in. We had quite a few weekend cases on top of the left-over backlogs from the week. Whatever you guys did, we had zero trays on the shelf Monday morning. Thank you."

As Rob thanks the group for their weekend work, Melissa and Cindy hang up the VSM on the wall behind him. It is handwritten with sticky notes and highlighter marks but the point is clear that the staff themselves created it.

"Ok, here's our first Value Stream Map courtesy of Melissa and Cindy," Rob shares as he waves to the VSM now on the wall.

No one seems impressed except for Melissa and Cindy.

"Go ahead and explain what we've learned from doing this Cindy," Rob purposefully asks Cindy as he knows she is respected amongst the group.

"Well, we decided to start with case carts as that seems to be what our Customer is focused on and is the first step in the process. From there we estimated how long each step takes, how long the instruments sit waiting to be worked on and some of the issues we're facing in trying to process all the trays every day." Cindy seems comfortable as Melissa jumps in.

"We also made notes on how many ways we're doing things and how we don't really do a good job of managing ourselves." Melissa realizes that everyone is giving her the "you are not our boss" look. "What I mean is that we had to calculate how many people, washers and sterilizers we need to get all the trays done. It seems like we should be able to do it, but we never do."

"That's okay Melissa," Rob interjects. "The point I like is that we've been able to put some structure around our process and that's exactly what this is, a process. It's something we can measure. It's something we should be able to control and standardize."

"Let's share with the group where you want to go from here," Rob suggests to Cindy.

"Well, we liked the idea of starting at the top with case carts. We talked a bit to Rudy and he was interested in helping us do a process flow diagram on case cart picking to see if we could make some improvements. We also thought the OR might see our efforts and give us some credit for making things better." Cindy looks for Rudy who is trying to stay in the back and not make any waves as the newest staff member.

"I think that's a great place to start," Rob adds. "What do you guys think?"

The group shrugs and mumbles their approval.

"I think starting with case carts makes a lot of sense," Richard adds.

"Ok, we'll start with case carts!" Rob claims. "We only have about two more minutes, but I'd like each of you to come up and read the details of the value stream map for now. I'll talk with Rudy and ask for two more volunteers to start working on detailing out the case cart pick process and we'll get started right away."

While the meeting was not a smash hit with high fives and excited staff engagement in a value stream map, it did start engaging the staff in the process. Rob realizes that picking Melissa and Cindy was a safe bet but knows he is going to have to select a less enthusiastic team member in the next step to drive change.

"Jackie, can I talk to you for a moment?" Rob asks.

"Um sure," Jackie's mind quickly tries to think why Rob wants to talk to her.

"Even though you don't pick case carts very often, I'd like you to use your experience and join the case cart team to help us finds ways to improve how we pick cases," Rob asks.

Jackie looks at him and wonders if there's a hidden agenda. "Why me?" she asks. "Wouldn't it be better to pick Rudy or Melissa or Cindy?"

"I'm already going to pick Rudy. And yes, I agree that having Melissa on the team would be a good addition to you. I still want you to be on the team." Rob watches Jackie's body language to see if he is convincing her or not. "You've been here a long time. You have seen a lot of different things work and a lot of different things not work. Plus, this will be one of the easier lean projects we'll do, so why not join this one and let the others work on the projects to follow."

Looking around to see if anyone is listening, Jackie quietly agrees but adds that she cannot do it on overtime. Rob smiles and agrees.

Rob's case cart team does indeed meet and begin mapping out in details the case cart process. What they find surprises all of them. They first spend time observing Rudy picking case carts and then decide to watch other staff members pick case carts to compare. Their findings include the following points:

- Some staff use the case cart to pick to while others pick to a push cart or a shopping bag.
- Staff mark the pick list different for missing items or picked items.
- Staff were constantly interrupted during their picking, usually by the OR, and thus had to decided how and who should handle the request and then remember where they had left off.
- The pick lists were not in the order of the supply shelves or the supply shelves were not in the order of the pick list, requiring the staff to walk back and forth retracing their steps through the same aisles multiple times.

- Pick tickets were not updated, were missing items, had incorrect items and had incorrect storage locations.
- Observed times to pick case carts varied between staff members even when picking similar cases.

Starting with a blank piece of paper taped to the wall, they begin to hand-draw the process. Red markers were used to identify variances and issues. Once the current process was clearly identified and documented, they had other staff members review their work and add their comments. Items missed were added and after a few days the map was complete.

The team then created the new and improved standard method to pick a case cart. Rudy was utilized as the standard setter and felt satisfied knowing that the expertise he had developed in a short period of time was being noticed and used. Their final step is to standardize the new process through a documented standard work document.

~~~~~~
~~~~~~

Chapter Seven: Lean Operational Plan – Standard Work

Remember the difference
between a
boss and a leader;
a boss says "Go!"
a leader says "Let's go!"

-E.M. Kelly

Standard work is one of Lean's most powerful concepts and fundamental to every successful process. In fact, without standard work every process will eventually create waste and drift to a non-lean state. Use of standard work eliminates waste by consistently applying best practices and eliminating variance in work.

Standard work documents exactly how an activity or task should be completed. This includes the sequence of steps and desired method to complete the activity, quantities of work in process and the pace at which the process must be completed. If followed, standard work ensures staff completes activities the same way and processes are consistent and repeatable without variation. The documentation also assists with training and compliance and becomes the foundation for continuous improvement. Lastly, defining the process steps, time to complete and standard method of work provides the needed information for the department to plan its activities and resource requirements.

If standard work is so important and powerful then why are more SPDs not utilizing it? Good question. The answers are varied. Many SPDs claim they do not have the time or resources to devote to writing standard work. Leadership claims their experienced staff knows what to do and it is not needed. Some claim policies and procedures already exist, and thus standard work is already covered. Others simply do not know the importance of standard work nor how to develop it. I am sure there are other reasons for not utilizing standard work, but the point is these objections and reasons are insufficient to ignore one of leans' most powerful tools.

For those who claim their staff are experienced and thus know what to do, I would challenge them to create a PFD with their staff's input and see how many variations exist within the processes. While there are experienced staff members who indeed know what to do, the question becomes how can we ensure that they are always following the best practice and training others to do the same? We have encountered experienced staff members that have drifted from best practice to performing tasks according to how they feel the task should be done. Occasionally, their new way of completing a task is indeed a better way and thus would become the new standard work, but frequently their way is simply a deviation from how the task should be completed.

For those who claim their policies and procedures already cover their standard work requirements, I would challenge them to show how their P&Ps cover the step by step instructions to perform a task. Policies describe what a department, business unit or company is to become, do, or follow to support their greater vision. An example would be a policy that requires all instrument trays to have manufacturer's instructions for use on file before being processed for use. A procedure describes what the department will do to support the policy. An example would be a SPDs requiring all vendors to provide instructions for use upon delivery of their trays, staff to enter those instructions into their instrument management system for reference, and verification before processing the trays that instructions exist.

Typically, P&Ps do not provide the step by step instructions for how to perform a task that standard work would include. For example, standard work would describe the specific steps to accept vendor trays, how to enter the instructions for use into the instrument management system, specific forms to complete, visual inspections and where to place the trays upon receipt. Another way of comparing P&Ps to standard work is that P&Ps can be successfully followed while staff performs activities differently. The outcome may have supported the P&Ps, but the steps taken to get there differed. Standard work eliminates variance in task completion and describes in detail how activities are to be performed. Standard work thus supports policies and procedures while simultaneously ensuring adherence to how the specific tasks are to be completed.

Traditional work processes are typically full of variances in how staff completes the same activity. Work is done according to "how I was trained" and inevitably contains significant variances between shifts and individuals working side by side. Relying on experienced staff to train new staff based on their own preferences inevitably produces variance in work practices that result in:

- Defects that are untraceable to the process
- Inability to consistently train
- Lack of accountability to process adherence and outcomes
- Inability for leadership to follow-up on staff performance

Standard work provides the means to achieve process repeatability, discipline and predictability of outcomes. It allows you to go home and sleep soundly knowing that the department is performing tasks according to an agreed upon best practice. A great question to ask a SPD manager or supervisor is how he or she knows for sure that the staff is performing tasks per best practice when he or she is not there. We often receive a shrug of the shoulders and the realization that they do not know. A great follow-up question is to ask them if they have identified the best practice and standardized it into their training. The answer is usually silence as they know they have not. There are SPDs that have taken standard work to heart and have invested the time and effort into documenting best practices and training staff as well as holding them accountable. We applaud you!

Standard work is typically the first step in any process improvement initiative for, without standard work, there is no process consistency. Therefore, it is difficult to establish a baseline to improve upon. Continuous improvement is dependent upon standard work being implemented to support the new and improved methods of work while enabling staff and leadership to detect abnormal events and variance in processes.

Creating Standard Work

The steps to creating standard work are simple. State the task to be completed, identify the key process points to be monitored, document step by step instructions to perform the task and explain why the steps should be completed in the described method. Providing the reasons why a task should be completed per standard work provides staff with meaning and justification for how the task is to be completed and helps avoid deviation based on personal preference.

Standard work instructions are living documents that are easily updated as process improvements are made. This is another difference between P&Ps and standard work. P&Ps may require corporate or executive approval for changes since they dictate the direction and requirements the department must follow. Standard work, defined as specific steps to complete a task, should never require corporate approval and thus can be changed as needed based on departmental requirements.

Creating standard work instructions can be time consuming as the level of detail requires in-depth understanding of the task being performed and every step or possible step that should be completed. Some prefer to include photos while most are happy with simple verbiage for explaining how to perform the task. Two examples are provided:

Sample Standard Work Instructions with Photos

1. Prepare the decontamination area.

A. Check levels on chemicals, replace as necessary. Date all containers when opened.

B. Inspect cleaning tools open packages of new brushes and position for easy access.

C. Obtain lint free cleaning cloths and green towels and place under the work table opposite the sink.

D. Place clean dry white bath towels on the work table and area next to sink to absorb the moisture from items cleaned manually.

E. Check inventory of PPE and ensure supply is adequate.

F. Obtain metal basin and fill with enzyme and water per manufactures recommendations. 1 oz = 1 pump. The basin holds 2 gallons of water.

G. Wear appropriate PPE as per OSHA and hospital policy, including eye protection and mask.

WHY? Preparing the area prior to manual cleaning ensures having the right tools available at the time of need. Wearing the appropriate PPE is an OSHA requirement.

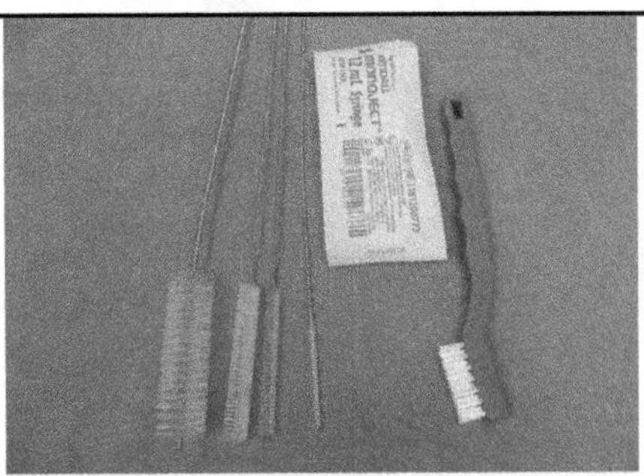

2. OR preparation prior to delivery to decontam.

A. OR staff removals the blade from the handpiece and discards any disposable parts in the appropriate sharps container.

B. Disconnect the handpiece from the console and attach the soaking cap to the cable connector.

C. Spray soiled instruments at point of use with Pro-Ez enzyme foam prior to coming to decontam. Gross contamination should also be removed at point of use as per AORN Recommended practices.

E. Cover and transport soiled instruments to SPD decontam from OR suites. Instruments received in decontam not in appropriate condition should be reported to the OR manager by the SPD staff

WHY? Removing gross contamination at point of use reduces the overall turnover time and prevents bioburden from drying on the instruments making it more difficult to clean.

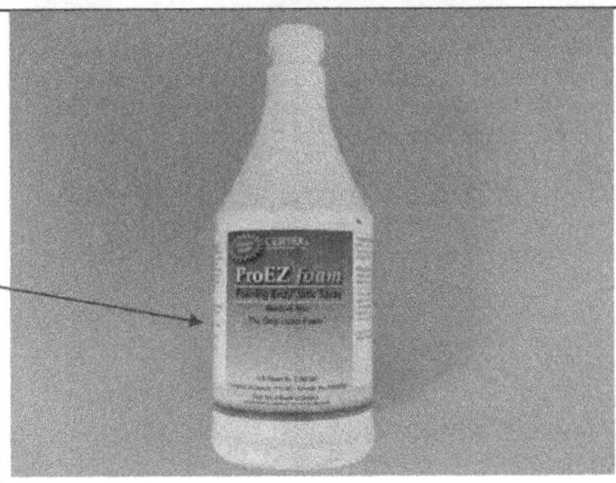

Sample Standard Work Instructions with Photos Continued

3. **Rinse and soak the shaver:**

A. Rinse the hand piece thoroughly under running tap water, flushing water through all channels.

B. Prior to soaking ensure the soaking cap is attached to the cable connector by twisting the cap onto the connector.

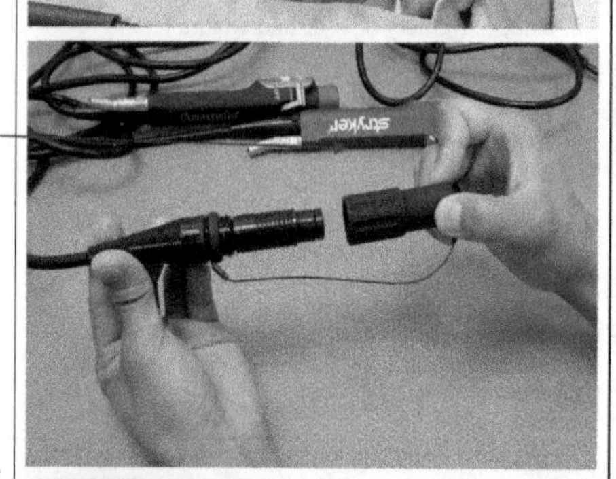

C. Soak the shaver in the basin of enzyme solution for a minimum of 1 minute and maximum of 15 minutes as per the manufactures recommendation. Do not immerse the power end.

Note: Prepare an enzymatic detergent solution according to the manufacturers instructions as seen on the bottle. (1 pump per gallon of water)

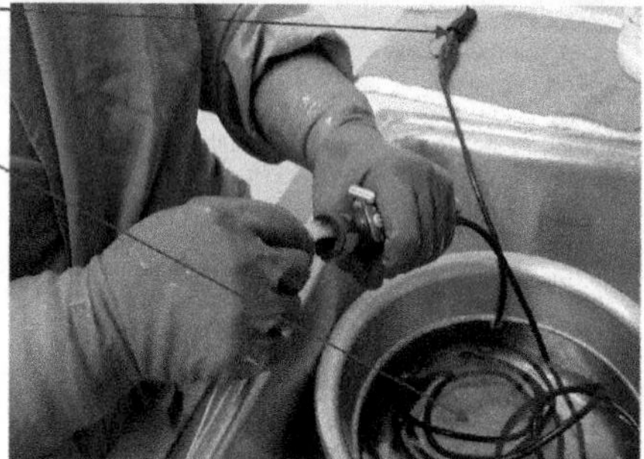

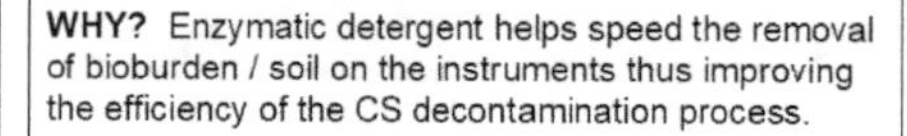

WHY? Enzymatic detergent helps speed the removal of bioburden / soil on the instruments thus improving the efficiency of the CS decontamination process.

Creating standard work instructions provides an opportunity to engage staff in the process as well. The initiative is often combined with process improvement projects as the time it takes to document the process will inevitably identify improvement opportunities. Having staff engaged in the process of creating them will help in the implementation of the work instruction since the content was developed by the staff themselves. Remember that every standard work instruction should be viewed as a living document that will and should change as processes change and improvements are made. It is unlikely that your first standard work instruction will be perfect the first time you draft it so do not worry when you find that you must change it after rolling it out to the entire department for use.

Creating work instructions is only the first step. Implementing them requires all staff to be trained and verified for competency including supervisory staff. Supervisors should then follow-up regularly with staff to ensure compliance and address any variances observed. This approach provides clear, up-to-date guidance that can be followed by even the most inexperienced SPD technician and thereby helps the department keep up with the ever-changing needs of its Customers. Regular supervisory follow-up helps identify problems in the process or practice that can then be modified or corrected, documented and trained as part of the continuous improvement process.

An important element of standard work that is frequently missed is the inclusion of the time required to complete the task. The most effective method is to use a “reasonable expectancy” or the time it takes a fully trained and qualified employee following standard work processes to complete the task one time without interruption or interference. By this definition, the time to complete the task represents a waste free environment for an experienced employee and provides a valuable baseline to measure actual performance against.

Frequently, SPD leaders and staff immediately balk at this definition claiming that it does not represent reality and that interruptions will happen. Also, not all staff have the same experience levels. They then derive time requirements based on estimates, averages or historical data. The fallacy with any of these methods is that value adding and non-value adding activities are not identified and separated and thus the "time standard" includes waste. The result is an acceptance of the current operational performance and no clear understanding of how much better the department could become.

It is worthwhile clarifying the different uses of time standards such as reasonable expectancies versus averages. Reasonable expectancies are best utilized to determine the opportunity for improvement while providing an expectation for staff when performing a task. Averages may be utilized to determine real life labor requirements given current performance but should not be utilized as an expectation for staff to perform to. The most effective method is to determine labor requirements based on reasonable expectancies and then compare the required staff to current staff to determine the department's current performance level. Since reasonable expectancies represent the standard work requirements without waste, this method provides insight into how "lean" the department currently is. The question will then become is 70%, 80%, 90% or higher an acceptable level of "lean".

Determining the reasonable expectancy for an activity will require direct on-the-floor observations of the task being performed. How the observation is performed is critical to ensure the results are valid. Observations are not only useful in setting time standards but can be utilized to determine what the standard work should be, what improvement opportunities currently exist and where process variations are occurring.

<u>How to Perform an Observation</u>

First, determine who should conduct the observation. Typically, a supervisor, manager, educator or lean process team member should conduct the observation. It is important that whoever conducts the observation understands the activity being observed, its impact on the overall process, quality requirements, and value-adding and nonvalue-adding activities. If the observation is being utilized to determine a reasonable expectancy time standard, then the employee being observed must follow the standard work instruction. Conversely, the observation may be utilized to provide information to create the work instruction or to identify opportunities for process improvements.

Next, define the activity to be observed. If you have a standard work instruction available, then this should already be defined. If not, determine the beginning and end of the activity and make sure the observation stays inside those constraints. Detail the individual steps within the activity to confirm everything is included. Decide what the unit of measure will be or what will be counted during the observation. Typical units of measurements for SPD observations include tray, peel pack, case cart, sterilizer load, washer load, deliver run and others.

Selecting an employee to observe is equally important. If you are setting a reasonable expectation for the activity that will become the standard for the department, then you must confirm the employee is trained to perform the activity according the standard work, routinely performs the activity so he or she is experienced and is comfortable being observed without feeling pressured to perform.

Begin the observation by recording the process steps as they occur. If you have already created standard work, then ensure the employee follows the work instruction. If not and you are using the observation to create standard work, then allow the staff to work as he or she normally would. Supervisors tend to want to correct the process immediately, but this will not help to identify and record variances and non-value activity. Take notes and do not stop the process unless there is a safety issue. Document value-adding and nonvalue-adding steps for review later. The goal is to find the most effective method to complete the activity while confirming quality and regulatory requirements are met.

Define clear transitions between individual steps. Look for exact movements, not general movement. Sound or audible signals can often be indicators of a process step change. Some activities may have a few steps while others have multiple. A benefit in documenting the observation down to discrete individual steps is to uncover opportunities for improvement or best practices. An example of how a detailed observation may provide insights is shown below. Even though both observations had similar total activity times, they each had different step times, indicating there may be opportunities to leverage the best practice from each to create a new standard as well as understand why there were variances.

Example of Observation Notes

Process: Set Assembly - General Major 62 instruments			
Steps	Description	Observation #1	Observation #2
1	Obtain instrument set from rack	1	1
2	Scan set and inspect and test instruments	6	8
3	Arrange instruments in tray according to count sheet	7	6
4	Print count sheet and bar code labels	1	1
5	Obtain container and lid	2	1
6	Put filters in lid, containerize set, add locks and indicator	1	1
7	Place on sterilizer cart	1	1
		19	19

Task grouping may be appropriate for when one or more tasks are too small to track their time or when the interval time is so short an accurate time is not possible. Sometimes it is better to watch 20, 30 or more and divide the time to get a measure per unit. Make sure a full cycle is observed so all activity is represented. Work towards getting a "units per hour" measurement.

An example of task grouping for SPD is best found in decontamination where trying to time individual steps is sometimes a bit difficult. An easier method is to set aside three hours or a long enough time frame to capture a wide variety of work activity. Then keep track of all labor hours spent in the decontamination room for all staff working. This will require you to keep track of when staff came in to work and when they left the area. Next, utilize trays as your key volume indicator and track how many instrument trays made it through the department and into either the automated washers or the manual wash pass through window. By the end of the observation you can divide the total amount of labor hours by the number of trays completed to calculate a time per tray average.

While you are performing the observation in decontamination, you will want to watch for workflow issues or best practices, adherence to standard work if applicable, waste in the process, quality issues and opportunities to improve. This type of observation is excellent if you are just starting to review decontamination and want to truly understand what's going on. While three hours may seem like a long time and it does indeed move a bit slow when you are simply watching other people work, it is a very valuable experience to see the staff working through real life experiences. Having taken many supervisors through this exercise, they frequently find staff doing things "not how they should be." These types of comments only point out that the supervisors themselves have not been actively following-up on staff performance in a manner that allows them time to see what is happening. Walking into decontamination and asking the staff how things are going is much different than standing there for three hours and watching what they do.

Below is a simple example of a task grouping observation for decontamination. The example does not show all three hours but gives you an idea of the concept. The example also does not take out waste which would be recommended if you are trying to set a reasonable expectancy and determine what could be possible. Task grouping observations are harder to set true standard work time expectations since many activities are occurring during the observation. They are very effective though in determining the current performance of the staff and department. In this example, both staff members had no work to do at the start of the observation and thus the first three minutes of the observation could be considered waste and removed from the observation. Remember since both staff had no work to do, the three minutes is multiplied by two resulting in six total labor minutes of waste. The other waste item identified was the receipt of trash on the case cart. In this situation, the trash should have been removed before arriving in decontamination. The amount of time required to handle the trash could be considered waste and thus removed. In reality, the trash will still have to be handled; however, when setting a standard to measure performance against these observations, is best to not include waste activities. Here, taking out the trash will become a reason why performance is not achieving standard.

What this observation example does not show is the details of how the staff is working. Are they handling instruments properly? Is the staff following manufacturer's instructions and department standard work? These types of notes and observations should be captured to help identify improvement opportunities.

A simple example from a recent observation was seeing the staff in decontamination stop using stringers to keep the ringed instruments open during the washer cycle. When questioned about the practice, staff stated there were no more stringers available and thus could not be used. After further investigation, it was found that the assembly staff was not prioritizing returning the stringers back to decontamination and had over 20 stringers sitting in assembly. Conversely, no one in decontamination thought it was important enough to ask assembly staff to return the stringers. The observation pointed out that even though a process was supposedly in place, a culture had evolved that allowed a lack of adherence by the staff.

Example of Task Grouping Observation Notes

Process: Decontamination			
Time	Description	Trays	Notes
11:05	John and Mary in decontamintion		No work
11:08	Receive case cart, scan, take to sinks		
	Both staff working same case cart		
11:15	Receive 2nd case cart, John scans, Mary stays at sink, John load case carts into cart washer		Good practice to have one staff handle incoming work and other stay at sink
11:20	4 trays to washer	4	
11:21	3rd case cart came down with trash		Trash shouldn't have come down
11:30	John leaves for break		
11:40	6 trays to washer	6	
1:00	Total labor (25 minutes x 2 staff, 10 minutes x 1 staff)	10	Total Trays
0:06	6 labor minutes per tray		

How Many Observations Should Be Performed?

The number of observations depends on the variance found in the activity. If you are seeing the same thing over and over and feel comfortable with the results, then you can move on. If you are experiencing variations in time, steps or outcomes then you may need to perform additional observations. Make sure you are observing the same tasks during each observation, identifying interruptions and variations and removing other activities that may be interfering. The objective of the observation will also determine how many you will need to do. If you are using the observation to identify opportunities for improvement and are documenting what is currently happening, then watching the process or activity one time or relatively few times will be sufficient. If your objective is to set a reasonable expectancy as a standard and performance measurement, then you will want to complete enough observations to cover potential variances as well as ensure that staff is following the standard work.

For typical SPD activities, the following recommendations will help guide you:

General Observation Recommendations

- Decontamination: At least two three-hour observations at different times of the day will help set a current performance baseline. As you make improvements to process and workflows, repeat the observations.
- Assembly: To be exact, each unique instrument tray should have its own reasonable expectancy. If your knees just buckled thinking of how many observations you are going to have to do, try taking one of the following alternative options:
    - Average trays per hour, assuming staff receive a variety of trays and performance measurement is either daily or weekly to consider variations in trays worked on.
    - Calculate a time based on instruments in the tray with a minimum and maximum amount of time.
    - Perform observations on the top 20% volume producing trays using the 80%/20% rule and then estimate the rest or move to average trays per hour.
- Sterilization: Observations can usually set a standard per steam load and low temperature load.

- Picking case carts: Observations can usually set either an average time per case cart knowing that some are faster, and some are slower or an average time per line item picked.
- Other tasks: Some tasks such as cleaning medical equipment or making floor pick-up runs can be observed a few times to create reasonable expectancies.

Setting the Expectation

The last step is to establish the reasonable expectancy. Remember, your objective is to set a standard to measure yourself against and for staff members to look to as the desired performance once they are trained and have become efficient performing the activity. The reasonable expectancy is not a reflection of your current average performance. Average performance or current performance may be utilized in budgeting resource requirements to reflect reality, but a Lean SPD department is always measuring itself against the waste free possibilities and thus always looking for ways to improve.

Depending on your observations, you may set the expectation by identifying the lowest or best repeatable value for each step or activity in observation and adding them together. Be careful that additional time spent on one step may provide the next step a means to be faster while being fast in one step may require more time spent on the following step. Do not assume that the fastest time in each step is always achievable if you attempt to add all fastest times together.

If each step is repeatable, then find the way to make it standard so that staff can replicate the performance. The intent is to find the reasons for variance or interruption and remove those issues. Identify the non-value activity and brainstorm how to remove it from the process. Gaining employee acceptance of the expectation is critical but not something that lends itself to a democratic vote. Staff members understand that expectations may well become the standard they are measured against. If they feel they are not able to meet the expectation, they will quickly voice their displeasure and lobby to have it changed. Understand that in any work environment you will have a bell curve of performance around measurements. Again, this is dependent on how you have set the expectation. If you used current average performance, then you may find a natural bell curve with high performers and low performers. Or, you may be surprised by how many people are now able to achieve the expectation once they began being measured against it. This impact will lead to the average changing as staff performance changes.

If you set the expectation observing an experienced staff member who is following standard work without waste or interruptions and is proficient at the task, then you may find most staff are unable to meet the expectation. This is not a bad situation though. It is okay if only 20% of your staff can achieve a standard that is set as a benchmark of proficiency. What you will want to clarify is the minimum performance required by all staff for the activity before remedial action is taken.

We are often asked what the industry benchmarks are for SPD productivity, task specific productivity and other items. Unfortunately, SPD does not have widely accepted benchmarks. Some organizations allow SPD departments to self-report their performance to create a database of benchmarks, but even these are limited in scope to the number of participants and how they have self-reported. While every SPD department decontaminates, assembles, and sterilizes trays, there is a wide variety of other activities that make it difficult to compare any SPD department to any other SPD department. To give you something to go by, here are the typical, reasonable expectancies we have found to be a good starting baseline. From here, you can begin to determine what your lean operational plan will be and what your expectations and standards should be.

General Expectations Guidelines

- Decontamination: A baseline average is 6 minutes per tray including all activities in decontamination from receiving case carts, scanning, breaking down trays, prepping for the washer, loading the wash, hand washing, loading cart washer and dressing in PPE. Lowest acceptable times observed reached 3 minutes per tray. Observations resulting in less than 3 minutes per tray (that included all activities in decontamination) showed potential short cutting the process.

- Assembly: A baseline averages at four trays per hour. Ten years ago, this may have been three trays per hour, but the proliferation of small trays, cameras and scopes, power and other small trays has increased the throughput per hour. High performing SPDs are now reaching an average of five trays per hour in assembly.
- Sterilization: Observations usually result in all activities associated with building a steam sterilizer load, loading and unloading the sterilizer, documenting the load and possibly putting the instruments away (if it is immediately adjacent) to be 15 minutes per load. Low temperature loads are between 4 and 7 minutes depending on the number of items.
- Picking case carts: This one will vary between hospitals as the definition of what is included in picking a case cart varies. Some SPDs are responsible for soft good plus instruments while others are only responsible for instruments. While it is hard to give a baseline, a good starting point is somewhere around four to six case carts per hour.

I am sure many of you have already raised your voice regarding where these guidelines are incorrect, do not reflect your reality and are unreasonable. That is okay. The best thing to do is get out pen and paper and go and start performing your own observations and creating your own standard work. Then start the never-ending process of trying to improve how your processes work.

Let us return to our fictional SPD and see how they are implementing standard work and reasonable expectation.

~~~~~~

City Hospital: Implementing Standard Work

Scene: It has been a month since Rob introduced the department to lean and today the case cart team is about to officially implement the department's first lean standard work.

"Good afternoon everyone. Today I'd like to introduce our first standard work on picking case carts. Remember how a few of you raised the issue of everyone doing things differently? Well today we are standardizing our first activity. No longer will we focus on how each of us performs our job but rather how we as a department have agreed to perform our jobs. I'd like to have our case cart picking team come forward and present their findings."

Jackie, Rudy and Melissa step forward to address the group and look a bit nervous in having to do so. Typically, the leadership team, specifically Rob the manager, has prepared and implemented all the departmental changes so having the staff present to their peers is a new experience.

"We spent time last week working with Rudy on how he picks case carts and what the best way to do it should be," Jackie begins. Rob hopes silently that Jackie's negative or pessimistic flare does not raise its ugly head but rather that she maintains a positive tone. "While we know that Rudy has only been here about four months, he actually does a really good job picking case carts."

"Well that's all I do every day," Rudy adds with a little blush in his cheeks.

"We looked at how Rudy picks case carts, came up with some improved methods that will help us do it quicker and added a quality check at the end to be sure the OR receives what they need. Once we came up with the best way, we wrote the standard work for case picking that Melissa is handing out now." Jackie seems to feel comfortable in front of the team and may have found a positive way to channel her energy.
~~~~~~

"I'll review the standard work that I just handed out to everyone," Melissa takes over. "You'll see we've broken down the process steps into printing the pick tickets, checking them against the OR schedule to be sure we have them all, picking the case cart and doing the quality check at the end. The actual delivery of the cart is going to be a separate work instruction."

Melissa reads through the standard work and Rob is starting to feel good about the employee engagement and acceptance of standard work. Perhaps implementing a Lean SPD is not as hard as he thought it would be.

"You'll see at the end we've listed how long it should take to pick a case cart. We came up with a time of 12 minutes per case cart," Melissa finishes. Suddenly, Rob's good feeling vanishes as the staff start vocalizing their disbelief with a 12-minute time standard.

"12 minutes? Really?" Latisha is the first to blurt out. "So much for getting more staff to help us get the work done," Latisha adds as she crosses her arms and lowers her head.

"I told you this is just to get us to work faster," Rachel states before going over to talk to Jackie.

Suddenly, the group is talking amongst themselves and the meeting has lost focus. Jackie is no longer addressing the group but agreeing with her friend Rachel that the standard work does seem to make people work faster.

Rudy is standing by himself unsure where he now stands amongst his new coworkers. Others start murmuring that the whole lean project is just another way to get more work done with less people.

"Everyone, listen up. The 12 minutes is our lean standard that Rudy has proven can be done! They even watched him for an entire shift and, after taking out the waste and making sure he wasn't interrupted, he could do 12 minutes for the entire day. The team didn't just make it up." Rob is scrambling trying to get the team back on track and somehow return to the positive meeting that he thought he was going to have.

"Great. Cindy is crying," Vlad whispers under his breath. Rob notices Cindy, one of his best employees, about ten feet away wiping away tears. Things have gone downhill he thinks to himself.

"Remember that our lean journey is all about continuous improvement and trying new ways to eliminate waste and create a quality product for our Customer. Just as Jackie said, we've even built in a quality check to be sure our case carts are correct. Let's give this a try and see how it works and if we need to change, we can." Rob is trying his best but realizes that he may have to let everyone sleep on what they have just heard, resuming the conversation tomorrow.

"Ok, let's call it a day for our meeting and we'll start keeping track of how well our case cart picking goes and then we can determine if our standard work is working or not. Let's get back together tomorrow at the start of shift and see what progress we've made." Rob dismisses the group and heads over to talk to Cindy.

"Cindy, what's wrong?" Rob asks as he pulls her aside away from the others.

"I can't pick a case cart in 12 minutes. I'll fail." Cindy is definitely taking the 12-minute standard hard.

"Cindy, you're one of our best workers and you hardly ever have to pick case carts. I don't expect you to hit the 12-minute standard. Rudy, yes. He picks case carts every day as that's his primary assignment. You might pick a case cart once every two months just to help when we're short on staff. Remember, the standard is a reasonable expectation for someone who regularly performs the task and is proficient at it. You're one of our best tray assemblers and that's where you'll be setting the standard. When it comes to case cart picking, don't worry about the standard. Just do your best and help us out." Rob starts to realize that the delivery of the message is perhaps more important than he originally thought.

Cindy stops crying as she listens to Rob's explanation and seems to understand. She's now embarrassed and is thankful it's time for her to go home.

Later that night, Rob goes back over the day and starts to formulate how he can better roll out standard work. Perhaps he will roll out the standard work first without the time standard and then, once everyone is comfortable with the work instructions, he will show how the time expectation can be achieved and perhaps test it out first on actual staff.

I should have better explained what the time expectation will be used for, he thinks to himself. If Cindy took it that hard, how many other people thought they would lose their job if they could not meet the standard? Rob suddenly realizes that communication and how a message is presented can make or break the lean implementation.

The next day, Rob addresses the group again and apologizes for the rough start. He goes on to explain how the time expectation will be used as a baseline to help identify opportunities for improvement, not to punish staff who cannot achieve it. The point, he stresses, is to continuously find ways to improve the department's performance in both quality and efficiency while keeping the work environment fun and enjoyable. There will be a minimum standard of performance, as there always is, but the intent is not to make people work harder or faster, but smarter and with less waste.

In the end, it was a rough start, but the learning continued for both Rob and his staff along their Lean SPD journey.

~~~~~~
~~~~~~

Chapter Eight: Lean Operational Plan – Continuous Flow

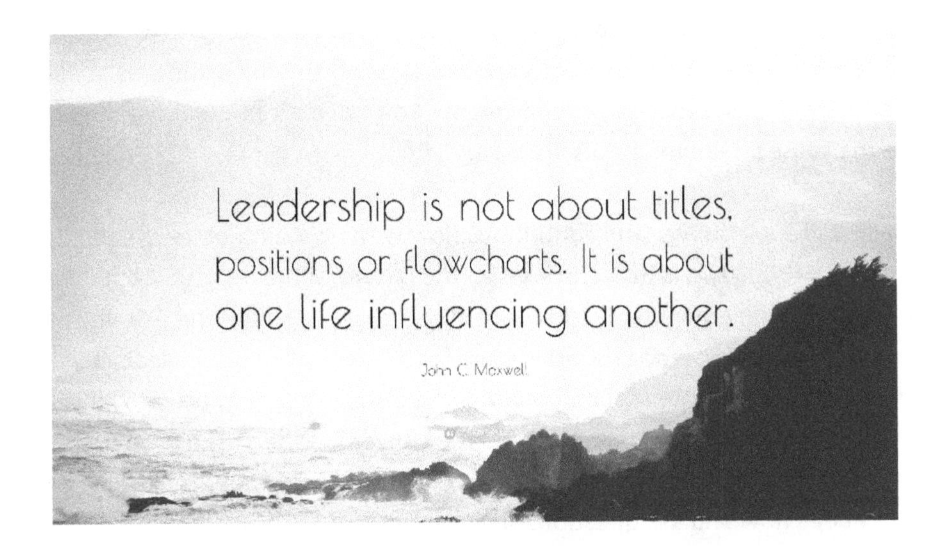

Continuous flow is a powerful lean concept that applies perfectly to sterile processing departments. In fact, it is a perfect foundation for many process improvement projects from which most aspects of the department can be improved including throughput, quality and employee engagement. First let us define what continuous flow means and what it does not mean to a sterile processing department.

Sample Definitions of Continuous Flow:

- To move through a process without stopping
- To reprocess an instrument set with minimal or no wait time
- To move a patient through surgery with minimal or no wait time

These simple definitions talk to flow of the instruments through the department. The underlying reason why this is so important starts with the Customer's expectation that instruments will be reprocessed in an acceptable amount of time and returned to sterile storage to be used when needed. The OR and other internal Customers do not want their instruments and equipment sitting in SPD unusable and unavailable should they be needed. Continuous flow supports the Customer requirements of on-time instruments and acceptable turnaround times.

Let us define continuous flow in terms of actual sterile processing workflows. The following graphics depict the various stages of continuous flow as applied to a typical sterile processing department. You will notice how these are very like the value stream maps discussed earlier.

The first graphic shows true continuous flow with no wait time between activities. While this is unrealistic given the nature of the activities, batching of trays through equipment, cooling of trays before handling and just normal working conditions, it does set the stage for a "perfect" scenario against which to measure potential improvement. Perhaps more importantly, it is a good teaching tool to help understand the concept. When used properly, staff can begin to view their working environment against the backdrop of continuous flow and ask questions such as:

- Am I working on an activity that adds value and supports continuous flow?
- Why are instruments sitting in the department and not moving?
- What are the resource requirements to achieve continuous flow?
- What time standards do I have to work to, to achieve continuous flow?
- Why are there backlogs?

Process Cycle Time: Continuous Flow

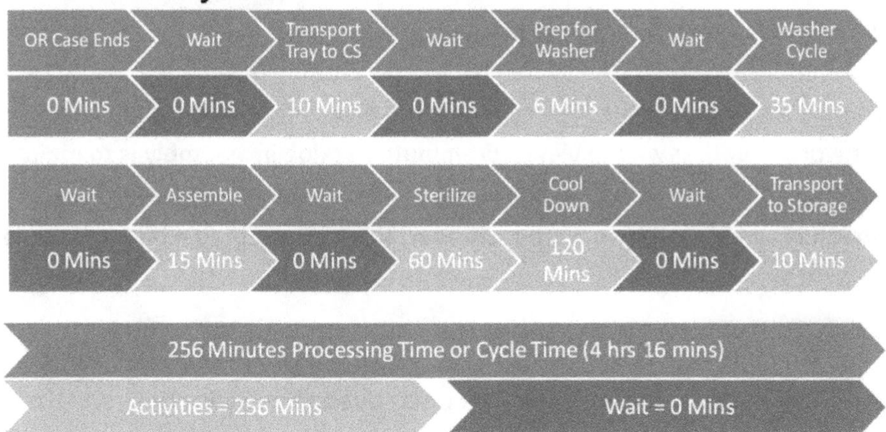

The following graphic takes a more realistic view of continuous flow in a sterile processing department. When these two graphics are shown to SPD Customers such as the OR, they quickly understand that true continuous flow is unrealistic, but they readily agree that they would be happy with and accepting of a realistic continuous flow time frame. In the example below, you will notice wait times have been included and shaded a dark gray while activity times have increased slightly and colored a lighter gray.

Example - Realistic Continuous Flow

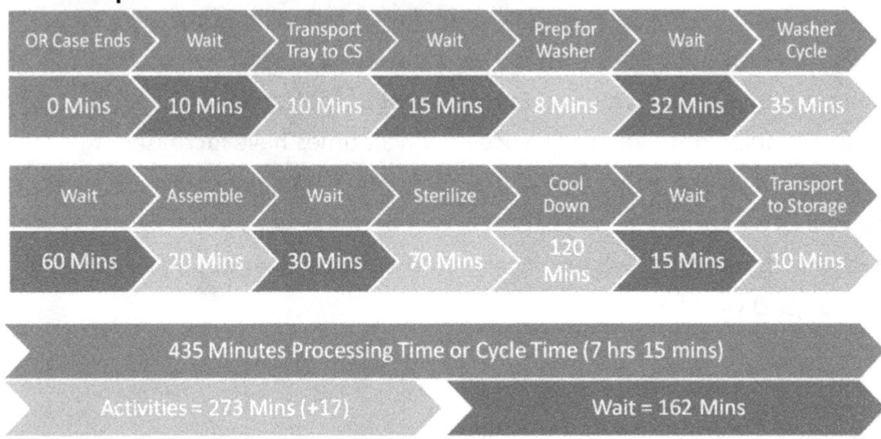

The longest wait times in this example are found waiting on assembly staff for 60 minutes, waiting at the instrument washer for 32 minutes and waiting at the sterilizer for 30 minutes. An assembly wait time of 60 minutes is acceptable for two reasons. First, instruments are typically too hot to handle when they come out of the washer and need to cool. Secondly, assembly is labor intensive, and it is okay to have a small backlog of work waiting to be completed to ensure the staff can maintain productivity and not be waiting for work. Another way to view a 60-minute backlog in assembly is to maintain one hour's worth of work per assembly staff member. If you have three staff and they can assembly four trays an hour, then an acceptable backlog would be 12 trays.

The 32-minute wait time in front of the washers and 30 minutes in front of the sterilizers represents typical wait times due to batching of instruments into the equipment. Since instrument washers and sterilizers are designed to batch process multiple trays at once instead of single piece flow, backlogs naturally will occur as the staff prepares the loads.

The reason this example is acceptable to every OR we have talked to is because of this explanation. With a realistic continuous flow processing trays in 7 hours and 15 minutes, the first instrument trays used in the morning will be back on the shelf sterile around 5pm. Every OR we have talked to has exclaimed that if that could happen all the time they would be overjoyed.

Unfortunately, there is a few of you reading this book that realize your department is not performing to this standard or at least you know of someone else's department that is not! Let us look at a broken continuous flow example. Here you will notice how wait times have increased throughout to levels that become problematic. Activity times have increased as well as a natural side effect of the increased backlogs and wait times. The example below shows where most wait time occurs per our observations of broken SPD workflows:

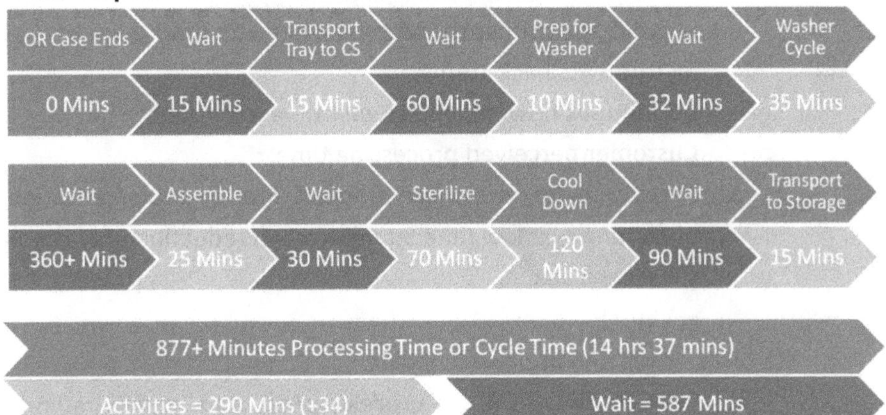

Again, the wait in assembly is by far the greatest with instruments sometimes waiting for days to be worked on. In these situations, staff shortages, an acceptable view of backlogs and a lack of process management are the usual underlying causes. It does not have to be this way though.

We have found many SPDs claim that they prioritize their work based on the OR schedule. Having trays waiting in backlogs to be assembled is acceptable if the OR receives what it needs. While this may sound reasonable, it is an outcome-focused mentality versus a process-focused mentality that 9 times out of 10 leads to trouble. In fact, almost every broken SPD department we have helped turn around has this exact problem of wait times and "acceptable" backlogs.

Once the SPD understands the concept of continuous flow, you can reinforce the concept by sharing the multiple benefits of implementing continuous flow. Besides happy Customers and less backlogs, continuous flow will help improve operational performance in all areas. Proven benefits include the following:

- Reduces processing time
    - Customer perceived processing time starts when they send you dirty instruments and ends when you send the instruments back sterile.
    - Continuous flow minimizes wait time and reduces the Customer perceived processing time.
    - Actual activity time is also reduced through implementation of continuous flow time standards and reduction of waste in the workplace.

- Reduces errors and improved quality
    - With continuous flow, "process speed" and "quality" support each other.
    - As instrument trays are processed closer and closer to the time of use, SPD staff identifies lost and extra instrumentation quicker and can notify the OR and find their correct home easier.
    - Less sets on the shelves in assembly means less phone calls from the OR, fewer interruptions, less looking through stuff and less errors.

- Reduces space requirements and clutter
    - How much space is currently utilized for instrument trays, carts, storage racks, case carts and other items waiting to be processed?
    - Continuous flow minimizes space requirements and creates a clean organized workplace with minimal inventory in process at any time.

- Reduces backlogs
    - Less wait time equals fewer backlogs as instrument trays move through the process in a timely manner.
    - There will be less OR phone calls looking for that instrument tray that has been sitting in assembly for 18, 24, 36, 48, or 72 hours.

- Improves staff productivity
    - Continuous flow improves productivity through better processes, less clutter and improved staff mentality and attitude.
    - Staff strives to keep the flow going, helps promote flow and "pushes" and "pulls" instruments through to reduce backlogs while gaining productivity.

Implementing Continuous Flow

Let us look at how to implement continuous flow. At a high level, the department should do its best to staff decontamination as a "push" function, putting as much labor and resources as required to prevent any backlogs, remove bioburden as soon as possible and maintain continuous flow as best as it can. It is understandable that decontamination will have uneven flow of instruments from the OR and other Customers, but staff can and do set the pace for the rest of the department's continuous flow. Once the instruments are through decontamination, the rest of the department should be able to staff and maintain a stable and predictable flow of work through the department.

There are eight steps to implementing continuous flow:

- Balance the production line
- Align staff schedules
- Create standard work
- Set staff performance standards
- Train to standard work
- Reduce interruptions
- Develop key performance indicators
- Create leadership routines

Balance the Production Line

Balancing the production line or process directly relates to determining resource and equipment requirements. The intent is to create a balanced flow of work through the department where no one area represents a significant capacity constraint or overabundance of capacity. The graphs below depict a typical SPD that is out of balance and one that is in balance. The first two dark bars represent average and peak trays arriving into the department per hour. The following lighter bars represent the capacity of each process step in the department. Shorter bars mean the process step is under capacity and represents a bottleneck or capacity restraint. Taller bars represent adequate or over capacity. Remember that too much capacity can be considered a waste of resources and should be minimized while maintaining adequate redundancy should a piece of equipment go down for repair or become unavailable.

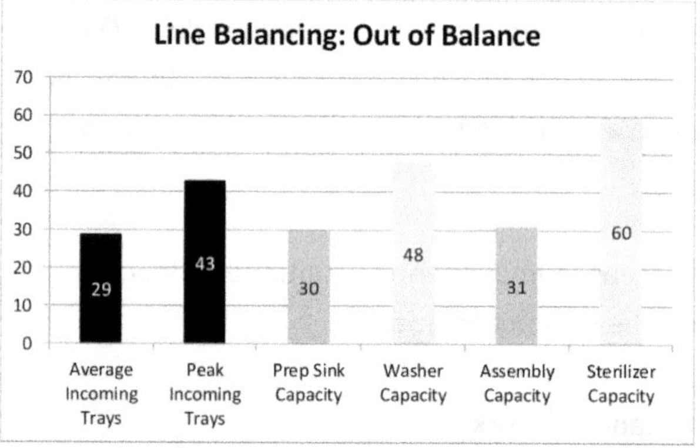

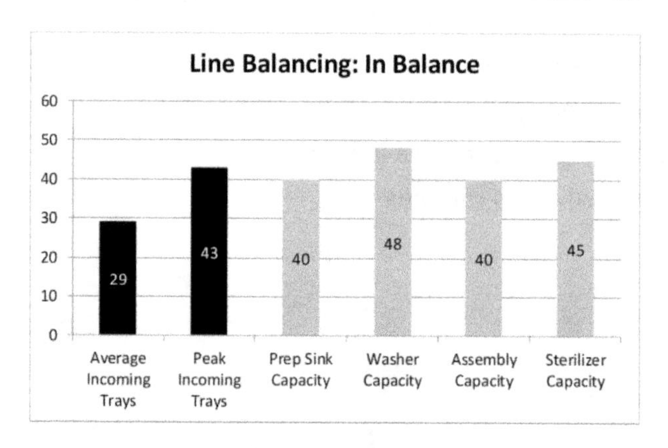

It is worth noting that even if you have balanced physical pieces of equipment such as prep sinks and instrument washers, the equipment itself cannot process a workload without a staff member assigned to the area. The capacity restraints in the first graph may be due to lack of prep sinks and assembly stations or they could represent lack of staffing for prep sinks and assembly stations. Our experience has shown a combination of both scenarios where some departments do not have enough assembly space and stations to keep up with the workflow while others have enough stations but struggle with providing staff to maintain a balanced production line.

While the graphs above may be sufficient to drive a balance in many SPDs, we have found value in looking at line balancing by the hour of the day to identify bottlenecks, backlogs, and process constraints. Utilizing simulation software that accepts department specific inputs on workloads, equipment and staffing and performance preferences, simulation graphs can be generated showing the forecasted hour by hour workflow and potential backlogs in the department.

Simulation software can be a powerful tool in designing future department workflows and resource requirements as well as helping identify improvement opportunities for current departments. The following graphs depict a typical department simulation that is currently experiencing backlogs in decontamination and assembly. The graphs are interrelated meaning that assembly can only work on instruments that have been decontaminated and sterilization can only sterilize trays that have been assembled. This interrelation is critical when understanding the impact that staffing has on equipment requirements. For example, if assembly is continuously backlogged then the sterilizers are sitting idle waiting for work and thus look like they are underutilized or overcapitalized. If assembly were to maintain continuous flow, then suddenly workload on the sterilizers would increase during peak processing hours.

Simulation Software Graphs

- Medium Gray Bars represents cycles or labor hours working during the hour.
- Dark Gray and Light Gray Bars represents backlog accumulated.

Cart Washers – No Backlogs with 3, 4 or 5 cycles ran each hour

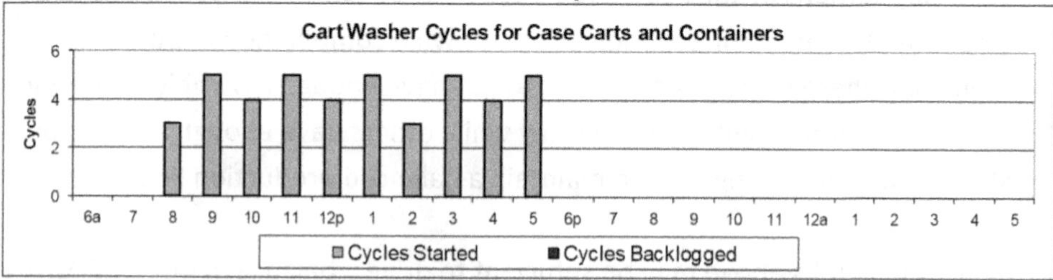

Prep Sinks and Instruments Washers – Both experiencing backlogs

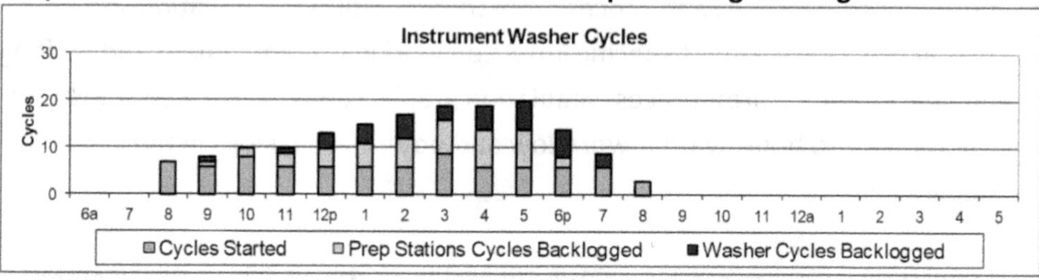

Assembly – Backlogs growing through the day relying on 3rd shift to catch up

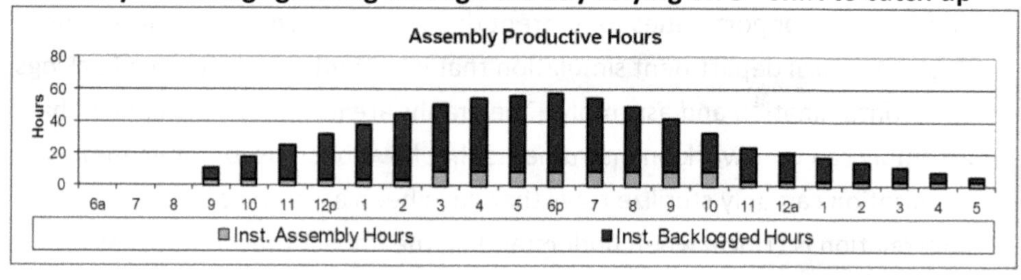

Steam Sterilizer – No Backlog because the sterilizers are waiting on assembly

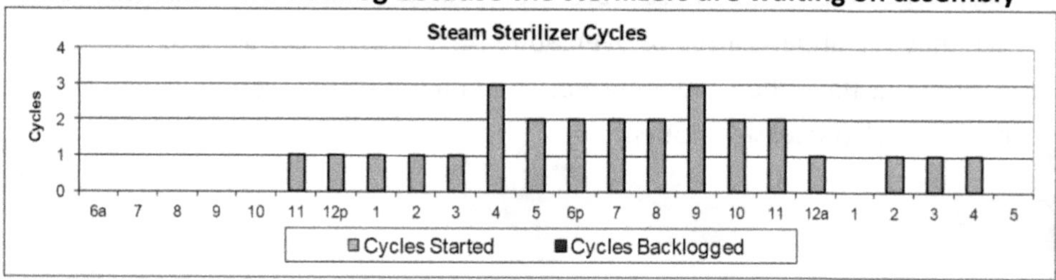

Simulations such as these provide valuable insight and opportunities to observe the impacts of different scenarios, staffing schedules, workload volumes and equipment selection to find the best fit for the department. Slow days, average days and busy days can be simulated to help determine resource requirements. The impact of purchasing new equipment with faster cycle times can be easily seen as well as what happens when a piece of equipment is down for repair. For new construction, running simulations is critical to forecasting the right amount of equipment and space for the forecasted workloads and future growth before the department is equipped and built. For current departments that may not have the opportunity to replace existing equipment, simulations are valuable in understanding what the department is capable of and how staffing directly impacts continuous flow. In fact, the impact of staffing is often the biggest factor when running simulations and determining how to balance the department's processes. Lack of assigned staff, undertrained or underproductive staff has the same effect as increasing equipment cycle times and thus creates backlogs.

While balancing the line is simple to do on paper, achieving it can be difficult, especially if the department is truly understaffed. We have found some departments to be too understaffed to effectively handle their workload while others claim they are understaffed but in reality, they have the correct number of staff but are not working at the right time of day. Lean SPD provides many tools to help eliminate waste and thus utilize your labor resources on value added activities. In the end, though, there is a certain amount of staff that you will need to be successful which is where the staffing guide discussed earlier is a critical management tool to utilize. Making sure the resources you do have are working at the right time of day and right day of week leads us to the second step in implementing continuous flow: aligning staff schedules.

Align Staff Schedules

Aligning staff schedules simply means to schedule staff to work when the work arrives. To do this you first must understand when the work is arriving, how much is arriving and what resources are needed to process the work. Let us look at an SPD that processes instruments for the OR, Labor and Delivery and various clinics while also picking case carts and performing other support functions. The following graph shows how you can visually see the arrival of work by hour of the day. In this case, the department would need to collect data from various sources to determine these average arrivals.

SPD Workload Arrival Pattern by Hour

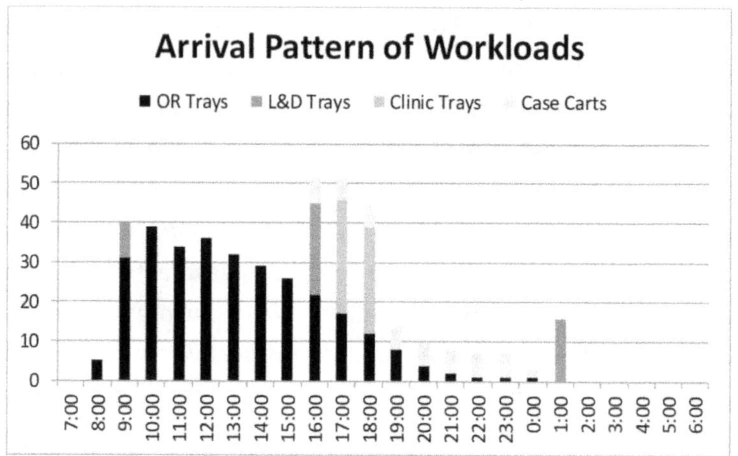

In the above graph, the OR Trays start arriving in mass in the 9:00 hour due to the first cases beginning to finish. The OR peaks during the 10:00 to 12:00 hour and then slowly decreases throughout the day as fewer cases are completed. L&D Trays are used throughout the day but in this example, the department only picks them up three times a day at 9:00, 16:00 and 1:00, thus creating three specific spikes in arriving workload. Clinic trays are delivered by courier and arrive during the 17:00 to 18:00 hours. Case cart picking starts at 16:00 and continues until midnight.

Once you know what and when work is arriving, you will then need to determine the resource requirements to process the work in a continuous flow manner. This means figuring out how many people are needed to do the work each hour utilizing standard work and time standards in your calculations. Once you put time standards to the workloads you can then create a staffing requirement graph as shown below. Note that even though the clinics seemingly provide a lot of workload during the 17:00 and 18:00

hours, when you convert their volume into resource requirements the demand is not as great as it seems due to the shorter time standards associated with these trays, at least in this example.

SPD Staff Requirements by Hour

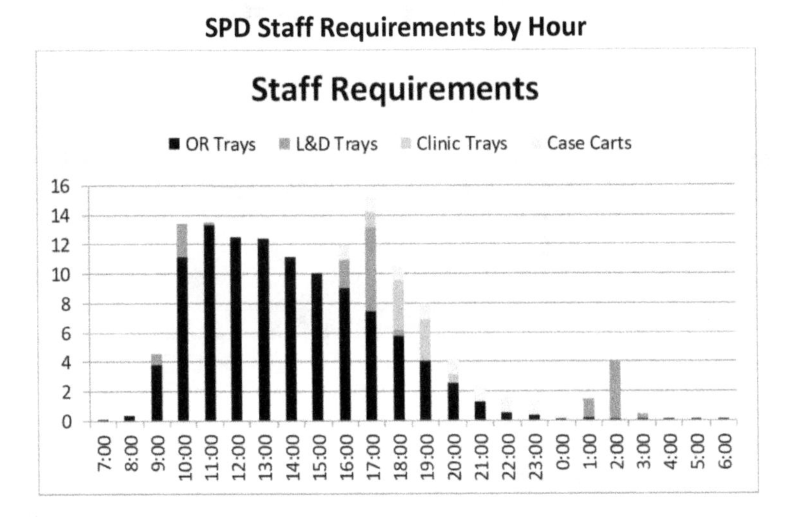

Staffing requirements should also be based on the flow of the work through the department so that the OR Trays that arrive in the 9:00 hour impact decontamination staffing immediately but do not require assembly staff until the next hour. While this data collection and calculations may take some time, the point being made is that if you desire to reduce backlogs and move towards continuous flow you should schedule your staff based on the arrival of the work.

The last step is to overlay the current or actual staff schedule by hour. The following graph shows a traditional SPD staffing schedule based on 7AM, 3PM and 11PM starts in a manner that resembles the backlogged simulation graphs shown earlier. The staff scheduled line shows five staff starting at 7AM, ten at 3PM and four at 11PM. Due to the lack of staff from 10:00 to 15:00, the department creates a backlog of trays waiting to be processed and then works throughout the day trying to catch up. By moving more staff from the evening to earlier in the day, the department can minimize backlogs, reduce the total cycle time for reprocessing instruments and move closer to continuous flow. The objective is to match your staff to the incoming workload which often results in creating a mid-shift starting at 10AM or 11AM.

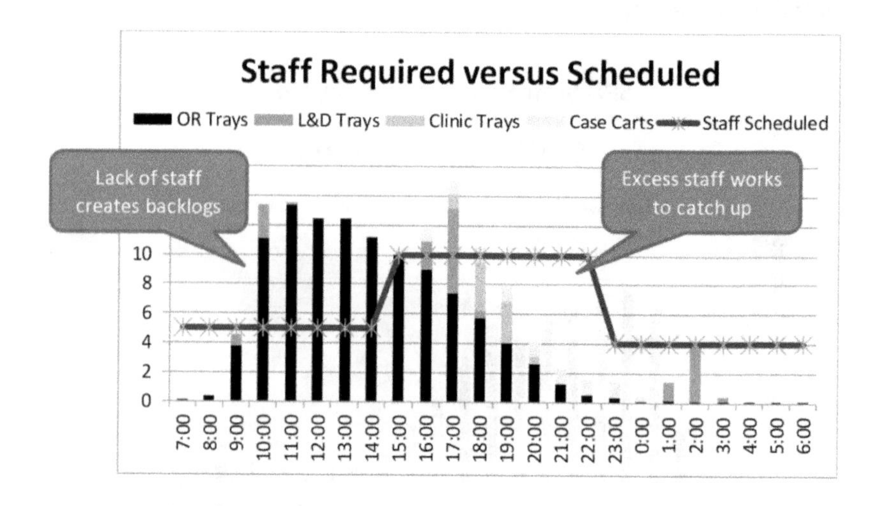

You can also add in other activities performed such as equipment testing, department cleaning, restocking supplies and other tasks. Make sure that the staff scheduled in the graph is representative of the staff assigned to work on the workload represented in the graph. For example, if you chose to show only instrument reprocessing and case cart picking in your graph as the major activities you perform, then be sure to only include staff scheduled that work on those activities.

Create Standard Work

After balancing the production line and aligning staff schedules, the next step is to create standard work for the activities. To successfully plan for continuous flow, you will need to ensure all staff are performing tasks according to a predictable and standardized method. Without standardization, variance in performance will lead to variance in workflow and out of balance processes. Without repeating the benefits of standard work instructions, it is worth stating that continuous flow works best when staff is working in a predictable and repeatable process.

Set Staff Performance Standards

Along with standard work, performance standards must be established so that staff understands the level of quality and productivity the department is planning for. Continuous flow planning, like any operational planning, is based on staff and equipment performing to a standard of performance. Whether the standard is a time-based expectation for assembly staff to complete four trays per hour or decontamination to sonic all instrument trays for quality, setting performance standards allows the department to plan operational performance to meet expectations.

Train to Standard Work

Perhaps a bit obvious at this point in the book, but staff must be trained per the standard work as well as the performance standards planned for. Training should also be viewed as an on-going process instead of a one-time event. Many SPDs excel at creating new hire training programs with dedicated time in each area under the supervision of an educator, proctor, or qualified and experienced staff member. Common failures in the training cycle occur after the new hire exits their training period. The worst explanation we often hear of why on-going training is not being performed is that "everyone has been here for years and knows what to do." While being in the department for years would hopefully equate to quality performance according to standard work and performance expectations, it is not guaranteed. In fact, continuous and on-going training is a critical part of the lean process.

Since most SPDs we visit have human beings working in them, we must remind everyone that humans tend to drift from standardized methods to personal preference. Even the best employee may find themselves performing a task slightly different than the documented method. In some cases, the tendency is driven by our natural desire to find the easiest way to accomplish a task. Sometimes the easiest way leads to an improved lean method while other times it simply represents laziness that leads to less than desirable performance.

To combat process drift, SPDs often perform annual competency checks and document that everyone is competent to perform the tasks they perform.

Not only are competencies valuable, but they are a required part of any Joint Commission or quality audit process. Unfortunately, again we find failings in many competency programs.

Some competency documents are merely self-assessments of what activities the employee feels they can perform. Other times, an educator or supervisor completes the competency based on what they feel the employee can do and is completed in a matter of minutes. The most effective competency programs contain a review of the standard work on how to perform the task and the performance expectations, a demonstration of how to perform the work and direct observation or return demonstration by the staff member performing the task correctly.

To complete an effective competency on just one employee takes time, which is something many SPDs claim they do not have enough of. These same SPDs may then spend hours dealing with process breakdowns, variance in staff performance and quality impacting issues. The correlation is often direct. The leaner a department becomes the more time they find they can train. The more time the department spends training, the leaner they find themselves becoming. The initial investment of time is well worth the effort and will lead to improved performance.

To help reduce the labor requirements in performing annual competencies, we recommend breaking them down into monthly units. This allows the department to spend quality time in each area reviewing the details of the tasks and ensuring everyone is on the same page, the standard work is understood and opportunities for improvement are raised.

Example Competency Schedule

- Jan: Decontamination Automated Wash
- Feb: Decontamination Hand Wash
- Mar: Flexible Scopes and Specialty Items
- Apr: Assembly – part 1 by service line
- May: Assembly – part 2 by service line
- Jun: Steam Sterilization
- Jul: None due to vacations
- Aug: Low Temp Sterilization
- Sep: Process Management and Navigator Positions
- Oct: Customer Service
- Nov: Hospital Competencies
- Dec: None

Reduce Interruptions

The first five steps have focused on creating an environment to support continuous flow. The next three steps focus on making it happen, starting with reducing interruptions. If there is one thing that disrupts continuous flow causing quality errors and reducing quality of life for staff, it is interruptions. Cleaning, disinfecting, inspecting, assembling and preparing instruments for sterilization requires attention to detail and focus. SPD technicians who are interrupted in the middle of a task are prone to missing a step, overlooking a quality defect, or having to start over again, reducing their productivity. Continuous flow works best when the balanced process can work without interruptions.

So how do we eliminate interruptions? While there is no magic solution, there are common sense suggestions. First, identify the main activities in the department that would benefit the most from an interruption free environment. We have found that decontamination and assembly are the two highest priority areas to focus on. Next, identify all the activities or reasons the staff are interrupted. In assembly for example, your list may include phone calls, answering the door, conducting floor rounds, unloading the instrument and cart washers and helping the OR look for an instrument. Often the tasks that interrupt the staff are short duration tasks that can be grouped together and assigned to a utility person to handle. With clear assignment and responsibility, staff assigned to assembly can stay focused on their task while the utility person answers the phone, unloads the washers, and performs Customer service activities.

A second suggestion is to implement a "navigator" position. In the SPD environment, especially in large departments, a navigator can play an important role in not only reducing interruptions but also maintaining workflow. Like the lean concept of "water strider", an SPD navigator can be assigned in either decontamination or assembly with the objective of maintaining a continuous workflow, providing staff with prioritized work, handling the various small tasks, and minimizing disruptions to staff. Like the utility assignment, a navigator could handle all incoming phone calls, managing the workflow out of the instrument washers to assembly workstations and finding missing instruments needed for assembly. By navigating the workflow, the navigator is providing a non-interrupted work environment in decontamination and assembly so staff members can focus on their specific tasks, maintain a balanced production line and continuous flow with greater efficiency and quality.

In decontamination areas where two or more staff are assigned, the navigator position can provide value similar to assembly. Commonly the first person in decontamination is the navigator with subsequent staff being assigned to work prep sinks. The navigator receives all incoming dirty case carts and items, scans instruments, unloads the case cart, breaks down rigid containers, loads case carts and containers into the cart washer, stages instruments at the prep sinks to be cleaned and assists with loading the instrument washers. The other staff members remain focused on cleaning instruments.

Every department may find that their solution to reducing interruptions is unique and that is okay. The best thing you can do is involve your staff with the concept of uninterrupted assembly and instrument cleaning and see what solutions they can come up with. Here is a helpful note from our experience in implementing a utility or navigator position. These positions can be the ultimate multi-tasking assignment and work best with staff that like to and are capable of juggling multiple responsibilities in a fast-paced environment. Steady Betty might be better suited working an assembly table while Hyper Hank may be a great utility player.

Develop Key Performance Indicators

While an entire chapter was devoted to measurements, it is worth noting that implementing continuous flow should coincide with key performance indicators that help measure how well the work is flowing. In the perfect SPD, you would have measurements of how long it took to process each item and a calculation of mean, medium, minimum, and maximum values for your processing time and how that compares to planned continuous flow. I have never seen a perfect SPD or tracking system that easily provides this data so we must move to plan B. There are tracking systems that log the time the instruments arrive in decontamination and when they are returned to sterile storage, so the data points do exist. The difficulty comes in generating useful reports. Perhaps by the time this book is published we will have improved functionality and reporting in instrument tracking systems.

A very easy method to measure your continuous flow is to measure your backlogs. The most common measurement is number of instrument trays in assembly at 7AM, 3PM and 11PM. Backlogs can also be measured in decontamination if you are having issues with workflow in that area. By measuring the backlog, a correlation to continuous flow or planned workflow is easily made. Bigger backlogs equate to non-continuous workflow. Minimal workflows equate to better continuous flow. Since perfect continuous flow is not realistic or desirable, planned backlogs are acceptable. Based on your line balancing, staffing levels and staff schedules, you should be able to set measurable goals for the specific times of the day. 7AM, 3PM and 11PM are used as an example only but do tend to be valuable times to measure your backlog.

7AM assembly backlog should be very minimal depending on the amount of overnight cases being performed, such as a trauma. 7AM should also be minimal or zero to ensure all instruments are sterile and ready for use by your Customers. 3PM is typically the largest backlog of the day due to the completion of most OR cases by this time flooding SPD with dirty instruments. 11PM is where the department's performance throughout the day is deemed a success or not. Continuous flow departments have minimal backlogs at 11PM. Non-continuous flow departments are still digging out from a mountain of instruments accumulated throughout the day.

The following graph represents a real SPD that implemented continuous flow strategies over a 20-week period and successfully reduced their average 11PM backlog of trays in assembly. Implemented changes include aligning staff schedules with incoming workload, moving weekend shifts to midweek shifts, setting assembly performance standards, measuring individual and departmental performance, creating a utility assignment to reduce interruptions for assembly staff and requiring supervisors to follow-up on performance throughout the day. Key to their success was that they set a goal and measured their performance. Remember the saying "You can't improve what you don't measure!"

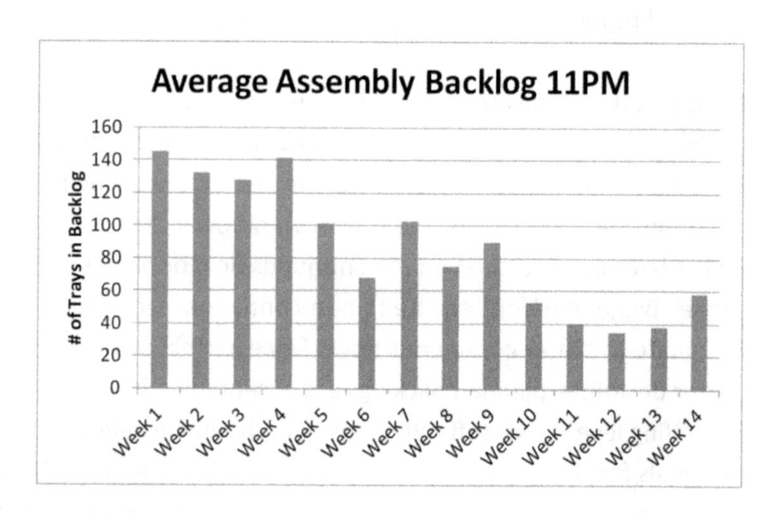

Create Leadership Routines

The last step in implementing continuous flow is to create leadership routines. The following chapter is devoted entirely to leadership routines so we will only hit the highlights here that pertain to continuous flow. Assuming you have implemented the first seven steps of continuous flow, the last step focuses on sustaining your improvements and identifying further opportunities to improve. This is accomplished by creating leadership routines to follow-up on your continuous flow implementations. Your leadership team should be on the floor measuring backlogs, identifying situations where instruments are sitting longer than planned, ensuring staff is aligned to workloads and working to standards, confirming standard work is being followed and removing interruptions from the process. The leadership routines you develop and hold your team accountable to will directly determine the long-term success of your department and your lean implementation which is a great introduction to our next chapter. First, let us revisit Rob in City Hospital as he introduces continuous flow to his team.

~~~~~~

City Hospital: Continuous Flow

Scene: It has been two weeks since the roll out of the case cart standard work and the staff has settled into their new routine. Rudy has been following the new standard work with success and the initial apprehension has dissipated. Rob has carefully thought how best to introduce further lean concepts to his team to help reduce backlogs and improve quality. The OR has patiently been waiting for him to improve the department's performance.

"Good afternoon everyone," Rob opens and wonders if he always says the same thing. "Today we'll continue our lean journey and talk about how we go from having this," he points to the backlog of trays, "to creating a continuous workflow."

Realizing that no one is grasping the continuous workflow comment he continues. "I've talked to other SPD Managers and have heard that they found the most benefit from the lean concept of continuous flow where the instruments never sit for very long in any one area but rather keep moving through the department. All of them told me that they used to have backlogs just like us but found some good improvement opportunities through lean."

"Just hire some more people and that backlog will be gone in a day!" Latisha adds.
~~~~~~

"Well, you never miss an opportunity to point out we need more staff, that's for sure!" Rob responds. "The unfortunate truth is that I've been told we will not be able to hire any additional staff, period. The hospital has to cut operating expenses so that's a no-go option for us."

Rob realizes that his last comment was a definite downer and scrambles to regain some momentum. "But there is a solution that other hospitals have found that helped them reduce their backlogs while not having to hire more people. Give me two minutes to explain. Remember a while back I asked everyone to have an attitude of curiosity and be open to new ideas? Now's the time I'm asking you to hear me out. I'm committed to this department and I'm committed to each of you." This last comment seems to have evoked a subtle response from the group.

"Here's the plan or at least the direction I'd like us to go. In continuous flow, the instruments move through our department with minimal wait time. There will be some wait time but not to the extent that we currently have with over a hundred trays sitting in our department at seven in the morning." Rob feels a bit more comfortable and continues.

"The first step towards this is identifying how much work we can complete at each step of the process to see if we have the capacity we need and if our process is balanced. Does that make sense?" Rob asks the group as he realizes that if they do not grasp this concept, nothing going forward is going to work. He then waits silently until someone talks.

"Kind of but not really," Vlad speaks up which surprises everyone.

"Ok, here's what it means to me," Rob tries to remember what the other SPD Managers shared with him. "The case carts come to us in decontamination, your favorite job Vlad. We need to determine if we have enough staff every hour to handle the incoming workload. To do this, we need to know how long it takes us to process them and what the standard work should be. Then I need to be sure you have those people available to keep up. If we need to change our processes or give you more training, we'll do it. The important part is to work together to figure out how we can eliminate backlogs first in decontamination and then move through the process."

"How do we do that without hiring more people?" Rachel adds somewhat sarcastically but the question is valid.

"That's where I need all of your help. I don't work in decontamination. I used to but you are the ones who are in there every day and see what works and what doesn't. We need to leverage the knowledge we already have to figure this out." Rob looks to see if anyone is following with him.

"Roberta, what things can you think of that would help us keep the flow going?" Rob hopes that Roberta is in a good mood today and he is happily relieved at her answer.

"I definitely think we need to get rid of the interruptions," Roberta shares. "When I'm able to just do my job and nobody bothers me or I don't have to answer the phone or help the OR or whatever, I can get a lot done. It's probably the same for decontamination."

Rob remembers one of his visits to another department and takes over. "Ok, so let's talk about how to eliminate interruptions. One of the departments I talked to implemented a navigator assignment in decontamination when they get busy. This person is responsible for just about everything in the room except for working at the prep sinks. They receive the case carts, do the scanning, breakdown containers, load the cart washer and stage instrument trays at the sinks for the rest of the staff to handle. They said that the navigator allows the staff at the sinks to work uninterrupted and stay focused on their cleaning."

Roberta is engaged and continues the conversation. "Well, that sounds good, but we need the people here to make that happen. We need all the people in assembly, so where are we going to get another person for decontamination to be a navigator?"

"The department I talked to had the same issue when they started," Rob happily shares as Roberta's question gives him the perfect lead to another continuous flow concept. "What they found was that it was more important to focus staff in decontamination at the beginning, even if it meant there was one less person in assembly. They bought into continuous flow 100%. They shared that it felt really weird but, in the end, it worked."

Rob prepares for another possible bombshell with his next statement. "They also found that they didn't have enough people in the department at 11AM when a lot of the work was coming to the department from first cases. So, they created a mid-shift and had people move from second shift."

"I'm not moving," Jackie is quick to speak up.

"What they found was this," Rob ignores Jackie's comment for now and continues. "When they matched their staff to the incoming workload, assigned navigators to handle all other tasks and let the primary people assigned to decontamination and assembly focus on their tasks," he looks at Roberta as he knows that assembly is her specialty, "their continuous flow improved immediately."

"Here's what I'd like to propose to get us started," Rob knows that baby steps are best and wants to end on a positive note with some forward movement. "I'd like each of you to just observe what's happening in your area as you work and think about why the trays are sitting there, not moving. Remember we must find improvements without adding people which means we need to find ways to eliminate time spent on things that don't keep the trays moving. Think of it this way. If you're not keeping a tray moving through the process, then you're not adding value and we need to eliminate that. Also, I'll be asking the supervisors to take the time to observe what we're doing, why we're doing it that way and how we can improve our throughput. We can also use our process flow diagram to focus in on things we can change."

Rob adjourns the meeting satisfied that the concept has been addressed and some discussion had. He understands that one ten-minute shift change meeting is not going to solve all the problems, but it can kick start a thought process. The journey continues.

~~~~~~
~~~~~~

Chapter Nine: Leadership Routines

This quote is perhaps the defining statement that should represent the leadership team's on-going focus and reason for being. For many departments, the leadership team's focus is on the outcome and not the process. They focus on getting the OR what they need today at the expense of fixing their process issues. Every day they deal with the same issues, bottlenecks, process breakdowns and defects that cause them headaches repeatedly. I feel for them. Wear their shoes for a day and you will often find they are exhausted from fighting fires and yet, they still somehow manage to get through the day without cancelling surgeries. Ask them if they have time for process improvement and they will quickly answer you no way. Nevertheless, a supervisor or manager's first responsibility should be to continually improve the processes.

The solution is not working harder. As the cliché says, the answer is in working smarter. Leadership routines are all about working smarter and realizing that if you are on the leadership team, you are no longer a technician. For many technicians who are promoted to supervision positions, this change in role is often a tough one. Being a good technician does not automatically mean someone will be a good supervisor. Even those who have the potential to be a good supervisor must be trained and given clear objectives and expectations. I am often lost at how organizations can be so effective at training and setting expectations for their employees but fail to do it for their leadership teams.

This is where Lean leadership routines can help. In simple terms, leadership routines refer to what the leadership position should do daily to ensure operations are performing to plan. The key word is "should". I enjoy asking SPD supervisors, "What is the most valuable activity you could perform that the hospital is paying you to do." If you are a supervisor reading this book, ask yourself that question. If you are a manager, ask yourself that same question. Then look at how you spend your day.

We often find SPD supervisors and managers focusing most their time on administrative or technical work with little time spent on managing the actual operational processes. This is where the "leadership rubber" hits the road and operational performance and lean success is often won or lost. At the start of this book we highlighted Lean production and Lean management systems. Leadership routines are a critical aspect of Lean management.

Leadership routines identify the key activities that the supervisor, manager or other leadership position should perform on a routine basis to make sure operations are performing to plan. This includes ensuring staff is working to standard work and time standards while following up on a regular basis to understand what is impacting their ability to be effective. Leadership routines should also include walking the floor, Genba Walk in Japanese, to observe workflow, backlogs, opportunities for improvement, variance to standard work and learning to see waste from a lean perspective.

It is also beneficial for leadership to set aside time routinely and frequently to perform formal observations of the work activities on the floor. In a formal observation, the supervisor or manager observes actual performance while not intervening, records all steps and time to perform, identifies interruptions, identifies variance to standard work and identifies waste and opportunities to improve. These observations should uncover improvement opportunities and ideas for improving the overall performance of the department.

In David Mann's excellent book *Creating a Lean Culture,* he shares four key attributes for effective Lean management systems that create the structure for leadership routines.

- Leader standard work
- Visual controls
- Daily accountability process
- Leadership discipline

Leader Standard Work

Leader standard work defines the key tasks each leadership position must do at certain times each day to ensure that processes and people are working to plan. It does not define every minute of their day but rather key activities throughout the day. It helps them focus on managing the process instead of focusing on the result of getting work done. By improving and managing the process, the result or outcome will become easier and easier to accomplish!

A sample leader standard work for a SPD Supervisor could include the following tasks:

- 7AM: Shift start-up, staff assignments, hand-off from previous shift
- 8AM: Verify staff in decontamination completed start-of-shift tasks (this should be easily accomplished through a visual control as well)
- 9AM: Production check: review department actual performance to plan (such as number of trays assembled from 7AM to 9AM versus plan)
- 10AM: On-the-floor compliance check: target certain tasks to observe whether standard work is being followed
- 12PM: Production check: review department actual performance to plan

- 2PM: On-the-floor compliance check: target certain tasks to observe whether standard work is being followed
- 3PM: Production check and report shift performance to plan and opportunities for improvement, end-of-shift handoff to next supervisor

This example is a great starting point, but every department should develop a leader standard work that best fits their environment. In a large complex department, it may be beneficial to perform production checks and explain variances every hour during the peak production times. On the floor supervisors must identify variances to plan and then ask the questions required to understand why there was a variance. Remember that a variance is any deviation from plan or accepted practice. Managers should then review the shift's performance with each supervisor and discuss the variances and determine if correction action is required. This will then lead to the leadership routine attribute of accountability.

The following is an example of a very detailed leader standard work utilized in an environment where supervisor routines had never been established. To help drive the new culture, the supervisor's daily routine was scripted out in detail. As the leadership team becomes comfortable with their routines, the standard work can change and evolve. Often, the standard work may detail out 50% of their daily time while leaving the other 50% open for administrative work, meetings or other activities. The most important activity to accomplish every day is direct process and people management tasks. In the example, this would include the department Genba walk, reviewing shift operation plan and production results and performing observations.

2nd SHIFT SUPERVISOR LEADER STANDARD WORK			
"People respect what you inspect"		Date: ________	
TIME	TASK	✓	REASON FOR MISS / COMMENTS
3:00 - 3:15	Review Daily operations plan and adjust/plan staffing accordingly		
	Shift hand off with night Lead while walking department		
	Huddle with day shift staff		
3:15 - 3:30	Print daily copy of leader standard work		
	Count and record backlog		
	Review previous day Standard Work with Manager		
	Check email		
3:30 - 4:00	OR Rounds - touching base with OR staff		
4:00 - 4:30	Department gemba walk - production plan review (manage accordingly)		
4:30 - 5:15	Cover Lead tech lunch - decon/washer/assembly backlog		
5:15 - 6:00	Lunch		
6:00 - 6:30	Employee engagement - talking to staff (issues, process, concerns, improvements) - production plan review (manage accordingly)		
6:30 - 7:00	Review shift operation plan and manage as needed - meeting production or not		
7:00 - 7:30	Production plan review (manage accordingly) - record decon/washer/assembly backlog		
7:30 - 8:00	Check productivity in Rosebud -		
8:00 - 8:30	Admin time (familiarize with regulatory standards, review vacations) - production plan review (manage accordingly)		
8:30 - 9:00	Observations for process imrpovement		
9:00 - 9:30	Production plan review (manage accordingly) - record decon/washer/assembly backlog		
9:30 - 9:45	Over see implant room exchange		
9:45 - 10:30	Observations for adherence to standard work - production plan review (manage accordingly)		
10:30 - 11:00	Monitor and double check cases picked for next day		
11:00 - 11:30	Walk the department with night Lead		
	Finalize shift report		
	Put standard work in Managers box		
Mon 3PM	CPU leadership meeting		
Wed 3PM	CPU staff meeting/in-service		

The following graphic is a slightly different example from a large hospital SPD that requires the supervisors to update their production numbers every hour and identify variances to plan. The key components include backlogs, staffing levels and throughput by hour.

DAILY OPERATIONS PLAN - 2nd SHIFT DATE: ___________

Shaded cells require input

	3p	4p	5p	6p	7p	8p	9p	10p	11p
ASSEMBLY BACKLOG	76	82	84	90	80	70	56	31	11
PLANNED BACKLOG	76	76	82	86	74	65	46	22	0
VARIANCE	0	6	2	4	6	5	10	9	11

DECONTAMINATION PERFORMANCE

	3-4p	4-5p	5-6p	6-7p	7-8p	8-9p	9-10p	10-11p	TOTAL
DECONTAM STAFF	3	3	3	2	1	1	0	0	13
TRAYS COMPLETED	28	34	24	16	15	9	0	0	126

ASSEMBLY PERFORMANCE ASSEMBLY TRAYS PER HOUR 4.0

	3-4p	4-5p	5-6p	6-7p	7-8p	8-9p	9-10p	10-11p	TOTAL
ASSEMBLY STAFF*	7	7	5	7	6	7	6	6	51
TRAYS COMPLETED	22	32	18	26	25	23	25	20	191
PLAN TRAYS	28	28	20	28	24	28	24	22	202
VARIANCE	-6	4	-2	-2	1	-5	1	-2	-11

It is important to note that leader standard work will grow and change as operational requirements change. Initially, leadership may only be able to perform rounds to identify opportunities for improvement, variances in work practices and obvious incorrect practices. Once an operational plan and technician standard work have been established and implemented, leaders can begin to follow up on performance and adherence to standard work as part of their routine.

Visual Controls

Creating visual controls for your leadership team will make their life easier! Visual controls are any visual communication method that allows anyone entering an area to know whether the process is on schedule and working to plan simply by looking at the visual. Examples include white boards, computer monitors, full/empty bins or full/empty staging racks. In a SPD, these visual controls could track the status of the following production processes:

- Backlog of case carts in decontamination
- Trays assembled every hour
- Sterilization loads every hour
- BI's ready on time
- Scheduled tasks completed
- # Case carts picked

By simply looking at the visual, people can immediately tell when the process is not working as planned without asking questions or bothering anyone. Visual controls also remind the staff of what the expectation is and how well they are achieving it. Visual controls make the leader's standard work easier to complete and more effective. Simple is better when it comes to visual controls. Manual logs, white boards and processes that force someone to write the number, input the date or explain the variance involves the staff and keeps people engaged.

Lastly, visual controls only state the current condition. They do not tell you why the condition is the way it is. This is when leadership and staff must ask themselves a few questions. Why is the number, status or visual the way it is? Why are we below or above plan? Why are there no case carts in decontamination? Why have we assembled 27 trays when the plan was 33? Once you ask why, you will probably have to ask why again and again and again. There is a lean concept known as "5 Why's" explained in the Lean Term glossary that states that you should ask "why" five times to get to the root cause of the issue. Leadership routines should be designed to drive this information to the surface, raise up opportunities for improvement, identify waste and identify excellence, top performers and opportunities to praise employees.

Daily Accountability Process

A daily accountability process is a structured approach at all levels of leadership to meet regularly and review operational performance, identify operational issues and assign and review action items while holding each level of leadership accountable to improving their area of responsibility.

Being held accountable daily helps everything work better. Leadership routines are not about doing a task because the boss said so but rather about improving operational performance.

A daily accountability process is not just for supervisors either. All levels of leadership should have a built-in accountability process in their routine. Supervisors should meet daily to review performance and document their findings and opportunities. SPD managers should meet weekly with supervisors to assign and review action items. Directors should meet weekly or bi-weekly with managers. Vice Presidents should meet monthly with directors.

Three main points of accountability are managed through the process:
1. Adherence to the Lean management system, 2. Departmental performance tracking and 3. Action item assignment and implementation of improvements. To create a Lean culture that the staff see and believe is going to stick, try combining the accountability process with a visual control by posting action items assigned visually in the department on an accountability Board. Everyone then sees who is assigned to implement the action items currently assigned and whether they are on schedule or behind. The accountability board becomes a central meeting place for the leadership team to meet and discuss progress and hold each other accountable. This is an excellent area to also post departmental performance metrics as well.

Leadership Discipline

Now that you have created leadership standard work and routines, posted visual controls and implemented daily accountability processes, the next step is to be disciplined and follow through by using the system to improve and sustain operational performance.

Leaders who are not disciplined in their daily responsibilities create a culture where no one is disciplined. Discipline is not just for supervisors either. CEO's,

COO's, Vice Presidents and directors must all be disciplined to follow-up on the lean management system below them to ensure that everyone understands the importance of managing process and people versus just getting things done today. Remember, if it is not important to your boss then it probably will not be important to you and therefore will not be important to your employees. If you hold a leadership position, then you need to be disciplined to do what needs to be done. Discipline is simply this: *Doing what you are supposed to when you do not want to.*

An excellent lean tool to guarantee leadership discipline is the executive "Genba" walk. The term "Genba" is a Japanese word defined as "the place where the work or action is happening." For an SPD, the Genba includes decontamination, assembly, and sterilization areas.

The executive Genba walk accomplishes two critical items. First, it makes the executive walk through the actual department versus having a meeting in their office or a conference room. Walking the floor not only shows the staff members that the executive is interested in their area but assists in educating the executive on how the SPD operates and where opportunities to improve exist. Secondly, the Genba walk supports the accountability process by having the executive grade the SPD's performance on utilizing the Lean tools available, their leadership team's adherence to their leader standard work and the level of staff engagement. There is nothing more motivational to a manager than to take an executive walk through the department and grade how well the department is running. Human nature ensures that the manager will pay more attention to the items that their executive pays attention to. The saying that "whatever is important to your boss becomes important to you" holds true in a Lean SPD with the Genba walk and follow-up. What is important to the executive becomes important to the manager which becomes important to the supervisor which becomes important to the staff. Without the executive Genba walk, many lean implementations slowly fade away, being replaced by whatever budget or project the executive places importance on.

The following page shows an actual SPD executive Genba walk utilized by a large level 1 trauma hospital. Genba walks can and should be customized to your needs and operations. This executive Genba walk example will probably be used by the hospital for a couple of years and then modified as the department matures in their lean journey. David Mann provides examples in his book of executive Genba walks as well as the scoring system used in our example here.

A sample Executive Genba Walk with rating definition is shown below.

CS Executive Gemba Walk

Date:

Location:

Shift:

INTENT

Diagnostic Questions

Decontam — Rating

- Is the room properly staffed for current workload?
- Are decontam observations performed, how frequently and what improvements have been implemented? ______
- Staff question: What process improvement has happened in the past month in this area?

Assembly

- Is planned vs. actual trays assembled being recorded and variances explained?
- Are assembly observations performed, how frequently and what improvements have been implemented? ______
- Staff question: Ask someone what their current assembly productivity is – what is expected?
- Staff Question: What process improvement has happened in the past month in this area?

Sterilization

- Is planned vs. actual loads being processed, recorded and variances explained?

Lean Management Systems

- Supervisor- show me your standard work-is it being used-describe how it has helped you be more effective? ______
- Do leader observations result in action items that are visually managed with clear accountability? ______
- Are the supervisors regularly ensuring compliance to standard work? Are process deviations documented and acted upon? ______
- Manager- show me your standard work-is it being used-describe how it has been Effective? ______
- Show me your 5S Audit, is it current and all areas using 5S methodologies?

Assessment: Rate this area/areas from 1 to 5 on the scale below and note the rational for this rating

1 = Pre-lean	2 = Starting	3 = Recognizable	4 = Stabilizing	5 = Sustainable
Focus on results not process Reactive problem solving Work arounds No visual processes No Standard Work No staff engagement	Visuals highlight problems/delays, do not drive improvement Some improvement with task assignments Some standard work Occasionally staff are engaged, offer some suggestions for improvement	Visual/cycle tracking charts in some areas Follow up on improvement opportunities Standard work for all leadership positions More Customer focus Some staff can speak to production expectations not fully engaged in identifying opportunities and driving improvement	Visuals for most activities and maintained Accountability board highlight problems and drive solutions Customer perspective is given Standard work is a daily working record and reviewed updated as needed Most staff participate in Process Improvement, are engaged in bring suggestions to the leadership and volunteer for work groups	Visuals/cycle tracking charts for all areas-drives improvements-identify and act on problems. Accountability is routine Customer perspective is a given Leader Standard Work reviewed with manager daily and acted on always Full staff participation in improvement, drive change and identify opportunities

~~~~~~

City Hospital: Leadership Routines

Scene: The team recently began addressing continuous flow issues by starting in decontamination. Rob knows the OR is most frustrated with the department's inability to process the instrument trays in a timely manner so that there is no backlog at 7AM still sitting in SPD. Their first process improvement is to ensure that instruments never sit waiting in decontamination. The team has implemented new staffing patterns in decontamination including a navigator position during peak volume times. They have also standardized daily decontamination tasks for setting up the room, performing daily tests and manually cleaning instruments prior to going into the automated washer. Rob has now called together his supervisors to discuss their role in sustaining the new improvements.

"Ok, let's get started," Rob closes the door to his small office and sits down with Dwight, 1st shift supervisor, and Becky, 2nd shift supervisor.

"We've already had a lot of discussions about lean and what that means to the staff, but we need to clarify what that means to the three of us as well. Have the two of you had a chance to put some ideas together on what your leaders standard work would look like?" Rob waits silently for an answer.

"I've been busy getting the new tray changes input and sorting out case carts everyday with the backlogs we've been experiencing," Dwight offers.

"What about you Becky?" Rob asks hoping for some type of positive response.

"No. I've been swamped just trying to get as many trays done as possible, and we've been short staffed the last two weeks," Becky explains with no remorse that she has not completed anything Rob had asked her to do.

Rob sits silently looking at both supervisors and does not say anything for what seems like an eternity.
~~~~~~

"You two do realize that you set the example for the department. How you act and perform is how your staff will act and perform." Rob is hoping this is not going to backfire on him. "If you only focus on what the OR currently needs and don't take time to start managing processes and people or showing support for the lean concepts we're preaching, then this entire effort is going to eventually fail."

This comment upsets Dwight and he has been around long enough to feel comfortable voicing his displeasure. "Well then *you* come out on the floor and try facing the OR every day, and you'll see what I have to deal with. It's not as easy as you make it out to be."

"Dwight, I know," concedes Rob. "I used to be a 1st shift supervisor as well. I did the same thing you're doing and every day I faced the challenges and dealt with the same issues. I got the job done but it never improved and every day I couldn't wait for 3PM to come and clock out. That's the exact point I'm trying to make. If we keep doing the same things we've always done, then we'll never change, never improve and never make things better. If that happens, I may no longer be calling this office mine." Rob decides it's time for tough love.

"The hardest part of any lean journey, at least this is what I've been told, is starting. We all experienced a rough start with our first standard work instruction and getting people to accept time standards. Now it's time the three of us take an honest look at how we spend our time. I'm including myself as well," Rob leans in to make his point.

"I asked both of you a week ago to write down what you thought your daily routines should look like, what you should be measuring and how we can start improving. Neither of you did it. If the staff starts to see that the two of you aren't disciplined enough to do what you're supposed to do, then why should they do what we're asking them to do?" Rob notices Becky is becoming self-defensive by crossing her arms, leaning back in the chair and staring at the wall.

"Becky, I'm not trying to be a jerk and I'm including myself in this as well," Rob directs to her.

Becky glances at him a bit emotionless and states, "OK, what do we do?"

"We'll start with focusing on sustaining the changes we've rolled out to the team. This includes the daily decontamination set-up checklist, the navigator position and keeping continuous flow in decontamination. I'd like each of you to physically go into decontamination at least three times during your shift and observe backlogs, how well we're keeping up with the workload, if the daily checklist has been completed and if the staff is adhering to the navigator position and work assignments. I'd like you to record what you've observed, improvements we can make and how the individual staff performed. Every day we'll meet right here and discuss your findings. As for me, I'm going to walk the floor once during each of your shifts to see how things are going as well." Rob sits back and waits for Dwight or Becky to comment which neither readily do.

"Dwight, would you like me to join you the first couple of times?" Rob asks.

"That's okay. I've got it," Dwight seems to be less stressed than Becky but Rob knows that Dwight has the tendency to say things are okay when they are not. Rob, Dwight and Becky draft a simple supervisor routine sheet to fill in that will keep them on task. They agree to talk each day. Rob knows that he has not done a good job in the past holding his supervisors accountable to any type of routine much less ask them to identify opportunities to improve while holding their own staff accountable. Since he has not actively managed his supervisor's performance, they naturally have not actively managed their staff either. At least we are taking a step forward, Rob thinks to himself as Dwight and Becky leave the room. For Rob, this process is just as uncomfortable for him as it is for his team, but he understands that it is the right approach and vows to not let it fail no matter how hard it may seem.

~~~~~~
~~~~~~

Chapter Ten: Problem Solving

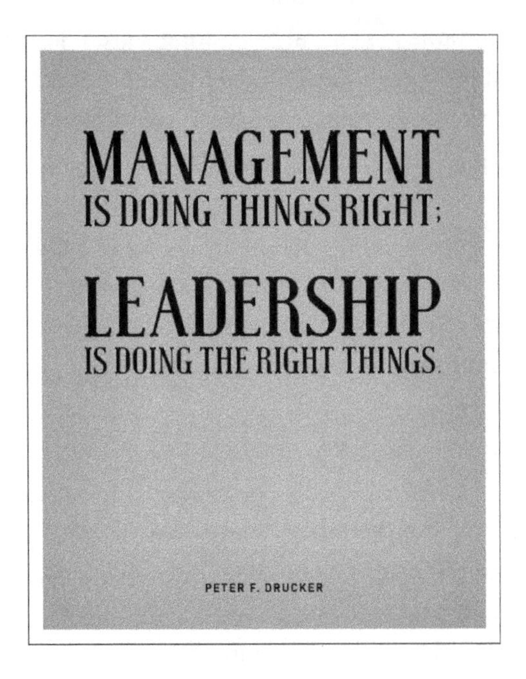

So far, we've introduced basic lean concepts and covered four of the eight steps to creating a Lean SPD: Customer requirements, measurements, Lean operational plan and leadership routines. If you follow these steps in order, you will find yourself measuring your actual performance versus planned performance while your leadership team is actively identifying issues and off-plan situations. So far so good, except now you must solve the problems you are identifying!

Fortunately, being an effective problem solver is a skill every person can learn. As a leader, problem solving is a skill you cannot survive without. Whether tasked with solving a problem by yourself or through a team, solving people issues or process issues or systematically improving your department utilizing lean techniques, problem solving is a fundamental attribute of every leadership position.

While everyone can learn problem solving skills, they do not always come naturally to everyone. To help individuals improve their skills, lean promotes the use of systematic problem-solving methods of which there are numerous effective approaches. It is worth stating though that many managers, SPDs and lean implementations in general have done a great job in measuring performance and identifying issues but fail miserably at acting to fix the issue. While following a formal systematic approach to problem solving is beneficial, it is not as important as simply doing something.

We will first review the lean approach of 5 Why's as a simple and straight forward problem-solving methodology and then explain the popular PDCA and DMAIC methods. Lastly, we will cover the lean concept of A3 Thinking as an organized method to approach a problem.

5 Why's

The 5 Why's is a simple but systematic method to identify the root causes of a problem. It refers to the practice of asking "why" five times to understand why a defect or failure occurred in a process. Each successive why dives deeper into the cause of the issue being investigated. "Five" is a relative number that forces you to analyze and continue asking questions until there are no more why's to answer. You may need more or less why's. In theory, the root cause is eventually identified and then acted upon. The technique is used to ensure the real cause of the problem is addressed and not just a symptom.

Let us look at two examples of how asking why repeatedly can help solve an operational problem.

Problem Statement: Assembly area was unable to assemble the planned number of instrument trays in each hour.

- Why? One of the staff left the assembly area.
- Why? There were no more trays to assemble.
- Why? Decontamination was backlogged and did not keep up with the production schedule.

- Why? Eight case carts were brought to decontamination at once.
- Why? The OR runner assigned to bringing case carts was too busy transporting patients to maintain his delivery schedule of case carts to decontamination.
- Why? One of the OR runners called in sick and no one was assigned to cover his absence.
- Root Cause Failure: A failure to ensure an upstream task was completed per plan by providing absenteeism coverage caused a downstream variance in planned production. This example also highlights opportunities for decontamination processes and leadership follow-up to have identified the problem before it became evident in assembly.

Problem Statement: The wrong instrument set was picked and placed on a surgical case cart.

- Why? The wrong item was picked from inventory.
- Why? The item picked from inventory was mislabeled.
- Why? The assembly technician mislabeled the item prior to sterilization.
- Why? The technician placed the wrong label on the item.
- Why? Labels for multiple sets were pre-printed and accidently mixed up.
- Root Cause Failure: Staff waited to label multiple trays simultaneously, known as batching, instead of doing them one at a time using continuous flow.

5 Why's is a simple but effective method that is often overlooked as a problem-solving technique. Most problems experienced by SPD can be resolved by using this technique and thus help the SPD staff start to address issues in a manner that is quick, easy and understandable.

Once you reach the root cause, a corrective action is developed and either initially trialed or immediately implemented using standard work. Either way, taking action is better than waiting to find the perfect answer to the problem. Try out a solution, measure the results and then determine if the corrective action was sufficient, needs to be adjusted or did not work at all. If the problem still exists, try asking why again and again until a new root cause is identified. Continue the process until your problem stabilizes and is no longer an issue.

PDCA and DMAIC

Both PDCA and DMAIC follow a similar approach to problem solving. Both help ensure that root cause issues are identified and addressed instead of simply treating the symptoms. Problems are clearly recognized and measured against clear objectives and standard processes.

PDCA Elements

- Plan – Take the time to plan what you're trying to do and ensure you understand the real problem and root cause being addressed. Gather information on the current state and conditions. Plan your action items for correcting the problem and establish a clear goal for what the outcome should be.
- Do – Implement your planned changes and how you'll measure success to the goal.
- Check – Follow-up and measure the new process performance and determine if the changes are meeting expectations.
- Act – If the new changes are successful then ensure they are standardized, and methods implemented to sustain the improvements. If the outcomes aren't successful, then return to Plan and start over with incorporating the newly learned lessons and what didn't work.

DMAIC Elements

- Define – Take the time to identify the problem, current conditions, the improvement opportunity desired, and establish a clear goal for the expected outcome.
- Measure – Gather data on the current process or operational performance you wish to improve.
- Analyze – Identify the root causes of the issue.

- Improve – Develop and implement new processes and operational improvements to eliminate or reduce the root causes and improve performance.
- Control – Measure the new operational performance to determine if the changes were successful and then manage and sustain the improvements.

Both PDCA and DMAIC follow basic problem-solving approaches for identifying root causes and implementing solutions. The common steps are explained below.

Define the Problem

The first step is to clarify which problem should be addressed based on Customer and operational impact to ensure resources are spent on addressing an issue that is worthwhile. Take the time to understand the problem based on facts, measurements and results versus perception.

Usually there is no shortage of potential problems to address. If you are measuring your operational performance against planned performance, then you should already have a sense of opportunities that exist. Quality issues, low productivity, not meeting schedules or Customer expectations are all typical candidates. If you are still not sure, then ask your Customer how you are performing and how you could improve. There is usually someone out there willing to tell you about a problem you have!

Defining the problem also addresses the severity of the issue. How many people or surgical cases does it affect? How costly is the problem? What is the impact on quality, schedules and productivity? How much time is lost due to the problem? Who is complaining the loudest?

A useful technique for establishing the significance of the problem is to perform a Pareto Analysis. A Pareto Analysis ranks the issues being compared by order of magnitude from left to right, biggest to smallest or most significant to least significant. An example of a Pareto Analysis data collection and matching graph is shown below for instrument errors as reported by the OR.

Data Collection for Pareto Analysis

Cause	Talley	Total
Not returned from previous case	~~////~~	5
Not working, no replacement available	//	2
Missing not noted by Assembler	~~////~~ ~~////~~ ///	13
Instrument not listed on Count Sheet	///	3
OR tech unfamiliar with instrument	//	2
Unknown cause	~~////~~ //	7

Pareto Analysis Graph Showing Categories in Order of Occurrences

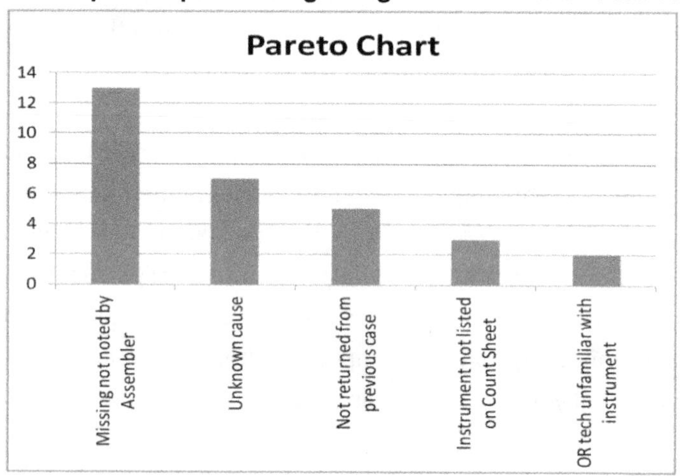

<u>Obtain, Chart and Evaluate the Data</u>

Most formal problem-solving approaches rely on facts and data to drive resolution and measure success. This entails measuring current performance as compared to planned or expected performance or utilizing data that may already exist. Even if the accuracy of the data is questionable, it is still the best place to start. The data may provide clues where to look for the source of the problem. It may also indicate what additional data is required to accurately evaluate the impact of the problem.

Data by itself is often overwhelming or incomprehensible unless put into a graphical form. Showing data in the form of graphs and charts helps to understand and communicate the meaning of the data. The specific type of graph or chart you use will depend upon the nature of the data and the purpose of the analysis. Common charts used to display data are:

Frequency Distributions or Histograms

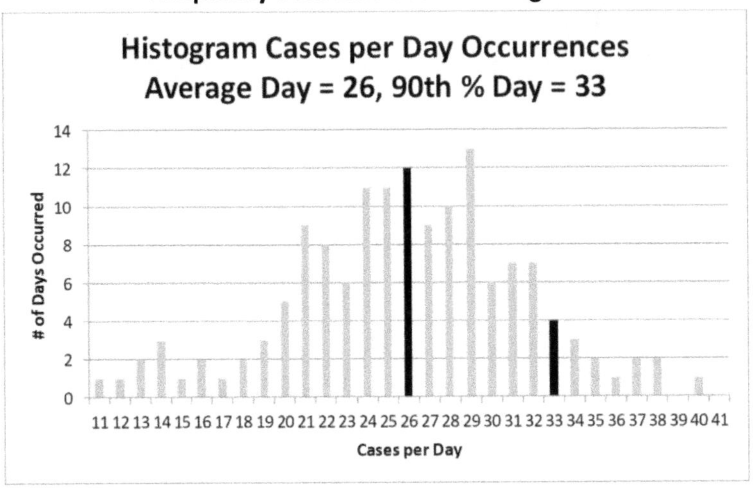

Bar Charts Showing Occurrences by Magnitude

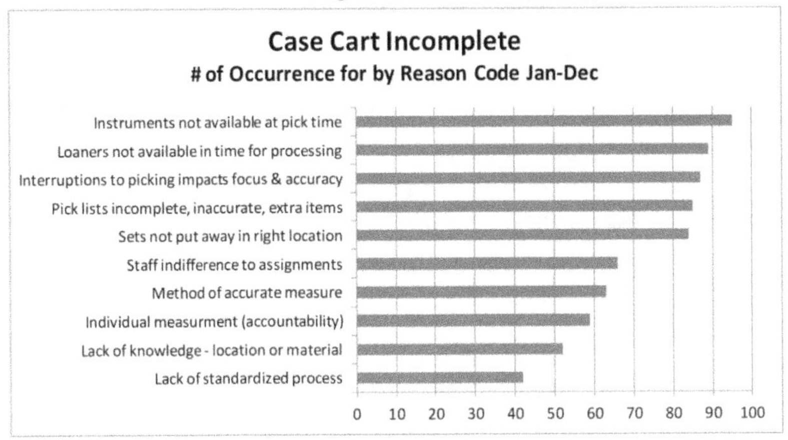

Line Charts Showing Performance Versus Goals and Limits

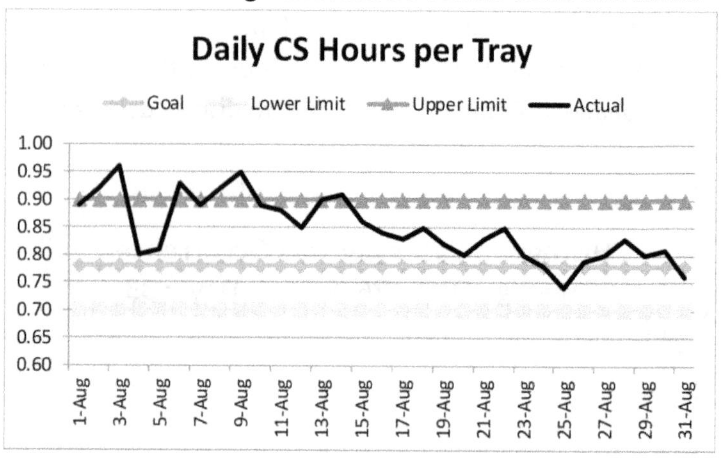

Scatter Diagram – Showing No Correlation Between Data Points

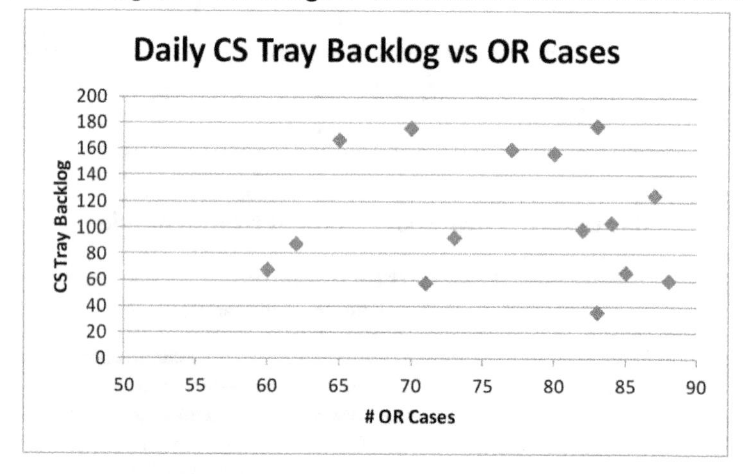

Scatter Diagram – Showing A Correlation Between Data Points

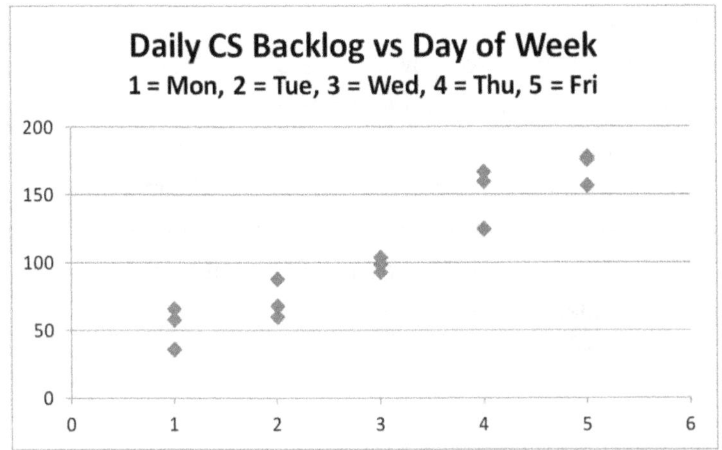

Graphs and charts will reveal the variations and magnitude of the problem sources or opportunity to improve the process. When any of the sources of variations become large in magnitude, they become readily identifiable when shown visually. A timeline chart of the process will show a pattern variation such as a sudden change or jump in the level of the data or a trend outside the norm or average.

Determine the Root Cause(s)

Finding the root cause may be quick and easy for some problems and difficult and time consuming for others. Asking the 5 Why's may be sufficient or an in-depth study of the various causes will need to be performed. Depending on the stability of the current process, it may be necessary to identify and eliminate process variations due to instability before determining root cause issues. If processes are unstable, meaning that no standardization exists and various methods and processes are utilized that produce varying results, it is often difficult to understand root cause failures.

When determining root causes, there are six categories or factors that contribute to problems and process variation: material, machinery, methods, measurement, manpower and milieu. Milieu considers environmental factors.

A commonly used tool for defect analysis, brainstorming and identification of the potential reasons for problems or process variation from the 6 M's is the cause and effect diagram, also known at the Ishakawa or fishbone diagram. The technique includes brainstorming the problem with a small group of people for generating as many ideas as to possible causes. Then, record these ideas on a Fishbone Diagram to provide a picture of the meaningful relationships between an effect and its causes. This process, along with the Pareto diagram, is also effective in determining what new data may be needed to further identify and solve the problem.

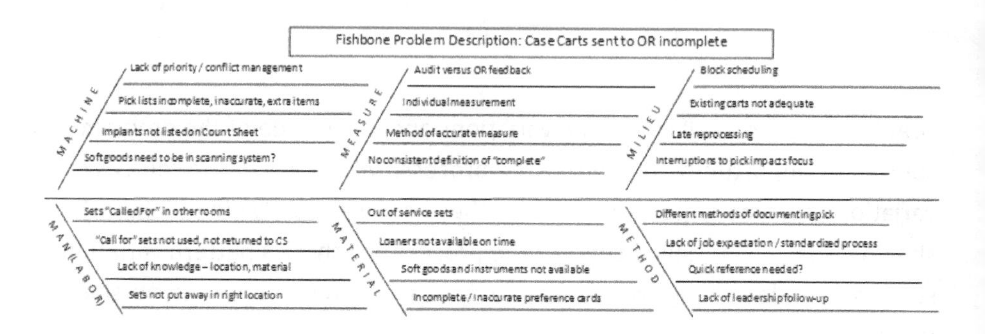

When the most likely causes have been identified, they are evaluated to assign a reason and prioritize these conditions. Then steps are taken to eliminate the variation or defect. Continue these problem identification and elimination activities until the process data indicates the situation is stable and controlled.

Make the Change

Implement the suggested changes and measure the results. Continue this cycle until the changes result in a process that is both in control and meets the requirements. At this point, it is now possible to establish controls to regulate this stable process so that it will continue to meet the requirements.

Sustain the Improvement

Sustaining any improvement is critical if you want your process to continuously improve and not slide backwards. Sustaining improvements is commonly a combination of leadership routines and process measurements to identify any drift or variance at an early stage. Corrective action can be taken as soon as variations begin to materialize. Controls and control measurements can be utilized to monitor processes for conformance to standard rather than waiting to inspect the final product at the end of the process.

The SPD key performance indicators are a form of high-level process controls commonly used to understand process issues. In addition to these, specialty controls or measurements may be tracked to monitor specific processes.

A3 Thinking

The term A3 refers to the international paper size of 11" x 17" or legal-size paper in the U.S. and is utilized to organize the problem statement and action plan on one page. The A3 sheet is designed to help ensure a structured approach to solving the problem is followed, root causes rather than symptoms are identified and addressed, and clear goals and measurements are utilized. John Shook advises in his article, "Toyota's Secret: The A3 Report, seven simple steps to effectively sequencing the problem resolution using the A3 Report":

1. Establish the business context and importance of a specific problem or issue.
2. Describe the current conditions of the problem.
3. Identify the desired outcome.
4. Analyze the situation to establish causality.
5. Propose countermeasures.
6. Prescribe an action plan for getting it done.
7. Map out the follow-up process.

According to Art Smalley and Duwark Sobek in "Understanding A3 Thinking, 2008", the process includes the following list of questions:

- What is the problem? What are the symptoms? Impact?
- Who owns the problem?
- What is the background. What are you talking about and why?
- What are the current conditions?
- What are the root causes of the problem?
- What is the specific improvement in performance you need to close the gap?
- What are possible countermeasures for the problem?
- How will you choose which fix to propose?
- What is the cost and benefit of the selected countermeasure?
- What is the implementation plan and schedule?
- How will you know if your plan is working?
- What problems are likely to occur during implementation?
- How will you ensure follow up and continuous improvement?

Using A3 methodology in your problem solving helps to quicken the pace of learning and understanding the problem and instills ownership of the problem and a commitment to change. It creates a consistent and systematic approach to thinking and communicating about problems, promotes collaboration and prevents waste in the problem resolution process.

What Are You Talking About A3 Report

Plan - Background

Why are you talking about it?

Plan - Current Condition

Where do things stand today?
What is the problem?
Show visually if possible.

Plan - Goal

What specific outcomes are required?

Plan - Root Cause Analysis

What is the root cause of the problem?

Do - Countermeasures

What is your proposal to reach the desired state?
How will the recommended countermeasures impact the root cause to address the problem?

Check - Effect Confirmation

What activities and step will be required to implement the plan?
Who has what responsibilities and time line?
What are the indicators of performance or progress?

Act - Follow-up Actions

What issues can be anticipated?
Ensure ongoing PDCA
Capture and share learning

Incomplete Case Cart Delivery A3 Report

Plan - Background

Case carts are picked by CS staff and delivered for each OR case. Timely and complete delivery is required to ensure on-time start of the case. And ability to effectively perform the surgery

Plan - Current Condition

- In the past month 17% of first and second case carts are received to the OR missing instruments or supplies.
- of these 13% resulted in delayed case starts.

Plan - Goal

On time and complete should be met 100%. Acceptable target within one month is 98%.

Plan - Root Cause Analysis

Events
15
10
5
0
Not...
Sets put...
Item not...
Priority...
Loaner not...
Item...
Loaner not...
Not on...
Set out of...

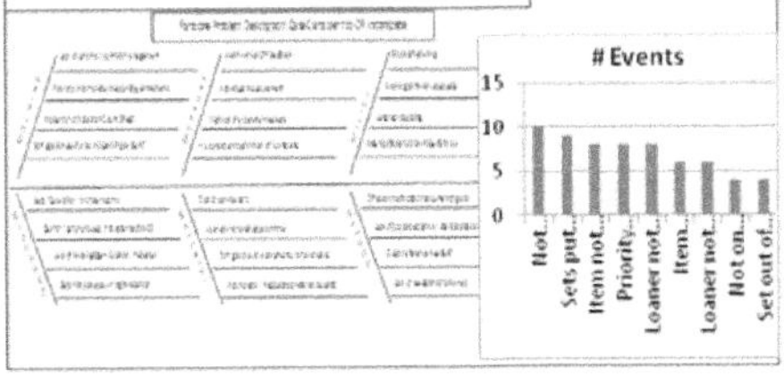

Do - Countermeasures

-Implement Standard Work for case pick, case cart layout and missing item communication.
-Begin pick later in the day to reduce double-handling. Manage pick routines with viual management heijunka board
-5S to reduce clutter in case build area

Check - Effect Confirmation

-See the attached Action Item Plan for step and responsibility details.
-Implement 1st and 2nd case complete and on-time metrics.
-Determine long-term staff schedule adjustments

Act - Follow-up Actions

-Staffing shifted to later hours.
-Review on-time delivery stats daily and at weekly Director meeting
-Determine sustaining steps

Chapter Eleven: Employee Engagement

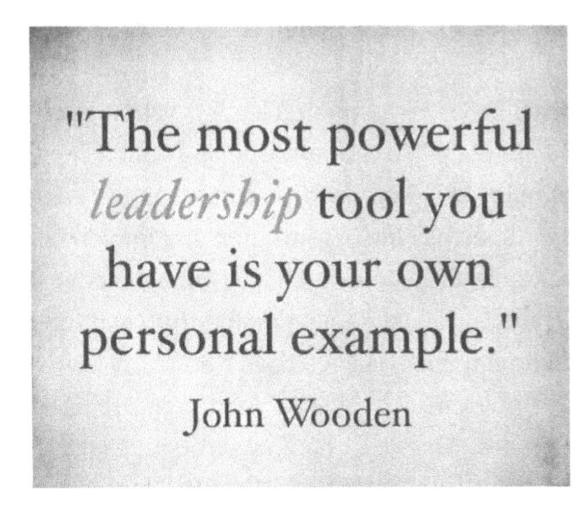

Definition of Engagement

"This is about how we create the conditions in which employees offer more of their capability and potential." – David Macleod, blog: Engaging for Success

Many companies are fond of touting their employees as "their greatest asset." But what does this mean? If the employees closest to the work are not creatively engaged and actively proposing ideas to improve processes, products, marketing, inventory turns and operations in general then we have in fact wasted our greatest asset.

A key pillar in Lean thinking and methodology is employee engagement and includes the following elements:

- Cultivates an alignment of individual goals and values with those of the organization
- Provides motivation for employees to contribute to the organization's success
- Encourages active employee involvement in continuous improvement processes

- Provides employees with a sense of well-being, belonging and satisfaction

It is well known that without effective employee engagement, changes made to processes and work areas are destined to backslide or fail altogether.

A point often missed by well-intentioned leaders is that employee engagement does not come from simply opening your arms and minds to ideas from your employees. Suggestions must be actively solicited, visually acknowledged, shared across the organization and implemented with swiftness using a standardized methodology. Timely feedback, recognition and follow-up are crucial to maintaining momentum and furthering employee's willingness to engage. We have frequently seen organizations reach out to their employees for improvement suggestions only to never follow through on them. This lack of follow through results in employees withdrawing from actively engaging with the attitude that management never listens to them anyway.

An example of this comes from a first-hand experience helping a hospital address their sterile processing struggles. Upon arrival, the department was paying time and a half plus $5 an hour to incentivize staff to work overtime, utilizing OR scrub techs on overtime to assemble trays in sterile storage, had nurses picking their own case carts and needed the weekend to work off the backlog of trays piling up in the SPD. As for space, the department was too small, had only one cart washer when two were needed, and was constantly fixing broken and old washers with double the cycle time of newer models. In short, the department was broken, and the result was unhappy OR Customers to the point of melt down as first cases weren't ready and IUSS rates out of control. The interesting point of this story is that the management team was not deficient or ignorant. The SPD Manager was well qualified and understood the situation she was being asked to manage.

After asking her why she thought things were the way they were, she compared her dire situation to her previous job with a simple answer. "My previous job wasn't like this at all. I think the difference between the two is that where I came from the management listened."

Her frustration wasn't towards the situation she was in and the uphill battle she faced every day but rather with her perception that management wasn't listening. Her story ended well though as management did listen and took the necessary steps to approve needed capital and budget resources to address the issues. Unfortunately, the delay in action had already negatively impacted the department with Customer dissatisfaction and high employee turnover. The environment was not conducive to a positive work environment and the employees simply left. The staff didn't feel they were being heard, disengaged, and eventually moved on to other jobs further deteriorating the situation.

When we first wrote this section, we struggled with expanding it to include a full dissertation on employee engagement but realized there are entire books dedicated to the subject and one chapter would not suffice. We then continued with writing what you'll find below on the elements of an employee suggestion program which on the surface sounds boring and old school. What we've compromised with is the following. Employee engagement is not something you can implement. It's not a program, although we still believe in the employee suggestion program detailed below as a component. Employee engagement is a result. It's the outcome from a positive work environment. It's the result of motivational management who listens and responds. Leadership teams who truly care about their staff as the most important asset of the hospital naturally create environments where employees become engaged. Staff engage when they feel safe, treated fairly, listened to, and respected.

This is where lean often falls short. Lean is full of tools, measurable indicators, best practices, and ways to be more efficient and remove waste from processes. Unfortunately, tools and operational best practices are not always equal to motivational management techniques. Strong lean leaders may be viewed by staff as boring and non-emotional to the point of only caring about the financial results and not the staff. Finding a balance isn't easy! Our suggestion is to leverage what you can from your leadership team. Utilize people with natural motivational skills to motivate the staff towards a lean environment and utilize others with natural organizational and process skills to implement lean. If you're lucky you'll hire a motivational positive leader who has excellent process skills and can combine the two to create an atmosphere where the staff wants to participate.

No matter where you are in your lean journey and leadership skill development, one lean tool you can utilize and we recommend is to implement an employee suggestion program. If you invest your time and energy into the program, honestly listen to your staff, and act to implement their suggestions, you'll find your environment improve and your staff become engaged.

I've often thought of naming an employee suggestion program the "Optimizing Operations Program Suggestion" to utilize the acronym OOPS to have a fun play on words. As with any Lean concept, a standard system is needed to successfully launch and a sustain an employee engagement program as simple as a suggestion system. While the components of the system may take on a variety of forms, the essential elements include:

Operational Improvement Suggestion Program Essential Elements

- Process to capture ideas or suggestions
- Venue to encourage discussion among the team
- System of timely review and approval
- Formal documentation of the change
- Visual sharing and recognition

<u>Process to Capture Ideas or Suggestions</u>

Any format can be used, but the following basic elements in this example should be included. The main intent is to keep the suggestion process simple and easy to use while simultaneously requiring some logical thought processes to ensure reasonable submissions.

! Process Improvement Idea Form !	
Problem Statement	Assembly technicians are continually interrupted to answer phones and service window
Improvement Idea	Assign a single technician to handle all interruptions (Customer Servic role). Obtain a hands-free headset to answer the phone. Allow all other assemblers to focus on assembly tasks.
Date Submitted	August 25th
Submitted By	John Johnson
Expected Benefits	Fewer interruptions and distractions to assembly staff. Better quality and accuracy in instrument sets. Improved productivity.
Other Stakeholders	Who else might be impacted or have valuable input? Customers using service window such as L&D and Cath Lab.
Implementation Steps	1. Order hands-free phone 2. Review plan with Service Window Customers 3. Explain idea and plan to all CS staff 4. Make daily assignments for Customer Service role 5. Follow-up on Customer feedback and measure improvements in quality, productivity and timely response
Approval Status	Approved Sept 10th
Implementation Date	Trial to start Sept 29th
Results	

One option to simplify the above example is to eliminate the implementation steps from the suggestion and focus on those only after the suggestion has been approved for next steps. Another option to simplify the process is to remove the paper requirement all together and have conversations with your staff and listen to what they say. If you're the leader of the team, take notes, ask clarifying questions, and post the suggestion yourself. Staff may feel uncomfortable putting their thoughts to paper for various reasons but give them a venue to talk about how things could be better, and they may open up. Some may feel comfortable talking in a group setting while others prefer one-on-one. Leaders take the time to understand their employee comfort levels and how to encourage them to engage. Again, employee engagement reflects the work environment.

Venue to Encourage Discussion Among the Team

Lean Employee Engagement programs should be distinctly different from the old "suggestion box" where ideas withered and died, and employees mostly ignored it. Lean Employee Engagement programs are "visible" throughout the entire process from suggestion to approval to implementation and become a standard part of weekly discussions. Keeping the process visible and actively discussing suggestions, progress, and opportunities encourages employees to participate and increases their level of buy-in.

One effective venue to accomplish this is to place an "idea board" on the wall in a high-traffic area where it is frequently seen and easily reviewed by all staff. Schedule weekly staff meetings at the board to specifically discuss ideas and progress while recognizing employees who have participated in the process. The use of an "idea board" not only helps the team build upon and share ideas, it also provides a natural accountability mechanism to ensure leadership or staff assigned to implement the ideas is making progress. The weekly discussions are also the perfect time to reinforce staff adherence to newly implemented processes.

This "idea board" might contain sections for the following:

- New Ideas: Using the process improvement idea form or something similar, post all new ideas for all employees to see, comment on and build upon. Encourage this positive discourse.
- To Do: As ideas are approved, move the idea card to the second section and detail the tasks to be completed to implement the idea. This is the developmental stage.
- In Progress: Ideas that are in process of being implemented are moved to this section.
- Complete: Ideas that have been completed with results posted are shown in the last column or area of the board.
- Idea Metrics: Keep track of the number of ideas submitted and implemented to see how well the team is engaged.

Idea Boards also show the staff that leadership does listen and act on what they hear. It helps correlate employee input to action.

<u>System of Timely Review and Approval</u>

A common error in implementing an employee engagement system is not setting a plan for timely completion. The following diagram illustrates the basic steps in the cycle that can typically be completed in three or four days. Of course, some ideas may be implemented immediately and other, more complex ideas requiring input from multiple stakeholders, may take longer. The intent is to hold everyone accountable to completing the process in a timely manner. Long delays in implementation can seriously degrade a process improvement program and lead employees to believe that leadership is not serious about listening to their ideas.

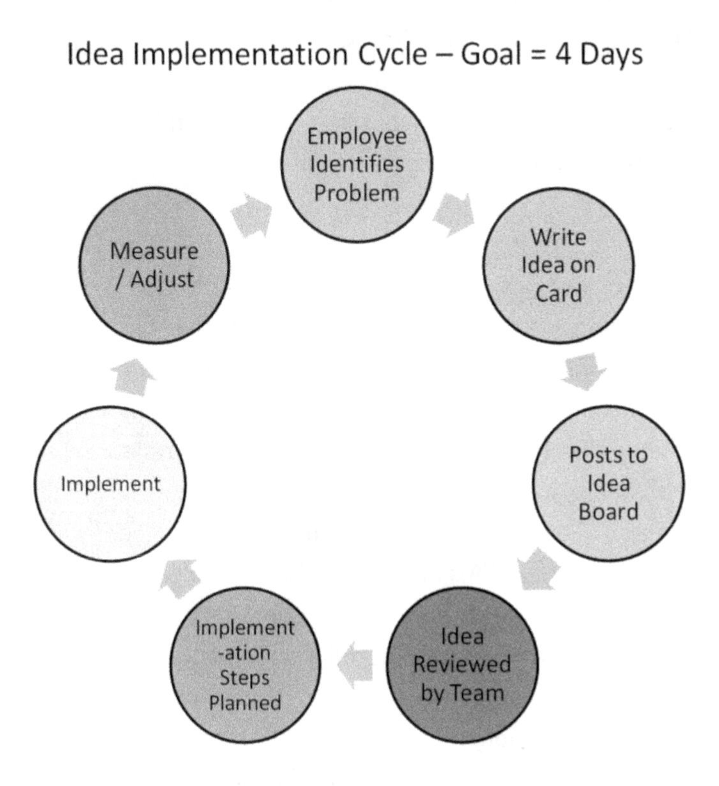

Particularly during the early stages of a Lean transition, ideas should be encouraged, accepted and implemented frequently and swiftly. As a leader, resist the temptation to over analyze and reject suggestions. Instead, use the opportunities to coach and improve the development and presentation of ideas. In fact, it is often better to allow employees the opportunity to implement ideas even if they have a high probability of not improving the process or succeeding. If the employees understand that their ideas must show a measurable improvement and the process is followed to evaluate the effectiveness of the idea, staff will learn from each implementation and gain confidence that their input is valued and trusted.

Leadership should focus on facilitating idea creation and implementation to ensure a continuous improvement culture grows and flourishes. Remember that not every implementation will be successful. In baseball, a successful batter fails two-thirds of the time. In basketball, a successful shooter fails fifty percent of the time. In both these cases the athlete is still considered successful. The extent of failure or success is up to you and your department. The point is you should not expect perfection. People learn from their mistakes and a lean environment encourages people to take chances to improve the process without undue fear of failure.

Formal Documentation of the Change

Even the smallest of changes should be documented because it encourages review and idea sharing. Plus, do not forget what you have learned about standard work! Every change must be standardized, trained to and added to the routine training and competency programs. Documentation provides the structure to ensure that the change is thought through, implemented correctly and trained consistently to all employees involved. Formal documentation also allows for leadership to quantify their team's efforts over time. The number of suggestions and successful implementations, benefits to the department, measured performance improvements and staff participation can all be captured, reported on and shared if documented properly.

Visual Sharing and Recognition

The idea board described earlier is the first and best method for immediately sharing ideas. However, to share ideas outside the immediate department, consider a monthly newsletter, flyer, bulletin board or verbal presentation that is distributed to other areas letting them know of your department's Lean efforts and successes. Not only can you inform and educate your Customers on the improvements you are making for them, your communications can lead other teams to become actively engaged in improving their areas. As the saying goes, "Nothing breeds success like success". Use this opportunity to also recognize the ideas and effort of your employees in the Lean transition, giving them the motivation to continue developing ideas and staying engaged.

One visual sharing that provides a true measure of the level of engagement of your team is to measure performance indicators of employee engagement.

Employee Engagement Metrics:

- # of improvement suggestions versus implemented suggestions
- # of improvement suggestions per employee and % implemented

# of Improvement Suggestions versus Implemented Suggestions

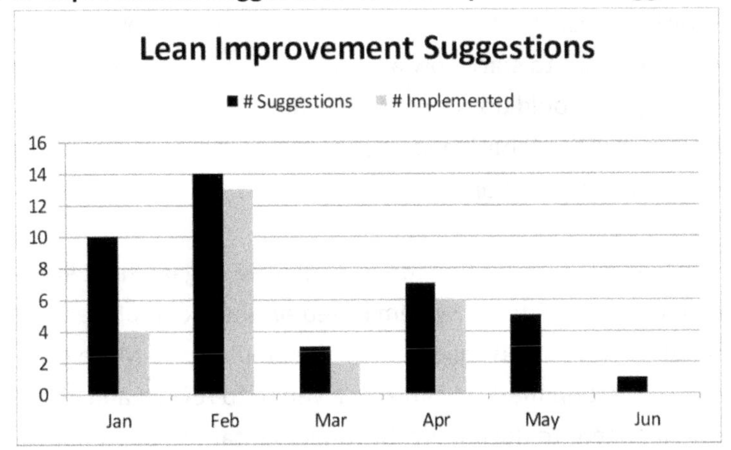

# of Improvement Suggestions per Employee and % Implemented

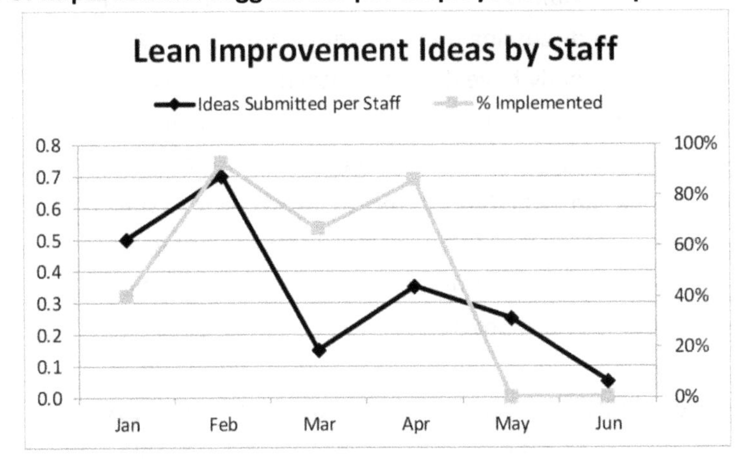

A high performing lean department will receive one suggestion per month per employee with over 75% of them being implemented. From the above graph, how would you rate this department's lean employee engagement and implementation performance?

Implementing an Employee Engagement Program

The six employee engagement essentials outlined above provide the "what to do" for implementing an employee engagement program but the how is perhaps even more important. How you communicate and set expectations from the start is critical to the long-term success and employee buy-in. Our recommendations are to start slow and easy with obtainable expectations. The worst thing you could do is to open the flood gates for suggestions that range from excellent to foolish and not have the time or system in place to handle the volume of ideas or manage them.

A successful lean implementation for an employee engagement starts with the leadership team creating a system based on the six employee engagement essentials before anything is rolled out to the employees. Make sure you have a solid suggestion method in place, a venue to review and discuss the suggestions, a system to document the implementations and visual measurements ready to go. A best practice is to start with the weekly discussions of performance at the future idea board and set the routine of meeting weekly and discussing department performance. A subtle point here is that you should already have departmental performance measurements in place before asking for improvement suggestions. The objective is to create performance measurements, or KPI's, that focus the staff's attention on the operational measurements that matter the most. As you start to discuss them and create awareness of how well the department is performing or not performing, you will have a natural pathway to introduce the employee engagement or idea board program.

Once you are ready to announce your idea board and start asking for suggestions, be sure to set expectations that are manageable. This includes letting the employees know the goal for the first three months is to receive and approve just one appropriate suggestion a week and implement 50% of the suggestions. The objective here is to stress the word appropriate and explain that suggestions should relate to the key performance metrics for the department or the department charter if you have one. Implementing 50% of the suggestions means you are implementing something new every other week. For most departments new to lean, this pace of improvement often proves to be so fast they have a hard time keeping up even though they usually claim it will be no problem.

Again, the how to implement the program should be based on slow and reasonable expectations that will increase the likeliness of success and employee engagement. Starting slow never hurts if you keep moving forward. Plenty of departments have attempted to start too fast only to fail miserably and then find it difficult to gain the momentum back again.

In the end, having an engaged employee base may be the strongest asset you will ever have in your lean journey. Most successful, if not all successful, lean companies will point to employee engagement and involvement as the core foundation of their lean programs. This also points to the importance of culture in lean transformation and how many lean implementations are considered cultural change agents more than anything else. Since entire books are written on corporate or organizational culture, we will not dwell any further on the subject except to say that engaged employees equal operational success.

~~~~~~

City Hospital: Employee Engagement

Scene: Everyone in SPD has come to realize that Rob is not letting the Lean SPD idea go and that he seems intent on following through with each implementation. The staff also noticed the change in Dwight and Becky as they began to visit decontamination every day and observe the staff's adherence to the standard work and checklists. Since the supervisors never used to come into decontamination at all, the impact was noticed immediately. Today, Rob has asked Dwight to lead the discussion with the
~~~~~~

staff on employee engagement as part of Dwight's leadership development. Rob knows that his success and his department's success rely heavily on his supervisor's ability to lead and sustain the lean improvements.

"Let's get started," Dwight calls the group together. "Before we start, I want to make sure everyone remembers to sign up for the hospital's customer service training class. This is mandatory for everyone in the hospital, not just us, and needs to be completed by the end of next month. The class is about two hours I think and is held in the East Wing Conference Center."

Most of the staff is not hearing anything Dwight is saying as he is standing in front of a large board that is covered up by an OR drape. It is obvious he is going to "unveil" something today.

"Hey Dwight, what's behind you?" Richard asks.

"I'll get to that in a moment," Dwight replies with a slight smile. "First I'd like to share something personal." This catches everyone's attention as Dwight normally does not share personal stories.

"Three months ago, when we started our Lean journey, I was skeptical. To tell you the truth, I thought it was just another idea that Rob had and, given enough time, we'd move on and get back to doing our work. Then something happened that I had never considered. Rob called Becky and myself into his office and basically told us we weren't doing our job."

Rob was not prepared for this and suddenly wonders where Dwight is going. The meeting was to introduce the idea board and how it was to be used, not to share personal stories. Rob had committed to letting Dwight run the meeting, so he bit his lip and continued to listen.

"I was a bit pissed off to tell you the truth. We work our butts off every day to get the trays done and there Becky and I were in Rob's office listening to him tell us we needed to change." Dwight had everyone's complete attention now.

"All of you know that Becky and I come into decontamination every day and make sure you're doing what you're supposed to be doing, the checklist is complete and we're following the standard work we implemented. Well, that wasn't very easy for me." Dwight looks a little nervous as he continues. "First, it made me realize that I really didn't know what a supervisor should be doing."

This comment hurts Rob the most as it is indicative of his ability to train and support his supervisors, so they are successful.

Dwight continues, "All these years, I have been focused on making sure the trays get done and the OR has what they need. I carry this phone around every day as if it's the reason for my being. What I now realize is that anyone can carry this phone and get the OR what they need. You don't need me to do it."

"The second thing I realized is that I was wrong in thinking that we all know what to do and don't need someone checking on us to make sure we're doing what we should be doing. So, when Rob told us we had to go to decontamination every day and fill out our leadership routine checklist, I felt like he didn't trust us or thought we didn't know what was going on." Dwight takes a deep breath.

"What I learned is this: The checklist isn't about Rob not trusting us. Following up on what you guys are doing in decontamination isn't about not trusting you either. Well maybe I don't trust Vlad," Dwight smiles and gives him a wink.

"Here's the point," Dwight takes a deep breath. "Rob's helped me understand that I needed to spend more time with all of you because my job as a supervisor is to make sure you have what you need to get the job done, know what to do and together come up with ideas of how we can get better. For all the years I've been a supervisor, I've spent most of my time working on trays or projects and very little time trying to figure out what we can do to get better. Going to decontamination was a bit of a surprise for me. The first time the checklist wasn't complete, I wasn't sure what to do but I had to report to Rob what I observed and how we could get better. I'll be honest with you, I was a bit uncomfortable asking Vlad why the checklist wasn't done and assumed he just didn't do it." Dwight again smiles at Vlad who is smiling himself as if he knows where the story is going.

"What I learned is that Vlad did have a valid reason for not getting the daily checklist done. He was tracking down missing instruments for a first case that for some reason weren't where they were supposed to be. Here's where the lean checklist made me realize Rob was right when he told me I hadn't been doing my job. Before lean, I would have accepted Vlad's reason and maybe told him to check in with me if he couldn't get the checklist done. Today, using our leadership checklist, I must report to Rob the reason why the checklist wasn't done and not just Vlad's reason, but the underlying process reason. Not to bore you with all the details, but what I ended up doing was asking the question why and continued doing it until I found out what happened. Vlad's reason led me to the case cart which led me to the missing sheet which wasn't accurate which led me to 3rd shift which led me to the case picking process specifically for add-on cases. The result was that the person on 3rd shift who picked the add-on case at 5AM didn't understand the standard work we've implemented and failed to mark on the missing list the trays needed." Dwight paused to clear his throat.

"Before Rob got on to me about doing my job I would have simply stopped at Vlad's reason and continued on. Today, we're training the 3rd shift on our case picking processes, so the problem doesn't happen again. I get it now, Rob," Dwight looks at Rob.

"That's a great story Dwight, thank you," Rob responds proudly and somewhat surprised.

"So, today I'd like to introduce our idea board," Dwight pulls the drape off the board. "From now on, every week, we're going to meet at this board and discuss what Becky and I have observed and learned during the week what changes we think should be made and, most importantly, review what ideas all of you have for getting better. Becky, you want to explain it to them?"

"Sure Dwight," Becky responds as she walks up to the board.

Becky consumes the rest of the meeting explaining the idea board, how people can post ideas, what happens to an idea when it is posted and how it can move from an idea to being implemented. For an example, Dwight has already posted his idea of training the 3rd shift on case picking so the board already has its first improvement suggestion. She goes over the graphs at the end of the board measuring the department's key metrics including their new measurement of employee engagement. Jackie, Roberta and Rachel add their comments as usual and the team adjourns.

Over the course of the next two months, the staff slowly settles into a weekly routine of meeting at the board and discussing their performance and ideas. As expected, the ideas trickle in the first couple of weeks but then increase as Rob, Dwight and Becky spend more time on the floor observing and asking the question why until they find the root cause of the issue. The staff submits various ideas including organizing the extra instrument inventory, assigning one person to unload the cart washer and stage containers where assembly staff can easily find them, running Bowie Dick tests at 6AM instead of midnight to keep the sterilizers running when the department is busy, using water proof loaner tray tags that are attached to the tray upon receipt and having one person stock all the assembly stations in the morning. The most important and valuable part of the process is that Dwight and Becky are managing it instead of Rob, and the staff is starting to submit suggestions and take an interest in seeing how the department is performing better.

~~~~~~
~~~~~~

Chapter Twelve: Eliminating Waste

Eliminating Waste, the seventh step in creating a Lean SPD! This is where we pause to let that sink in – the seventh step. How many of you or others that you know would have jumped right to eliminating waste as the first step? It is quite common to do so.

In our experience, the most common lean implementations in SPDs focus on either Kaizen events to identify and eliminate waste or 5S programs to clean up and organize the department to eliminate waste. In both cases, skipping the first six steps often leads to short term gains that are not sustained over the long run and little to no fundamental change in how the department functions. Supervisors continue life as normal; staff returns to former habits and the lean implementation is soon a memory.

Before we dive into eliminating waste and what that looks like in a SPD, it is worth stating how important the first six steps are. As a refresher, the eight steps to creating a Lean SPD are listed here again:

The Eight Steps to Creating a Lean SPD

- Customer Requirements (Lean management system)
- Measurements (Lean management system)
- Developing a Lean Operational Plan (Lean management system)
- Developing Leadership Routines (Lean management system)
- Problem Solving (Lean management system)
- Employee Engagement (Lean production)
- Eliminating Waste (Lean production)
- Continuous Improvement (Lean production)

The common theme for success in the first six steps is implementing a Lean management system and engaging your employees as the foundation for all future operational improvements and lean initiatives. In short, start with the management system before attempting to fix the production system.

The well-known biblical story of building a house on sand or on rock to withstand the storm is applicable. Building your lean transformation on a strong lean management system with engaged employees is like building your department on a solid rock foundation. When the storm hits, things go wrong, mistakes happen, trays go missing and staff leave, your department will withstand the temptation to backslide, return to old bad habits, or give up. Instead, your team will maintain focus on identifying root cause issues and staying true to lean principles. Starting your lean transformation at step seven and holding a Kaizen event is like building your house on sand. When the storm hits, the house is easily swept away because it has no foundation to hold on to. Improvements are soon lost as leadership fails to follow-up, performance is not measured, and staff becomes complacent with the status quo, whatever the status quo may be.

With a lean management system in place and employees who are ready and willing to participate in the process, let us now look at waste as traditionally defined in lean terms and how it applies to the SPD.

Waste, or Muda in Japanese, can be simply defined as anything that does not add value to the product or service. The hard part is in being able to see waste or conversely being able to see value. It is not easy for those unaccustomed to looking for it. It is even harder to see if you have worked in the same environment for years. Getting out and seeing how others run their SPDs is a great opportunity to expand your thinking and knowledge base.

Usually, the first impulse when talking about waste is to dive into definitions of the eight wastes of lean. We will get to that, as well as show you how those wastes apply to SPD, but first we will start with defining value. Think of this as focusing on the positive instead of the negative!

Value is first and foremost defined by your Customer and, in some aspects of healthcare, defined by regulatory agencies. The question to ask then is who are the SPD Customers and what do they value? This takes us back to the first step in a Lean SPD, defining Customer requirements.

Let us use the OR as our Customer and surgical instruments as our product for example. A typical OR values clean, complete, sterile and on-time instruments. Translating this into SPD operations, the OR values SPD activities that clean, complete, sterilize and deliver on-time instruments. Anything besides these activities is a candidate for waste.

Using our knowledge of value stream mapping and process flow diagrams, let us look at an actual process flow diagram of a decontamination department. While this is a simplified version, it helps to explain the concept. The following diagram has three shades of gray. Dark Gray represents activities that do not add value but are considered "must do" activities. Medium Gray represents activities that do not add value and are candidates for being eliminated. Light Gray represents activities the Customer values.

Decontamination Process Flow Diagram Example

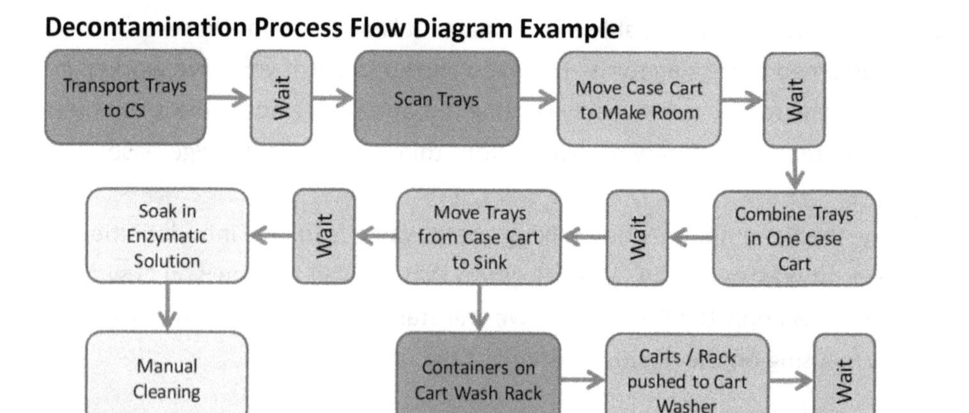

Look at the process flow above and ask yourself how your decontamination process works? If you followed an instrument tray through the process, what would that tray experience? How much time does the tray spend being cleaned (value add activity) versus being moved or waiting? If you look at your operations through the lens of value, you will soon not only see the steps that add value, but you will start to see a lot of waste.

~~~~~~

<u>Case Study – Decontamination Observation</u>

A typical hospital performing 60 surgical procedures a day and sterile processing department with 27 full-time staff were experiencing backlogs in decontamination that frequently lasted until 10pm nightly. To better understand the situation, a four-hour observation was performed. Staff performed their activities as they normally would while the observer simply recorded what they saw. The following bullet points from the observation uncover multiple opportunities for improvement in waste elimination, employee engagement, quality and throughput. This example also demonstrates the power of observation and the importance of leadership
~~~~~~

getting out into the department and simply watching what is happening. Names have been changed for anonymity purposes.

- *3:15pm Shift change begins as first shift staff leave decontamination empty. One fully loaded washer is sitting, waiting for someone to select the cycle and start the load. It is unclear how long it has been waiting. 7 case carts are backlogged with dirty instruments. 28 dirty instruments are sitting at the hand wash station.*
- *3:30pm Judy comes into decontamination and puts on PPE.*
- *3:45pm Judy comments, "It's just a job," as she unloads empty baskets from the washer return racks. Judy notices the loaded washer and starts the cycle.*
- *Judy loads multi-level Ortho trays without separating out levels and leaves lids on, inhibiting the effectiveness of the washer to clean the instruments*
- *The washer auto load mechanism is not working as Judy states, "I can't wait for it," and then struggles to manually push the rack into the washer. How long has it not been working?*
- *3:50pm Natasha joins and goes to the hand wash sink to work. Judy unloads empty racks from the cart washer and then loads two case carts into cart washer.*
- *3:53pm Both staff breakdown case carts, piling more hand wash instruments onto hand wash rack, combining dirty trays from multiple case carts into one case cart and putting containers on the container rack for cart washer.*
- *OR varies in how they return trays. Some are sprayed some are not. Some dirty instruments are placed on top of towels and others are not. D&C tray is very bloody and drying.*
- *Judy focuses on keeping the cart washer running to free up space for more case carts.*
- *Per Natasha, there is no department standard for decontamination.*
- *Most instruments are opened by staff for washing but some are not. They are all jumbled in a pile versus facing up towards the spray arms.*
- *White scum film built up on washer #1 and #2 but not #3 or #4. Why?*

- *Consolidated dirty case cart is staged at the sink. Staff member walks to other side of the room to another sink countertop next to a non-working table top sonic washer to get gloves. Why not keep gloves closer by?*
- *4:15pm Natasha leaves for a birthday party in the breakroom. Judy says she is too busy to go.*
- *Judy places a tray on the washer rack, filling it up, but then left it waiting for a washer that is running while two other washers are empty.*
- *Judy is cleaning clinic items that just arrived while the OR trays sit waiting.*
- *Shift supervisor Matt and a case cart transport person bring in 6 more dirty case carts from the OR and leave them as is in decontamination. Judy says per their policy, the transport person is supposed to open the carts and scan the trays but does not do that. They also always get multiple case carts this time of day because no one will bring them down between 3pm and 4pm.*
- *Judy stops cleaning clinic items and starts breaking down case carts and scanning instruments*
- *4:23 Matt helps start the cart washer. He moves case carts to make room and then leaves. He makes no comment about backlogs or scanning and offers no encouragement to Judy.*
- *Judy manually carries the washer rack from the return module to the loading module at the washer instead of using the transfer cart. This is a safety issue.*
- *Using the pushcart at the sink to put trays on after prepping and then transferring trays to washer rack on the loading module, why not use the transfer cart and bring the rack to the sink and load there instead of multiple handlings with the push cart?*
- *4:26 Natasha returns.*
- *The lower spray arms on the washer rack is not working. The cart washer spray nozzles are not working. Neither Judy nor Natasha ever notice. How long have these machines not worked and what kind of maintenance do they receive?*

- *Natasha is breaking down case carts while Judy is breaking down carts. They could put the container rack in the middle of the room between sinks and push the case cart to the sink for single touch as they break down and prep instruments and load containers on rack in one step.*
- *Stryker System 6 came back jumbled, not in slots on rack. Instruments are mixed up between trays.*
- *Natasha does not think they test their sonic, but the SPD manager thinks in-house BioMed group does. Manager cannot confirm.*
- *Judy manually pushes in washer rack into washer #3. Even though the auto load module on that washer works, manually pushing the rack in caused the working auto load module to error.*
- *Natasha scans instruments on the hand wash cart that have been sitting since start of shift. Some were already scanned by first shift.*
- *Judy loads mayo floor trays onto a single level washer rack and runs them on an instrument cycle instead of the utensil cycle. She again carries two racks from the return module to the washers.*
- *4:59pm Judy goes to dinner. 50 trays are backlogged at the hand wash station. 27 trays are backlogged at the other prep sink.*
- *Natasha uses the sonic washer as a soaking step for dirty trays and then continues to use the sonic with dirty water for daVinci cleaning.*
- *5:20pm Four more case carts arrive. Natasha breaks down carts and loads the cart washer.*
- *Natasha hand wipes Stryker scopes with enzymatic solution but there is no disinfection of any hand wash items.*
- *The daVinci flushing is not according to the poster IFU's. Dirty sonic water is being used to hand flush syringe instruments. The poster says to flush until water is clean. How can Natasha know this?*
- *CTRC Flexible scopes are in plastic bins on the cart sitting in decontamination. Two were already processed in decontamination and considered clean but are still sitting on the lower shelf of the cart in blue clean bin. A dirty scope in a gray bin is sitting on top of a plastic cart and nobody was aware of it. The dirty scope had been sitting for over an hour, maybe over two hours, after procedure. According to IFU's, the staff has to soak the scopes for 10 hours to ensure dried*

bioburden is removed. A handwritten note for midnight staff is placed by sink.

- *5:45pm Judy returns from dinner, breaks down the case cart and loads the cart washer.*
- *5:59pm Natasha uses the same dirty sonic water again for the next daVinci instruments.*
- *6:05pm Judy starts to work on OR trays.*
- *There is no continuous flow in decontamination at any stage, even at the washers. There are 5 trays sitting on manifold in front of an empty washer for an hour. Judy is putting multiple level trays on a pushcart.*
- *6:31pm Judy unloads/loads cart washer. There is a six-foot long empty metro rack in the middle of room. Why? Transfer carts in middle of room are not being used. Judy then used a transfer cart to move the washer rack from return rack to washer, but the cart did not align well so she struggled manually to push manifold onto load module.*
- *6:40pm End observation*

I will let you determine what opportunities were uncovered in this case study!

~~~~~~

Our decontamination process flow diagram and case study help understand how to see waste in one area. Now walk through the entire instrument reprocessing flow from receipt to delivery and document steps and time spent on the value-add activities of cleaning, completing, sterilizing and delivering and you have identified your value stream. Add in all the other steps and you have identified your waste. Some waste you must live with. Transporting dirty trays from the OR to decontamination adds no value but is required based on the location of your SPD. Testing your equipment does not add value directly to the instrument tray as viewed by the Customer but is required by regulatory guidelines and is a good quality practice. Spending money on personal protective equipment for staff does not add value to the instrument tray but is required for employee safety.
~~~~~~

As you become more comfortable identifying value and waste in your processes, you will soon find yourself having lean debates over whether an activity adds value or is waste. An example is in "completing" an instrument tray for the OR. While the OR values complete trays, it is questionable whether they value the time spent by SPD in trying to complete the tray. In true lean terms, looking for missing instruments to complete a tray is a sign of waste. Why did the tray show up missing instruments in the first place? What processes can be changed to guarantee the tray stays complete throughout the cycle of use?

Often, the OR, our Customer, argues that they cannot maintain their operational metrics, such as room turnover times, while ensuring every individual instrument is returned to the correct tray. So, what to do? Assuming we are going to have trays missing instruments, a reality for every SPD I have been to, then completing trays can be viewed as value add but should be managed and reduced to the minimal amount of time, effort and resources as possible. One SPD measured the amount of time it took an employee to find and replace a missing instrument and then improved the process to reduce the time to less than one minute on average.

If you follow the logic shared above for identifying value and waste, you will probably identify plenty of improvement opportunities in your SPD. Diving deeper into lean, let us review and understand the traditional eight wastes of lean to identify waste that may be hidden or hard to see. The eight wastes of lean are listed here and then explained in more detail. The wastes are listed in an order that seems to be most relevant to SPDs:

The Eight Wastes of Lean

- Waiting
- Defects
- Excess motion
- Transportation
- Underutilized people
- Excess inventory
- Over production
- Excessive processing

Waiting Waste

Definition: Staff waiting to work or product waiting to be worked on. It is important to note that waiting waste is not only about labor. Product waiting to be worked on is an important waste to eliminate and often the most common in sterile processing departments.

How to See Waiting Waste: Look for machines that are sitting idle, product waiting to be worked on or staff waiting for work to arrive from the previous process. Staff waiting for work rarely just sits there doing nothing, so seeing this waste is a bit hard. Look for staff slowing down while waiting for work to arrive or performing other activities that may or may not be value add or necessary at that time.

Examples of Waiting Waste in SPD:

- The biggest example of waiting waste in an SPD is instrument trays waiting to be worked on such as those sitting on staging racks in assembly. For a refresher on this waste, go back and review the chapter on continuous flow.
- Incomplete case carts waiting for trays
- Backlog of case carts in decontamination waiting to be worked on
- A washer breaks down and is waiting to be fixed
- Washers and sterilizers waiting for work backlogged in the department
- The OR waiting for a case cart or instrument tray

- Staffing schedules not aligned with available work leaving periods of over and under capacity causing both staff and product to wait

A more difficult form of waiting to identify is staff waiting for something, such as a physical item, information or another person, yet they are currently working while waiting. Staff waiting usually does not mean he or she is standing there with nothing to do, although I have seen this in a few decontamination areas when staff was waiting for dirty case carts. Usually, the staff has been told he or she must wait for the tray, documentation or something else and, in the meantime, performs another activity to keep productive. This type of waiting is not easily observed by walking into the room and requires active discussions with staff to identify these times. Frequently, the wait is viewed as normal and nobody questions the wait since that is the way it always is.

Another form of staff waiting that is hard to see is the slow down effect. When staff realizes that they are running out of work or the next case cart or delivery is going to be late, they may slow down their current work pace to fill the available time. This phenomenon is seen in all industries and can be described as "work expands or retracts to fill the available time." In assembly, staff may increase productivity when tray backlogs are large and conversely reduce productivity when there are few trays to work on. Walking into a room and seeing everyone working does not mean the process is functioning properly. You must understand what the planned process performance for the area is, how the area is currently performing to plan and the causes of the variances.

Remember when we introduced the concept of the perfect SPD at the beginning of the book? Think of the perfect SPD as having zero wait time for anything! Have your staff and leadership team keep notes for a week of every time they waited for something and then see what opportunities you uncover. Combine your observations with the goal of continuous flow and you will probably have enough work for the next year to perfect your processes!

Examples of waiting with root cause why questions may include the following:

(Remember the staff is usually still working on something else while they are waiting).

- Staff waiting for a supervisor to help them, bring them something or answer a question
    - Why was the supervisor needed in the first place?
    - Does the staff not have the necessary information at their workstation?
    - Are certain tools, instruments or materials not stocked conveniently for the staff to use?
    - Does the staff need additional training?
- Staff in decontamination waiting for a dirty case cart
    - Are the case carts being transported timely from the OR?
    - Is the staff schedule in alignment with dirty case cart arrival times?
    - If there are peaks and valleys in dirty cart arrivals, what can the staff do to stay productive?
- Staff waiting for elevators
    - This one is included for fun!
    - If staff members do have to wait on elevators, how can you reduce the number of times they wait on the elevator? I have seen one SPD responsible for picking up dirty instruments, equipment and commodes from multiple nursing floors given an elevator key to lock out the elevator for their own personal use during their runs.
- Instrument trays waiting to be assembled
    - Is enough staff scheduled in assembly at the right time of day to keep up with the incoming workload?
    - Are staff members allowed to assemble without being interrupted?
    - Are staff members working to planned productivity?
    - See the continuous flow chapter for more details on this one.

Eliminating Waiting

Now that you have learned to see waiting waste, look at what you can do to eliminate it. For waiting waste, the first place to start is with continuous flow. Most waiting waste in SPD is with instrument trays not flowing through the department and backlogging.

As a review, the eight steps to implementing Continuous Flow are shown again here.

- Balance the production line
- Align staff schedules
- Create standard work
- Set staff performance standards
- Train to standard work
- Reduce interruptions
- Develop key performance indicators
- Create leadership routines

If you can successfully balance your production line so that product and people are evenly matched, you will eliminate probably 80% of the waiting in your department. For the rest of your waiting try the following suggestions:

- Plan Ahead: Can the items, person or information be planned for in advance, so you do not have to wait for it or them?
- Reduce Activities: If an activity has waste in it, such as waiting on an elevator, is there a way to reduce the number of times you perform the activity? An example is running to the OR to deliver or pick-up items. If every trip to the OR requires an elevator trip up and down and thus two "waiting on elevator" experiences, how can deliveries be coordinated with pick-ups to reduce the number of trips?
- Communication: If you could better communicate (earlier, quicker, more accurately) could the waiting be reduced? A very common form of communication waiting is email. How many times have you heard someone say they are waiting for so-and-so to reply to their email? If you have a department or area that receives and processes large

amounts of emails, perhaps that department could assign one person on a rotating basis to answer a live phone number allowing "Customers" like yourself to receive immediate information versus waiting for an email response. The other department may find that this "phone person" can triage a large percentage of the phone calls and eliminate most email work, a win / win for everyone!

- Backfill the Waiting Time: Sometimes you must live with waiting based on how your workflows and processes are designed. An example of this may be a required staffing position in the OR quick turn room or scope room or any other room where you are required to staff the position no matter what the workload is. These staffing requirements are usually customer service focused with the Customer requiring immediate service without warning. These positions can also have periods of no work followed by a swarm of activity. While the staff member is waiting for the swarm of work, make sure they have a secondary work assignment or activity that they can perform to maintain their productivity. If you want to dig into lean processes, you could start asking "why" fives time to understand why your Customer needs someone there all the time. You may find opportunities to improve elsewhere that reduce or eliminate the need for the position to be filled.

Defects Waste

Definition: something that does not meet the Customer's requirement.

How to See defects waste: The time to see defects is before the product or service reaches the Customer. Look for ways to measure, view and confirm product quality within each process step. At each handoff in the process, such as decontamination to assembly, create quality checks to confirm the product was passed on per quality expectations. After the product has been sent to the Customer, any defects identified will require a Customer feedback mechanism.

Examples of defects waste in SPD:

- Dirty instruments caught in assembly and returned to decontamination
- Incorrect documentation or packaging caught in sterilization and returned to assembly
- Incorrectly labeled instrument trays
- Incomplete or incorrect instrument trays
- Soiled instrument trays
- Incorrectly scanned or stored instrument trays
- Incomplete or incorrect case carts
- Instrument count sheets not accurate/maintained
- Late instrument trays or case carts
- Product sent to the wrong Customer
- Incorrect or incomplete case cart preference cards / pick lists
- Sets returned by the OR with instruments missing
- Set returned by the OR missing original basket or container

Defects cause waste twice. The first waste is the time spent incorrectly making or delivering the product or service. If you did not do it right, then your time as well as the supplies and materials that were used were all wasted. The second waste is that you must deal with a defect. You respond to it, research it, report it and then usually reprocess or remake the product or service that was defective. Additional waste was experienced by your Customer as well.

The examples of waste in an SPD listed above are the first waste in the process. Now look at some resulting examples of defect waste, or the second waste.

Examples of Secondary Defects Waste in SPD

- OR staff going to get another tray to replace defective one
- OR staff looking for or waiting for a non-defective item
- OR staff reporting the defect
- SPD staff responding to, researching and reporting on the defect
- SPD staff reprocessing the defective item

- Additional materials, supplies, utilities or effort in reprocessing the defective item
- Customer and/or patient waiting
- OR sitting idle

I have attended a few joint SPD and OR meetings where they discuss SPD quality metrics and the issues and problems they are facing. Afterwards I tell them the meeting was a waste! With a smile and friendly banter, I then explain that I did not mean the meeting time was wasted but that any time spent on defects is considered a waste in lean.

Eliminating Defects

So, the million-dollar question is how do we eliminate defects? While this topic could be a book unto itself, let us focus on the common types of defects a typical SPD faces. While our intent is not to provide specific answers to your individual issues as that is the job of your Lean oriented team, we can provide some examples to help stimulate thoughts.

Incomplete Trays

This defect is a prime candidate for traditional data-based problem-solving skills that rely on measurements to help identify the root cause. Using examples from the previous chapter on measurements, the first place to start is to understand the scope of the issue. The following graphs are from the measurement chapter and represent traditional metrics that many SPDs track, such as % complete and # incomplete instrument sets.

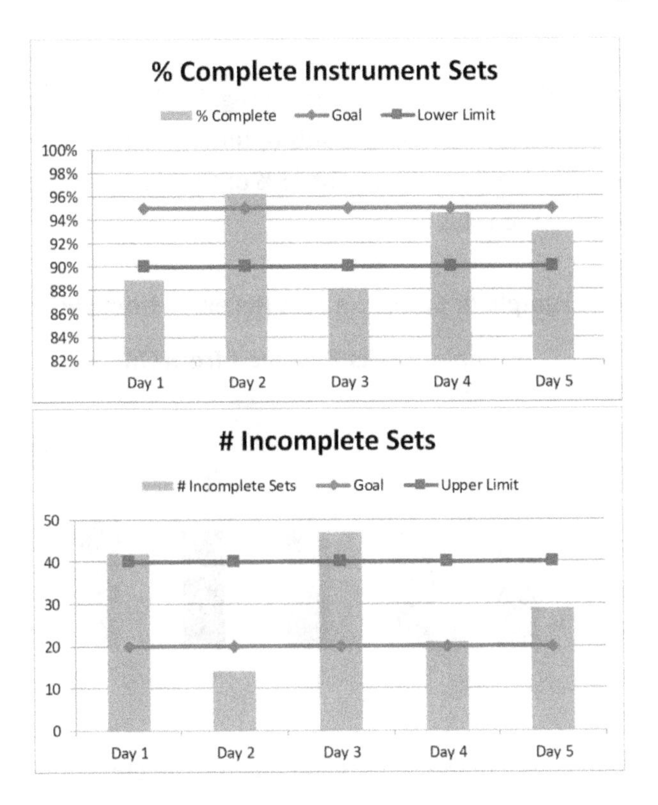

Though these outcome measurement graphs only indicate that there is an issue. To better understand root causes and potential solutions, process measurements are needed that will provide more information and give direction to improvement efforts. Using value stream skills such as process flow diagrams, you will find the following potential process areas to measure that will help determine where in the process defects are occurring.

- # incomplete trays received from the OR – measured by OR service line and if possible, by OR staff member
- % complete tray on first attempt – measured by SPD staff member
- % complete trays sent to OR – measured by SPD staff member
- % complete trays and # incomplete trays by OR service line
- Ability to query the data by OR service line, OR staff member, SPD staff member, tray name, instrument name, date, and any other potential data field

Using graphs from the measurement chapter again, the following metrics show an OR that is indeed returning a sub-optimum number of trays incomplete or "mixed up" to SPD, about 35% of the time, and causing extra work to reassemble the trays.

Example of Complete Sets Received from OR

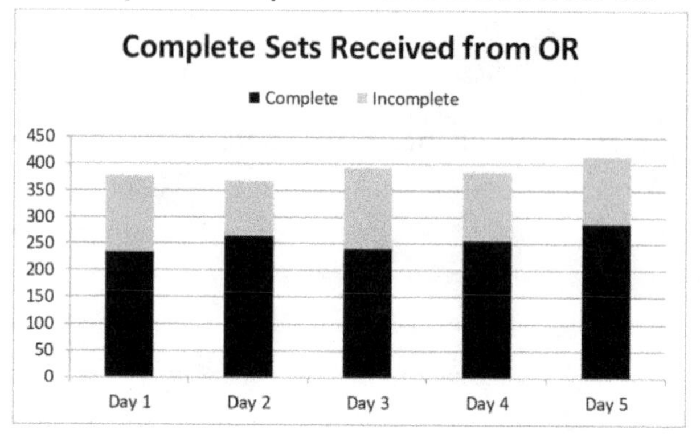

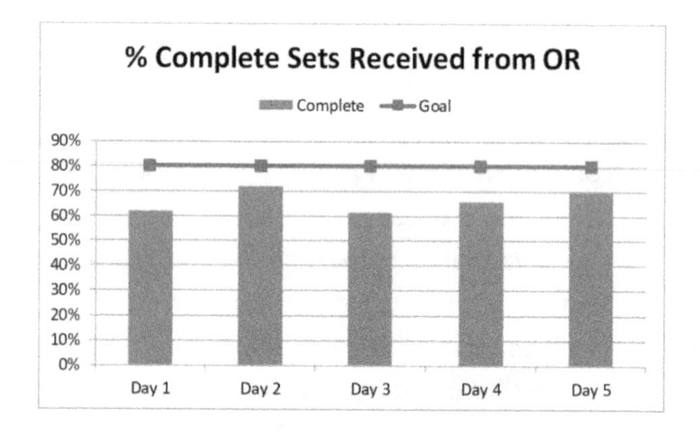

While a typical SPD can complete most the instrument trays, they still end up with a portion of trays that they are unable to complete and thus require additional data to understand the root causes. The following graph is an excellent Customer facing graph that shows how the SPD is adding process value in completing a large percentage of trays, about 70%, that were received from the OR incomplete. Since the OR only sees and "feels" the outcome focused measurements of incomplete trays sent to the OR, it is valuable to educate them on the overall process and how the SPD is indeed improving the complete tray percentage. In the end, the outcome measurement is the most important measurement, but internal process measurements are critical to focus everyone on the actual process improvement needed versus just complaining about the issue.

Example of SPD Ability to Complete Sets Received from OR Incomplete

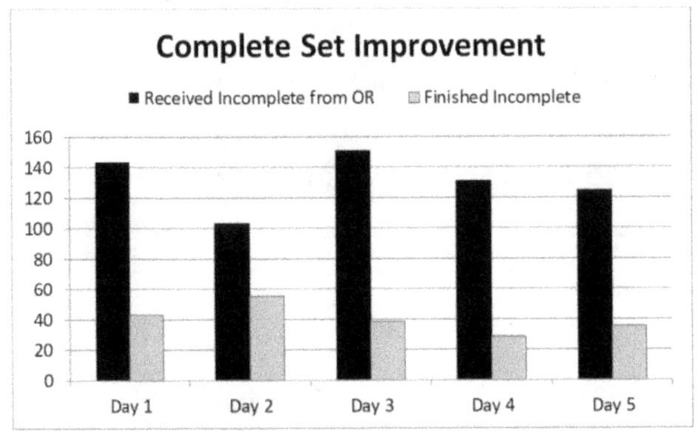

The use of an instrument tracking system makes gathering this type of information much easier, but you can gather data the old-fashioned way as well. One hospital trying to tackle the issue of incomplete trays started to collect data manually from the SPD staff assembling trays and then entered the information into a spreadsheet for analysis. What they found was not only valuable but gave them a focused direction to improve. It was also very valuable to the OR as they were just as vested in improving the outcome and realized they had work to do on their end. The hospital chose to have each person assembling keep track of any instrument tray they were not able to complete by copying the count sheet and highlighting the missing instruments. From this data, they could provide the following process measurement data.

Missing Instrument Data for One Month

- 287 = Total number of missing instruments
- 99 = Total number of trays missing instruments
- Missing instruments by OR service line
  - 96 = General
  - 86 = Ortho

- 32 = Neuro
- 18 = Ortho Spine
- 16 = Plastic
- 7 = CVT
- 5 = GYN
- 1 = Lithotripsy

- 15 trays accounted for 50% of the missing instruments
- 19 instruments accounted for 50% of the missing instruments

Top 15 Trays Sorted by # of Missing Instruments

Tray Name	# Missing Instrument
Synthes Consign Neuro Fix IMPLANT Set	23
Ortho Spine Tray "A"1	16
Anterior Cervical Fusion Tray # 1	16
OPSC Ortho Hand Tissue Tray # 1	15
Laparotomy Tray #2	14
Laparoscopy Tray # 1	8
Ortho Hand Tissue Tray #1	7
Ortho Minor Tray # 1	6
Lap Chole Tray # 1	6
Orhto Minor Tray #2	6
OPSC Laparoscopy Tray # 2	6
Minor Tray # 4	6
Total Hip Tray "A" 1	5
Plastic Tray # 1	5
Total Hip Tray "A" 3	5

Top 15 Instruments Sorted by # of Missing

Instrument	# Missing
Clip Towel Peers 5 1/2"	25
Clamp Kelly Cvd 4 1/4"	15
Screw Low Profile Tit Self-Drilling 5mm	15
OB Scissor Mayo St 6 3/4"	14
Clip Towel 4 1/4"	9
Screw Low Profile Tit Self-Drilling 4mm	7
Hook Skin Joseph Sgl	7
Clip Towel Sm 3 1/2"	7
Scissor Bandage Black Handle	6
Forcep Adson W/Teeth 1x2x4 3/4"	6
Scissor Mayo St 5 1/2"	5
Clamp Pean Cvd 6 1/4"	5
Clamp Mosquito Cvd 5"	4
Clamp Kelly Cvd 6 1/4"	4
Clip Towel Edna 4"	4

With hard data to go by, the OR began to focus their attention on the service lines and specific trays that were causing the largest amount of missing instrumentation. This focused attention enabled them to utilize their limited resources to return the highest value possible. In reviewing the data, it was obvious that a few very common instruments such as towel clips, Kellys and Mayo scissors were causing most the problem. Even without an engaged OR working to reduce the issue, a SPD can utilize this data to ensure they have enough back-up inventories of single instruments on hand to replenish the common missing instruments. While this solution does not solve the underlying root cause issue and thus does not produce a lean solution, it does at least improve the outcome measurement of complete trays. In this situation, an accounting system charging back the cost of the instrument inventory to the OR service line would be a nice way of closing the loop.

While every SPD would be very pleased to have an OR actively engage with them in reducing missing instruments and return the trays to decontamination "complete", the story should not end there. Here is where we will incorporate our City Hospital SPD to finish the story. The SPD provided the OR great data on missing instruments but failed to look deeper into the data to see what information it might provide concerning their internal processes.

Many SPDs we have visited keep track of assembly data to see who is "producing" or assembling the most trays. High performers are often praised and allowed a bit of slack due to their high performance. A typical review of their assembly data might produce the following graph:

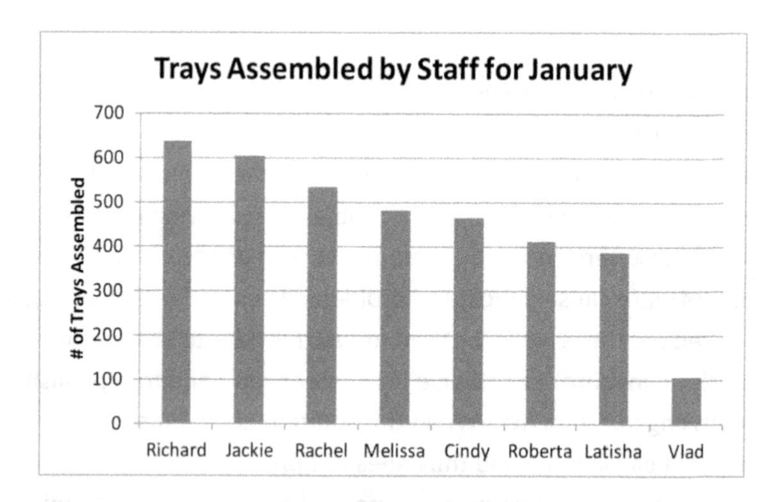

From this graph, Richard and Jackie are the high performers, and Rob (the SPD Manager) puts up with some less than desirable behavior and comments from them because of their performance. But let us dive into the missing instrument data to see what else we might learn. If Rob were to measure missing instruments by staff member, he might find the following results:

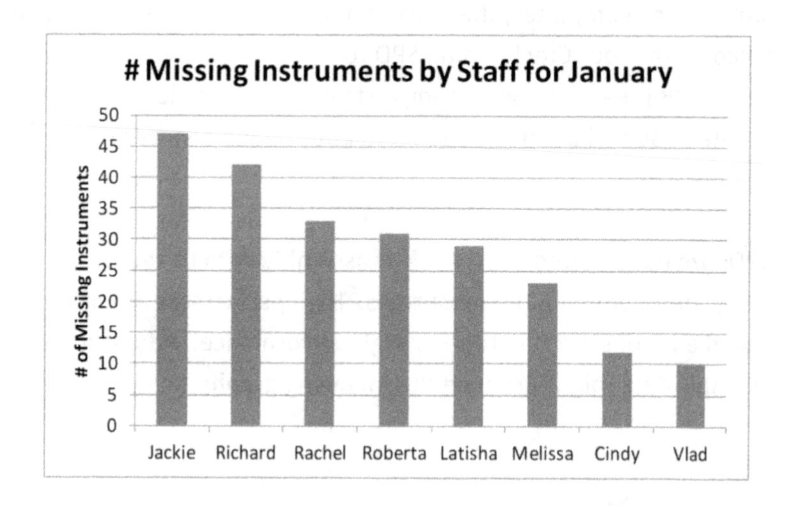

Suddenly, Richard and Jackie's high production seems to be tarnished by their high number of missing instruments. At first glance, the impulse may be to state that the more trays one assembles, the more missing instruments that person will have. Plus, the ratios show staff members have less than one missing instrument per tray assembled which seems reasonable. But what if we looked at the data as a ratio of trays assembled to missing instruments to see who can assemble the most trays before having a missing instrument. The results would look like this.

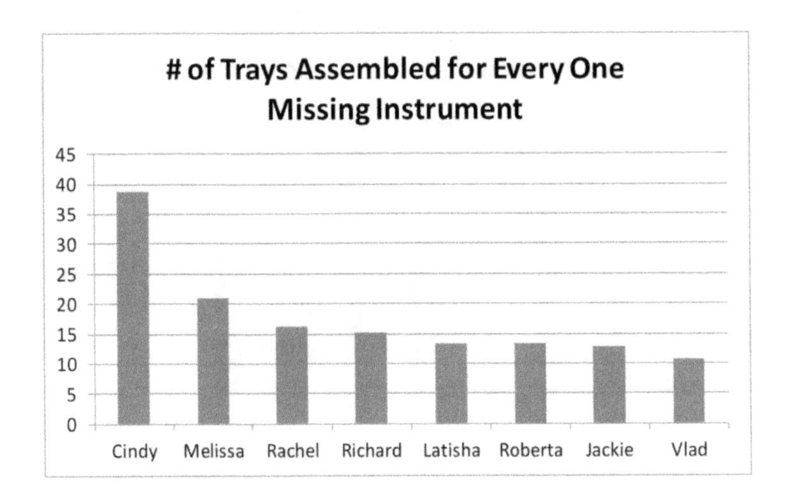

From this view, Cindy is by far the most effective at assembling trays without missing instruments. She can assemble, on average, 38 trays before having a missing instrument. Something Cindy is doing is producing far better results than the rest of the team. The question now is to find out why and if it is repeatable for others to follow. Here is where further investigation can lead to either an explanation or a process breakthrough. Perhaps Cindy is only assembling trays from CVT and GYN who return their trays complete, while Jackie works General and Ortho who do not return their trays complete 100% of the time. Perhaps Cindy takes the time to find the instruments she needs and thus produces a lower number of trays during the month but does so with a much greater quality outcome. From the OR's point of view, Cindy is probably the staff member they want working on their trays.

In the measurement chapter, we stated that how you view the data will often give you a better view of what is happening. The graph below combines trays assembled with missing instruments by staff member and allows for a quick visualization of outliers in the process. In this case, most staff member's blue line, representing # of missing instruments, is roughly the same level as his or her trays assembled (red bar), except for Cindy and Melissa. You can immediately see there is a variance in performance amongst the staff. If you could add a line or bar for expected or planned performance, you would have a great visual for detecting performance issues or opportunities.

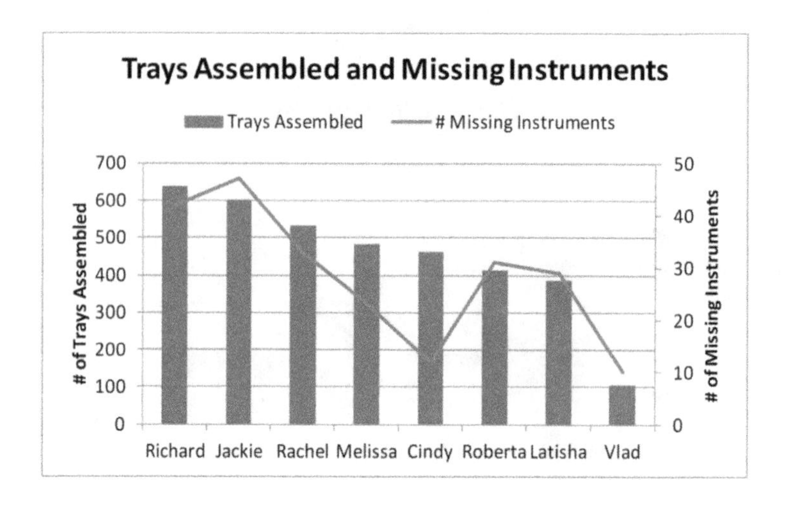

To conclude the missing instrument discussion, graphs and measurements are always susceptible to manipulation and thus everyone needs to be upfront on how the numbers are tracked. For an SPD tracking missing instruments, how they define their process will make a direct impact on the missing instruments measurement. Consider the following four different processes a SPD could take when managing missing instruments:

- All instrument sets can be sent to sterilization no matter their status.
- Only complete instrument sets or those only missing non-critical instrument can be sent to sterilization.
- All instrument sets unable to be completed after first pass are placed in a non-conforming status for further follow-up.
- All incomplete / non-conforming instrument sets are sterilized but then held in SPD for completion unless requested for use by the Customer.

Whichever process you are following may make a dramatic impact on your outcome measurement of % complete sets sent to the OR. In one of the leanest SPD we have visited, they chose to follow the fourth bullet point. Their reasoning was that they wanted the tray sterile in case the OR absolutely needed it even with missing instruments. But they also wanted to keep the tray if possible, to try and complete it before giving it to the OR, thus improving their % complete instrument sets metric.

Lean departments also do their best to improve both outcome measurements as well as process measurements. The following process measurement graphs show both first pass and final Customer facing measurements. Both measurements could be graphed separately or jointly.

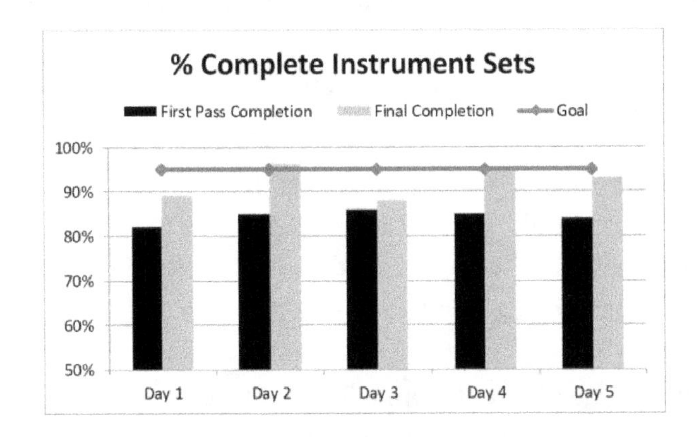

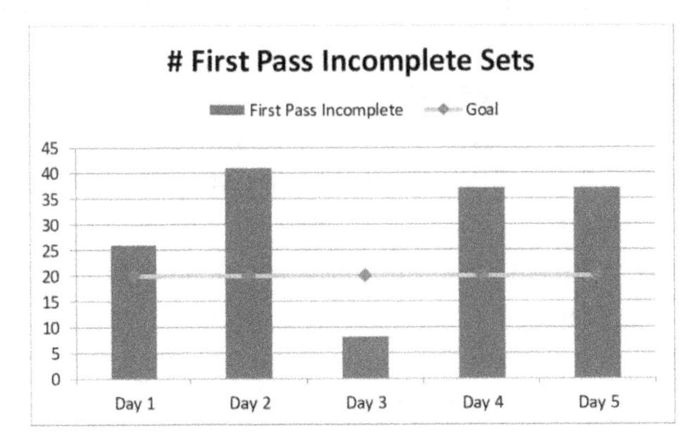

It is important to note again that continuous flow also improves % complete sets, especially on first pass attempts. This is because continuous flow departments have very little backlog of trays sitting in assembly, making it easy for staff to look for missing instruments. Additionally, continuous flow departments find it easier to keep all instrument trays from the same case cart together throughout the process making it easier for staff to "put the puzzle back together." One very Lean SPD department was so good at keeping a continuous flow going that they could call the OR within 90 minutes of the case ending and tell them what instruments were missing and what case the instruments were used in. On the opposite end of the spectrum, we have visited SPDs where over 200 trays are backlogged in the SPD assembly room, making it almost impossible for a staff member to attempt to find a missing instrument that was accidently returned to the wrong tray by the OR.

Another interesting measurement that seems to be somewhere between outcome and process is the number of trays currently in sterile storage that are incomplete. A large hospital we visited tracked this metric with the goal of having zero trays in inventory missing instruments. Through a combination of OR process improvement, SPD process improvement, extensive and well-organized back-up inventories, and a continued drive to complete every tray possible, the hospital eventually reached their goal! Imagine walking through your hospital and not being able to find one tray with a missing sticker!

Let us summarize the different steps a SPD can take to reduce and eventually eliminate missing instruments or, stated positively, to ensure every tray is complete:

1. Provide relevant and specific data to the OR on how the instruments are being returned. Without good data, it is difficult for the OR to act and utilize their limited resources to improve their processes.
2. Measure and track SPD staff performance on missing instruments and then follow-up with each staff member. Remember the saying, "People pay attention to what you inspect, not what you expect," is relevant here as well. If you simply say you expect everyone to do their best in finding the missing instrument and completing trays but do not measure it or inspect how each person is doing, your words will be ignored. If your department is measuring and holding people accountable to producing as many trays as possible but not measuring their quality or completeness, you may have staff sending incomplete trays without trying to find the instrument.
3. As needed, invest in a reasonable amount of back-up inventory that is justified by your hard data of most common missing instruments. As

you continue to lean out the processes and reduce process variation that creates missing instruments in the first place, you will reduce the amount of back-up inventory needed.

4. Make the effort to organize your back-up inventory. Staff should be able to find exactly what they need within one minute. Conversely, they should be able to return an extra instrument to inventory within one minute.
5. Work to maintain continuous flow and minimal backlogs in assembly while keeping all trays from the same case cart together throughout the process. This should make it easier for everyone to complete trays, find missing instruments and identify extra instruments that belong in other trays.
6. Chose a process design that fits your department and hospitals operations. A suggested option is to hold incomplete trays in SPD during the day in hopes that the missing instruments will be found in another tray. At a certain point in the evening or early morning hours, all trays still incomplete are then sterilized and placed on a labeled "incomplete shelf." These incomplete trays are then turned over to a specific person to manage and either find or order the missing instrument. Once the missing instrument is obtained, the tray is opened by the original assembling technician and completed and then re-sterilized. In this scenario, the outcome measurement of trays sent to the OR complete increases as trays are held in SPD in the incomplete state. In case the OR must have the tray, even in an incomplete state, the tray is held in a sterile state, so it is immediately available.
7. In each step, the Lean management system works together with the Lean production system in that your process design and selection determine the operational process, resource requirements, standard work instructions and staff expectations for both productivity and quality. Leadership then follows-up on the performance to plan, identifies variances and improves the process.

Incorrect Instruments in Tray

Correcting the defect of incorrect instruments in a tray combines the three elements of training, technology and employee engagement. Incorrect instruments are typically a symptom of a staff member's lack of knowledge, incorrect knowledge, lack of paying attention or caring to pay attention or interruptions while assembling the tray. Let us review how training, technology and employee engagement can help reduce and eliminate this defect.

Training should be near and dear to every SPD leader and staff member. It was not so long ago that surgical instrumentation consisted mostly of stainless-steel items that were relatively easy to reprocess through repetitive and standardized processes. Today, instrumentation has evolved to include power equipment, minimally invasive specialties, robotics, intricate cannulated items, low temperature sterilization items, rigid and flexible scopes, cameras, delicate items requiring special handling, vendor specialty sets and any multitude of items that have individualized and specific instructions for washing, assembling, testing and sterilizing. Today training has become an essential element for every SPD.

Unfortunately, too many SPDs fail to have the resources to commit to produce an effective training program. New hires are placed with a "preceptor" or simply an experienced technician for on-the-job training. Frequently we hear from these new hires how they are taught different ways and methods for performing a task from various "experienced" staff members and thus conclude that they can determine their own best way. Experienced technicians on the other hand rarely go through remedial training per se but simply sign off on an annual competency with their supervisor under the premise that they have been doing the job for so many years that they know what to do.

Based on the knowledge required to be an effective sterile processing technician in infection control, instrumentation, cleaning, testing, sterilization, regulatory requirements and customer service, training is no longer just nice to have but rather a must have. Training must also become an on-going event for all staff members no matter their years of experience. Placing an incorrect instrument in a tray is not a mistake only made by new hires.

Measurements will also help identify training requirements for both topic selection as well as staff member selection. Incorrect instrument defects should be measured, and Pareto analyzed to determine which instruments, trays or services require immediate training as well as which staff members require additional training.

Even with extensive training, human beings by nature will make mistakes. Asking someone to remember every instrument on the count sheet, while assuming they will never make a mistake, is no longer a viable option. Fortunately, technology can assist. Anything you can do to remove the reliance on human memory, the better. Implementing instrument tracking systems that incorporate on-screen assembly can reduce the possibility of placing an incorrect instrument into a tray. Adding in photos of the instruments assists the staff in identifying the correct and incorrect instruments. Bar codes or etching 2D matrix on the instruments allows for scanning of the instrument for electronic identification. Perhaps someday the instruments will be manufactured with built in RFID technology allowing for immediate identification without individual scanning.

Another way to leverage technology is to build verification steps into the process that help ensure the staff member is utilizing the technology as well as verifying the correct instrument. We have seen plenty of SPDs with on-screen assembly technology that the staff ignore during the assembly process using their memory instead. They then quickly click the screen once the tray is complete and move on. Technology is great if your staff uses it. Thus, consider options that require the staff members to verify each step along the way. This could include verifying each instrument one-by-one on the screen as they assemble, answering on-screen questions to help confirm they perform critical steps or build in specific requirements based on problematic trays or instruments.

Perhaps the best option is to combine a rigorous training program with technology solutions to support the training and staff member. Rigorous training may have to be defined though. Having a yearly competency performed for annual reviews is not rigorous nor comprehensive nor effective. The best training programs are continuous and focused. The twelve months of the year are designated for specific training topics while leadership or senior staff members are assigned as specialists in each area and are responsible for developing and delivering the training. While formal Staff Development Manager positions are preferred, they are not to be the sole repository of expertise or training delivery. These educators should oversee the education and training program, develop the structure and assist in delivering the training. A sample training program is shown below that works well for most SPDs:

Month	Topic	Owner
January	Hospital Competencies	SPD Manager
February	General Decontamination	1st Shift Supervisor
March	Hand Wash / Power Decontamination	1st Shift Supervisor
April	Scanning and Documentation	1st Shift Lead Tech
May	Assembly – General, GYN, Plastic, URO	2nd Shift Supervisor
June	Assembly – Ortho, Spine, Neuro	2nd Shift Supervisor
July	Steam Sterilization	3rd Shift Supervisor
August	Low Temp Sterilization	3rd Shift Supervisor
September	Case Carts and Distribution	2nd Shift Lead Tech
October	Customer Service	SPD Manager
November	Infection Prevention	Educator
December	Annual Competencies	Educator

The key to success in a training program as shown above is that every staff member, no matter his or her years of experience, goes through the training. Remember that a Lean SPD is based on standard work where every activity is performed the same way no matter who is performing it. Training programs should be designed to support standardization of work and ensuring every staff member understands the documented and standard method for performing a task.

Having addressed training and the use of technology to reduce incorrect instruments in a tray, let us look at how employee engagement can help. In short, employee engagement helps everything. The more employees are engaged, the more they care. The more they care, the better quality they produce. If there is one thing that can be repeated in lean, it is that a successful lean department must find a way to engage employees in the process. Share the hospitals and department vision and objectives. Make reviewing operational performance and key performance metrics part of everyday life in the department. Measurements are not only for leadership; they should be known and understood by everyone. Share the defect rates. Ask the staff to help identify why incorrect instruments are in the tray.

Once the staff members start to participate, you will find ways to help them improve the quality of their work. This is where interruptions come into play. We covered this topic in the continuous flow chapter to ensure assembly meets their throughput goals to maintain flow and reduce backlogs. Now, we will look at interruptions as a source of defects. Assembly staff must be able to work without being interrupted. The patient and surgeon are counting on it. Interruptions cause staff to start over, forget where they were and make mistakes.

To summarize, reducing incorrect instruments in trays requires a focus on the following:

- Collect data to help understand where the issues are.
- Create an ongoing training program that all staff participates in.
- Leverage technology to remove the reliance on human memory.
- Leverage technology to verify process steps are being performed and performed correctly.
- Eliminate interruptions for your staff while they work.
- Engage your staff in the process and finding ways to fix the issues.

Dirty Trays

Finding bioburden in a sterile tray is not only embarrassing for an SPD, it is also potentially harmful to our patients and upsets the doctors, nurses and scrub techs. This is one of the biggest "we screwed up" defects SPDs face. As I write this book, hospitals across the country are looking at ways to guarantee flexible scopes are effectively cleaned to eliminate the possibility of further patient infections after having realized that thousands of patients were treated with contaminated scopes. It is a serious subject.

The answer to eliminating dirty trays is not a single solution, step or lean concept. It is the culmination of all the lean concepts. Dirty trays are all about process breakdown or even worse, a lack of process development in the first place. It starts with understanding the cleaning requirements at point of use in the OR. AORN states that decontamination starts in the OR with the removal of gross bioburden. From there, efficient and timely transportation to the SPD decontamination department helps eliminate dirty trays by reducing the amount of time the bioburden has to dry. The longer bioburden dries, the harder it is to remove. If you do find that dirty instruments sit for periods of time, then follow the recommended practices of maintaining moisture through enzymatic spray solutions, transport gels or moist towels.

Once in decontamination, SPD staff must follow the instructions for cleaning which should be available at their workstation with verification by the staff members that they followed them. This may require additional investment in sinks, sonic washers, lumen flush ports, technology or other required resources to meet the need. In almost EVERY SPD we visit, the decontamination process relies on staff memory to do the right thing. This is not good. Ask yourself this question: How do you know your staff is following the instructions for cleaning for every instrument every time and can you prove it in a court of law? The more you think about that question, the more you may not be able to sleep at night.

Think about the variations in instrumentation and the multitude of cleaning requirements for standard stainless-steel instruments, lumens, cannulated items, laparoscopic instruments, power equipment, vendor trays, eye instruments, robotic instruments and rigid and flexible scopes. A large hospital that we consulted with was recently cited by CMS for not ensuring their hinged stainless-steel instruments were maintained in a fully open position facing the spray arms in the automated washer.

Here is where Lean SPD departments can utilize technology to ensure the standard work instructions for cleaning are readily available at the decontamination station. Staff scan the tray or instrument, review the cleaning instructions, perform the cleaning per instructions and then confirm their success on the screen. How many of you can do that?

Eliminated dirty trays also required the washing equipment to be tested and verified. American SPDs are doing a better job at weekly or daily testing of their washers, but how can we verify that the washer performed correctly during every cycle? How can we guarantee the staff selected the proper cycle? We need to.

Dirty trays are also a sign that inspection post cleaning also failed. Processes in assembly for inspection of instruments must be part of the standard work. Here is where the quality versus quantify discussion is often raised. In lean, there is no give or take between quality and quantity. Quality is defined and processes are built in the most efficient manner to meet the quality requirements. When a SPD staff member says he or she does not have time to inspect the instruments and maintain productivity, this is considered a symptom of either an unrealistic productivity expectation or a staff member struggling to meet performance expectations. Quality inspections in assembly are critical. In the measurements chapter, we discussed internal process measurements, such as "good catches" in assembly when finding a dirty instrument. Use those good catches to determine the root cause and then eliminate it.

Throughout the process, leadership routines should provide regular rounds for observing staff performance, identifying variance to standard work, improving adherence to cleaning instructions and improving processes.

Leadership follow-up is critical to ensuring ongoing compliance, continuous improvement and staff maintaining their personal vigilance for following the standard work and doing the right thing. Remember it is what we inspect that gets the attention, not what we expect.

Once the instrument moves to sterilization, the dirty instrument is destined for the OR but the tray sterility then becomes the issue to be maintained. We will talk more about "holes in wrappers" and break downs in sterility next.

Let us summarize then how to eliminate dirty trays from our list of defects:

- Define, develop and standardize your processes. Start in the OR with removal of gross bioburden, continue with effective transportation and finish with the actual cleaning processes.
- Write standard work instructions for decontamination and perform annual training at a minimum.
- Leverage technology to provide cleaning instructions at the workstations with a confirmation by the staff member that they have followed them.
- Regularly test your equipment and document the results. Remember that if it is not documented, then it never happened.
- Follow-up regularly on staff performance, take the time to stop and observe staff working and create an atmosphere of excellence.
- Get your staff engaged and hold them accountable for being a part of the solution.

Holes in Wrappers

Just in case you are reading this book and do not have a SPD background, wrappers refer to the blue wrap used to wrap around an instrument tray that does not have a rigid container or case to protect it. The wrap is porous to steam or hydrogen peroxide penetration during sterilization but maintains a sterile barrier afterwards until opened or damaged. The defect happens when the OR staff receives a wrapped instrument tray and finds a hole or holes in the wrap thus invalidating the tray's guarantee of sterility.

Most OR's are good at finding holes in wrappers. Some are pickier than others, but there is usually no shortage of people claiming a tray is unsterile and then pointing out a hole, tear or slit in the wrapper. The problem is in understanding the root causes and eliminating them.

In theory, a hole in a wrapper can happen at any time after the tray has been wrapped. In a typical hospital, this includes the following process steps:

- Transport from the assembly table to the sterilization area
- Loading the tray onto the sterilization cart and into the sterilizer
- Unloading the tray from the sterilization cart and transporting to sterile storage
- Placing the tray into or onto the sterile storage shelf
- Moving the tray in sterile storage, trying to get to another tray
- Stacking trays on top of each other
- Handling the tray from sterile storage to a case cart or directly to the OR for the surgery
- Handling the tray in the OR
- Returning an unused tray back to sterile storage

Within each process step is the potential to create a tear, hole or damage to the wrapper. The first four steps are typically handled by SPD employees while the last four steps can be either SPD or OR employees. The hard part is in determining where the hole in the wrapper occurred and what to do to stop it from happening again. Here is where problem solving skills along with basic lean principles for process design, standard work and training come into play.

Problem solving skills will help identify potential causes or the exact cause of the hole in the wrapper. To be successful you will need to collect all the data you possible can on the issue. Consider these questions:

- What tray was it?
- When and where was the hole found?
- Who found it?
- What kind of hole is it (a pin hole, cut or tear)?
- Where on the wrap is the hole?

- Where did the hole align with the tray (along the corner, ridge, handle, foot, other)?
- Who handled the tray from assembly to sterilization to sterile storage to case cart to OR?
- Was the tray previously picked for a case but not used and returned to sterile storage?
- Where in sterile storage was the tray stored? Are there stacking of trays in that area?
- Are there sharp ridges, shelf edges or other reasons the hole originated in sterile storage?
- Where was the tray put once picked from sterile storage? In a case cart?

Once you collect all possible data, you can record it in a spreadsheet for easy review along with other defects for future analysis. The objective is to identify common trends that may have caused the hole in the wrap. Most hospitals have already taken the easy steps of addressing the physical aspects that cause holes in wrappers such as sharp edges in sterile storage and on the tray itself. Smooth shelf liners are installed, rubber corner protectors are utilized on the trays, an additional towel is placed under the tray when wrapping it and blue plastic carrying trays are utilized to protect the tray. These measures could have been identified through process flow diagramming, measurements and Pareto analysis, as well as basic common sense. What becomes harder is when these process improvements are implemented and holes in wrappers still occur.

From our experience, holes in wrappers that occur after the physical aspects are addressed are most commonly a result of employee handling or mishandling. To address this, we again return to employee engagement combined with standard work instructions and training and a dose of leadership observation. First, realize that holes in wrappers are typically so small you never see them until you have opened the tray in the OR and take the time to look at the wrap holding it up to the ceiling lights. Even though the hole or tear probably happened earlier while being handled by someone else, he or she never realized it. This is perhaps a training issue as well as an adherence issue. Every step within a process should be documented and standardized including how to carry, handle, put away, move and maintain the sterility of wrapped trays. Many hospitals may have procedures on how to clean instruments but how many of them have documented how to handle instrument trays in sterile storage or move them to a case cart when picking a case? It is this level of detail that can make the difference between a world class Lean SPD and an average SPD.

Once you have documented in detail every step of the process, you then turn to training and employee compliance with the standard work to ensure that the results are achieved. As sad as this is, we have experienced many hospital staff members who in the rush of the moment disregard their training and grab a tray off the shelf, dragging it across another tray or shelf edge and disregarding the acceptable method for handling a tray. It should be no surprise when they later find a tear in the wrap. Additionally, we have seen many storage areas packed so tight with trays stacked on top of each other that it is practically a miracle when they do not have a hole in the wrapper.

So here is our summary to eliminate holes in wrappers:

1. Keep detailed records of every defect to find patterns, physical characteristics or staff relationships. The more information you have the better you will be at finding the root cause.
2. Document and standardize each process step from the end of assembly to handling by the OR.
3. Fix the easy physical aspects of sharp corners, edges, shelf liners and other aspects.
4. Train the staff on the standard process and how trays are to be handled. Let them know that holes in wrappers are largely caused from staff handling.
5. As always, incorporate leadership follow-up with rounding and occasional observations of staff handling trays, picking case carts and OR staff handling trays to inspect what you expect.

Lastly, remember that every person who potentially handles the sterile tray prior to opening it in the OR is a potential cause for a hole in the wrapper.

This means that the OR staff themselves must be involved and acknowledge their role in maintaining sterility of their trays as they handle them. It is truly a team effort.

Trays Not Available or Late

Along with finding bioburden in a tray, not having the tray available when needed is also one of the most embarrassing defects a SPD can have. The common root causes for such a defect seem to be process, lack of adherence to process and inventory. Working in reverse order, inventory is usually something the SPD has little to no say in. The inventory is what it is and if the OR schedules four cases requiring the same type of instrument tray and there are only three in inventory, then the SPD must "quick turn" the first tray used in time to be used on the fourth case. While this sounds straight forward, it commonly causes strain on both the SPD and the OR if the proper processes are not in place.

Developing a quick turn process starts with identifying the need. This can be accomplished through the case cart picking process or a review of the scheduled cases and instrumentation needs as compared to on-hand inventory. Once you have identified the need, you should then identify which previous case the instrumentation can be obtained from for the quick turn. I have seen SPDs simply list the instruments that will need to be quick turned on a white board in hopes that when one shows up in decontamination the staff will notice and alert the team. A proactive approach, such as using quick turn cards, is probably a better solution.

Quick turn cards identify the tray for quick turn and are placed with the tray in advance, so the OR staff understands that the tray they are using is required for a later case. The case, room number and time needed is written on the quick turn card so that when the tray is returned to decontamination it is immediately noticed and prioritized. Some of the most effective quick turn processes assign one specific staff person to oversee and manage the quick turns.

Returning to our root causes, process or lack of adherence to process, let us assume that the hospital has enough instruments for the cases and thus the issue is not a lack of inventory. Unfortunately, there are broken SPDs that struggle to ensure they are processing the correct instruments the OR needs on a timely basis. First, if you implement continuous flow and eliminate backlogs then this issue goes away as all instrumentation is returned as quickly as possible to sterile storage. The following bullet points highlight some of the issues that cause instruments to be late or not available when needed:

- Incorrect OR preference cards and thus the instrument requirement is not known
- Lack of process to identify the instrument is needed; this is often the case with vendor supplied instruments as many hospitals do not associate vendor sets on the doctor preference cards
- Lack of process to identify instrument priorities and process per those priorities
- Lack of staff following the designated process and working on instruments that are not priority
- Too many priorities so that everything becomes a priority

To solve most of these, always start with implementing continuous flow solutions and then focus on creating a prioritization process. Even the best continuous flow departments sometimes find themselves behind a backlog and are forced to prioritize. Here is where organization and technology can play an important role. First, every department should be organized, especially to find a specific instrument tray quickly. Instrument tracking systems are valuable tools to help locate instruments if staff adheres to scanning processes. Clearly labeled staging areas help staff place the correct instrument in the correct location. If you segregate your instruments in assembly by OR service line, then clearly label those areas. Once you are organized and can find specific trays quickly, the next step is to create a process to prioritize your work. Instrument tracking systems can help here again by tying into OR scheduling systems and displaying instrument tray priorities based on the OR's needs. Case cart missing lists or quick turn lists provide easy priority lists.

As with every process, staff adherence is critical and thus occasional leadership follow-up should be built in to ensure staff are following the priority process. We have all seen staff members assemble a tray they "preferred" to versus what was the priority at the time.

Here is our summary for correcting trays that are not available or are late:

1. Develop and adhere to a quick turn process that proactively identifies specific instruments requiring quick turns and confirms they are managed through the process.
2. Implement continuous flow practices.
3. Implement a prioritization process when backlogs do exist accompanied by an organized method to track and know where every instrument tray is always. Ensure that only "true" priorities based on the OR schedule are on the list. Avoid creating too many priorities based on types of trays as eventually everything becomes a priority and thus nothing is prioritized.
4. Utilize "missing lists" when picking case carts to understand what trays are still needed for case carts and assign specific responsibility to oversee completing the carts.
5. Make sure OR preference cards are accurate.
6. Ensure staff follows standard work processes through active leadership routines.
7. A vendor tray process needs to be in place to identify, track and manage vendor trays so they are always available and on-time.

<u>Incomplete Case Carts</u>

Just like missing instruments, this defect is also a prime candidate for traditional data-based problem-solving skills that rely on measurements to help identify the root cause. Using examples from the previous chapter on measurements, the first place to start is to understand the scope of the issue. The following graphs are from the measurement chapter and represent traditional metrics that many SPDs track such as % complete and # incomplete case carts.

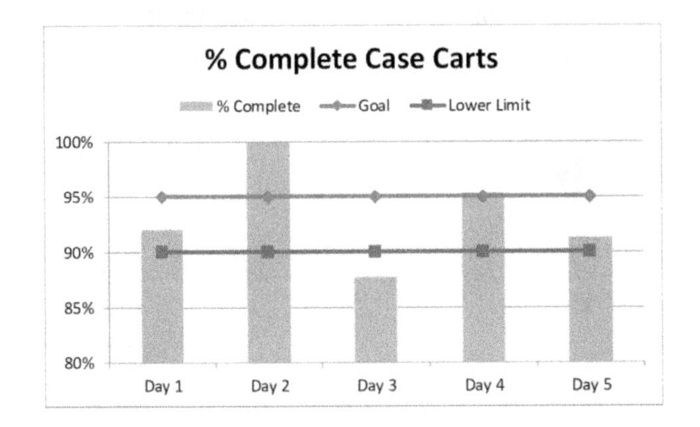
% Complete Case Carts
% Complete
Goal
Lower Limit
100%
95%
90%
85%
80%
Day 1
Day 2
Day 3
Day 4
Day 5

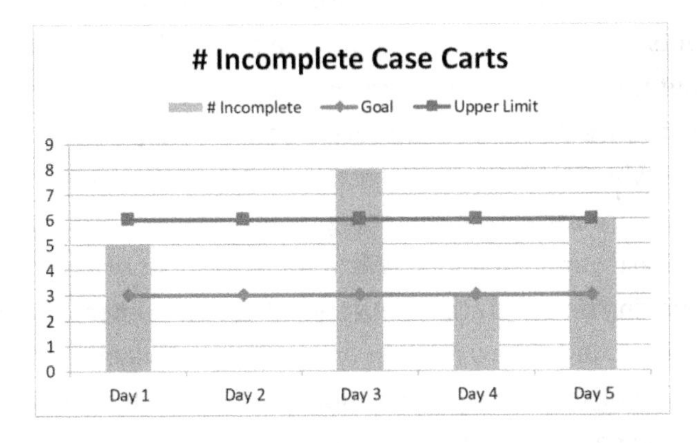
Incomplete Case Carts
Incomplete
Goal
Upper Limit
9
8
7
6
5
4
3
2
1
0
Day 1
Day 2
Day 3
Day 4
Day 5

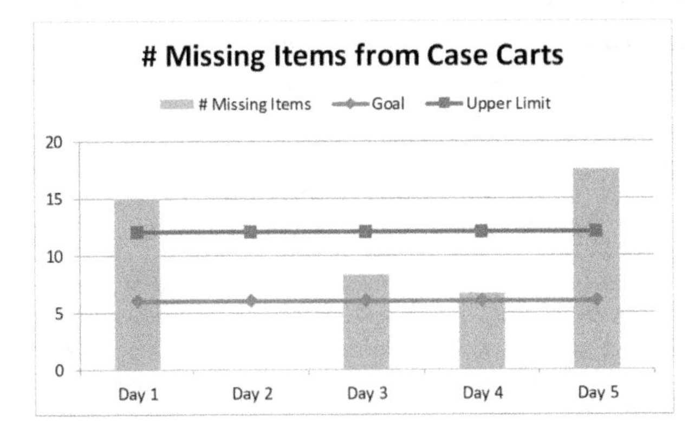
Missing Items from Case Carts
Missing Items
Goal
Upper Limit
20
15
10
5
0
Day 1
Day 2
Day 3
Day 4
Day 5

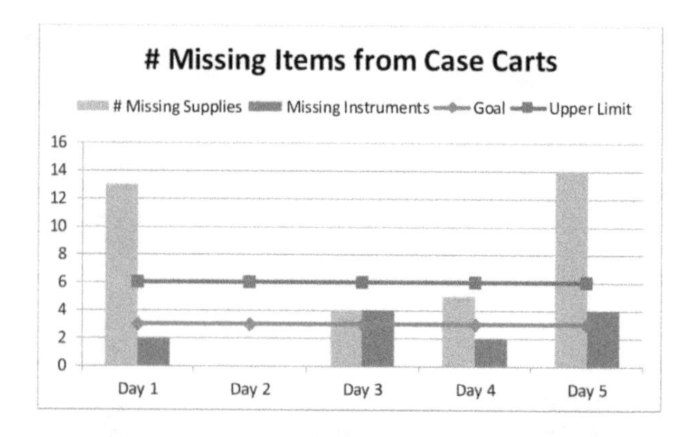

These measurements are outcome measurements though and not process measurements. They help us understand the scope of the problem but nothing about the root cause, the process breakdown or other factors involved. Just as we dived deep into the process measurements and root cause analysis when solving missing instruments, you can do the same thing for incomplete case carts. The first thing to do is capture the reason codes for why the case cart was incomplete. Were soft goods out of stock, back ordered or waiting on a materials delivery? Were instruments backlogged and not processed in a timely manner and thus not available? Did the staff member make a mistake? Did the vendor not deliver the needed item on-time? Create an easy method to capture what seems to be the root cause at the time of case cart picking as a starting point. The following Pareto graph shows an example of incomplete case cart reasons.

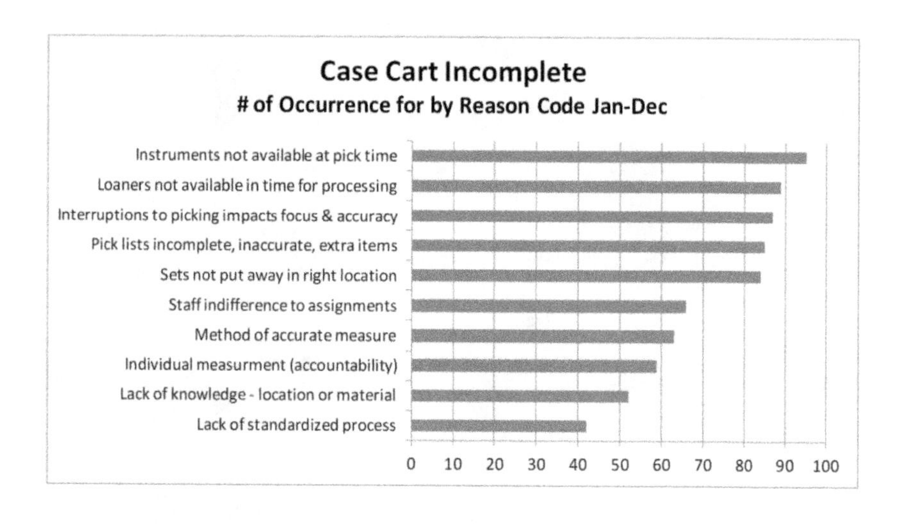

Using problem solving skills, start with one reason and determine what needs to be changed so that the issue does not happen again. You may find that certain days of the week, staff members, types of cases or certain items are producing most your issues and thus help you focus on finding the root cause and eliminating it. Having the data is the key to understanding the problem. As the saying goes, "You can't improve what you don't measure."

There are a few common reasons why case carts are incomplete that apply to most SPDs and can be reviewed regarding supplies and instruments:

Common Reasons for Missing Supplies

- Supplies are backordered – sometimes you cannot do anything about this one
- Case picking is scheduled before supply restocking
- Par levels or Kanban levels are set incorrectly (either too much or too little)
- Case preference cards that create the pick list are incorrect and the staff does not even know supplies are missing
- Needed supplies are still in the breakout room or returned to the supply area and need to be placed back into storage
- Supplies are not ordered consistently or in a timely manner

Common Reasons for Missing Instruments

- Case picking starts too early and instruments are still being processed
- SPD is backlogged or understaffed, and instruments are waiting to be processed
- No priority system to identify what needs to be process based on case cart requirements
- Case preference cards that create the pick list are incorrect
- Case preference cards do not contain specialty items such as vendor sets and the need has not been adequately documented and communicated

While the solutions to these reasons may be straight forward and simple to implement, the fact that they exist is not always a sign of an inept staff or management. It is often a simple but slow decline in processes and process management to the point that everyone was accustomed to "the way things had always been here." Lean solutions will not only implement lean production practices, such as standard work activities, clear responsibility and assignments, organized work areas, workflow improvements and other improvements, but must also include lean management solutions to ensure the improvements are sustained.

~~~~~~

Case Study – Incomplete Case Carts

A Level 1 Trauma hospital with 24 OR's and a 24/7 SPD was looking for ways to improve their SPD performance and improve their Customer satisfaction with the OR. The OR had brought to their attention issues with case carts and requested the department look into the issue. A team of three technicians was assembled and tasked with understanding the issues and finding a solution to provide 100% complete case carts. Having recently completed a process flow diagram exercise, the team decided to first spend time observing the case picking process and track reasons why the case carts were incomplete. Their findings included the following:

- *Missing supplies were found in the OR unused return supplies which accumulated in a large pile until someone put them away.*
- *Missing supplies were found in the breakout room, waiting to be placed into storage.*
- *Missing supplies were ordered too late and not available when needed.*
- *Missing reusable items such as graduates and basins were in SPD waiting to be reprocessed.*
- *Missing instruments were in SPD waiting to be reprocessed.*
- *Excess disposable gowns were overflowing in stock and returned every day from the OR.*
~~~~~~

Based on their observations and data collection, the team outlined seven process improvements and presented these to their peers and the SPD Manager for approval to implement. The details of one improvement is shared below with a summary of the others following:

Improvement: Set aside one hour from 8AM to 9AM for coordinator to breakdown incoming supplies and restock to shelf.

1. *Benefits: Eliminates supplies backing up in breakdown room and causing staff to search through boxes to find supplies, increases stock on shelves, gives coordinator uninterrupted specified time to complete the job.*
2. *Action Items:*
    a. *Create job assignment as part of coordinator's daily report.*
    b. *Create training material for competencies in performing activity.*
    c. *Train coordinator on new process and expectations.*
    d. *Update staffing guide with activity requirements.*

The additional improvements included the following:

1. *Set aside 45 minutes at 7AM for a technician to restock unused returned supplies.*
2. *Set aside 30 minutes every morning at 9AM for coordinator to reorder supplies to ensure they are received according to schedule and train a back-up person to perform activity.*
3. *Work with materials management to update par levels based on usage reports.*
4. *Purchase additional graduates to meet minimum needs.*
5. *Move case picking to start at 8PM instead of 3PM to allow more time for instruments to be reprocessed and available.*
6. *Correct OR preference cards requesting extra disposable gowns to eliminate overstocking and daily unused returns.*

All the team's recommendations were implemented, and their case cart complete measurement improved from an average of 76% to 97% within one month.

~~~~~~

Let us summarize the different steps a SPD can take to reduce and eventually eliminate missing supplies and instruments from case carts or, stated positively, to guarantee every case cart is complete:

1. Collect the data specific to the missing items and the reasons why they are missing. Without good data, it is difficult to take action and focus your resources to improve their processes.
2. Measure and track staff performance on missing items for every case cart and follow-up with each staff member on why he or she was not able to complete the case cart. This provides the opportunity to engage your staff in understanding the root causes or at least thinking about why they were not able to complete the case cart. Engaged staff will then be more likely to suggest improvements as well as make the extra effort to complete the case cart versus passing it off to the next shift or to OR.
3. As needed, confirm your par levels or Kanban levels are accurate to ensure you have what you need for the case cart.
4. Work to maintain continuous flow and minimal backlogs in instrument assembly while simultaneously moving case picking to later times in the evening to improve the likelihood that the instruments needed will be available.
5. No matter how good you think you are, you should always have a documented system to handle incomplete case carts. Whether for supplies or instruments, design procedures that guarantee the missing items are documented and communicated. Root causes should be addressed, and action items developed to eliminate the issues from happening again. While the item is missing, institute an exception process to manage the incomplete case cart that either finds alternate methods to complete it (borrow from sister hospital for example) or work with the OR on alternative replacements. Do not leave the incomplete process to chance and your Customer scrambling to adjust.
~~~~~~

6. In each step, the Lean management system works together with the Lean production system. Your process design and selection determine the operational process, resource requirements, standard work instructions and staff expectations for both productivity and quality. Leadership then follows-up on the performance to plan, identifies variances and improves the process.

Excess Motion

Definition: Unnecessary movement while performing a task or process.

How to see excess motion waste: Look for staff movement that could be reduced, eliminated or that is not directly adding value. Staff leaving their workstations is usually a sign of excess motion. Not having the supplies needed to do the task at hand without walking somewhere to get them is excess motion.

Examples of Excess Motion in SPD:

- Staff assigned to assembly walking back and forth to a printer to retrieve a count sheet or bar code sticker
- Workstations not supplied with the needed items and thus not set up to minimize walking, reaching or bending
- Delivering case carts when they are not needed or used
- Walking back and forth to retrieve a container or wrap a tray
- Ergonomically poor workstation layouts requiring excessive or repetitive reaching, bending, etc.
- Non-linear or non-continuous workflow from decontamination to sterile storage requiring excessive storage racks, transportation routes and handling
- Looking for items that should be readily available
- Searching for missing or poorly located supplies or instruments

Seeing excess motion is not always as easy as it sounds. Often, SPD technicians and leadership team members have grown so accustomed to their current work environment and current "motions" that they do not consider them excess. They simply see the motion as part of the job. In lean terms, they view the motion as value adding when in fact it can be reduced or eliminated and should therefore be considered waste. This takes us back to our earlier discussion on being able to see waste or inversely see value. Seeing excess motion assumes you understand what the absolute required motion is or could be.

During an assessment at a hospital, we spent time on the SPD assembly floor simply watching the staff work while training the supervisors to see waste. If you have ever stood in assembly and watched the staff work, you probably thought that it is a bit boring. During our observation, a staff member left their workstation, the first sign of potential waste, and retrieved a loaner sheet from another workstation to attach to the loaner tray they were handling. After assembling and wrapping the loaner tray, the technician started to assemble a second loaner tray only to stop again and walk over to the same workstation to retrieve another loaner sheet. The supervisor had never taken the time to stop and watch people work with the intention of seeing waste. She immediately picked up on the opportunity to stock loaner tray sheets at each workstation to eliminate the walking.

Sometimes excess motion is a sign of other wastes, but sometimes other wastes cause the excess motion. Every time a technician leaves their workstation to retrieve a missing instrument or return an extra instrument, he or she is experiencing excess motion waste that was caused by a waste upstream in the process. Excess motion is perhaps easiest seen when technicians must leave their workstation, but there are usually opportunities to eliminate excess motion even when they are not leaving their workstation.

One example was in an SPD where the assembly table was a bit smaller than desired, and the computer keyboard and mouse were in the way of the technician assembling and wrapping trays. Every time the technician started the assembly process, he or she used the keyboard and mouse to scan the tray and begin assembly before pushing them out of the way to make room for the tray and wrapping. The technician even attempted to balance the keyboard on top of the barcode printer to make more room which then caused additional excess motion when a label needed to be printed. Even though this type of excess motion takes only a few seconds, it becomes aggravating when you must do it repeatedly throughout the day. Staff satisfaction with their work environment suffers and eventually staff starts looking for solutions to make the job easier. This is the good side of human nature; finding an easier way to do things helps eliminate waste. In this case, the technicians had been moving their keyboards and mouse for over two years and no one had attempted to eliminate the wasted excess motion.

Eliminating Excess Motion

As with every lean waste, the first step in eliminating the waste is to identify it. For excess motion, it is best to categorize waste into two categories, non-value adding or value adding, that could be performed better and with less motion. To understand and identify excess motion, we perform observations to give us the knowledge we need to drive out waste. Let us look at the four major areas in most SPD operations of decontamination, assembly, sterilization and case cart picking to better understand where excess motion may be hiding.

Decontamination

By definition, the value adding activity in decontamination is cleaning or decontaminating the instruments. Anything beyond this is technically waste. In most SPDs, you will have some waste due to room layouts, washer and sink locations and constraints or waste that is non-removable. A typical decontamination usually has the following activities that represent the basic workflow and "motion" in the area.

- Receive dirty or used case cart
- Scan trays and remove from case cart
- Move case cart to cart washer for washing
- Separate rigid containers from instruments and place on cart washer rack
- Move instruments to sink for manual preparation
- Move instruments to automated washer for washing

Do you remember the "decontamination process flow diagram example" from earlier in this chapter with color coded steps showing value and non-value adding steps? I have included it here again as it helps drive the point home in eliminated excess motion. Look at all the Medium Gray steps in the process. Most of these represent excess motion.

Decontamination Process Flow Diagram Example

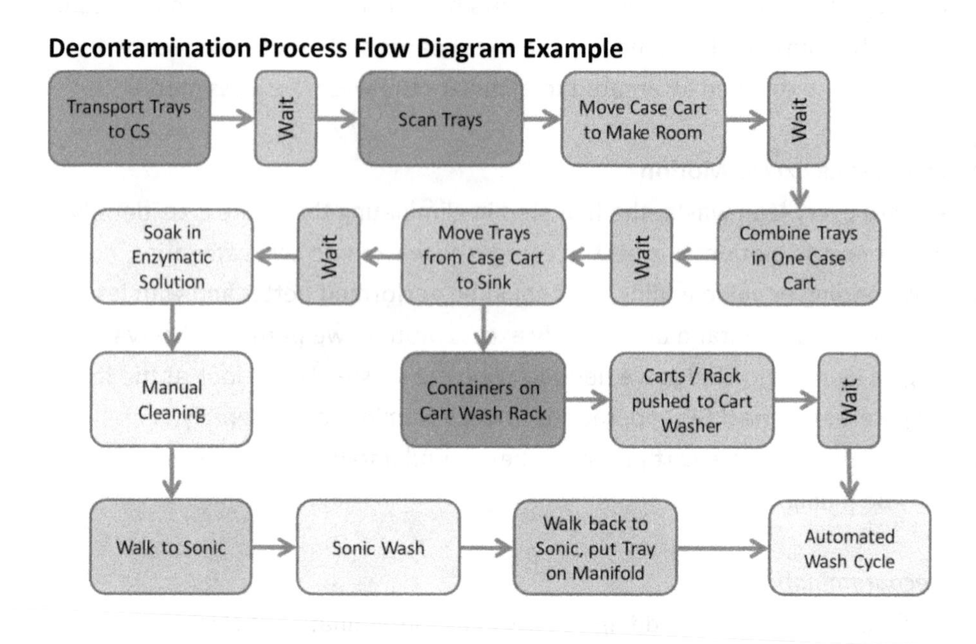

To eliminate the excess motion, you have two options: 1. Eliminate the motion or step in the process or 2. reduce it. By implementing continuous flow practices, the wasted steps shown above "move case cart to make room" and "combine trays in one case cart" can be eliminated. By utilizing new lean sink designs that incorporate sonic washing in the sink, you may be able to remove the motion and waste of walking to the sonic and back. By rearranging where the sinks are in relationship to the instrument washers, you may be able to reduce the amount of walking and motion. Guaranteeing the staff has all the necessary tools to perform their task without having to walk or move away from the direct task of decontaminating instruments will also help reduce excess motion.

Another excess motion opportunity is found in the earlier bullet points outlining the basic workflow steps as well as in the diagram. The bullets mentioned removing the trays from the case cart, pushing the case cart to the cart washer and then moving the trays to the sink. These three steps could be rearranged as moving case cart to the sink and allowing the technician at the sink to work directly from the case cart and, when empty, the case cart is moved to the cart washer.

Another opportunity stated above mentioned providing staff with all the necessary tools needed to perform a task without having to walk or move away from their direct task. This is where Lean 5S or workstation standardization effort may be implemented. 5S is a lean tool providing managers and staff a system to achieve greater organization, workplace standardization, effective cleaning habits and process efficiencies. The five S's are as follows:

- Sort
- Set
- Shine
- Standardize
- Sustain

Sort means to remove all the garbage/items, unused or unrelated, from the workplace while only keeping those items specifically needed to perform the required tasks. *Set* refers to staging everything required to perform the task in its proper, orderly and labeled place with identification for ease of obtaining and use. *Set* also means to return the item back to its proper location after every use. *Shine* means implementing daily and systematic cleaning efforts to maintain the environment. *Standardize* refers to ensuring Sort, Set and Shine are performed in the same manner regardless of who is doing the task and doing it on a frequent interval to maintain the workplace is in perfect condition. *Sustain* is the self-discipline to consistently follow the first four S's. Leadership routines are a great tool to ensure your 5S efforts are sustained.

5S provides an immediate visual impact in the workplace and is a great first step in the improvement process. It is an easy way to start and can be a great momentum builder if properly sustained. It is all about "controlling the conditions" and eliminating waste and frustration associated with searching for items, which makes it a great tool to eliminate excess motion. While the function of 5S is often viewed as focused on organization and housekeeping, 5S is also about establishing standard work, taking pride in one's workplace and instilling the discipline for future improvements.

Within decontamination, observing how staff members work to determine where you can eliminate excess motion will also help you understand how 5S can further improve the workflow and processes. It will help remove waste and improve throughout, productivity and staff satisfaction by ensuring that the staff at the sinks can remain at the sink and perform their tasks without looking for any needed tools, items needed have clearly identified and standardized locations and quantities, and the work environment is clean and orderly

Assembly

Some of the same principles outlined in decontamination apply easily to all areas, including assembly. Start by performing observations to understand the current state then move into 5S activities to organize and eliminate waste. An examples of excess motion waste in assembly would be when a staff member makes multiple trips from the assembly workstation to retrieve an instrument tray for assembly instead of simply staging multiple trays at the assembly workstation once the trays exit the washers. Staff having to move items on their workstation to make room for tray assembly also represents excess motion. Page printers and bar code label printers not within reach require excess motion to retrieve printed items. Finding and matching up containers with trays often has excess motion.

The actual job of assembling a tray can have excess motion as well depending on how technicians handle the individual instruments. How many times do they pick up and move the same instrument? More than once is considered a waste. Motion to retrieve missing instruments is waste as well. Some hospitals have designed service specific assembly tables, pre-stocked with the most common missing instruments experienced from the corresponding service, all within reach of the technician assembling the tray.

Sterilization

Sterilization is a straightforward activity that involves arranging the instruments on a sterilization rack for steam sterilization or placing them directly into the low temperature sterilizer chamber. The items being sterilized are documented either electronically or manually, load parameters are checked and documented according to the instruments sterilization instructions for use and load stickers are then applied. Observations for excess motion may find waste in the staff's motion while placing the instrument trays on the rack or rearranging them, during scanning routines that require multiple back and forth movements to the computer, while recording or documenting one tray at a time instead of recording them all at once or when moving the sterilizer racks out of the way due to space constraints or backlogs.

Case Cart Picking

For most people reading this book, they already know what picking a case cart entails. Just in case you are new to sterile processing, here are the basics. A staff member obtains a list of required items for a surgeon to perform a surgery. The list contains supplies as well as instruments, the amount needed, hopefully the location to find them and sometimes whether the item will be opened and used or held just in case the doctor needs it. The goal for eliminating waste from the case picking activity is to accurately pick all needed items in a timely fashion. While hospitals are getting better at implementing best practices from non-healthcare industries, some have yet to organize their case picking storage in a manner that minimizes labor requirements for picking the items.

First and foremost, the objective should be to reduce the amount of walking a staff member must do to pick the items needed. Secondly, excess motion should be eliminated from how the staff handles the case cart, push cart and other items during the process. This is where a "spaghetti diagram" comes in handy. A spaghetti diagram traces a staff member's movements through a physical area on a floor plan over a certain period of time. The diagram should allow you to see the chance for excess motion through travel patterns that repeat, backtrack, go outside the typical work area and so forth. Let us look at an example spaghetti diagram for a case cart picking process.

The following spaghetti diagram shows a staff member obtaining a pick ticket or preference cart print out from the printer station in the lower section of the room, getting a case cart to fill and then walking through the storage aisles picking the needed items and then taking the case cart out through the top end of the room. The printer station and the storage shelves that items were picked from are color coded in blue.

Spaghetti Diagram of Picking One Case Cast with 15 Items – Walking 814 Feet

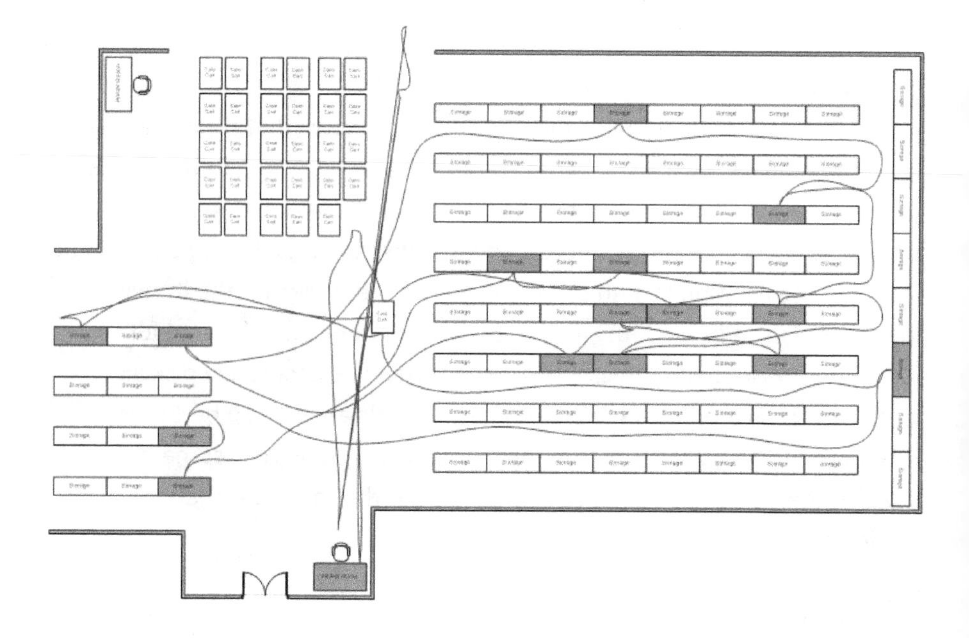

As you can see from the spaghetti diagram, there is no systematic pattern to the picking process. The staff walked to the same storage aisles multiple times to pick different items resulting in excess motion. In total the staff walked 814 feet from the start of the picking process at the printer station to returning to the printer station to start the next case cart.

There are two things you can immediately determine from this exercise. First, rearranging the sequence in which the items are picked could save time. Second, rearranging the physical location of the items could also save time. The following spaghetti diagram shows what happens when the items are listed in order of the picking locations so that items stored in the same area are listed together. The item locations have not changed, but the order they are listed on the pick list has been organized in a manner that minimizes the walking required. Total distance walked in this improved process is 536 feet resulting in a savings of 278 feet walked for one case cart.

Spaghetti Diagram of Picking One Case Cast – Improved Pick Order – Walking 536 Feet

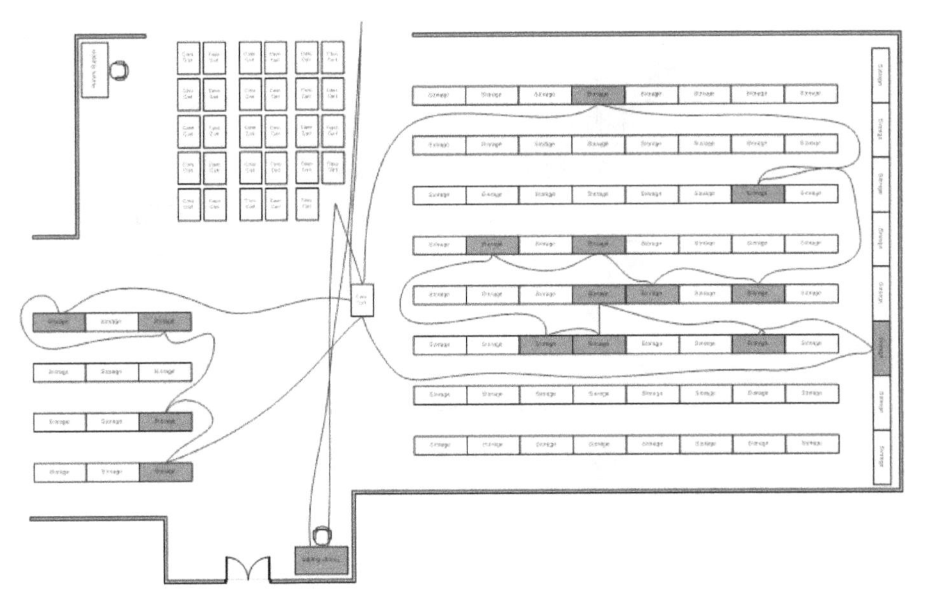

The last step would be to rearrange the actual storage locations of the supplies as well as streamline the staff members walking to the case cart at the beginning of the process. In the previous examples, the staff member walked to the case cart and moved it to the center of the room before starting to pick items. In this last example, staff begin by picking the items at the left of the room, perhaps surgical packs for example, and then deposit those items in the case cart on the way to the other side of the room.

Supplies were also rearranged to position the high-volume items closest to the front of the aisles in hopes that the staff member would not have to walk all the way to the back very often. In this example, only two items picked were moved closer to the aisle but the impact results in less steps walked even though they still had to go to the back wall. Total distance walked in the second improved process is 443 feet resulting in a savings of 371 feet walked for one case cart as compared to the first diagram.

Spaghetti Diagram of Picking One Case Cast – Improved Supply Locations – Walking 443 Feet

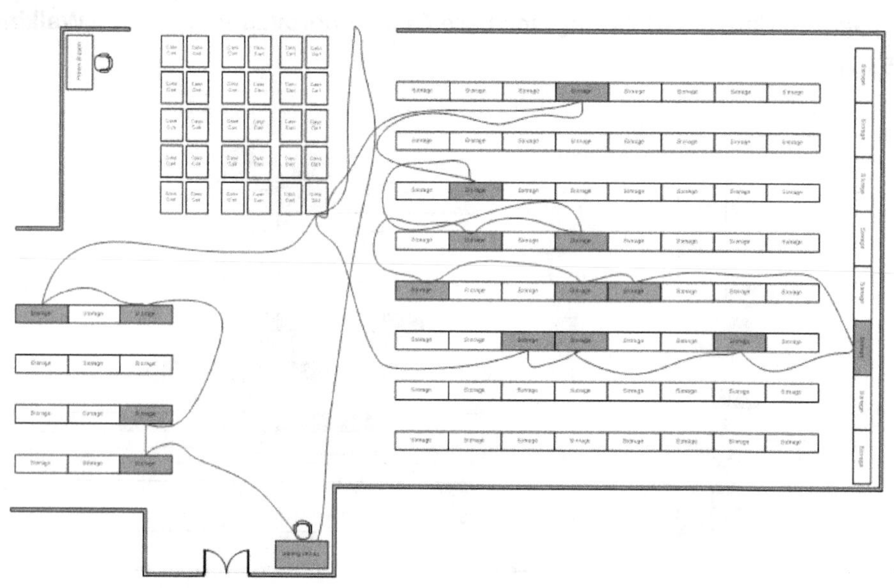

Transportation

Definition: Moving product from one place to another. When something is being transported it is not being worked on and value is not being added.

How to See Transportation Waste: Transportation waste is one of the easier wastes to see although eliminating it can be difficult. Simply stated, anytime you are transporting or moving an instrument tray, a case cart or other materials, you are not adding any value. Moving something from point A to point B, no matter how important the movement is, usually results in no change to the product or service. Thus, if no value is added, then the activity is waste. Your options are to eliminate the transportation all together or, if it is 100% necessary, then reduce or minimize the effort put into the transportation.

Examples of Transportation Waste in SPD:

- Moving dirty case carts from the OR to decontamination
- Moving dirty case carts in decontamination to make room
- Transporting an instrument tray from the sink in decontamination to the sonic cleaner across the room instead of having the sonic cleaner next to the sink; this may be considered excess motion as well
- Unloading the instrument washers and placing the trays on a staging rack and then moving them to an assembly station and then to the sterilization station
- Moving unassembled trays to an assembly workstation and then moving them again to another assembly workstation when the trays are not completed Moving incomplete trays to the incomplete rack where they wait for the instrument to be found
- Transporting trays to sterile storage
- Transporting trays and case carts to the OR
- Moving clean case carts once or multiple times before actually needing the case cart

Everyone's initial reaction when they see this type of list is that most items are 100% necessary and, for the most part, they are right. The physical design of the department and its location play a significant role in the amount of non-value adding transportation required. If you are involved in designing a new department then think through the flow of product and materials through the area and the staff effort required. Then you can predict waste and decide how it can be eliminated or reduced. If you are stuck in a department that was not designed efficiently then you will be faced with finding creative ways to reduce the amount of transportation and the effort put into it.

Eliminating Transportation Waste

As you should now know, the first step in eliminating waste is identifying it. Assuming you have walked the floor and performed "waste observations" to identify opportunities, let us talk about actions you can take to reduce and eliminate transportation waste.

- Moving dirty case carts from the OR to decontamination: While this is necessary, find ways to transport two carts at once instead of one at a time. The transportation of the carts was not eliminated but the labor effort put into the activity can be reduced.
- Moving dirty case carts in decontamination to make room: Moving case carts to make room is usually a sign of an undersized decontamination area or lack of continuous flow. Our experiences show that lack of continuous flow is the most common reason. By not providing enough staff at the right time of day working to planned standards, decontamination could easily backlog with multiple case carts piling up. A large teaching hospital performing 90+ surgical procedures daily had this exact situation and spent 4 to 8 hours of labor a day moving case carts through their decontamination room. We nicknamed the process the "case cart conga dance" as up to 20 case carts slowly moved in a line through the department to the cart washers. The cart washers posed no capacity issue either as the department had three new high-speed washers. The issue was a lack of continuous flow staffing at the right time of day working to standard work and supervisors who actively followed up on the process. With a restructuring of the staffing patterns and a little bit of

supervision, the conga dance disappeared, and the staff assigned to moving the carts was freed up to perform value adding work.

- Transporting an instrument tray from the sink in decontamination to the sonic cleaner across the room instead of having the sonic cleaner next to the sink: This waste is simply a design function. Move the sonic washer closer to the workflow and/or purchase a sonic equipment sink where the sonic is built into the sink well.
- Unloading the instrument washers and placing the trays on a staging rack before moving trays to an assembly station and finally sending them to the sterilization station: While these steps are necessary, minimizing the effort put into them can be looked at. Can washers and assembly stations be positioned closer together? Can trays be taken directly from the washer to an assembly workstation and avoid any staging step in between? Can trays be transported two or more at a time, minimizing the labor used? Can sterilizer racks be positioned next to assembly workstations and the entire rack transported to the sterilizer area by one person? You may classify some of these actions as the waste of excess motion and that is fine. The point is to find waste and eliminate it.

  A large level 1 trauma hospital who processed multiple implant trays a day due to ortho trauma cases had designed their workflow such that implant trays were staged on racks by the washers in the front of the room and then taken to the back of the room by the implant specialist who would restock the implant. Next the trays were taken back to the front of the room and placed on the rack to be assembled by an assembly staff member. After assembly, the tray was then taken to the back of the room again where the sterilizers were located. Process changes were implemented to have the implant specialists assemble the tray and thus reduce the transportation between the front and back of the room.
- Moving unassembled trays to an assembly workstation and then moving them again to another assembly workstation when the trays are not completed: If you are going to move trays to an assembly

table, then try to only do it if the staff assigned will be able to complete the trays. Moving them again is waste.

- Moving incomplete trays to the incomplete rack where they wait for the instrument to be found: There are very good processes being utilized to manage incomplete trays as a "non-conforming product" and separating them from the normal flow. This adds waste to the process. Minimizing the distance traveled is one option, but the best option is to eliminate the missing instrument in the first place, or root cause elimination, and find methods to have backup instrumentation available close by to keep the tray moving in the "conforming" completed process.
- Transporting trays to sterile storage: This is another necessary waste by design, but if possible, you can place the sterile storage in such a way that transportation to and from is minimized. Additionally, try to transport multiple trays at once so the labor per tray utilized is reduced.
- Transporting trays and case carts to the OR: This is another necessary waste that can be reduced by transporting multiple trays at a time, reducing the distance traveled through physical design considerations and only transporting items being used. Cancelled cases and transporting items to the OR only to have them be returned due to more cancellations via more transportation is double the waste.
- Moving clean case carts once or multiple times before actually needing the case cart: Moving case carts multiple times is often a sign of a multi-step case picking process, lack of adequate space or poor processes. Multi-step picking processes are typically caused by staff picking supplies first in the afternoon and them moving the case cart to a waiting area for needed instruments to be processed. After adding the instruments, the case cart is then moved to an OR based location where more supplies are added. In many of these examples, starting the picking process too early in the day results in many case carts not being completed due to unavailable instrumentation. Delaying case cart picking until the evening or night shift has proven to reduce multiple handling and transportation waste.

In review, transportation waste isn't hard to see but it does take effort to eliminate. Most SPDs are stuck where they are, and transportation is a part of their life. If this is your case, then try to minimize the effort required to transport your items and then set standards for your staff to follow and hold them accountable. If it should take 5 minutes to transport two case carts to the OR and the staff have twelve case carts to transport, then hold them accountable to getting the job done in 30 minutes.

Underutilized People

Definition: Lack of engaged staff whose knowledge and intelligence are not being leveraged to eliminate waste and improve the workplace and processes. Listen to staff members' ideas and engage them in the workplace decisions. Encouraging ideas is vital to the ultimate success or failure of Lean practices. A successful company realizes that their biggest assets are their employees.

How to See Underutilized People Waste: Seeing underutilized staff is both easy and hard. It is easy in that most managers can readily tell you which staff members are engaged, and which are not. It is hard to tell in that most SPD managers feel that "productive" staff is an indicator of utilized and engaged staff when in fact it may not be the case. Remember that Lean departments have engaged staff actively involved in improving how the work is done and thus improving the department's level of quality and productivity. This is different than a person being productive but never improving how the work is done.

In working with SPDs, there is a correlation between departments with active process improvement cultures and engaged staff and those who are trying to get the work done today. Remember the difference between being process focused versus outcome focused? Departments who are outcome focused become reactive firefighters very skilled at getting the Customer what they need but never fixing any underlining process or performance issues. Every day is a hold your breath and hope for the best. Proactive departments are those that focus on processes to ensure the outcomes happen in the most efficient and issue free manner. They are always looking at how they can eliminate the fires and leave their firefighters hat at home and let the process work. These proactive departments are also very good at engaging their staff, listening to their ideas and leveraging their knowledge.

The following bullet points have proven to be symptoms of underutilized people waste as well as symptoms of either broken SPDs or departments that are on their way to becoming broken.

Symptoms of Underutilized People in SPD

- High turnover of staff
- Excessive call-ins and sick days
- No process improvement culture or active program
- No departmental performance measurements tracked and posted
- Lack of standard work for activities
- Staff admitting that they do tasks differently from each other
- Lack of organized and up-to-date training program and competencies
- Lack of employee satisfaction surveys or low scores
- Backlogs, disorganized work areas, OR complaints
- Lack of leadership routines and standard work for supervisors
- Dictator style leadership

These symptoms are basically symptoms of a poorly run SPD and thus staff who have no desire or intention of becoming engaged.

Eliminating Underutilized People

A typical first step in understanding the level of engagement and utilization of people in your department is through an employee satisfaction survey. Find out how they feel and if they feel they are part of a team that is working to improve the department or rather a cog in the SPD wheel chained to his or her workstation. If you as a leader of the department truly intend to eliminate underutilized people waste, or stated more positively to create an engaged staff, be prepared to invest time and effort into it. People will feel good about engaging and participating in something only if they see others engaged and caring about it. Rarely does an employee start a movement on his or her own, so the leadership team must begin the culture transformation and become engaged and involved themselves.

The leadership team must also allow their staff members to have a say in things and listen to their ideas. It is often a great recommendation to allow staff to implement their initial improvement ideas even if the leadership team is skeptical of the outcomes. If there is no safety or patient risk impact, allowing the staff to try new ways of improving the work environment and taking the chance of failing or succeeding will set the tone that you want and are willing to trust engaged staff. Obviously, there will be limits, but allowing staff members to fail on their own will tell them you trust them and are taking the engagement seriously. If you shut their ideas down right from the beginning, you will lose the opportunity and the staff will retreat and simply "do their job" instead of improving it.

It is also important to have a clear vision and list of measurable objectives for the department that can direct the staff's efforts to improve things. If you simply ask them for their suggestions on how to make things better, you will get the common answers of "pay us more", "make the OR send the instruments back in the correct tray", "let me work first shift." Focus the conversation and questions to how we can make our performance measurements better or how we can cut our missing instrument rate in half? Reinforce a process-oriented culture that measures performance and works to improve the measurement through process enhancements.

You might be surprised at the level of competence and great ideas your staff has if they feel that their input is valued, and it is safe to talk. In the same hospital that had the case cart Conga, a bright young staff member was assigned to decontamination with two tenured staff. The young staff member worked hard to keep up with flow and reduce backlogs and therefore started making suggestions to the others on how they could make things better. The tenured staff shut her down, spit in her drink at lunch and bullied her into retreating. Fortunately, the situation was identified, and the leadership team made the uncomfortable decision to confront the tenured staff. While this type of culture does not change overnight, leadership's role in developing and maintaining a positive culture for staff to engage in is critical.

Employee engagement can also be measured just like any other key performance measurement. Common measurements to know how well you are eliminating the waste of underutilized people is to measure how many improvement suggestions you received from the staff and set a goal of one suggestion per staff per month. One per month should not be that hard, but we are continuously amazed at how a department of 20 to 30 people can go an entire month without one provided improvement suggestion. That is a sign of underutilized people. In addition to measure the number of suggestions you need to show the staff that their voice is making a difference, so you need to measure how many of the suggestions were implemented. Again, do not be afraid to let staff fail. If you let them ride the bike you also should let them fall. When they do, they will get back up and try again. If you never let them ride the bike, their enthusiasm vanishes.

In all of this, there is reality. Some staff members just prefer to come to work and do their job and go home. Others come to work and prefer to talk about making improvements while doing no work. It is up to leadership to manage their staff and to encourage them to participate in a manner they are comfortable with. Some will provide suggestions privately one-on-one but never in a group. Others love being heard in a group setting and sometimes must be reminded to let others talk. In the end, the goal is to create an environment where the staff actively works with the leadership team to improve how the work is done, resulting in improvements in performance measurements and increased staff satisfaction.

Excess Inventory

Definition: Having too much of anything that is not needed at the time it is needed.

How to See Excess Inventory Waste: There are two ways to see excess inventory: visually and calculated. Visually refers to physically seeing what should be in inventory, perhaps through visual management tools, versus what is in inventory. Calculated refers to inventory reports, documents or analysis that shows excess inventory as compared to needed amounts. For SPDs, excess inventory can be grouped into SPD managed inventory items and OR managed inventory items that impact SPD.

Examples of Excess Inventory that SPD Manages:

- Excess reprocessing supplies on hand tying up purchasing dollars and storage space
- Supplies that expire
- Workstations over stocked causing disorganized work area
- Extra instrument bins with instruments that haven't been used in the past year

Most of SPD managed excess inventory can be easily managed and reduced through purchasing procedures and 5S activities in the work area. OR Managed excess inventory that impacts SPD is a harder issue to attack.

Examples of Excess Inventory that OR manages that impacts SPD

- Obsolete or unused instrument trays in inventory
- Excess peel packs of single instruments stocked just in case but not used
- Instrument trays with too many instruments that are not used during surgery
- Surgeon preference cards not updated that drive excess inventory of supplies and instruments

These OR managed items increase storage space requirements, tie up capital dollars in inventory, and increase SPD workload every time unused instruments are reprocessed.

Eliminating Excess Inventory

Let us start with the SPD managed excess inventory. Step one is to conduct a 5S workshop and clean up the department by removing all the inventory and items that are either not needed or have become obsolete, expired or are cluttering the workplace. Step two is to standardize your supply reordering system. Only order supplies based on actual usage at an interval that is cost efficient but also minimizes labor requirements to order, receive and stock supplies. The third step is to confirm that inventory is being rotated so that items do not expire. Step four is to continue your 5S with workstation organization and a sustainable cleaning and organization process.

The last step and one that usually takes the longest is cleaning up the extra instruments. Determine what instruments you need on hand and then remove the rest. Next, create organized bins or locations to store the instruments you are keeping and then label each bin. Assign staff responsibility for maintaining the instruments in an orderly fashion and give them dedicated time to do it. Then, create standard work that dictates what to do with an extra instrument found in a tray as well as what to do when there is an instrument missing. What you do not want is the "homeless" bin of instruments piling up again. Technicians must adhere to the standard work of returning extra instruments to their correct labeled home or peel pack them per their actual home or use. The standard work should probably first address the process to complete instrument trays; an extra instrument in one set is most likely the missing instrument in another set.

Once you have cleaned up your department, removed excess inventory and have a handle on your extra instrument inventory, look at the OR managed excess inventory. The easiest items for an SPD to tackle are unused instrument trays and peel packs in inventory. Since most SPDs have access to usage data through their sterilization records or scanning systems they can utilize hard factual data to determine what trays and peel packs are simply sitting on the shelf and not moving. Manually, you could walk through the storage aisles and look for sterilization stickers that are 12 months or older and you would probably be safe in saying that those instruments are not used anymore. At this point, present your data to the OR director with two options. The first option is to move the items to a temporary storage location out of your work area to free up valuable space. Agree to a length of time the instruments can stay in the temporary storage location, and if they still are not used, then move to the second options. Option two is to agree that the instruments are no longer needed, and they can be broken down into singles, used to create new trays or peel packs or removed by selling or donating them to worthwhile cause.

The harder OR managed excess inventory is in dealing with extra instruments inside the tray that aren't used or at least assumed to be no longer used and surgeon preference cards that are inaccurate. Tray optimization is a term often utilized when leaning out instrument trays and removing individual instruments that aren't utilized. Optimization can also be used to combine similar trays into one standard tray or standardizing multiple trays into one. These efforts require the OR's involvement and if positioned correctly can not only help remove waste from the SPD workflow but also benefit the OR staff during surgery. How you go about making this happen differs between OR's and is a topic we'll leave for future discussions but it's safe to say that there's opportunity to be gained with the OR's help and assistance.

<u>Overproduction</u>

Definition: Producing more of something than is needed, faster than it is needed or before it is needed.

How to See Overproduction Waste: Overproduction is a less obvious waste in a sterile processing department. Here is why: Typically, the department is reprocessing items that their Customer has requested for them to process. Thus, everything they do is because of a Customer request. You could argue none of it was overproduction. There are a few circumstances in SPD though that could be considered overproduction:

- SPD building case carts too early and having the cases cancelled
- Excessive 'stat' or quick turn processing or IUSS (immediate use steam sterilization) for items the OR then does not use
- Pre-counting supplies for floor trays such as 4"x4" gauzes only to have the person assembling the tray recount them again
- Assembling instrument trays that are not needed while priority trays that are needed sit on the shelf waiting

These examples are overproduction waste in that the time spent was either totally wasted, such as building cancelled case carts, or wasted due to other staff's decisions or efforts. The fourth bullet point though brings up an argument that we have run into with traditional lean practitioners applying strict lean principles to sterile processing. Overproduction in manufacturing terms can apply to producing any product that has not been ordered by a Customer. Thus, they would never manufacture a product to fill inventory in hopes of a Customer purchasing it. Traditional lean practitioners have used this thought process to state that SPDs should not assemble or process any instrument tray until it is scheduled by the Customer for use. The obvious danger with this is what if the OR unexpectedly needs the instrument tray while the patient is on the table and SPD does not have it ready. Another way to look at this thought process though is to realize that when the OR sends an instrument tray to SPD for reprocessing they are effectively sending a Kanban signal telling SPD to refill the inventory item. Every SPD Customer I have spoken with absolutely desires all their instruments to be reprocessed in a timely manner and returned to inventory ready for use and not sit in the SPD department waiting for a case to be scheduled requiring the instrument.

With this type of thinking, most of the work SPD does is considered requested by the Customer with the expectation that it will be completed in a timely manner and thus overproduction is typically not an issue.

Eliminating Over Production

Based on the examples given, eliminating overproduction focuses on ensuring that tasks are performed only when they are certain to be needed, done in a priority order and not redone by someone later in the process.

Excessive Processing

Definition: Performing extra steps beyond the standard work instructions or putting more effort into the work as required by the Customer.

How to See Excessive Processing Waste: Seeing excessive processing can be difficult, but once you understand the waste you will probably start to see it throughout the department. Remember, excessive processing is not overproducing too much of an item, that is over production. Rather spending too much time and energy on the item you are supposed to be producing. Often, work that people consider as value adding or beneficial and necessary is excessive processing. Rework or redoing a task that another person has already done is one of the easiest to see. Harder to see examples include staff spending more time or working beyond the standard work instructions, spending time on a task that should have been avoided if the staff members working on the upstream process had done their task correctly, used quality audits and double checked that the same information had not been entered more than once.

Examples in SPD:

- Quality checks or audits performed on instruments to confirm accurate assembly; lean would ensure the assembly process produces correctly assembled trays thus eliminating the need for quality checks
- Staff reassembling an instrument tray left from an earlier staff member who started but did not complete the tray
- Staff spending more time and effort on cleaning or assembling a tray than is required by the standard work instruction
- Staff spending time correcting the state of the instruments because the upstream process did not properly perform their task, such as the OR not spraying or removing gross contamination from instruments at the end of the case causing additional processing in decontamination
- Staff manually recording sterilization records while simultaneously scanning the information into the tracking system
- Staff manually recording tray inventory against next day's requirements to produce a priority list only to have the case cart team also produce a priority list based on missing instruments

Eliminating Excessive Processing

Understanding Customer requirements and creating and adhering to Standard Work is key to eliminating excessive processing. Take the time to watch the workflow and how staff perform their tasks to identify any non-value adding activities. Watch for redundant processing steps and ask the question, "How can we stop doing this activity and still produce quality products and services?" For example, we have seen quality audits being performed in SPDs with reportedly improved results of less defects. While quality audits represent excessive processing their use usually represents an underlying issue with process quality, staff adherence to standard work or staff carelessness all of which should be addressed through employee engagement and active leadership routines. The goal would be to reduce the quality audits to the point that the process and regular follow-up is ensuring quality products and the audits are no longer needed.

~~~~~~

City Hospital: Eliminating Waste

Scene: Rob is preparing for his monthly department review with his manager, the Perioperative Director, and is proudly printing out his Key Performance Metrics all of which show improvement across the board. It has been three months since he kicked off the Lean SPD initiative and he is feeling good about the progress. It has been three months since Karen gave him 90 days to make a difference.

"Come on in Rob," Karen looks up from her desk smiling. Rob feels a bit relieved to see her smile. He also notices all the inspirational messages in her office and for some reason feels drawn to the one that says, "A successful manager hires good people and then gets out of their way." He wonders if he is a successful manager and that is why Karen does not spend too much time with him.

Karen begins right away. "Ok. I want to do something a little different today. We'll go over your department measurements, which it looks like you're ready to share," Karen notices the color graphs and Rob's smile. "But I've also asked Deana and Beth to join us in about 10 minutes to share how the OR feels about the improvements you've made."
~~~~~~

Rob's smile fades a bit as Deana and Beth are not always the most SPD friendly people but he realizes that they are his Customer and in the last 90 days his department has made a lot of progress.

"Alright sounds good. Shall I start with my KPI's?" Rob asks.

Rob and Karen review the department's performance for the past week and month as well as the recently added 90-day trending graph. He has not forgotten his meeting with Karen three months ago when he was given 90 days to make a difference.

"Wow, you've made some great progress. Backlogs are down. You're measuring quality and seem to have a handle on it. Complete case carts and instrument trays are all showing improvement." Karen pauses and then waves in Deana and Beth who were waiting outside the door.

"I can stay for only a little bit," Deana offers up. "Dr. Ancline wants to meet about new equipment before he leaves today."

"OK. We can make this quick," Karen says. "Rob and I were just reviewing the progress he's made in the past 90 days and it looks pretty good. Not only is he measuring multiple performance metrics but they've all improved since we last met; every single one of them." Karen slides the KPI graphs to Beth.

"I've noticed the staff seem to be a bit more relaxed," Beth adds as she looks at the graphs.

Deana is not too interested in the graphs. "Shall I share what we discussed earlier?" Deana asks Karen.

"Sure. First though I want Rob to know that, Deana, Beth, myself and the other Coordinators all appreciate the work you've done Rob. You've taken control of the department and we appreciate it. In preparing to see you today, I asked Deana and Beth how the improvements in SPD have helped them out and I was a bit surprised by their comments, so I asked them to come in today to share."

Rob sinks into the chair, again, waiting for the bad news.

"Karen told us about how the department is improving, and I guess I could say that things are getting better, but it's just that my staff doesn't feel like it is better," Deana states in her direct approach. "We still have issues we're dealing with and I agree with Beth that the staff do seem a bit friendlier, but we're still having issues."

"Your graphs do look great, and I know you're on the right track but I agree with Deana that we aren't feeling it in the OR yet." Beth adds.

Karen sees Rob is losing the excitement he had when he first came to the meeting. "Rob, you are doing good work and the numbers prove it. Don't take these comments as if we're unhappy with you or think you're failing, because you aren't. You are actually doing things in that department that no one has been able to do for many years." Karen again smiles at Rob, making him feel a bit better.

"I asked you to reduce the backlogs and you've done that and more. Now we have to figure out why your improvements aren't making the difference in the OR that we need." Karen seems to have a calming influence over everyone.

"Um, well I'm not sure what to tell you. I'm getting my staff involved in making things better. Our backlogs are down to the mid-sixties and our error rates have all dropped." Rob states.

"Something that would help us is if we didn't have to run and get things that should have already been ready when we need them," Beth interjects. "Is there any way you can help us by having someone make sure everything is ready to go in the morning?"

"I can't add any more staff if that's what you're asking for," Rob responds not knowing what to say.

Deana and Beth add a few more comments and then leave to finish their day while Rob and Karen talk for a few minutes.

"Here's what I think," Karen leans in towards Rob. "We need to continue improving the KPI's and you're doing that, but we also need to do something physical in the OR to make an impact on the nurses. An improvement in your graph may impact them by reducing three issues to two or even one issue, but they still have an issue and that's what I think they are saying."

Rob's thinking a mile a minute now and realizes something. "You know what? You're right. As long as there's one thing wrong, the nurses will always feel we're not getting the job done. But if I had someone there to handle the one thing that was wrong, then the nurse wouldn't have to worry about it. The issue is still there, but if I take care of it then it goes away for them."

With a smile on his face, Rob continues. "That's what I think Deana and Beth were trying to say when they said the nurses weren't feeling it. They don't care if my graphs look better; they just want someone to deal with the issues for them. I could have all the issues in the world but if I dealt with them for the OR and they didn't have to, they'd think I was great!"

"Well let's not go that far," Karen remarks. "But I think you are correct in that they need to feel the difference. Perhaps you can assign one of your morning team members to be in the OR Core and do nothing but get the OR what they need, kind of like a liaison or Customer service person."

Rob and Karen come to an agreement that the department is going in the right direction and the lean project is working. However, they need to do something to ensure their Customer is "satisfied" while the SPD continues its lean improvement journey. Rob leaves the meeting with mixed feelings. Rob's boss is happy with him and the department is improving, but the improvements were not impacting his Customer how he thought they would.

Perhaps he had not done a good enough job listening to his Customers? He knew they wanted complete instrument trays and case carts on-time without errors, but what he did not realize is that they wanted someone there to help them when there was an issue.

~~~~~~
~~~~~~

Chapter Thirteen: Continuous Improvement

Our Job is NOT to reprocess surgical instrumentation.

Our Job is to CONTINUOUSLY IMPROVE how we reprocess surgical instrumentation.

Continuous Improvement is the last and perhaps most important step in creating a Lean SPD! It embodies the true essence of lean, that you can always be better. To continuously improve is to get a little better every day. It's not about being the best but simply being better than you were yesterday. To dive even deeper, think of it as not only the department getting a little better but every single employee finding a way to be better today than yesterday. Once you put it in terms of every person in the department getting better you suddenly realize the task is bigger than you ever thought.

Taiichi Ohno, of Toyota Production System fame, once said the following.

"If you are going to do Kaizen continuously (incremental change for the good), you've got to assume that things are a mess. Too many people just assume that things are all right the way they are. Aren't you guys convinced that the way you're doing things is the right way? That's no way to get anything done. Kaizen is about changing the way things are. If you assume that things are all right the way they are, you can't do Kaizen. So, change something!"

Continuous improvement is about change. Never ending change. Change creates friction and is often uncomfortable. Most people avoid change. To create a culture of continuous improvement is to create a culture that accepts and embraces change. This is not easy. Culture can defeat knowledge, expertise and effort every time. Culture can be good and bad. The question is how do we create a positive culture which accepts change for continuous improvement to flourish.

Developing a Culture of Continuous Improvement

Healthcare organizations are finding themselves in a more competitive world than ever before. To survive or die is often a very potent motivator for change. These competitive challenges require an approach to change and improvement that is rapid, produces positive results and is sustainable. It requires the development of a continuous improvement culture in which every individual is growing, learning and contributing to the growth and improvement goals of the organization and that allows employees to have complete ownership over the quality of their work. While executives managing the financial health of the healthcare system can identify with a need for change, front line staff in the sterile processing department may not feel the same urgency or need for change. Within the basement walls of sterile processing, the competitive marketplace pressures seem far removed from trying to find the missing instrument or confirm all case carts are completed for tomorrow's cases.

So, what is culture anyway? In its simplest terms culture is how people are incentivized to think, act, talk and work every day. In an organization, it is based on a system or structure that allows desired behaviors to happen consistently. Changing culture is not an overnight process though. Companies who have successfully developed positive, continuous improving, Customer focused cultures have spent years developing, maturing, and adjusting to changing conditions to be successful.

Lean can be best described as a journey. It is not a one-time process improvement effort, value stream mapping exercise or Kaizen event. It is a way of life. Lean is also a maturing process. Companies do not immediately "do lean" and perfect it the first time. It takes practice, experience and effort to mature into a lean organization. Companies and departments who have successfully implemented lean, first started with simple process improvement tools before maturing to active lean leadership routines to finally employee engagement and continuous improvement culture. This maturing factor is the result of cultural change. Whether the culture changes and produces the lean maturity or the lean maturity produces the cultural change is debatable but the two are interdependent. You cannot be successful in lean in the long run without a positive continuous improvement lean culture.

Peter Drucker, management consultant and author, is credited with stating, "Lean culture is the sum of its individual habits. Lean management is a systematic way to shape those habits".

Management, or Leadership, has the most direct impact on creating and sustaining culture; both good and bad. Simply put, you are truly blessed if you are lucky enough to have a manager who naturally develops positive culture where employees are engaged, processes are improving, and Customers are satisfied with operational performance. However, not all are naturally gifted in this area. In fact, it is quite hard to find someone who is gifted in managing processes and operational performance while simultaneously being gifted in managing and motivating people. Whether this is a left brain / right brain dilemma, I am not quite sure!

This is where we could dive into an entire book on leadership and developing the leadership skills to motivate and manage people. While the lean concepts we have presented will help develop positive leadership skills, we will stay focused on processes and tools you can utilize to engage your staff on the lean journey to develop leadership routines to support a culture of continuous improvement.

Since lean is traditionally seen as evolving from the Toyota Production System, it seems right to go back in time to understand how the Japanese initially began their own lean culture transformation. In fact, we need to travel to post World War II with the introduction of American Edward Deming to the Japanese Union of Scientist and Engineers.

In 1950, Deming trained engineers, managers and scholars in statistical process control and concepts of quality. His message to Japan's chief executives was that improving quality would reduce expenses while increasing productivity and market share. Japanese manufacturers applied his techniques and teachings and soon were experiencing world class levels of quality and productivity. Deming's teachings helped create products with improved quality at a lower cost that resulted in a market demand for Japanese products. Hopefully you will have absorbed enough lean knowledge to know that Deming's teachings were the foundation to today's lean methods.

Japan's entry into the U.S. car market was viewed by most Americans as nothing more than "cheap Japanese cars." What most of us did not realize was that the cheap cars would soon exceed the quality of American cars and Japan's market share would continually grow for decades to come. Ironically, Japan's embracement of Deming's teachings went largely unnoticed in the United States until Ford Motor Company hired Deming to help them in 1981 over 30 years after he shared his teachings with Japan.

Having lost nearly $1 billion per year for three years, Ford desperately needed a cultural and operational performance change. Their decision to hire Deming was aimed at improving the quality of Ford's automobiles. Surprisingly, Deming did not talk about quality, but rather management and he questioned the company's culture and the way its managers operated. He told Ford that management actions were responsible for 85 percent of all problems in developing better cars.

By 1986, Ford had turned the profitability corner and credited their quality culture and turnaround directly to Deming's teachings. That same year, Ford's earnings exceeded General Motors and they became the most profitable American auto company.

During this period, Deming published his book *Out of the Crisis*, offering his famous 14 Points for Management theory. He states that management's failure to plan for the future brings about loss of market which leads to loss of jobs. Management must be judged not only by the quarterly dividend but by innovative plans to stay in business, protect investment, ensure future dividends and provide more jobs through improved products and services. Long-term commitment to new learning and new philosophy is required of any management that seeks transformation. The timid and the fainthearted and the people that expect quick results are doomed to disappointment.

In short, Deming was stating what American companies were feeling; if they did not change and continuously improve, they would go out of business.

His 14 Management Principles were Deming's foundation for creating a continuous improvement culture. The philosophical and management basis for pursuing quality, according to Deming, is by designing systems that foster an attitude of doing things right the first time. At the philosophies core is recognizing the Customer as a priority and developing people as the most important resource to achieve that quality by enabling continuous improvement throughout the enterprise. It further defines the culture where employees oversee their own jobs, design their own standard work and are authorized to make changes to improve the standard work.

This philosophy applies directly to the Lean Pillar of Employee Engagement where employees are respected and developed as key contributors to the department's success.

The website Mindtools.com, "Essential Skills for an Excellent Career", has a nice summary of Deming's fourteen points with easy to understand bullet point snippets to help explain each. The summary is shared below. The website is https://www.mindtools.com/pages/article/newSTR_75.htm.

Deming's 14-Point Philosophy (as explained by Mindtools.com):

1. **Create a constant purpose toward improvement.**
    - Plan for quality in the long term.
    - Resist reacting with short-term solutions.
    - Do not just do the same things better; find better things to do.
    - Predict and prepare for future challenges and always have the goal of getting better.
2. **Adopt the new philosophy.**
    - Embrace quality throughout the organization.
    - Put your customers' needs first rather than reacting to competitive pressure and design products and services to meet those needs.
    - Be prepared for a major change in the way business is done. It is about leading, not simply managing.
    - Create your quality vision and implement it.
3. **Stop depending on inspections.**
    - Inspections are costly and unreliable, and they do not improve quality. They merely find a lack of quality.
    - Build quality into the process from start to finish.
    - Do not just find what you did wrong; eliminate the "wrongs" altogether.
    - Use statistical control methods and not just physical inspections alone to prove that the process is working.
4. **Use a single supplier for any one item.**
    - Quality relies on consistency. The less variation you have in the input, the less variation you will have in the output.
    - Look at suppliers as your partners in quality. Encourage them to spend time improving their own quality. They should not compete for your business based on price alone.
    - Analyze the total cost to you, not just the initial cost of the product.
    - Use quality statistics to ensure that suppliers meet your quality standards.

5. **Improve constantly and forever.**
    - Continuously improve your systems and processes. Deming promoted the "Plan-Do-Check-Act" approach to process analysis and improvement.
    - Emphasize training and education so everyone can do their jobs better.
    - Use "Kaizen" as a model to reduce waste and to improve productivity, effectiveness and safety.
6. **Use training on the job.**
    - Train for consistency to help reduce variation.
    - Build a foundation of common knowledge.
    - Allow workers to understand their roles in the "big picture."
    - Encourage staff to learn from one another and provide a culture and environment for effective teamwork.
7. **Implement leadership.**
    - Expect your supervisors and managers to understand their workers and the processes they use.
    - Do not simply supervise but rather provide support and resources so that each staff member can do his or her best. Be a coach instead of a policeman.
    - Figure out what each person needs to do his or her best.
    - Emphasize the importance of participative management and transformational leadership.
    - Find ways to reach full potential and do not just focus on meeting targets and quotas.
8. **Eliminate fear.**
    - Allow people to perform at their best by ensuring that they are not afraid to express ideas or concerns.
    - Let everyone know that the goal is to achieve high quality by doing more things right and that you are not interested in blaming people when mistakes happen.
    - Make workers feel valued and encourage them to look for better ways to do things.
    - Ensure that your leaders are approachable and that they work with teams to act in the company's best interests.

- Use open and honest communication to remove fear from the organization.

9. **Break down barriers between departments.**
    - Build the "internal customer" concept. Recognize that each department or function serves other departments that use their output.
    - Build a shared vision.
    - Use cross-functional teamwork to build understanding and reduce adversarial relationships.
    - Focus on collaboration and consensus instead of compromise.
10. **Get rid of unclear slogans.**
    - Let people know exactly what you want. Do not make them guess. "Excellence in service" is short and memorable, but what does it mean? How is it achieved? The message is clearer in a slogan like "You can do better if you try."
    - Do not let words and nice-sounding phrases replace effective leadership. Outline your expectations and then praise people face-to-face for doing good work.
11. **Eliminate management by objectives.**
    - Look at how the process is carried out, not just numerical targets. Deming said that production targets encourage high output and low quality.
    - Provide support and resources so that production levels and quality are high and achievable.
    - Measure the process rather than the people behind the process.
12. **Remove barriers to pride of workmanship.**
    - Allow everyone to take pride in their work without being rated or compared.
    - Treat workers the same and do not make them compete with other workers for monetary or other rewards. Over time, the quality system will naturally raise the level of everyone's work to an equally high level.
13. **Implement education and self-improvement.**
    - Improve the current skills of workers.

- Encourage people to learn new skills to prepare for future changes and challenges.
- Build skills to make your workforce more adaptable to change and better able to find and achieve improvements.

14. **Make "transformation" everyone's job.**
    - Improve your overall organization by having each person take a step toward quality.
    - Analyze each small step and understand how it fits into the larger picture.
    - Use effective change management principles to introduce the new philosophy and ideas in Deming's 14 points.

Challenges in Developing and Sustaining a Culture of Continuous Improvement

Most likely, everyone reading this book will acknowledge that building a culture of continuous improvement is not easy. Many have tried but few have succeeded. A successful continuous improvement culture is one in which the employees are educated, engaged and incentivized to work toward the goals of the organization. It is an environment in which a leader can walk away and the employees can sustain themselves in pursuing higher targets of quality, productivity and Customer service by implementing process improvements. This process takes time (years and even decades) and a commitment.

Continuous Improvement may be initiated at any level of the organization structure. It may be strategically developed and driven from the executive levels of the organization. It may be started as a grass-roots initiative by employees recognizing that there is a better way of completing a process. It may begin at a department level by a forward-thinking, progressive manager. In any event, the eventual growth, success and sustainability of a continuous improvement culture requires the support and engagement of the top leaders in the organization. Only by this level of commitment and dedication to the fundamentals can a culture of continuous improvement be developed.

One of the fundamental challenges every organization faces in this journey is with employee engagement. Employees at all levels of an organization are resistant to change. It is a natural tendency to continue doing what we know and what we are comfortable. The table below, adapted and modified from Healthcare Kaizen, Graban and Swartz, shows some of the common reasons for resistance to continuous improvement and possible counter measures.

Common Barriers	Counter-Measure Approach
People do not think we need to change or improve.	There is always room for improvement. Take a team approach to finding and seeing possibilities. Do not just look for "problems." The definition is too narrow.
Others are resistant to change or fear getting in trouble with coworkers.	Let us learn from their experience; engage them in the team process development.
Lack of time and lack of confidence in self or others	Re-evaluate priorities and enlist expert resources to help facilitate change and growth.
Reward for firefighting	Plan for success and to avoid problems; improve processes to address known "fires." Dis-incentivize reactive behavior by evaluating failures, planning your time, leaving a percent for unknowns and building in continuous improvement.
Fear of getting in trouble for admitting we have problems	Process issues are generally the result of management design. Department managers and supervisors must feel non-threatened in raising long-standing issues. Keep in mind also, mistakes are not failures, they are simply the process of eliminating ways that will not work to come closer to the ways that will.
We forget to follow up on ideas, and people give up when they do not receive a response.	Establish a routine for accountability including a detailed action item capture, assignment and follow-up technique. Ensure the feedback loop is closed on all ideas.

Administration only wants cost savings	Process improvement is a long-term approach to improving organizational performance with less risk of destroying value when compared to short-term approaches. Ensure top level commitment to the continuous improvement process.
Lack of trust in organization and fear of losing jobs	Open some channels: communication and shared successes. Gain executive commitment to reallocating "freed" resources to more improvement.
Perceived lack of control if I let people do Kaizen	Empower people to do their best.
My people jump to solutions.	Great! Now improve your role as a coach and change-agent to improve results.

Steps to Developing a Culture of Continuous Improvement

While it is difficult to list the perfect method to developing a positive and continuous improvement culture, the following points provide a good roadmap to follow:

- Communicate Expectations
  All expectations should be communicated clearly and regularly. These expectations might include punctuality to work and from breaks, attendance to regular meetings and training, participation in continuous improvement projects and completing assignments on time.

- Follow-Up on Expectations
  Communicating expectations will only go so far if you do not follow-up and let everyone know that they are expected to adhere to the expectations. Creating a culture of "adherence" is the first step to creating a culture of continuous improvement.

- Assess Current Knowledge and Skills
  In sterile processing both clinical knowledge and processes and continuous improvement skills are required. Routinely gauge staff competencies on work processes and develop and measure contribution capabilities to process improvement.

- Deliver Information and Appropriate Training
  To implement change, you must provide a clear vision and understanding of the change required along with the skills and tools necessary to see opportunity, evaluate process and make change happen. Remember that people do not naturally see waste or value. It is a learned skill and requires an investment in your people.

- Explain to Everyone Why They Matter
  In SPD it is easy to become disconnected from your Customers. People need to know that the job they do makes a difference and can have a significant impact on the patient's outcome. Routinely engage employees with the Customer including observations within the OR. The ideas, thoughts and questions may generate new ways of doing things.

- Provide Encouragement
  Praise employees for advancement, certifications or mastery of a new skill. Commend them on contributions to process improvements. Public acknowledgement on excellence can lead to heightened motivation and encouragement to further their skills development.

- Allow Room for Mistakes
  Continuous improvement is often a case of trial and error with the target of excellence ever-present. Your people must feel safe if they experiment and do not succeed. Hold them accountable to prevent them from repeating the same error but give them coaching to grow.

- Engage Customers, Suppliers and other Stakeholders
  Without the engagement of these groups, your continuous improvement journey will be only partially successful. You need their involvement. Many sterile processing staff laugh at the idea of the OR doing anything to help them or administration executive leadership even knowing where their department is but it should not be this way. Actively engage and communicate with your internal Customers and stakeholders. Invite vendors to participate.

- Develop Leaders as Change Agents
  While change can be initiated at any level, a shift in culture requires leadership. This is often overlooked with the expectation that if we introduce the continuous improvement process and provide "management support," then we can develop the front line and the groundswell from the employees will create the desired culture shift. Unfortunately, many attempts at Lean have followed this path and most often failed. Your efforts are usually only as good as your leadership. Therefore, develop your leadership.

Requirements for Successful Continuous Improvement Programs

- Consistent Messaging
  The organization and department's purpose must be clear to everyone while providing value to the Customer, developing smooth value stream processes and engaging everyone in improving the processes and flow. Whether communicated through a SPD Charter, Key Performance Metrics, Vision and Mission statements or weekly team meetings, consistently remind staff what their objective is.

- Knowledgeable Leaders
  I am sure you have gotten the message by now that leadership is critical to the success of your lean journey. You must invest in your leadership team. Leaders must understand and preferably have experience in continuous improvement processes. They must "walk

the talk" and demonstrate the desired culture. Some say leaders are born leaders, other state that leaders can be developed. I believe both to be true. Either way, budget time and money to invest in your leadership team.

- Committed
  A simple fact in life is that nothing survives, thrives and becomes successful without a commitment to the effort. Continuous improvement processes and cultural change will only happen if the organization is committed to the long-term success. This starts at the top with executive and managerial commitment and investment of time and effort. The lean journey cannot and will not be successful with a management proclamation and kick-off event only to then assume the staff and local department supervisor or manager will handle it from there. The entire organization must be committed to the cause and realize that the commitment will take time, effort and work.

- Encouraging
  Employee engagement will only happen if staff feel encouraged, respected and invested in. Developing your staff starts with encouragement. Not every staff member will be excited about engaging in process improvement projects, but you may be surprised who is just waiting to be asked to help.

- Investment
  Lean journeys, cultural change and continuous improvement transformations do not happen without investment. Success comes through investment, training, obtaining expert resources and providing the staff what they need to improve. Investments include financial, time, materials and emotional support.

Using the Eight Steps to Creating a Lean SPD to Enable Culture of Continuous Improvement

The entirety of this book has led to this moment and this point. The 8 Steps to Creating a Lean SPD is about the 8 Steps to Creating a Continuous Improvement Culture. Let us review the eight steps with a view of how they can and will lead your sterile processing department through the lean journey to becoming a continuously improving department.

Customer Requirements (Lean Management System)

A Perfect or Lean SPD identifies their Customer expectations, how well they are meeting them and exactly what, where, who and why they are not meeting them.

By focusing on your Customer requirements and how well you are meeting them, you will continuously and naturally identify opportunities for improvement. I have not met a sterile processing department that is perfect and do not envision I will, but I am happy to report there are some who are working towards perfection. Remember the daily question you can ask yourself, "We weren't perfect today, but where was the opportunity to improve?"

Measurements (Lean Management System)

A perfect or Lean SPD measures their performance historically and in real time. It can identify an off-schedule or off-plan situation immediately and take corrective action.

We covered a multitude of measurements in the Measurement chapter and hope every reader realizes that measurements by nature point out opportunities. It does not guarantee that you will naturally transform into a culture of continuous improvement, but if you take your measurements seriously you will have plenty of data that will point you to where the improvement opportunities exist. Continuous improvement cultures thrive on measurements. They embrace them instead of fearing them.

Understanding how you are performing should not be a negative experience, but rather a positive identification of where your next process improvement, Kaizen event, value stream map or 5 Why's exercise needs to take place. Those interested in becoming the best they can welcome the analysis of where they can improve.

Developing a Lean Operational Plan (Lean Management System)

A perfect or Lean SPD develops a detailed operational plan and ensures everyone knows what should be happening, when it should happen, how long it should take and what the results should be.

Developing an operational plan and ensuring every employee understands the plan and his or her role in it is perhaps the key to developing employee engagement and discovering where we can improve. Without a plan, no one knows how things should work, how long things should take or what the work standard should be. By defining how the department should operate will give you the baseline to understand where you can improve. Remember the Perfect SPD exercise? If you can define the perfect or Lean SPD, then you can engage everyone in identifying where the opportunities are to improve.

Developing Leadership Routines (Lean Management System)

A perfect or Lean SPD clearly identifies what leadership routines or activities should be performed on a regular basis to ensure operations are performing to plan and variances to expectations are identified.

If your leaders are not actively assessing operational performance and identifying improvement opportunities, then you have a long road ahead in your lean journey. Leadership routines are the cornerstone to every successful lean transformation and continuous improvement culture. There is a reason we included leadership quotes throughout the book.

Now to review the basics of leadership routines:

- Leader Standard Work: Identify, document and hold accountable your leadership team, especially supervisors, to completing key leadership activities on a regular basis to identify operational performance and opportunities for improvement.

- Stand Up Meetings: We did not cover this initially, but it is beneficial to have a quick "stand up meeting" or shift change meeting to address the day's plan, expectations and staff's preparation for success. It is also a quick and easy way to reinforce lean expectations, results and focus for the day.
- Kamishibai Boards, Audits and Visual Controls: Utilize lean tools to enhance your leadership routines and create effective use of your time on the floor. Get staff thinking, talking and taking the initiative to improve.
- Accountability Meetings: Instill leadership discipline through accountability meetings where leads, supervisors, managers and directors are held accountable for identifying opportunities, understanding variance in performance and acting to make a difference and improve the outcomes for tomorrow. Create action item lists, assign responsibility, set due dates and follow-up.
- Genba Walks: Leaders, including senior management, must spend time in the SPD to see the work as it is done and identify barriers to excellence. Follow a structured format, score the department and show the staff that their work is important to senior level management.

Problem Solving (Lean Management System)

A perfect or Lean SPD utilizes a systematic approach to solving operational problems.

It should be obvious that problem solving is continuous improvement, but that is not always the case. Solving problems is sometimes confused with solutions that simply band aid the issue and ignore the root cause of the issue. While we have talked about the 5 Why's, PDCA, measuring performance and A3 analysis of problems, the main point here is that true problem solving is reliant on leaders taking the initiative to take action. Too many SPDs post performance graphs and record how well they are doing but somehow miss the point of acting to implement change. Take problem solving serious and implement change. Do something to make things better today.

Employee Engagement (Lean Production)

A perfect or Lean SPD has 100% employee engagement in actively finding ways to continuously improve Customer satisfaction and operational performance.

Employee engagement always leads to continuous improvement. Employee apathy always leads to status quo or declining performance. Creating a culture where your staff is engaged is all about creating a culture where the staff is working towards objectives and making the work environment more effective and fun. Employees in this environment are continuously improving. We spend most our time in the workplace; we might as well make it fun and productive!

Eliminating Waste (Lean Production)

A perfect or Lean SPD understands operational waste, exposes it and finds ways to eliminate waste from their processes to improve operational performance.

Understanding value, exposing waste and finding ways to eliminate waste and improve operations through problem solving and employee engagement provides an on-going process and structure for lean continuous improvement. There is no such thing as a waste free SPD or any other department, so you will never worry about running out of things to work on.

Continuous Improvement (Lean Production)

A perfect or Lean SPD never stops improving, never stops striving to raise the bar of performance and never stops finding ways to improve Customer satisfaction, employee engagement and operational performance.

Yes, this is our lot in life. To provide a life-saving and important service to our Customers while simultaneously striving for improvement. Is it hard work?

Yes. Can it be fun, exciting and fulfilling? Yes. It can be if you take the time and make the effort.

The Lean Journey

The lean journey can seem overwhelming and intimidating, but you should not worry. Hopefully the concepts and explanations in this book will help clarify what a Lean SPD journey can entail and provide ideas for where to start. The most important part is that you do not have to complete it tomorrow or even this year. You do though have to start now and take action. While the 8 Steps provide guidance, the following graphic provides a different way of looking at a typical improvement roadmap.

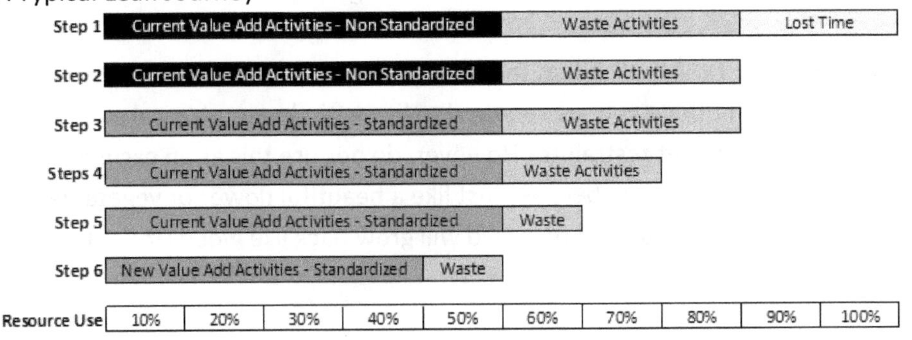

Step #1 in a typical lean journey starts by eliminated wasted or lost time through the implementation of clear work assignments, standard work and performance measurements. Lost time is defined as any resource used that is not actively working on an activity. At this point we are not even worried about whether the activity is adding value or waste. We are just focused on making sure that our resources are working on something. For labor, this means eliminating situations where staff are not working, talking to friends, wandering the hallways or disappearing while on the clock and being paid.

After getting a handle on lost time, Step #2 focuses on standardizing value add activities through standard work. Ensure your staff are performing tasks the same way and allow supervisors the time to follow-up on staff's performance to the standard work. At this point we are not trying to improve the standard work, decrease staff's time or eliminate waste from the activities, but rather standardizing tasks to create a culture of adherence to the "way we do it."

Now that you have reduced or eliminated lost time and standardized your activities, you can start working on reducing the waste in the process. This is best done in a structured, systematic method with laser focus and regular follow-up to ensure the waste is removed and does not return. A common approach is to start in decontamination and work your way through the process flow to assembly, sterilization, sterile storage and case cart picking. This requires the use of all the tools and concepts we have outlined and typically is not something that happens in a short period of time. That is why we have shown it as Step #3, #4 and #5 in the graph.

Eventually, you will realize that the remaining waste is either very hard to remove or something you are required to live with due to physical constraints, workflows or budget restraints. However, do not use this as an excuse to stop trying to eliminate waste because just like a beautiful flower or vegetable garden, the waste you have removed will grow back like weeds if not taken care of.

Eventually, you will start to focus your attention on the value-add activities and discovering ways to remove the waste from within the value. This may include performing a task in five steps instead of six, rearranging workspaces and flow patterns to reduce the time to perform the activity or finding that you can eliminate the value add activity by a change in process or Customer requirements.

It's been stated that up to 50% of the time, materials and resources used in a process can be eliminated through lean methodologies. Thus, we have made the previous graphic display what a 50% improvement would look like. In the beginning, 50% of the time and resources spent on the process were considered value add activities, 30% were considered waste and 20% were lost time. By the end, 40% were considered value add, 10% were required waste that could not be removed and 50% of the time, effort and resource use was eliminated. While this is just an example, if you take your "Perfect SPD" and total focus on value-add activities to heart, then you will be able to find just as much opportunity in your department! Let the games begin and the quest for perfection begin!

~~~~~~

City Hospital: Continuous Improvement

Scene: It has been one year since Rob's initial meeting with Karen, and he began to utilize lean methodologies to improve his SPD. Today he is welcoming three new employees to the team and introducing them to both the SPD team and the Lean culture that is now firmly rooted in the department.

"Good morning everyone," Rob realizes that yes, indeed, he starts each meeting with the same greeting.

"Welcome to City Hospital and congratulations on your new career. We are glad you joined the Operation Perfection Team. Today is the start of what I hope will be a very satisfying and fulfilling time for you here both professionally and personally. We take pride in our work, our culture and our SPD family, and we hope that you will too." Rob notices how young the new employees look and briefly drifts back to his first days in SPD and the lack of culture and process that existed.

"I see each of you has brought your New Hire Orientation folder with you. Excellent! Let's get started." Rob takes a seat in front of the three new hires and begins their introduction to the SPD Mission and Vision and the department's Culture of Continuous Improvement.

"You'll see by our SPD Charter that we have numerous Customers; the operating room is our largest and most critical due to the life and death circumstance of surgeries. We are committed to providing our surgeons the exact instruments they need in a clean, complete, sterile and on-time manner.
~~~~~~

Your work makes that happen and could be the difference between a doctor having exactly what they need to save a life of someone's loved one – their mother, child, spouse or friend. Your job is important." Rob pauses to let that sink in but realizes that for new hires it does not quite register their first day. He will take them to the OR later and let them see surgery up close and personal to drive his point home.

"We take our responsibility seriously and in doing so we've created an operational system that ensures we do the right thing every time, every day. We call it Operation Perfection or OP for short." Rob still does not feel the title is the best, but the staff voted for it and it has stuck ever since. "Our staff liked the play on words related to surgical operations and our drive for perfection."

"Let me outline the basics of the system and highlight where you fit in. First, we always put our Customers first and meet with them to understand their needs and expectations. That's why we post and live by our SPD Charter as it reminds us every day what our Customers are expecting us to deliver. For us to know how well we're doing, we measure everything we do. At least most everything. The point is we can't know how we'll we're doing unless we measure it. I'll take you to our Lean board later and explain our measurements and system we use to make sure we're identifying when and why we're not meeting the expectation."

Rob pauses for a moment as he realizes how much he has grown over the past year. He never could have spoken to a group of new hires in this fashion and with such business expertise had it not been for the opportunities he had to grow and learn under Karen's leadership. He hopes that these new hires will someday reflect on how much they have learned from him.

"We also believe that our business is to proactively anticipate what our Customers need and be prepared in advance to meet those needs. We continuously forecast our work and what resources we need to get the work done and create Standard Work instructions on how the work should be performed. In our line of work, there is no flexibility for individuals to determine how the job should be done; we follow strict regulatory guidelines, industry standards and our own internal policies and procedures. In short, we agree that everyone will follow the OP Way not their own way. This includes what activities we'll do, how we perform those activities, how long the activity should take and what resources and tools are needed to ensure we correctly perform the activity every time."

Rob takes a breath and considers how much of this the new hires are comprehending, knowing how critical it is for them to understand. "Our educator will take you through the Standard Work and show how it is developed as you go through training. I do want to be very upfront right now that we do have production standards and utilize agreed upon time standards for each activity. These standards are not meant to be used as a whipping stick to make you work faster, but rather they reflect the time we've planned, allocated and received a budget to work to. Our best staff can exceed the standards so don't worry about them being unachievable. They were all developed by our staff based on the Standard Work instructions. But do be aware that you'll be expected to eventually work within the acceptable range of the standard for us to succeed as a department."

Daryl raises his hand and asks, "What happens if I can't make the standard?"

"Good question Daryl," Rob answers him with approval. "We are here to provide support to everyone and especially new hires such as yourselves. A key tenant of our program is our training and education program. You should receive all the training you need to bring you up to speed, and we've recently introduced software at each workstation that allows you to access the work instructions for the task you're working on. We want to remove the reliance on our memories alone because we know that's a tall order to fulfill."

"Secondly, one of the key components of the OP Way is what we call Leadership Routines. You'll find that our supervisors are tasked with spending time on the floor actively observing how well everyone is performing their activities and staying within the Standard Work. We strive to make the work environment a supportive one where the leadership team is here to make sure you're successful. If either a supervisor or you notice that you're not working to standard, then we meet and talk about what is stopping you and address the root cause."

Rob again pauses to see how all three staff are absorbing what he is telling them. "We've found that most people can perform quite well with the proper support, training and experience. Occasionally, we may find that someone just can't meet the standard and as a team we must figure out where they can work to standard and how we can give them the opportunity to work in that capacity. Over the past year we've had two staff transition out because of this, but we found positions for them elsewhere in the hospital. The short answer is we're here to help make sure you succeed and just ask that you put forth the effort as well."

"Thanks," Daryl responds and turns the page in his orientation folder.

"Back to our leadership routines," Rob continues. "Just as we have Standard Work for you to follow, our supervisors have Standard Work to follow as well. Included in that is the observations I just mentioned, but we also ask them to identify why we aren't meeting our plan and/or what opportunities we must improve. You'll learn about our perfect SPD exercise in a bit, but in short, we believe that we're not perfect and therefore continually ask ourselves where we can improve. Every day our supervisors create a production plan on how things should go for the day. We look at the surgery schedule and calculate how many instrument trays we're going to process, how many people we need to get the job done and approximately what time of day the trays should come through. They then make hourly rounds checking on our progress and identifying if we're on schedule or not."

"I'll share that when we first started, everyone thought the supervisors were simply spying on them to see if they were working! That's not the case. We're all working. Instead, they were seeing if we were working on the right things, identifying what issues are stopping us from hitting our schedule and how could we improve? They are tasked with finding ways to help you become a better technician and help us become a better department. Every day I meet with Dwight and Becky and review their observations and findings for the past 24 hours. We prioritize immediate action items and then weekly decide as a group what issues to tackle as a department. The three of you will eventually be invited to help us fix the issues we identify."

"I forgot to tell you to turn to page six in your New Hire Orientation folder!" Rob remarks and thinks how he has naturally memorized the OP Way and sometimes forgets to follow the orientation folder.

"You'll see on page six the 8 Steps to Operation Perfection. We've covered one through four so far with Problem Solving being next. In fact, I put #5 and #6, Problem Solving and Employee Engagement, together because I truly believe that we can only solve our problems and serve our Customers effectively if we have engaged employees such as yourselves being part of the process. We have structured methods to solves problems and sometimes it may seem like a paper exercise, but we take our work seriously and expect people to participate in improving how we do what we do."

"What I ask of you, is to come to work not just to do your job but to help us figure out how you can do your job better. Help us eliminate errors, improve turnaround time, be more efficient, meet our Customer's expectations and create a work environment that you enjoy coming to."

"Rob," Dwight interrupts. "Karen is asking to meet with you in 10 minutes."

"Ok, thanks Dwight. I'll be right there." Rob looks at his watch and wonders where the time goes.

"Let's wrap up this section and then I'll turn you back over to Dwight who'll be with you until lunch. The seventh and eight steps to Operation Perfection include eliminating waste and creating a culture of continuous improvement. We'll teach you what waste is, how to see waste and conversely how to see value. In short if you think about what we do, we add value by cleaning, assembling and sterilizing instruments according to their instructions for use before delivering them to our Customers as a clean, complete, sterile and on-time product. That's the value we add. Anything we do that doesn't do one of these four activities is waste. Moving instruments is waste. Searching for instruments is waste. Walking is waste. Waiting is waste. Pulling an instrument for a case that's not used is waste. You get the idea."

Rob takes a breath and then finishes. "Everything we do is based on building and sustaining a culture of continuous improvement. We identify our Customer expectations. We measure ourselves and we develop a plan to succeed. We identify opportunities for improvement, figure out what the problem is, fix it and then start over. It's our never-ending search for perfection. Our Operation Perfection."

"Okay, that's it for me. Dwight, they're all yours!" Rob stands up and hopes that Daryl and others will accept the challenge to be part of the team above and beyond being a warm body. "I wonder what Karen wants now," Rob speaks his mind out loud as he exits the room.

~~~~~~
~~~~~~

Chapter Fourteen: Examples of Lean SPD

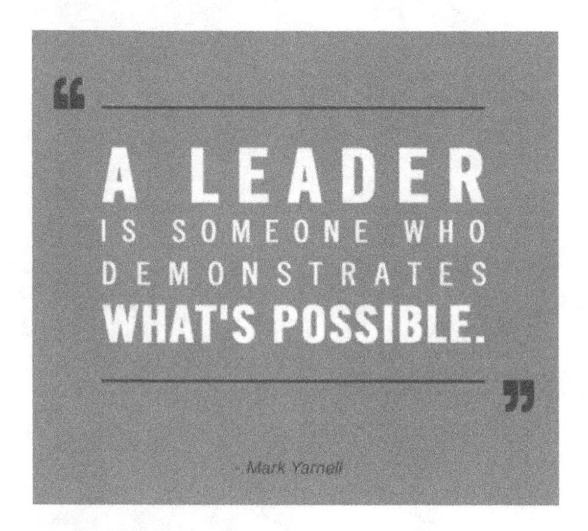

During a Lean SPD presentation to a group of hospital employees, a supervisor raised his hand and asked me if everything I was talking about worked. The answer is a resounding YES! This book is not a theoretical exercise on what should work but rather a collection of 14 years' experience and real-life learnings of what works! It is also a collection of what hospitals across the nation have successfully implemented in their own SPDs. So, let us look at some examples to help you get a sense of what may be in your future career path.

Continuous Flow

This is my personal favorite lean methodology to implement in SPDs. Mostly because it makes so much sense, staff understand the concept and it allows you to address so many underlying issues under one umbrella approach.

The following photos are the classic before and after results of Continuous Flow lean work to eliminate backlogs.

Before Lean and Continuous Flow – Major Medical Teaching Hospital 7AM Backlogs in Assembly

Every morning staff in this department fielded frantic phone calls from the OR staff looking for instruments. Staff would be pulled off their normal assignment to sort through racks, find what was needed, quick turn the trays if time allowed and then run them to the OR.

After Lean and Continuous Flow – Major Medical Teaching Hospital 7AM Backlogs in Assembly

This photo is the same staging racks after the lean implementation. The OR phone calls reduced dramatically, staff felt more relaxed and the department focused on quality initiatives as their next process improvement.

Before Lean and Continuous Flow – 10 OR Hospital 7AM Backlogs in Assembly

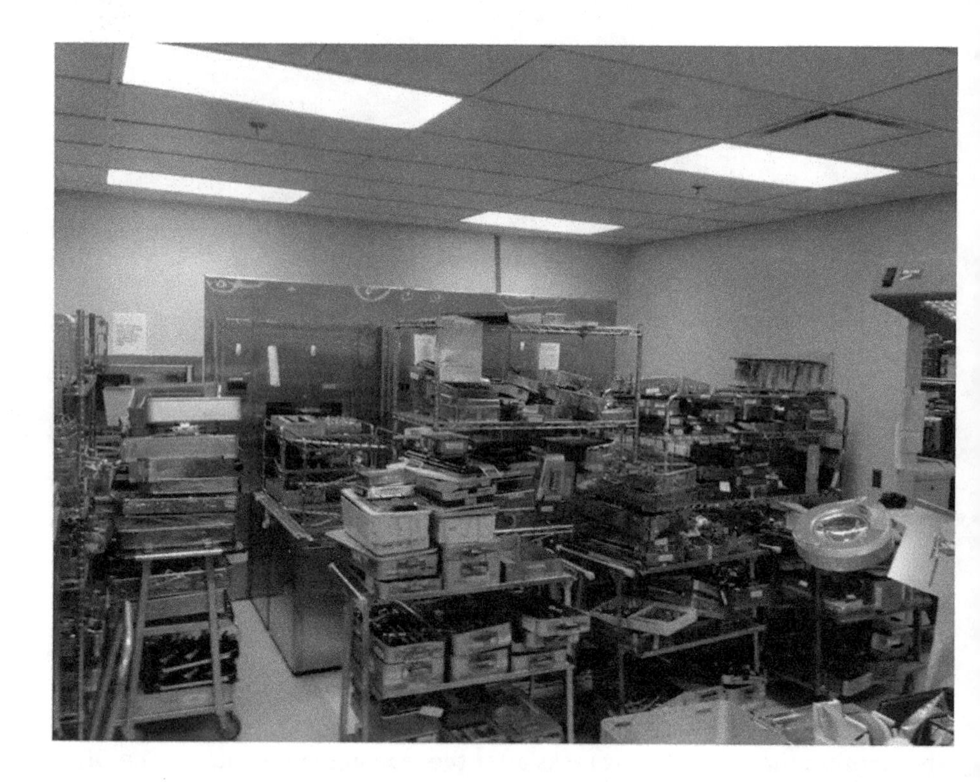

SPD staff in this smaller hospital had become so accustomed to backlogs that they did not think twice about the fact they could barely get to their washers to unload them. The OR had appointed one FTE to do nothing but find and ensure trays needed were processed. Every morning became a "priority" focus on processing trays needed for later in the day.

After Lean and Continuous Flow – 10 OR Hospital 7AM Backlogs in Assembly

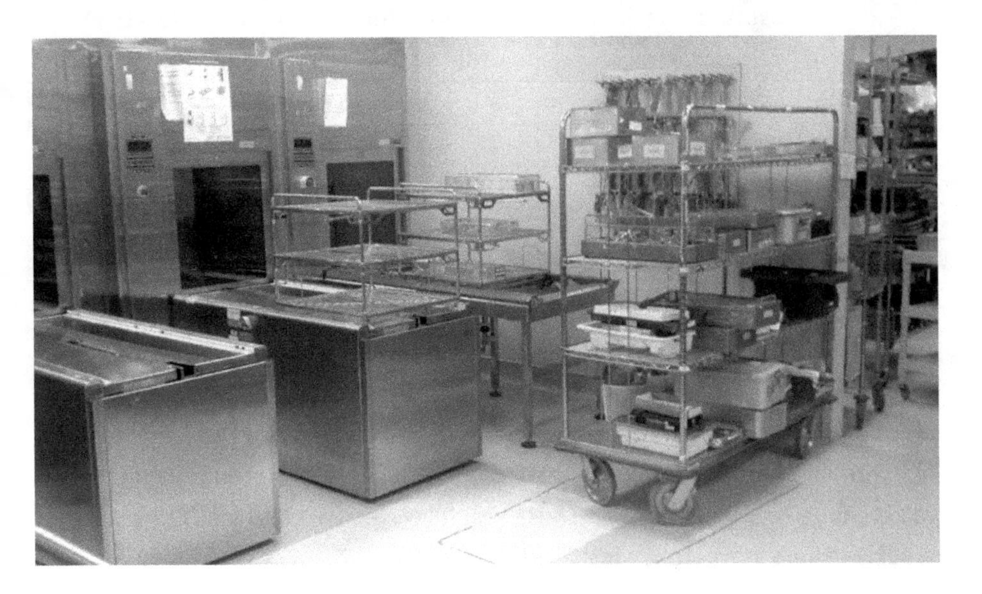

After continuous flow was implemented, the staff suddenly realized they had three washers instead of two! Just kidding! Their daily prioritization of trays was no longer needed. The dedicated OR FTE's job suddenly became much easier, and she migrated back to performing OR work. Finally, the SPD staff found that they did not need as many people assembling trays at 7AM anymore.

While photos can show the difference, the measurements behind the photos backed up the results. The metrics below show three areas that Continuous Flow helped improve in a Level 1 Trauma hospital with a unionized SPD that served 20 OR's. Not only did the backlogs vanish but quality and productivity improved

Impact of Continuous Flow – Level 1 Trauma, Union SPD, 20 OR's

Measurements	Baseline Min-Avg-Max	Results Min-Avg-Max
Assembly Backlog 7AM	0 – 63 – 146	2 – 12 – 31
% Complete Instrument Trays	90% – 96% – 99%	93% – 97% – 99%
Productivity = Hours per Tray	0.93 – 1.37 – 2.16	0.80 – 1.00 – 1.20

Notice how Continuous Flow not only reduced the backlogs, improved % complete trays and improved productivity, it also reduced the variance in performance. The spread between minimum daily results and maximum daily results in the beginning was large, signifying an unstable process. After continuous flow implementations, the process performance was not only stabilized and much more predictable, but processes also produced the results the Customer wanted. These results were also graphically displayed as weekly results in the following chart.

Weekly Impact of Continuous Flow – Level 1 Trauma, Union SPD, 20 OR's

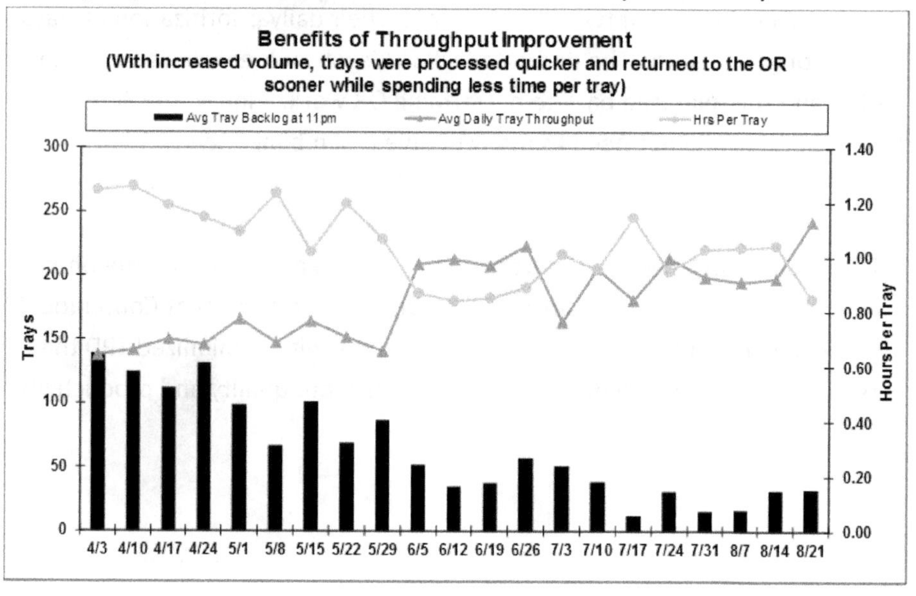

The graph above shows the results of continuous flow lean implementation in the measurable indicators: backlog, throughput and productivity. The bars represent the average backlog in assembly at 11PM each week. The team set the goal of finishing as much assembly as possible by 11PM or the end of 2nd shift and allow the smaller 3rd shift to focus on clean-up, sterilizer testing and picking case carts. The triangle marker line represents the average number of trays processed on an average midweek day. This measurement was intended to highlight how the same staff could process more trays during the week when they were used and needed and no longer rely on the weekends to catch up. In fact, weekend staffing was reduced, and hours added back to midweek schedules further enhancing the team's ability to maintain continuous flow. The circle marker line represents the average hours per tray spent by the total department and shows an improvement in productivity.

The following graphs, from a large SPD supporting over 90 surgical procedures per day, depict how continuous flow not only helped reduce backlogs but helped the department improve in other areas as well.

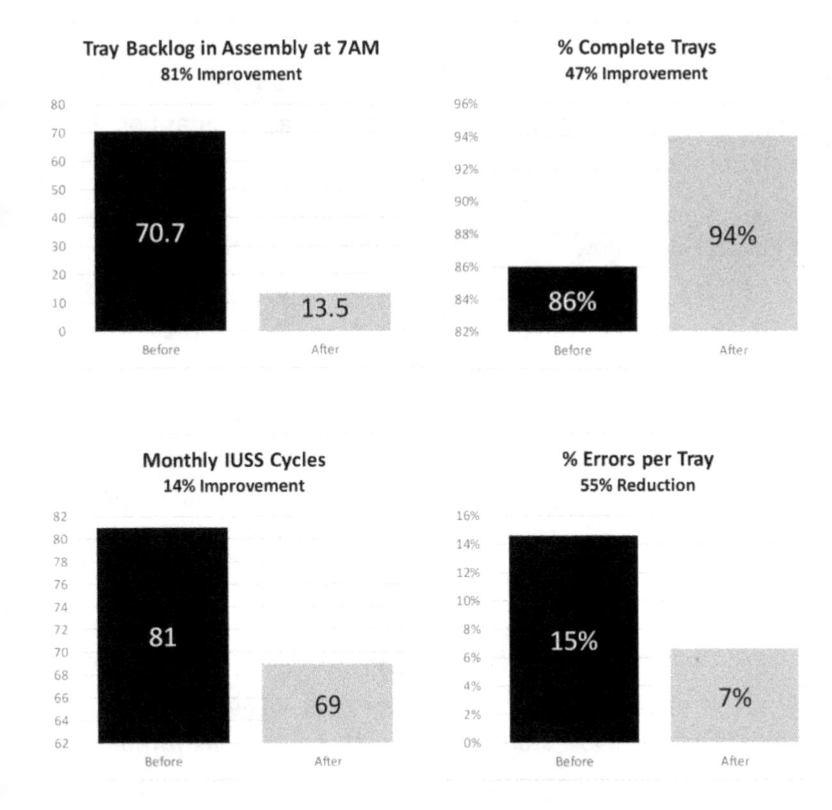

Decontamination

Decontamination presents multiple opportunities to implement lean concepts, some of which have been discussed in earlier chapters already. Common lean practices to help improve flow and quality in this area include the following:

- Linear Flow: Designing the flow of instruments, containers, and case carts so that they never backtrack and maintain as linear as possible movement forward to reduce waste.

- Floor Plan for Workflow: Often, you are stuck with what you have; but if you are designing a new SPD, then take the time to visualize and model the workflow through decontamination. Reduce the amount of walking and movement. Create a flow so that case carts and items move from the room entrance to the sinks to the washers without backtracking, crossing over or wasting movement. Design segregation of workflows as necessary, including manual wash, flexible scopes and automated washing items all receiving their own dedicated processing flow.

- Inline Sinks and Sonic Sinks: Recent SPD designs have incorporated the latest technologies, including sonic washing capabilities directly in the sink basins that allow staff to sonic wash instruments without ever leaving their sink work area. Placing the sinks in-line with the washers eliminates the need for walking and pushing washer racks on carts across the room to the load stations which in turn eliminates waste. The below photos show a new install of an in-line sink with sonic capability built into the sink basin. After using the sink and lean process, the Customer claimed that the workflow design and built-in sonic improved the quality and efficacy of the cleaning process and improved staff productivity. Their instances of bioburden left on the instruments went to zero and staff could work efficiently. Their design also allowed for the washer racks "manifolds" to return in between the two washers and automatically return to the sink station removing the need for staff to go to a return rack return window and manually move racks to the sinks.

Inline Prep Sinks Feeding Automated Washers

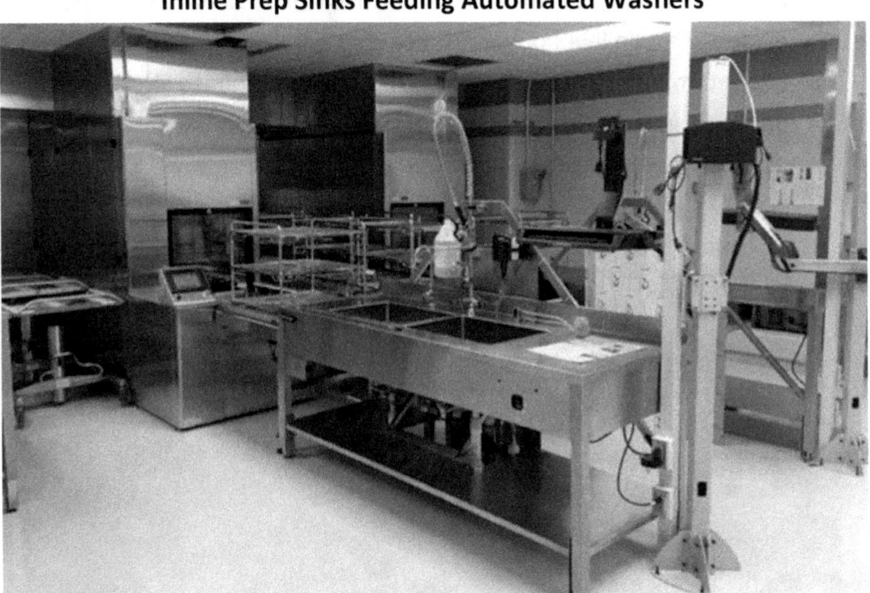

- While every activity within sterile processing requires Standard Work instructions, decontamination is probably the most susceptible to variance in practice and lack of documented control of what happens. Most departments rely on staff members to "remember" what to do and then actually do it for every possible instrument they handle during their shift. With the multiple instructions for use, varieties of instruments and multiple cleaning methods, it is difficult to imagine any SPD effectively cleaning or preparing its instruments for automated washing 100% correct 100% of the time.

Lean principles of error proofing can help. Only a few departments have taken this concept to heart in decontamination and attempted to provide their employees with instructions for cleaning at their workstation based on what is being handled at that moment in time. The tool to achieve this is typically an instrument tracking system that has built-in work instructions for each instrument tray that automatically appears on a screen once the instrument is scanned. Additionally, safeguards exist by way of an onscreen confirmation button that prompts staff to touch and confirm that a step is completed. Only at this level of control will SPDs have documented evidence and a level of confidence that what needs to be done in decontamination is being done. The following photo shows a properly set up decontamination sink with a monitor and scanning capability built into the workflow.

Inline Prep Sinks with Scanning and PC Screen Built In

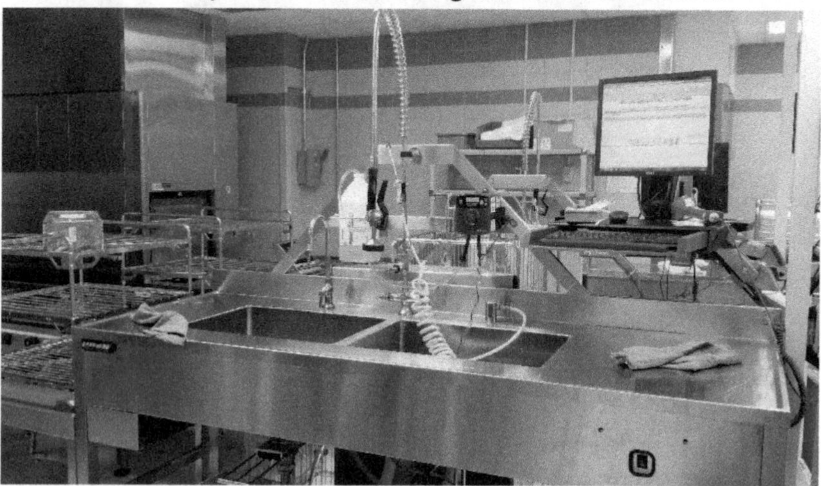

- Lastly, departments have found lean benefits in how their staff work in decontamination. In larger departments, navigator positions have proven to improve quality and productivity by assigning one person to handle all incoming case carts and dirty instruments, load cart washers and deliver work to the prep sinks. Staff assigned to the prep sinks thus stay at their station and focus on completing their task in an efficient and quality manner.

Assembly

Assembly typically represents the largest single labor requirement in every SPD as well as the last quality check before the instrument tray is sent for sterilization. Assembly is thus an important area where lean can have tremendous benefits. Typical lean concepts used in Assembly include:

- Linear flow
- Segregation of work assembly line style
- Navigator assignment and eliminating interruptions to assembly staff
- Standard Work
- Floor plan designed for efficient workflow
- Use of technology to ensure quality and reduce variance
- 5S
- Error proofing and automation
- Performance measurements

From these items, we have found that setting performance expectations and measuring performance, removing interruptions to staff and regular supervisory follow-up and coaching provide the greatest return to improving quality and productivity.

The following photo shows a unique and creative lean concept that helped eliminate time staff spent walking from assembly to the sterilization area. Staff members working the assembly stations on the backside of the room found that if they simply placed a gravity fed conveyor in-between the tables, they could place their completed trays on the conveyor and the trays automatically roll down to a pick-up point near the sterilizer person. The concept saved some walking and it was an excellent example of employee engagement.

Use of Gravity Fed Conveyor in Assembly to Move Trays to Sterilization

Another example of lean in assembly includes the spaghetti diagrams shown below and the rearranging of the assembly wrap tables to reduce movement and walking and improve efficiencies.

Use of Spaghetti Diagrams to Improve Workflow in Assembly

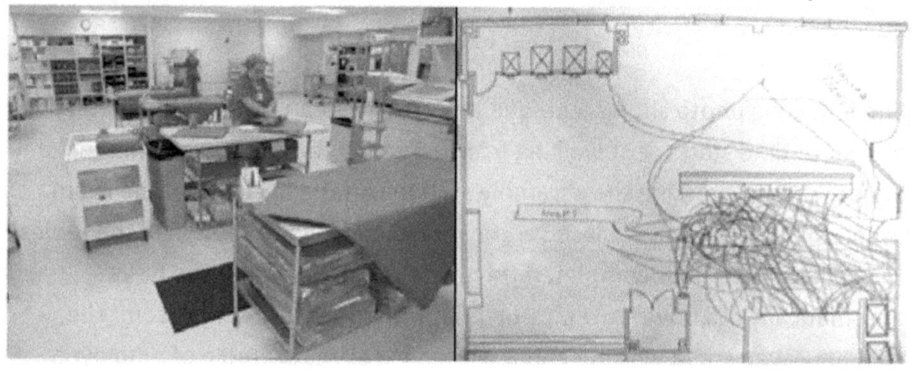

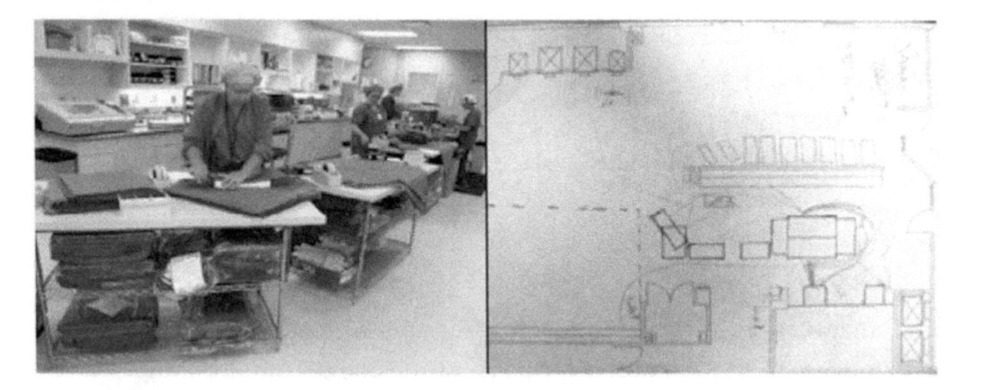

Sterilization

Lean quality control was introduced to sterilization activities years ago using instrument tracking systems that have built-in documentation and cycle selection controls. You scan an instrument tray requiring a biological indicator, the system warns you to include the biological. You scan a tray that requires a 6-minute exposure cycle and then select a 4-minute exposure cycle, the system stops you from continuing until the cycle selection and tray requirements match. You forget to read the biological after the one- or three-hour-time limit and the system reminds the user to do so. This technology driven processes are lean concepts and most people do not even know it!

Quick Turns

For those who work in SPD, the term quick turn or turnover is well known and may even cause an anxiety attack if the person has not figured out a systematic process to handle it. Quick turns represent instrument trays that are used by the OR and are then needed back for a subsequent case in less time than the SPD would normally process the tray. Lack of inventory, over scheduling of case types and Ortho doctors flipping between two rooms and reusing the same instruments sets are the typical culprits of quick turn needs.

The following Lean SPD examples have helped manage and reduce the anxiety of quick turns:

- Document tagging
- Process and workflow design
- Technology

Document Tagging

Document tagging is most commonly associated with multi-step processes in which the product or item is being passed from one person to another, requiring information to be collected along the way. Examples include paperwork processing in which each step is time stamped on the document tag for determination of how long each step took for cycle time evaluation. Another example is documenting product quality and parameters at each step of the process on the document tag to determine process improvement opportunities. A document tag is typically a piece of paper attached to the item that collects information as it moves through a process.

Below is an example of a Document Tag for an instrument tray needing to be quick turned. This was printed on plastic "luggage tags" or instrument tray labels for easy attachment to the tray and able to withstand washing and sterilization. The OR fills out the left side and when giving the tray to SPD for the quick turn. In some hospitals, a SPD based staff working in the OR may be responsible for identifying and tagging trays as well. Once the tray is in the hands of SPD, they begin the quick turn process entering in the time at each step along the way. At the end of the process, the SPD removes the tag and keeps it for record keeping. The department needs to ensure that they could meet the agreed upon turn time requested, thus meet their Customer's requirements.

QUICK TURN REQUEST Time: ______________	CS PROCESS
Tray Name: ______________	______________ Time Received in Decontamination
Room Needed: ______________	______________ Time Received in Assembly
Time Needed: ______________	______________ Time In Sterilizer
Requested By: ______________	______________ Time out of Sterilizer
Processing Requested	______________ Time to OR
☐ Hand Wash Only - 30 Minute Turn Around	______________ Room Delivered To
☐ Automated Wash - 60 Minute Turn Around	______________ Nurse Delivered To
☐ Wash and Sterilize - 150 Minute Turn Around	

Process and Workflow Design

Current OR designs no longer provide for a "flash" or immediate use sterilization area attached to OR's and instead rely on the SPD to provide services for quick turns and immediate needs. To accommodate this, some hospitals have designed small quick turn centers within the OR to provide expedited service. While designs may differ, the concept is simple and includes a small decontamination room with a sink, sonic and pass through washer. The clean side has one assembly table, a small steam sterilizer and possibly a low temperature sterilizer as well.

Technology

Instrument tracking or scanning systems are no longer designed to only track trays and build sterilization loads. They connect to OR schedules, prioritize work, provide process instructions, manage labor, provide task management functionality, provide real time messages and many other functionalities. The prioritization functions combined with the case cart requirements and OR schedule interface provide robust abilities to manage quick turns. SPDs have found ways to utilize their tracking system to identify the quick turn need in advance, identify where the trays currently are, immediately identify them as a priority or quick turn upon entering decontamination and track the tray through the process.

Performance Measurements

While most SPDs have some measurements process in place, few actively utilize the data in a manner that drives continuous improvement and a lean culture. At a minimum, we find many SPDs tracking its production numbers such as number of cycles run, number of failed BI's, and number of items processed. These types of measurements document quantity of work produced but do not provide any insight into whether it was good, bad or indifferent.

There are plenty examples of SPDs taking the next step of documenting errors, productivity, bioburden, missing instruments and other types of measurements that indicate operational performance which is great. Very few SPDs though take the final steps and compare actual performance to planned performance, create action items to improve, follow-up and implement improvements and maintain the discipline to create an on-going culture of continuous improvement. The following photos depict a Lean SPD department that lives their lean culture and documents it every day of the year by following through on its commitment to continuous improvement. The bottom slot in every column shows action items that have assigned responsibilities, due dates and whether the department is up to date on completing the task.

Lean SPD Performance Measurements Board – It's Not Just for Show, They Update It Daily!

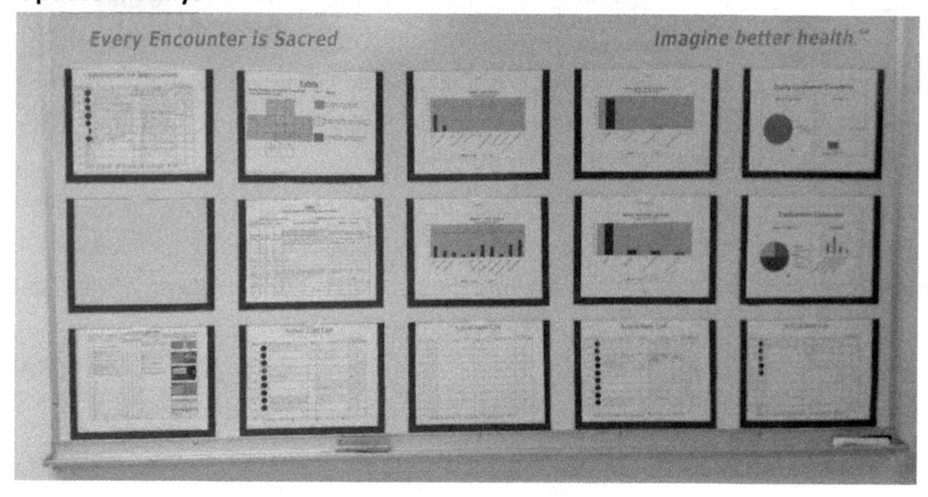

Floor Pick-Ups and Deliveries

This Lean example came from an SPD that had dedicated staff to restocking supplies on the nursing floors and wanted to relook at their processes due to a change in management. Using observations and data collection tools they focused on eliminating waste such as transportation, movement, redundancies and lost time while ensuring their Customer requirements were met.

In documenting their current process, the department realized it had split the task of restocking floor supplies between chargeable and non-chargeable items with separate staff responsible for each. This meant they had two people walking to the same floor and same location throughout the hospital. After observing the floor rounds the staff made and recording how much time it took, they compared how long it would take one person to do both chargeable and non-chargeable items together versus the current split system. The following chart shows their observation results and how one person doing both would save 50 minutes every time he or she performed the task. At this point, the savings or elimination of waste came from a reduction in walking time while the time spent inventorying and restocking remained constant.

Observation Comparison of One versus Two Staff Performing Floor Rounds

Activity	Minutes for One Person Doing All	Minutes for One Person Doing Half	Minutes for One Person Doing Half	Total Minutes for Two People
Walk to Supply Location	5	5	5	10
Inventory Supplies	10	5	5	10
Walk to Supply Location	5	5	5	10
Inventory Supplies	10	5	5	10
Walk to Supply Location	5	5	5	10
Inventory Supplies	10	5	5	10
Walk to Supply Location	5	5	5	10
Inventory Supplies	10	5	5	10
Walk to CS	5	5	5	10
Pick Supplies	30	15	15	30
Walk to Supply Location	5	5	5	10
Stock Supplies	5	2.5	2.5	5
Walk to Supply Location	5	5	5	10
Stock Supplies	5	2.5	2.5	5
Walk to Supply Location	5	5	5	10
Stock Supplies	5	2.5	2.5	5
Walk to Supply Location	5	5	5	10
Stock Supplies	5	2.5	2.5	5
Walk to CS	5	5	5	10
Finish – Total Time	140	95	95	190

Next, they focused on finding ways to minimize the waste in the actual inventory and restocking aspect of the task. The hospital was a small community hospital and did not have any form of electronic par levels or reordering in place and thus relied on manual inventory methods. None the less, they returned to performing observations and collecting data and presented the following chart.

 # Items Picked and % of Par Picked for Back-to-Back Floor Rounds

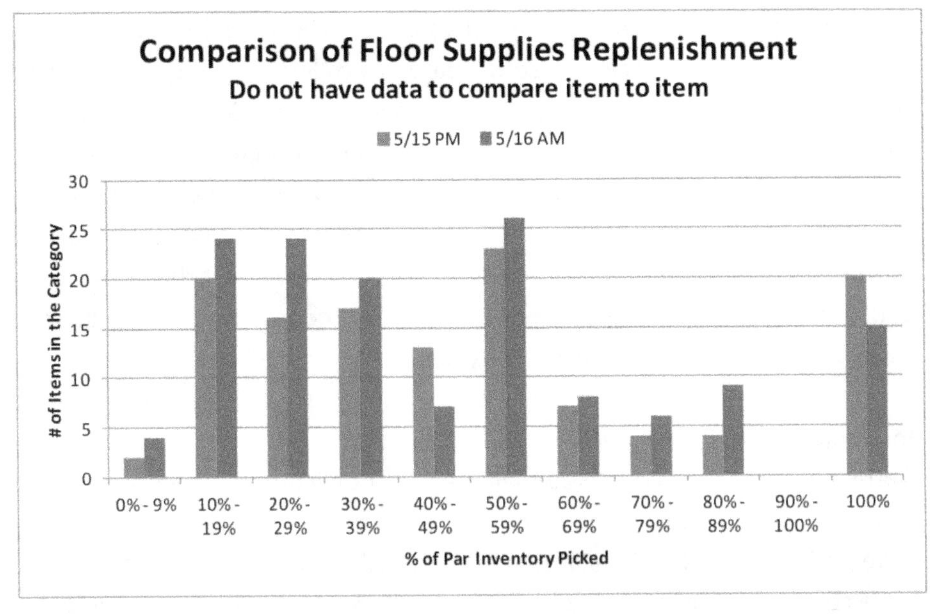

The data showed that 70% of the items restocked were less than 60% of the par level and quite frequently they were stocking far less as indicated by the large numbers in the 10% to 39% categories. For example, if the par level was 10 items, 70% of the time they were restocking less than 6 items out of the 10. In summary, the team felt that the restocking was occurring on a too frequent of basis and with proper setting of par levels, the restocking rounds could be cut in half.

The team also looked at ways to eliminate the walking to each floor to inventory the items needed and then the walking back to SPD to pick those items only to then walk back to the floor to restock them. Exchange carts were discussed allowing the staff to simply swap out a used supply cart with a fully stocked supply cart; but this proved too difficult to implement due to the numerous locations and permanent storage shelving already installed in the nursing units. Pushing a restocking cart to the floor and restocking in one trip was reviewed as an option but also proved difficult due to the number of different items in inventory.

The team eventually decided to try a Two-Bin Kanban system where reorder cards were placed in each supply bin separating the inventory in half and having the floor staff place the reorder card in a collection bin when they used the first half of the inventory. To eliminate the need for a SPD person to walk to each floor to pick up the Kanban cards, each floor assigned a support person to deliver the Kanban cards to the SPD every day at the end of his or her shift on the way out of the building. Since the floor staff had to come downstairs to leave, they had no problem simply dropping off their cards to SPD on their way out. SPD then pulled the items needed based on the Kanban cards and restocked the supplies every night in a single trip.

Instrumentation Inventory

Getting the OR to help right size their instrument inventory as well as the instruments in the trays has help reduce waste for SPDs as well. Many OR's have performed tray rationalization exercises where doctor specific trays were combined, trays standardized, and small packs or peel packs were created for unique items. These steps help standardize instrument trays making it easier for SPD to process and improve quality. By reducing the amount of instrument trays used in procedures, the amount of work SPD must perform is also reduced. These steps also help eliminate the need for nurses to open an entire tray for one or two instruments, also reducing the work SPD must perform.

Optimizing the actual instruments in the tray is another area that pays lean dividends to both the OR and SPD. By removing seldom or never used instruments from trays, the OR has less work to do on their back table and SPD has less instruments to clean and assemble. In some cases, up to 30% of the instruments can be removed from trays. What a great lean initiative!

Visual Management and Visual Aids

The following photos show real-life use of visual management and visual aids in sterile processing departments:

Procedure manual located at the workstation, making it easier for staff to use if needed.

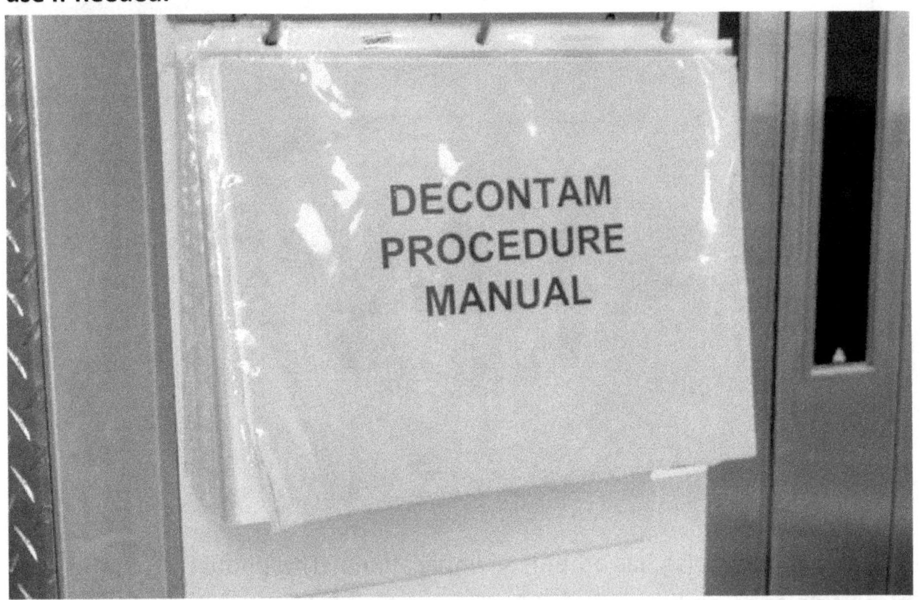

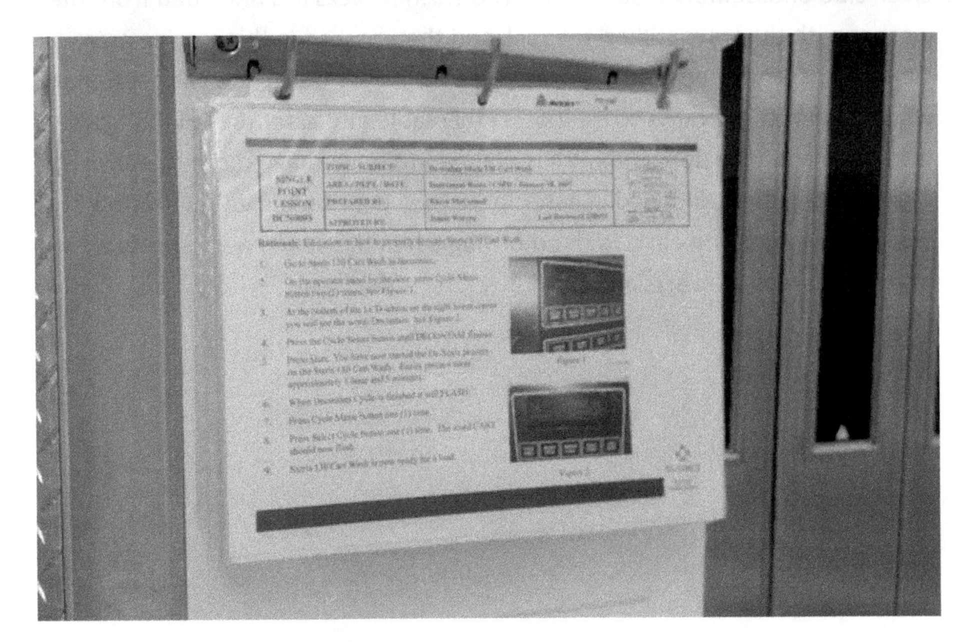

Cart staging locations identified on the floor. This helps to maintain a clean and orderly work environment as well as provide immediate visual if the area become backlogged.

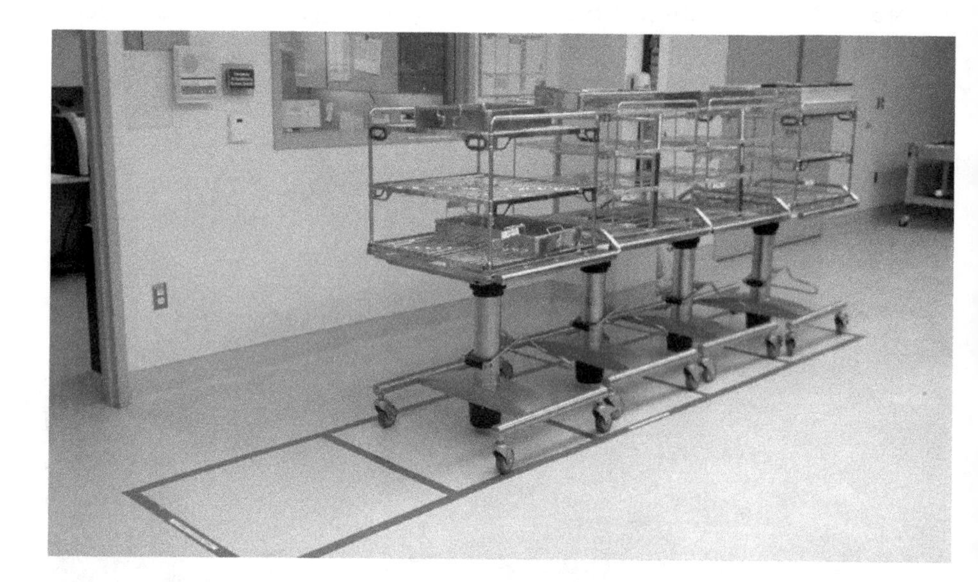

The above photo also has other lean implications. This photo is from the clean side or assembly area of SPD. The washer racks are unloaded from the washer with the trays still on the rack and then parked in this staging area. When an assembly person has completed his or her trays, he or she will then wheel one of these racks to their assembly table and assemble all the trays from the rack. The department has planned to never have more than five racks waiting or backlogged in assembly. They believe in continuous flow. This photo was taken early in the morning when the space was used as a parking spot for the carts and racks.

The photo below shows a visual aid (photo on the wall) depicting how the air hose should be wound and placed on the wall, eliminating excuses for doing it the wrong way!

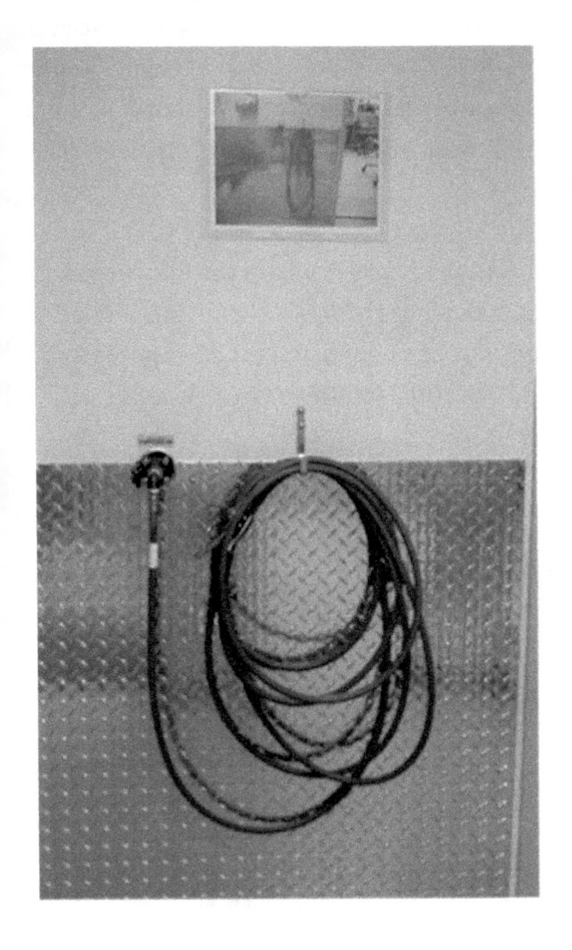

The following two photos show more visual management by placing Standard Work Instructions where the work occurs making it easy for staff to access should they need to review how to perform the task. Additionally, both photos show a time of day system that provides immediate visual feedback on the status of the activity. The left photo shows time cards representing hourly tasks that need to be performed. If the hour is showing 6:00 as shown in the photo, then that hourly activity has not been completed. Once complete, the staff simply turns the card around.

The photo on the left shows a manual BI read system where the BI to be read is placed in the hour slot at which time it needs to be read. With automated instrument tracking systems, this may not be needed, but for an easy-to-use manual method that provides immediate visual information on whether we have missed a BI read, it is effective.

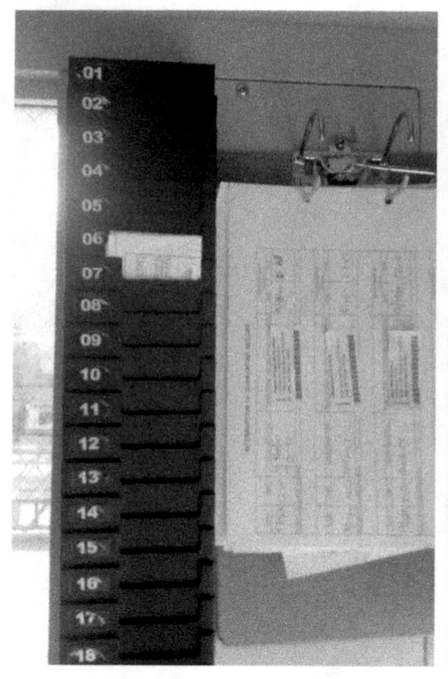

Chapter Fifteen: Lean Terms and Definitions

5S

5S – Opportunities are abundant in traditional processes to improve workplace efficiencies through organization and cleaning habits. Waste is often found in looking for needed items, workplace clutter, disorganization, and the inability to see problems as they happen. 5S helps departments become organized and improve efficiency. It utilizes visual management to remove all debris and unnecessary items while ensuring needed tools and items have clearly marked storage places visible from the work area.

The chart below shows the original Japanese words that all start with S, their English equivalents, and a short definition. You may find sources that use slightly different terms, but the intent and meanings are the same.

Japanese	English	Literal Translation
Seiri	Sort	Remove all rubbish, unused or unrelated items from the workplace.
Seiton	Simplify / Set	Orderly arrange all items required to perform the process or procedure. Set everything in its proper place for quick storage and retrieval.
Seiso	Shine / Sweep	Daily systematic efforts to keep the workplace clean and orderly. Everyone is involved.
Seiketsu	Standardize	Standardize the way of maintaining cleanliness and order. Perform the task the same way regardless of who is doing the work.
Shitsuke	Sustain	Make it a way of life. This is the self-discipline to consistently perform the practices and procedures in the preceding steps.

5S provides immediate visual impact in the workplace and is a great first step in the improvement process. It is an easy way to start and can be a great momentum builder if properly sustained. In fact, sustaining a 5S effort can lead to leader Standard Work, discipline and accountability board. It is all about "controlling the conditions" and eliminating waste and frustration associated with searching for items. 5S is about organization and housekeeping; but so much more, it is about establishing Standard Work, taking pride in one's workplace and instilling the discipline for future improvements.

Example: We have all been in areas where the space was too tight or too cluttered. Ample opportunity exists to organize, arrange and streamline operations.

You may find it useful in the home as well

<u>5S in Detail</u>

Step 1 Sort: Sort through your area and remove anything that you do not need by frequency of use. If used daily, keep it at or near the workstation. If used weekly, store it nearby but out from underfoot. If used less than monthly, then move it out of the work area. Red Tag techniques are useful in the sorting step. The red tag identifies the item, who moved it, the date it was moved and reason (not used, obsolete, broken, etc.). Items red-tagged are reviewed by all to determine actual use or disposition.

Hmm – this cubicle could use a little 5S!

Step 2 Simplify or Set: Set everything in order. Have a designated and labeled place for everything and confirm everything is set in its place. The intent is to be able to find anything in under 30 seconds. Can you find a needed instrument in assembly in under 30 seconds? Workplace organization is the key. It must be easily understood and team expectations to adherence must be high. Tools that can help:

- Color-Coding
- Shadow boards / boxes
- Signs and labels
- Audits

Step 3 Shine or Sweep: This step is much more than cleaning, but rather a systematic daily routine to clean and keep the work area orderly and looking "like new." Divide the work so that everyone has a role with a clear understanding of the improvement desired and expected result. Be sure to budget to allow it to happen. Safety is a major consideration of the Shine step.

Steps 4 and 5 are about establishing a culture of discipline and standard work. This helps demonstrate the ability to standardize work and sustain improvements, all necessary for successful process improvement. It is the reason that 5S is the foundational tool for all Lean transformations. Fail at 5S and mostly likely all your improvement efforts will also fail.

Step 4 Standardize: Create and implement the rules for the first 3 S's. Establish the guidelines, policies and the expectations for team member. Then enforce the rules.

Examples:

- **Sort**: When, where and how to sort, what red tag information to collect, how to disposition a red tag item
- **Simplify**: How much inventory to keep on hand, what visual organization standards, labeling and color-coding to utilize
- **Shine**: When, where, how and with what is cleaning and inspecting to happen

Helpful hints:

- Use someone from outside the area to review standards for clarity
- Maintain a consistency of application; correct every instance of non-conformance
- Correct anything less that sends that dreaded 'Mixed Message"

Step 5 Sustain: A successful 5S effort makes it look easy much like a championship team. But a great deal of work and dedication goes into that success. Keep your 5S efforts alive. Develop creative methods to share and learn about successful 5S steps. Make 5S part of everyone's daily work life. Develop a 5S audit, use it from day one and hold each other accountable.

5 Why's

5 Why's – A simple but systematic method to perform root cause analysis. Each successive question of why dives deeper into the cause of the issue being investigated. The number "five" is relative. The idea is meant to force the analysis and help us continue asking questions until there are no more why's to answer and theoretically the root cause is identified. An example in SPD would be the finding the cause of why the department was unable to assemble their planned number of instrument trays in each hour. Why? One of the staff left the assembly area. Why? There were no more trays to assemble. Why? Decontamination was backlogged and did not keep up with the production schedule. Why? Eight case carts were brought to

decontamination at once. Why? The OR runner assigned to bringing case carts was too busy transporting patients to maintain his delivery schedule of case carts to decontamination. Why? One of the OR runners called in sick and no one was assigned to cover for his absence. Thus, a failure to ensure an upstream task was completed per plan by providing absenteeism coverage caused a downstream variance in planned production. This example also highlights opportunities for decontamination processes and leadership follow-up to have identified the problem before it became evident in assembly.

Andon

Andon – A feedback system or signal, typically a visual but may be audible as well, for the production floor to indicate status. An Andon signal can indicate when a process is ready to advance, alert when assistance is needed or bring immediate attention to a problem as it occurs. Lean production empowers staff to utilize the Andon to stop the production process in real time to fix the problem immediately. A simple SPD application would be for any staff member to stop their work and thus the flow of instruments through the department when a problem or non-conforming issue arises to signal for a supervisor to come and assist in identifying the root cause issue and determine corrective action. See also "Stop the Line" definition.

Balanced Line

Balanced Line – A series of workstations or process steps that can produce the same amount work in each time period. When in operation, balanced lines allow product to flow through each process step without any backlogs developing. A simple balanced line example for a SPD is shown in the graph below with every step of the process capable of processing 40 trays per hour.

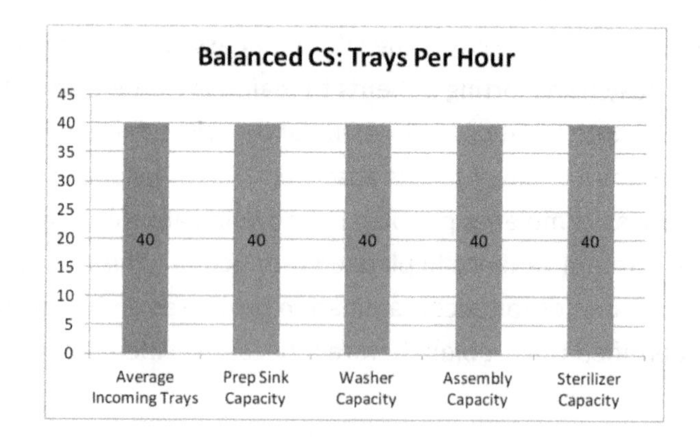

Continuous Flow / Single Piece Flow

Continuous Flow / Single Piece Flow – An operational state in which each individual product, such as an instrument tray, flows smoothly through the process with no interruptions and minimal wait time or backlogs. The inverse of continuous flow is batch processing in which many products are worked on together before moving them to the next step in the process. A SPD working to continuous flow would have little to no backlogs anywhere in the process and instrument trays would rarely sit waiting but rather continuously move through the department processes.

Cycle Time

Cycle Time – The total amount of time required to perform all the elements of work in each area or activity. Cycle Time in decontamination may include 1 minute to unload and scan instrument trays from a case cart, 5 minutes to prep and manually clean one instrument tray and 1 minute to load the tray into an automated washer for a total cycle time of 7 minutes. Total Cycle Time for SPD would then add decontamination, assembly, sterilization, and cool down cycle times together.

Discipline

Discipline – The adherence to a set standard or process by which to complete a task. Discipline is critical in any process to guarantee compliance to regulatory standards, quality of work, and overall effectiveness. In SPD, discipline is required at all levels from technicians following Standard Work Instructions to supervisors and managers following Leadership Routines designed to ensure work is accomplished in a timely and quality manner while identifying opportunities for improvement.

Document Tagging

Document Tagging is utilized to capture information and activity steps as the product or item moves through the process.

An example of Document Tagging in SPD would be the Quick Turn request tag attached to an instrument tray that is needed for a later case and needs to be processed via the Quick Turn Process. The Document Tag would include the needed information for the staff to know who needs the tray, when they need the tray, where they need the tray and any special instructions. Additional fields would include time into the department and time stamps along the way to provide feedback data on process performance and accountability to following the Quick Turn Standard Work Instructions. Another Document Tag found in SPD is the Vendor Tray form attached to the instrument tray identifying the date, time and doctor the tray is needed for.

Error Proofing (Poka-Yoke)

Error Proofing or Poka-Yoke are processes and methodologies for anticipating, detecting and preventing errors that adversely affect product quality, process efficiency and Customer satisfaction. It focuses on preventing defects at the source and includes any change to an operation, such as checklists or screens, fixtures, templates, gauges that help the operator reduce or eliminate mistakes that could lead to quality defects.

Error proofing examples that are common in the SPD include the visual internal and external indictors used with sterilizer loads and contents and the sterilizer parameter printouts themselves. On screen computer Count Sheets used to assemble instruments sets are another form of Error Proofing. As with many tools and processes, success relies on the proper use of specific tool – staff must use the onscreen assembly for it to be effective – while the best Error Proofing eliminates the chance of the error happening.

Genba Walk

Genba Walk – Genba is a Japanese term meaning "the real place" or "where the action is happening." Thus, a Genba Walk is to walk through the area where the action or work is happening. Genba Walks remind us to get out of our offices and spend time on the floor where the work occurs. The intent of a Genba Walk is to identify issues, verify information or data, observe first-hand the work as it happens not as it is designed, and talk with staff to understand the issues they are facing. Genba Walks should build a deep and thorough understanding of workplace performance. Genba Walks are excellent platforms by which a lean teacher or expert shares their knowledge with others by sharing what they see and questioning what is happening. In SPD, Genba Walks are extremely beneficial in observing flow of instruments and discussing why backlogs are or are not present, observing staff working to or not working to Standard Work, and building a more disciplined adherence to the lean practices implemented.

Heijunka Board

Heijunka Board – A Japanese word for a visual process of level-loading or smoothing out workload distribution. Instead of scheduling 75 minutes of work in the first period, 42 minutes the second period, 60 minutes the third period and 63 minutes the fourth period, Heijunka Boards would visually distribute the work as close as possible to 60 minutes every period. An SPD example would be case cart picking where the pick tickets would be placed into hourly slots based on the amount of work or line items on each pick ticket that closely equates to one hour of work. Case cart picking workload is thus evenly assigned each hour, expectations for each hour are known and visual and leadership can easily look at the hourly slots or Heijunka Board and determine if the staff is on schedule or off schedule.

Jidoka

Jidoka – Automation with a human touch or transferring human-like intelligence to a machine. This allows the machine to detect abnormalities or defects and stop the process when they are detected. Automation also prevents the production of defective products, eliminates overproduction and focuses attention on understanding the problem to ensure that it never recurs.

Within the SPD, low temperature sterilizers that can detect abnormal moisture in the chamber and thus abort the cycle before injecting sterilant is a form of Jidoka and prevents improperly processed items from being used and costly sterilant being wasted.

Kaizen

Kaizen - A Japanese term meaning "small, continuous improvement on everyone's part." It comes from the Japanese words "kai" (good) and "zen" (change). The intent is to create a work environment that focuses each employee on waste elimination as a normal part of the everyday work process. A **Kaizen Event** is a four to five-day, highly structured and coached attack on waste in a process or work area by a small cross-functional team of employees. They focus on designing and implementing solutions.

Kamishibai Board

Kamishibai Boards are flexible visual controls for performing audits of a process. Designed to help sustain process improvements they are also valuable in structuring leadership routines and bringing discipline to the audit process. A series of cards, each representing a specific audit activity, are placed on a board usually arranged by day of week for columns and time of day for rows. Each card has a specific audit task and is colored red on one side and green on the other. According to leader standard work, supervisors or other leadership team members perform the audit and place the audit card green side (lighter gray on Monday in photo below) out if the audit passed or red side out if failed. The entire board begins the week red (dark gray in photo) to ensure that if an audit is skipped it will remain red. All red audits require a root cause analysis such as 5 Why's and are added to the weekly leadership meeting.

Kanban

Kanban – A Japanese word meaning "signboard." A Kanban system provides a signal to do something and is commonly utilized to signal that an inventory item needs to be replenished. The signal can indicate that a process is ready for the next item, a staff member is ready for the next assignment or anything else that can utilize a structure communication or signal system.

The most common use is in inventory control such as supplies. Traditional supply management in hospitals relied on staff to visually count inventory items on a frequent basis and determine which supplies were low enough to reorder back up to their par levels. This system led to out of stock items, obsolete items still in stock, inability to find items, over stock of items, and visual counts that were more estimates than counts that consumed large amounts of staff time.

In SPD and OR departments, the most common form of Kanban utilized to managed supply inventories is the two-bin Kanban. Supplies are stocked in two bins with staff pulling supplies from the first bin. Once the first bin is emptied, the staff places the bin on top of the supply cart or nearby specified location and begin pulling supplies from the second bin. Supply staff then conduct a regular walk to collect the empty bins and refill them. The bin itself is the Kanban signal, visual counts are eliminated, reorder quantities are set, First-In First-Out supply management is automatically implemented, labor time spent on counting and replenishing supplies is reduced, supplies are maintained at the predetermined levels and stock is usually always available.

Electronic Kanban systems exist where the signal is an electronic magnetic other item that send the signal to replenish the first bin automatically and thus eliminates the need for staff to physically walk and pick up the signals. Grocery stores have perfected this system using electronic scans at the cash register automatically decrementing the inventory levels and once the reorder point is reached the computer automatically generates a restocking order for clerks to replenish the shelves as well as generate a purchase order to buy more items from the vendor.

Key Performance Measurements (KPI)

KPIs – Day-to-day operational metrics that give near real-time feedback on critical to success performance factors: quality, cost and schedule. These measures are designed to track actual performance and encourage progress towards critical organizational goals. KPI's can be a strong motivator to behavior so it is important to select metrics that drive the desired behavior and outcomes. Typical SPD KPI's include backlog of trays, error rates, complete instrument trays and productivity.

Leadership Routines

Leadership Routines – A key element of the Lean management system, leadership routines indicate the specific actions to be performed to ensure the leader's area of responsibility is performing to plan and opportunities to improve are identified and documented.

Minimum Interval Measurements

Minimum Interval Measurements – Otherwise known as short interval control, it is a structured process for identifying and acting on opportunities to improve the effectiveness and efficiency of a process. The work-level process engages team members to record production and quality data on scheduled intervals, such as hourly, and for team leaders to review performance data three or four times within their shift to assess where they need to focus their efforts and improve performance.

The idea is to look back to review previous results and assess the impact of previous action, then look forward to identifying next risks and determine and implement next actions to improve outcomes. Employees are trained to collect, analyze and react to this data to drive significant performance improvement. Within an SPD, measuring assembly throughput on an hourly basis to identify opportunities to improve is an example of a minimum interval measurement.

Pareto Analysis

Pareto Analysis – There is often more than one cause contributing to a problem. How do we know which to work on? A Pareto Analysis and Chart are both tools that can help separate the vital few from the trivial many. It is based on the Pareto Principle (80/20 Rule) that states that a few causes (20%) are responsible for most (80%) of the problem and focuses improvement efforts on the most frequent cause. An example of a SPD related Pareto Analysis of missing instruments is shown below.

Problem: Sets Missing Instruments when Delivered to OR

Cause	Talley	Total
Not returned from previous case	~~////~~	5
Not working, no replacement available	//	2
Missing not noted by Assembler	~~////~~ ~~////~~ ///	13
Instrument not listed on Count Sheet	///	3
OR tech unfamiliar with instrument	//	2
Unknown cause	~~////~~ //	7

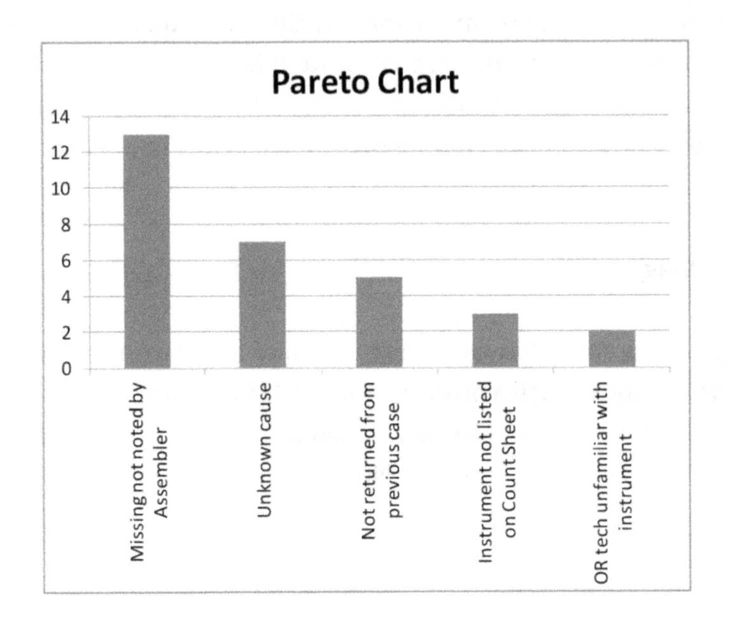

If you are already in a Lean mindset, then you probably thought to yourself that the "missing not noted by assembler" category is an indication of lack of discipline to Standard Work worthy of asking 5 Why's to correct the issue through error proofing which will then reorder the Pareto Analysis. Also, worthy to note is that categories such as unknown cause or other should be avoided as they do not provide actionable data.

Pull System

Pull System – A system in which Customer demand pulls products through the supply chain or triggers an activity to occur. This contrasts with a push system. A pull system in SPD could be the OR schedule pulling needed instrument trays through the process based on priority.

Push System

Push System – A system in which the volume and rate of production is determined by a schedule rather than by Customer demand. This contrasts with a pull system. A push system in SPD is typically seen in decontamination where the items are pushed through the cleaning process to avoid bioburden drying even if the instrument is not required by the OR.

Spaghetti Diagram

A Spaghetti Diagram is a visual representation of actual workflow of an item or staff or activity through a process. The key is that it represents actual workflow not what people tell you it should be like. Below is an example of a Spaghetti Flow of a staff member picking the supplies for a case cart.

Spaghetti Flow of Case Cart Picking

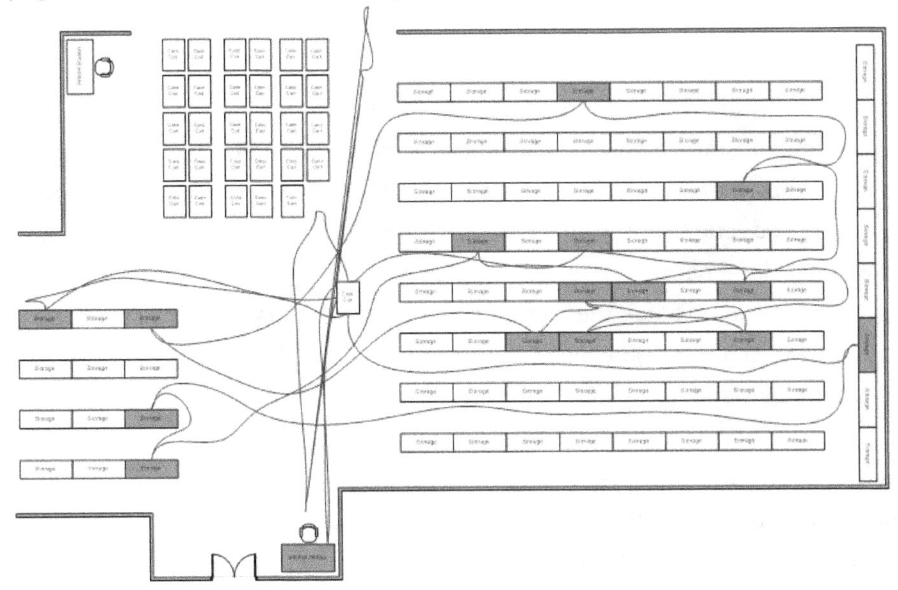

Standard Work

Standard Work – Documents exactly how an activity or task should be completed including the sequence of steps, quantities of work in process, the pace at which the process must be completed and defines the desired method to complete the activity which is usually also the most efficient. The implementation of standard work ensures that all employees involved in the task are completing the steps in the same way; the processes are consistent and repeatable without variation. The documentation assists with training and compliance and becomes the foundation upon which process improvement is conducted and that gains are sustained. Establishment of the process steps and time to complete each provides a better basis for the company or department to plan its activities and requirements.

Stop the Line

Stop the Line – Philosophy that every employee has the empowerment to stop production when a defect is found to take immediate corrective action. See also Andon definition.

Takt Time

Takt Time – Takt is a German-based word from Taktzeit, roughly meaning cycle time or time between occurrences such as arrival of scheduled trains at a train stop. In manufacturing, Takt Time is used to determine the desired pace of production that aligns with Customer demands. For example, if the Customer demand is for 200 items per day and the manufacturing area operates 16 hours a day the Takt Time would be calculated as 200 items divided by 16 hours equaling 12.5 items per hour that must be produced to meet the demand.

Within the SPD, Takt Time could be utilized given an overall even flow of product and/or a rough estimate of hourly production requirements if the total number of items to process for the day was known. Frequently though the SPD must estimate the number of items to process each day and due to clinical requirements of bioburden removal and Customer requirements to reprocess the instruments without delay they simple adopt the lean concept of Continuous Flow as best as possible.

Value Added & Non-Value Added

Value Added – Any task or process that transforms or adds value to a product or service to meet Customer requirements. It is an essential part of any business process and what the Customer is willing to pay for.
Non-Value Added – Activities or actions taken that add no real value to the product or service, making such activities or action a form of waste. Any activity that the Customer would not be willing to pay for.

Value Add vs. Non-Value Add Examples

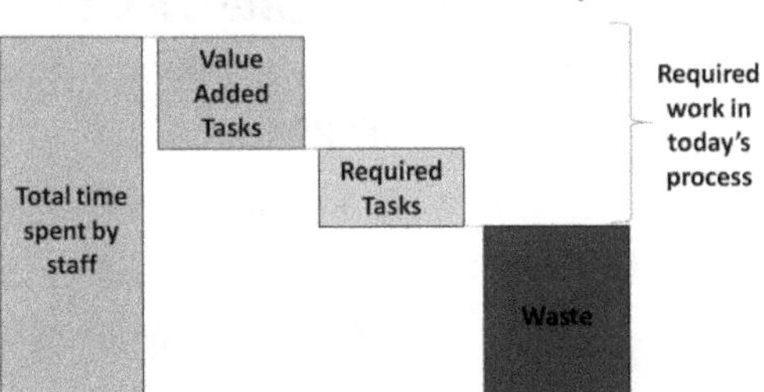

Examples

Role	VA Activity	NVA Activity
CS Decontamination Tech	•Scrub and flush soiled instruments •Load Cart Washer	•Wait for washer to be unloaded •Remove PPE to get detergent
CS Assembly Tech	•Prepare Instruments for Sterilization •Replace broken instrument with suitable	•Review surgery schedule of need •Assemble set missing instruments
Surgical Tech	•Prepare sterile field for surgery •Obtain surgical gloves and suture	•Search for missing instruments •Find misplaced case cart
What examples Value Add Activities and Waste can you think of in your daily work?		

Visual Controls

Visual Controls – Visual tools, indicators and systems that can immediately communicate the status of the workplace, actual versus expected performance and improve the communication of information. Visual management makes the current state and condition of the processes easily accessible and very clear – to everyone involved at a glance.

Waste

8 Wastes – Originally defined in the Toyota Production System as the 7 Types of Waste with Under Utilized People being added later. Waste is anything that uses resources but does not add value to transforming the product or service. They include:

- **Waiting** – Staff waiting to work or product waiting to be worked on. It is important to note that waiting waste is not only about labor. Product waiting to be worked on is an important waste to eliminate and often the most common in SPDs.
- **Defects** – Something that does not meet the Customer's requirement. Customers may be external or internal.
- **Excess Motion** – Unnecessary movement while performing a task or process.
- **Transportation** – Moving product from one place to another. When something is being transported it is not being worked on and value is not being added.
- **Under Utilized People** – Lack of engaged staff whose knowledge and intelligence are not being leveraged to eliminate waste and improve the workplace and processes. Listening to staff ideas and engaging them in the workplace decisions. Encouraging ideas is vital to the ultimate success or failure of Lean practices. A successful company realizes that their biggest asset is the employees.
- **Excess Inventory** – Having too much of anything that is not needed at the time it is needed.
- **Overproduction** – Producing more of something than is needed, faster than is needed or before it is needed.
- **Excessive Processing** – Performing extra steps beyond the standard work instructions or putting more effort into the work as required by the Customer.

City Hospital Cast of Characters

City Hospital Cast of Characters
The names and characters are fictional and do not represent any single department but rather a collection of the personalities we've worked with over the years. Something to think about is how difficult it is to "orchestrate" a group of unique individuals with different personalities, traits, work ethics towards a common goal. Being a SPD Manager is not easy!

Karen, OR Director: Calm and collected. Realizes that she's only as good as the people she is surrounded by and strives to hire the best and provide a culture where people can fulfill their potential. Karen was happy with Rob's performance and the department's turnaround. Her pleasure was short lived due to the reality of her position and the numerous other issues such as surgeon satisfaction, OR renovations, outsourcing transport, pre-op process changes, and audit surveys.

Deana, OR Coordinator: Passionate about her profession and expects perfection. Knows her stuff, prefers working with professionals, is a bit blunt at times, but surgeons and staff respect her as a true industry expert especially in orthopedics. Has a hard time relating to SPD and the struggles they have with producing clean, complete, sterile, and on-time instruments. Deana eventually took over running the OR Control Desk but not before she acknowledged Rob's work with the typical Deana comment "You've done a great job Rob, there's still problems, but you've improved it a lot." For Deana that's a big compliment.

Beth, OR Coordinator: The Service Line leader that everyone loves. Gives of her time and talents to help others. Seen as the peace maker and always tries to defuse situations. Is respected as a person but is sometimes taken advantage of by staff who use her soft side to their advantage. Beth moved on to the OR Educator role and found herself in an uphill battle when faced with training the staff on end of case instrument handling procedures to improve overall instrument management and processing. She suddenly found herself working to help SPD by changing how the OR operates.

Rob, SPD Manager: Worked his way up the ranks while receiving a college education. Has potential but is learning his job as he goes. Was a great technician and supervisor because he could do the work effectively by himself but is learning now how to manage through others instead of doing it all himself. New to lean but not afraid to try if it makes sense. In the end, Rob not only successfully turned around his SPD but began to help other departments through industry meetings and speaking engagements. Karen publicly acknowledged Rob's successfully work in SPD to the hospital leadership team and expanded his leadership responsibilities by managing the Surgical Support Specialists.

Dwight, 1st Shift Supervisor: Long-time employee, comes in early to spend time making sure the case carts are complete and the OR has what they need. Has never felt a need to manage his staff as they are mostly experienced long-time employees such as himself. Dwight eventually left City Hospital to become the SPD Manager at another hospital and successfully utilized his lean skills to transform the dysfunctional department. Dwight and Rob remain good friends and share lean ideas.

Becky, 2nd Shift Supervisor: Typically focused on the missing list and getting what's needed for tomorrow done. Usually spends some time assembling herself and prefers to avoid confrontation. Becky has flourished as a supervisor but still finds conflict hard and forces herself to address non-compliance issues with the staff.

Rachel, Technician: Quick to answer. Pessimistic, sarcastic, and points out why things aren't going to work. Rachel's pessimistic attitude has mellowed a bit after she was proven wrong a few times, but she continues as the "devil's advocate" whenever new ideas are presented. She performs well and is accepted for who she is.

Latisha, Technician: Reasonable and sees the benefit of ideas. Focuses on what helps her. Thinks they need more staff. Typically accepts change unless it's seen as making her work faster or harder. Latisha volunteered to represent the SPD in hospital wide lean initiatives and has found a new sense of self-worth through her interaction with other hospital staff and helping them improve their departments.

Melissa, Technician: Reasonable, good worker, and smart. Knows what to do and see variances but lives with it. Focuses too much on the OR. Naturally likes to take over which gets her in trouble with the other staff for being too bossy. Melissa continues to work in SPD, still gets in trouble, but maintains her performance and receives a "meets expectations" on her annual review.

Vlad, Technician: Quiet, prefers decontamination, a good worker but sometimes can be lazy. When pressed for ideas has good thoughts. Looks for affirmation from others as security. Stands over six feet tall and weighs over 250 pounds but affectionately known as the Ukrainian Teddy Bear. Vlad continues to work in decontamination. He recently started a volunteer program in the hospital's new Children's Waiting Area where he and other employees spend time playing games with the children of families having surgery.

Rudy, Technician: New employee and stuck on case carts for the time being. Trying to fit in but not sure if it's safer to kick butt and show the experience staff up or maintain a performance that's average, to fit in. Rudy eventually decided to show off his abilities and quickly moved up the ladder to become a Lead Tech before accepted a Supervisor position in Supply Chain.

Jackie, Technician: Frustrated, quantity versus quality objector, and is typically slower than the others and knows it. Time standards make her nervous. Usually quick to stir up support for not changing or putting down improvement ideas. Can be negative. Jackie adapted but it wasn't easy. It took time for her to relax and realize that standards and processes are there to support her not demean her. Her performance is adequate but not stellar, but she has found a niche in coming up with some of the best process improvement ideas.

Cindy, Technician: Hard worker and holds herself to a high standard. She keeps to herself but is always the first to help others. Assigned to train all new hires. Everyone likes Cindy but she's taken advantage of as others know she'll do the work that no one else wants. After Dwight left, Cindy was promoted to 1st shift supervisor and struggled through the transition from team member to supervisor. With the support of Rob, she eventually settled into her new role of motivating her staff while continuing to find ways to better process trays.

Richard, Technician: Likes to point out the issues with the OR and others to deflect any focus on himself or the department. Is smart but works the system, performs well enough to maintain a good review but needs to be managed. Unfortunately, Richard did not survive the lean transformation and found he was not comfortable with the transparency of performance combined with the culture of compliance to standard work. Richard continues to work in sterile processing, preferring departments that are disorganized allowing him to hide amongst the chaos.

Roberta, Technician: A high performer when she wants to be. Spends most of her time in assembly and can easily out assembly everyone else. Mood swings go from smiling and positive to negative with a chip on her shoulder, you never know which Roberta will show up for work. Staff respect her and when she's in a bad mood everyone stays away. Prefers to work alone with a "I don't need help" attitude. Roberta continues to pump out the trays but still comes to work with a little attitude every now and then.

Daryl, New Hire: Young single father who's working hard to make the best of his situation. His looks suggest someone you might not immediately think of as the poster child employee but once he opens up you realize he's the real deal; dedicated, passionate about doing the right thing, wants to be involved, and isn't afraid to put in his time. Like other young new hires though, he can be influenced by the work environment and culture both positively and negatively. Daryl thrived in the lean environment and eventually was promoted to Operations Coordinator overseeing instrument ordering and management, process improvement initiatives, instrument tracking solutions, and operational performance reporting.

~~~~~~
~~~~~~

CPSIA information can be obtained
at www.ICGtesting.com
Printed in the USA
BVHW030245220722
642761BV00007B/521